STATE, SOCIETY AND ECONOMY IN THE TWENTY-FIRST CENTURY

CANADA-INDIA PERSPECTIVES

STATE, SOCIETY AND ECONOMY IN THE TWENTY-FIRST CENTURY

CANADA-INDIA PERSPECTIVES

★ ★ ★

Shastri Indo-Canadian Institute
40th Anniversary Commemorative Volume

Edited by

A.S. NARANG

L'INSTITUT INDO-CANADIEN SHASTRI INDO-CANADIAN INSTITUTE

MANOHAR
2009

First published 2009

ISBN 978-81-7304-836-4

Published by

Ajay Kumar Jain *for*
Manohar Publishers & Distributors
4753/23 Ansari Road, Daryaganj
New Delhi 110 002

Typeset at

Digigrafics
New Delhi 110 049

Printed at

Salasar Imaging Systems
Delhi 110 035

Contents

Preface

This volume is a collection of selected papers presented at a seminar on Canada-India relations organized to commemorate the 40th anniversary of Shastri Indo-Canadian Institute. It also includes some special lectures held during the anniversary year in different universities. Since India's Independence, people-to-people links between Canada and India have grown steadily through academic, cultural and other exchanges. Shastri Institute as a unique bi-national organization has contributed in a very significant manner in promoting understanding between the two countries primarily through facilitating academic activities and exchanges. The Institute has been instrumental in building the foundation of trust, understanding and goodwill conducive to a positive relationship between these two great countries.

Seminars and special lectures during the 40th anniversary year were meant not only to consolidate the achievements but also to take note of the emerging trends, identify commonalities and differences between the two States and societies about what is happening around the world, bring to light the challenges that processes of enhancement of relations face, and areas of learning from each other. The end of the Cold War and the process of globalization has provided reason and opportunity to both countries, as to most states in general, to review their foreign policies particularly in the context of economy and trade and strategic relations. The result of these processes is a world that is smaller and more interdependent. In this context from the beginning of the century there has been a steady maturing of Indo-Canadian relations from one of engagement to one of partnership. The contributions in this volume focus on the different facets of political, economic and cultural aspects of this relationship, taking account of developments in the last sixty years. It is expected that the volume will provide an insight and will be of interest to those interested in the affairs of and relationship between these two countries.

AMARJIT S. NARANG

Acknowledgements

In preparation of this volume, celebrations of 40th anniversary year and successful functioning of the Shastri Institute, we have received enormous help from the governments of both India and Canada and several individuals. Government of India, through the Ministry of Human Resources Development (MHRD) apart from providing funds also helps us through advice and guidance through its Advisory Council and Administrative Committee. I particularly thank Shri R.P. Agarwal, Secretary Higher Education, Chairman of the Advisory Council, Shri Sunil Kumar, Jt. Secretary representing MHRD in Executive Committee and Administrative Committee, and Ms. Anupama Bhatnagar, Director MHRD for their sustained support. I also take this opportunity to put on record my thanks to Government of Canada for their financial and moral support through the Department of Foreign Affairs and Trade, and Canadian International Development Agency (CIDA). Canadian High Commissioners to India during anniversary year Dr. David Malone, Mr. Joseph Caron and Deputy High Commissioner, Mr. Kenneth Macartney have been very supportive along with other officials of the High Commission including Ghislain, Chaput, Faisal Beg, Bernard Francis and Priya Sinha. I wish to convey my thanks to them.

My colleagues in the Executive Committee, former President Prof. Gary Vanloon, Secretary-Treasurer Prof. Yvon Dandurand, members Dr Patricia Dold, Prof. Ranbir Singh, Prof. V.D. Kaushik and Prof. B.S. Ghuman, extended full cooperation and help in organizing various anniversary-related activities. I have been receiving utmost help from Vice-President/President elect Prof. Shiela Embelton and Chair of the 40th Anniversary Committee Dr. Stephen Inglis and other members. I wish to thank them all.

Sarmistha Roy, Director, Anju Taneja, Finance Officer, Prachi Kaul, Programme Officer, Reshma Verma, Librarian, and

Meenakshi Malhotra, Administrative Assistant at Shastri Institute Office have been assisting me in all possible ways. I also acknowledge the support of Executive Director James Liebenberg and, programme officers and staff of the Canada office. Several friends and colleagues encouraged and helped me in many ways including going through the papers and making suggestions. I thank them all sincerely. I owe grateful thanks to the contributors, who really have given shape to this volume. My thanks are also due to Shri Ramesh Jain of Manohar Publishers for his enthusiastic interest in the publication of this volume.

AMARJIT S. NARANG

Shastri Indo-Canadian Institute 40th Anniversary

Founded in 1968 by an agreement between the governments of Canada and India, the Shastri Indo-Canadian Institute completed in 2008, forty years of linking together Indian and Canadian academics in areas of shared interests. The Institute was conceived by Prof. Michael Brecher of McGill University to overcome the total information gap and lack of economic and cultural contacts between the two countries. The Government of India took an initiative in offering counterpart rupee funds—money accumulated through the sale of Canadian food aid—to support Canadian scholars in India; to promote greater knowledge and interest in India. To facilitate the task, Shastri Institute incorporated in Canada as a not-for-profit organization was set up. It began with three member universities, McGill, Toronto and the University of British Columbia. Its Canadian dollar budget was provided by the member universities while the rupee budget came from the Indian government. The Institute originally sought to encourage Canadian teaching and researches on India, focusing on the humanities and social sciences.

The Institute's success in sparking Indian studies among Canadian academics led to a reciprocal interest in Canada among Indian scholars. In the 1980s the Shastri Institute began to promote Canadian studies in India and later expanded its activities to include development studies and researches. The Institute was reinvented and restructured as a bi-national organization in 2005 and through the reorganization process it was bequeathed a unique structure. It has a unique bi-national organizational membership and governance. The Institute's membership has grown to 88 (50 Indian and 38 Canadian universities and institutes of higher learning). The Executive Committee of the Institute consists of equal members from each country and the presidentship rotates between the two on a yearly basis. In addition to traditional areas of Humanities and Social Sciences Shastri's mandate now also includes Science and Technology, Environment, Law, Management, etc.

Since its creation, the Shastri Institute has been connecting Canadian and Indian academics, scholars, performing artists, creative writers and students, encouraging them to explore and experience each others' unique cultures, traditions, languages and arts. During these years more than 920 fellowships have been awarded for Canadian faculty, researchers, students and artists and more than 370 scholarships to Indian researchers in Canada. The Institute managed 65 development and applied research projects in India funded by Canadian International Development Agency (CIDA). It arranged visiting lecture tours in India for about 25 Canadian academics including Margaret Atwood, Barbara Goddard, James Laxer, Charles Taylor, M.G. Vassanji, Rudy Wiebe, etc. It sponsored about 100 distinguished persons from India to provide public lectures in Canada including Dr. N. Ram, Dr. M.N. Srinivas, Dr. Kapila Vatsyayan, Dr. R.S. Swaminathan, etc. The Institute facilitated about 100 international internships for young Canadians to work with Indian research institutions, and business and non-governmental organizations. In its library programme, the Institute has sent more than 60,000 Indian books and journals to Canadian member university libraries. Over 9,000 resource material has been received by institutions in India.

For forty years the Shastri Institute has been instrumental in building the foundation of trust, understanding, respect and goodwill crucial to a positive relationship between the two great countries. The Institute has established a large network, accumulating a deep knowledge of higher education in India and Canada. Based on this substantial and growing knowledge, the Institute acts as a catalyst to establish and expand academic connections between India and Canada. Scholars today are using our programme to form both bi-national and multi-disciplinary partnerships.

During its forty years of existence by sharing ideas, books and periodicals, fostering exchange of students and faculty, supporting research, stimulating discussions and promoting academic collaborations, the Institute has been enhancing mutual understanding between two dynamic and diverse countries. We will continue to offer and expand a variety of programmes that respond to the needs and goals of our diverse membership. Initiatives to provide and support partnership-forming seed grants, development of courses to be jointly offered in India and Canada, internship for students and graduates and bi-national research directed toward millennium development goals are some of the new programmes we have started recently.

President AMARJIT S. NARANG

CHAPTER 1

India-Canada Relations: Patterns and Trends

A.S. NARANG

The new world order has dragged both Canada and India into the twenty-first century with a considerable political, economic and demographic change. Canada, now has emerged as a principal power in international affairs while India, apart from being a regional power, has also emerged as a global player. Both are active members of the commonwealth. Of course, Canada is primarily a doner country. In societal terms both are characterized by ethnic, linguistic and religious diversity and are pluralistic societies. In the framework of plurality both are secular state structures and devoid of state religions, apart from a charter of rights for all written into the basic constitutional documents for all. As polities both are federal states with parliamentary systems of government working in the framework of Rule of Law.

Of course, it also is true that Canada and India belong to two realms of history, two parts of globe, two processes of development, two narratives of everyday practices and have different memories of the colonial past and colonial present and differential or multiple modernities and finally both have different trajectories of social relations/cultural practices including structural transformation (Assadi 2004). Because of these similarities and differences, in the last sixty years Canada-India bilateral relations have been characterized by distinct warmer and cooler periods. Bilateral relations have not only grown significantly in many spheres during the period, but also went through periods of decline because of disagreements between the two governments over substantive issues. In fact, as Tyan Touchey points out, during the past sixty years the trend has not been very positive. Particularly from 1976 to 2001, neither country was wholly committed to fostering closer ties with the other. Even throughout the 1950s-1970s, both countries held starkly incompatible views on international relations and on nuclear non-proliferation regimes. At the same time, built upon shared values of democracy and pluralism and strong people-to-people links, there have been ongoing processes of understanding. Since India's Independence, people-to-people links with Canada have grown steadily, including academic, cultural and other exchanges. However, as stated earlier, the basic differences on international relations particularly on nuclear non-proliferation did not allow a close partnership either in strategic or economic relations. During the post-Cold War years Canada looked to China and Japan as new economic and strategic partners in Asia and bilateral relations with India entered a period of prolonged drift (Touchey 2007).

CORDIAL BEGINNING

In the early years of India's Independence there was a lot of commonality between India and Canada's understanding of international affairs and also cordiality in relations between the two. In spite of Canada's closeness and strategic relationship with the US, Canadian policy makers were freed from viewing South Asian affairs in the context only of US-Soviet relations. As Arthur G. Rubinoff points out, Canada's approach to the states of South Asia and its perspective on dealing with the newly independent countries of the post-war world stemmed from its participation in the British Commonwealth of Nations, which has previously been an exclusive club of non-Asiatic members. According to Mansur, the emergence of three new states—India, Pakistan and Sri Lanka—posed the problem of how the Commonwealth would accommodate the new Asiatic dominions without diluting its essential character. Canada worked on creating an intercontinental grouping that would serve as a bridge between the established Western democracies and the new multiracial Afro-Asian successor states of the British

Empire. Canada's relations with the South Asian region evolved from common middle power perspectives which resulted from participation in the Commonwealth of Nations. Its desire to retain the Commonwealth reflected Ottawa's belief that multi-racial organizations reduced international tensions in a bipolar world and provided a forum where Canada would not be overshadowed by its North American ally. These ties enabled Canada to have a counter-weight to Ottawa's relations with the US (Rubinoff 1994). As a former diplomat of Canadian foreign service of that time John C. Hadwen informs that Lester Pearson regarded Nehru a positive influence on behalf of India and for much of the underdeveloped or the less developed world. Pearson's respect and liking for Nehru was reciprocated (Hadwen 1994).

South Asian countries, Rubinoff points out, viewed the Canadian aid desirable since unlike assistance from the United States, the Soviet Union and China, it was considered unconnected with geographical and strategic considerations and more genuinely geared to development requirements. It was in the Commonwealth that the very first Canadian development programmes were established. After the US, Canada was the second largest supplier of food on a bilateral basis to developing countries. Canada's response to request for help from the countries of the region led to the adoption of the Colombo Plan for Economic Development (Rubinoff 1994).

The divergence between Canada and the US on their policy towards India, according to Rubinoff, was initially even sharper than in the case of their relations with Pakistan. Unlike the Americans, the Canadians were not suspicious of Prime Minister Nehru's socialism. In the early years after Independence there was a fundamental convergence in the approach to world affairs between New Delhi and Ottawa on such issues as the Commonwealth, the United Nations and the situation in Asia. The leaders of both countries saw themselves as representatives of middle powers who were interested in influencing world affairs in a constructive manner. They shared an identity of perceptions on the need to enhance relations between Asia and the West, to promote multilateral organizations, to foster Third World developments, and to settle military conflicts in Korea,

Indo-China and Suez. While the scope of their influence was different—Canada acted within the Western alliance, while India's domain was the Third World—both countries viewed their functions as establishing links between hostile camps. India's task was to temper China and build a bridge between that country and the West, while Canada's role was to moderate American policy towards Asia and Indian attitudes toward the US (Kapur 1991). The India connection gave Canada access also to non-aligned thinking. While they rejected neutralism for themselves, Canadians accepted, sooner than the Americans, the decision of the newly independent countries to opt for non-alignment. Although Canada joined NATO, its reluctance to accept US nuclear weapons on its soil enhanced Ottawa's position among the non-aligned countries. While the Canadian viewpoint was not often appreciated in Washington, it served a useful purpose in moderating Western policy. As Mansur puts it, Canada's membership in both NATO and Commonwealth gave it a 'rare opportunity to strive to narrow the gap between the United States, its closest ally and defender against Soviet threats, and India, a new state formed by a people with a very old and rich civilization' (Mansur 1992, quoted by Rubinoff 1994).

The way Canada-India relations were developing had both positive and negative aspects. The positive aspect was that when world affairs were dominated by the rivalry between the superpowers and by the nuclear factors, the Canada-India relations emerged as a partnership of sorts between an important Western interlocutor and an important Third World interlocutor. Canada and India had special qualities. Both had been active participants in East-West inter-bloc/and intra-bloc debates. Both avoided direct conflict with the superpowers. Both were not in the superpower league themselves; but both were powers in the world arena. These qualities helped them develop a commonality of interests, what Ashok Kapur calls, a semi-autonomous approach to world affairs and a semi-autonomous relationship (Kapur 1991). By semi-autonomous relationship Kapur means that Canada or India, have never, since 1947, functioned as a mirror image of the East-West block leaders (USA and USSR) in the Cold War era in their approach to South Asian affairs. In some areas—especially on international security and Indo-Pakistan issues, Canadian and US thinking has converged; here duplication between the North American states is evident. But in other areas, e.g. the China question in the 1950s, there was affinity between the Indian, Canadian and UK governments and a sharp divergence in approach between these governments and the US.

Thus, Canadian policies *vis-à-vis* India in the diplomatic strategic sphere have not been an extension of US policies even though there are areas of convergence between Canadian and US policies *vis-à-vis* India. Indian policies towards Canada were not an extension of Indian policies towards the US (Kapur 1991). As far as Canada is concerned, the beginning of this approach lay in the vision and version of Lester B. Pearson, Canada's Minister of External Affairs during the period 1948-58, and later as prime minister, for a new Canada in the post-Second World War period. He rejected Canada's pre-war disposition not to engage in international affairs. For him, post-war Canada had to, as a matter of urgency and policy, become more active in world affairs. For Pearson, Canada's outstanding contribution to the war effort justified its policy of staking a claim not only as a major player in the post-war peace process but also in the shaping of a new world order. He was convinced that isolationism could no longer be a principle of policy for Canada. In his words,

> everything that happens in the world affects us . . . consequently it is always foolish to assume that we can safely leave global matters of war and peace to the Great Powers while we modestly concentrate our energies on protecting our sovereignty and increasing our gross national product. If we withdraw into a foreign policy of narrow nationalism with economic growth as its main objective, Canada's voice might be heard, but it would not impress.

Likewise, to rely on 'sovereignty for the protection of Canadian interest is meaningless . . . unless you have the force and will to back up your insistence on its recognition.

For this reason international cooperation was essential. The protection of Canada's sovereignty could best be guaranteed by establishing "relations of friendship, goodwill and agreement with other countries so that insistence on the use of force will not be required". Such relations should extend beyond Canada's continental relationship with the US or that with Western European countries.

In short, to enhance world peace, and stability Pearson advocated the concept of participatory internationalism (Basdeo 2000).

Within the context of participatory internationalism, Pearson had special consideration for India. As early as December 1941, less than three weeks after war had broken out in the Pacific, he, at that time in the Department of External Affairs, revived the idea of appointing a High Commissioner to India. Pearson concluded that India would emerge as an independent nation after the war and, like China, the country could not be ignored. Canada could assist the young Indian government as it navigated the international stage by offering advise based on a similar history of colony-to-nation. Ottawa could also provide insight on how a future federal Indian government could accommodate states seeking greater powers while dealing with religious and cultural minority rights. Only Canada could uniquely assist India in meeting these objectives in contrast to the US or Australia because Canada could draw from its own largely peaceful political evolution and experience in dealing with minority rights. Lastly, Canada was not tainted by an imperialist past. In other words, the Canadians were not British. The final telling point used to sway the cautious government was that Ottawa could conveniently initiate this process without great expense and without assuming any embarrassing responsibilities. This vision was shared by Canadian prime minister, Louis St. Laurent.

In India, the first Prime Minister Jawaharlal Nehru and architect of its foreign policy was also endowed with liberal internationalism. He also had a sense of mission in building the New India. It was the 'kinship of spirit' to use Nehru's terms, between Indian and Canadian leadership that provided the framework for cooperation at the political level, and which subsequently led to greater people-to-people contact on appreciation of mutual differences, and respect for greater cultural understanding in the making of a new post-war world order. Nehru while not unmindful of the imperative need to defend India's own territorial integrity, had evolved an internationalist perspective much like Pearson, denouncing imperialism, military aggression and the selfish politics of the bi-polar world and called for a creative role for Asia in world affairs. He also advocated a policy of non-alignment through which he saw signs of a safer world guaranteed by alliances structured outside the power blocs (Basdeo 2000).

In this background working together within the United Nations and the Commonwealth, or in direct communication with each other, India and Canada helped to bridge the gap between the Orient and the Occident, and between the Communist and non-Communist blocs. They also helped to transform the Commonwealth into an effective multi-racial organization, and contributed substantially in easing tension in several of the world's trouble spots, including Korea, Indo-China and West Asia (Basdeo 2001). There was a fundamental convergence in their approach to international politics on issues, including the Commonwealth, the United Nations and the situation in Asia. However, this sort of relationship did not last for long. Apart from other factors, a basic reason for it, according to Kapur, was that these relations were more personality-based.

BUREAUCRATIZATION AND MOVING APART

Kapur recalls that E. Reid, the then Canadian High Commissioner in India, saw himself as the envoy to Nehru (not India). During the Nehru years, Canadians, Indians and academic experts, saw Nehru as India, and when Nehru did not deliver (on Kashmir, Hungary and ICC), disillusionment with India set in. Kapur points out that personalized foreign policy puts too many eggs in a single basket. It makes policy hostage to personality modes, personal style and personal preferences of leaders that are known to a small coterie of advisors. It creates a false sense of security, a false sense that a special relationship exists, a false belief that the size and activity of a small, closed decision unit can be managed. And when such expectations are not met, a disillusionment sets in. As bilateral relations become depersonalized, bureaucracies become more sensitive about divisive issues, and consequently controversies increase, bilaterally and internally.

Tracing the history of India-Canada relations from 1947 to early 1990s Kapur points out that in the early 1950s, leadership style and personalities in the two countries had a moderating influence in world affairs. Canada and India were ambivalent about the US. Nehru could be induced to accommodate Pakistan on the Kashmir issue. No major domestic controversies or domestic vetoes existed and the two countries had convergent interests in international, South Asian and bilateral issues. From the mid-1950s to 1960s Nehru and Pearson were not in affinity as were Nehru and St. Laurent. Mental outlooks and policy imperatives of St. Laurent and Pearson varied: Nehru's policies in Hungary and ICC were not helpful to the Western cause. Canadian leadership became less ambivalent about US in Cold War affairs, i.e. in NATO, East Europe and ICC affairs under Pearson. Nehru's attitude to Kashmir dispute after US/Pakistan pact was not considered helpful to Indo-Pakistan relations. Nehru was seen as a loser following India's defeat in 1962. At bureaucratic level, India's ICC role became a major divisive issue in Canadian government. This issue created a controversy in bureaucratic politics in Canada. State relations thus began to diverge.

During 1970, Kapur points out, Trudeau and Indira Gandhi were not in affinity in strategic affairs, but there was an affinity on Commonwealth and developmental issues. India was a functioning democracy and a useful Third World interlocutor. On the other hand, Canada and the USA were in accord on the nuclear question. Both suspected India's regional ambitions following the break-up of Pakistan in 1971. Above all, India's 1974 nuclear test created in-house and public controversy in Canada and it exacerbated bureaucratic politics in Canada. State interests diverged so the relationship changed from one of cooperation (1947-early 1950s) to one of diplomatic conflict (1974-early 1980s).

According to David M. Malone, former High Commissioner of Canada to India, India's nuclear weapons test of 1974, drawing on technology Canada had provided for other purposes, introduced a chill in India's relations with a country tremendously attached to the Non-Proliferation Treaty, all the more because Canada had renounced the nuclear weapons option for itself in 1945 when, having participated in the Manhattan Project, it would have been easy for the country to develop its own nuclear weapons. India soon had its own grievances arising from militancy among fringe groups of Sikh Canadians fuelling the Free Khalistan movement of the 1980s and sparking the Kanishka Air India tragedy of 1984 (Malone 2008). In that way developments in Indian Punjab also had a negative impact on ethnic politics in Canada. The desire to avoid malevolent terrorist reaction on Canadian soil created bureaucratic rethinking about future of Canada-India relations. Relations became depersonalized, i.e. emerging convergence of state interests led to a quest for cooperation. The affability of leaders on both sides, e.g. Brian Mulroney, Charles Joseph Clark and Rajiv Gandhi helped put the relationship on a positive basis. State interests began to change; a new focus emerged over the terrorism issue, the need to develop Canada-India economic relations, and South Asia as a source of valued immigrants. Canadian foreign policy regarding India was in a flux but the focus on terrorism, economic issues and immigration became firm. There was limited convergence and limited divergence (Kapur 1991).

Convergence till the end of 1980s however, remained limited. This in fact was a continuation of the 1970s negative state of affairs which according to Michael Breacher was due to increasing American influence over Canada and conversely India's political distancing from the USA and close ties with the USSR during the Cold War period. The Canadian government was also stung by allegations that for India's peaceful nuclear explosion in May 1974 the fissionable material used to construct India's first nuclear device had been obtained from the Canadian-supplied CIRUS nuclear reactor.

In general, as Rubinoff suggests, since South Asia had few economic or security concerns for either the United States or Canada compared to other regions of the world, it has been treated in a residual fashion by both countries. Within both the American and Canadian bureaucracies, relations with the South Asian States had a low priority. South Asian affairs in the American State Department were combined with the Near-

East until 1992, while in Canada's Ministry of External Affairs these were amalgamated with South-East Asia (Rubinoff 1994). Within that India always felt a US tilt towards Pakistan.

The Soviet invasion of Afghanistan provided Pakistan with yet another opportunity to court American assistance at the expense of US-Indian ties. To quote Rubinoff again, 'Pakistan was perceived as a frontline state resisting the advance of communism, while India was seen as endorsing pro-Soviet positions in Cuba, Kampuchea, Nicaragua and especially Afghanistan.' With regard to India-Canada relations the lack of congruency which surfaced over issues like Korea, Indo-China and Hungary transformed a once special relationship between India and Canada into one characterized by ambivalence or what Kapur terms 'Canada's own phase of benign neglect. Kapur, in fact, goes to the extent of saying that while US-Indian relations have moved from "very bad" to "improving", Canadian-Indian ties have evolved from "very good" to "very bad" to "making eyes again but avoiding the bedroom" ' (quoted by Rubinoff 1994).

Silver linings during 1970s and 1980s were that there were significant commercial interactions. Though actual progress in expanding trade and trade-related economic activities remained slow, these were moving. The business and trade delegations of the two countries exchanged ideas and also organized trade exhibitions. People-to-people links in the two countries were also growing steadily. After 1950 with changes in Canada's immigration laws, Indian immigration to Canada has been increasingly constantly. Adoption of the policy of multiculturalism helped immigrants integrate in the Canadian society and at the same time encouraged cultural interactions and exchanges between people of the two countries. Founded in 1968, the Shastri Indo-Canadian Institute (SICI) funded by the Government of India through counterpart rupee funds (money accumulated through the sale of Canadian food aid) to support Canadian scholars in India, soon became an important tool to overcome the total information gap and lack of economic and cultural contacts between the two countries. In due course it became a unique bi-national institute funded by two governments for cultural and academic exchanges and cooperation between the two countries. One very significant effect of SICI was that it received, along with some other agencies significant funds for Canadian International Development Agency (CIDA) projects. Immigrants and CIDA projects became the main societal and governmental links as both countries expressed rapid interest in the other.

ECONOMIC REFORMS AND THE NEW ERA OF COOPERATION

Starting in 1990s India's economic transformation attracted sufficient attention from the Canadian government and business community so much so that the Prime Minister of Canada, Jean Chretian led a Team Canada mission to India in January 1996 comprising two cabinet ministers, seven provincial premiers and 300 business persons. India's External Affairs Minister Inder Kumar Gujral paid an official visit to Canada in September 1996, which was reciprocated by Foreign Minister of Canada Lloyd Axworthy with a visit to India in January 1997. Axworthy during his visit said that India 'is emerging as one of the major world players of the 21st century. Canada recognizes this and we want to give India the priority it deserves in our foreign relations'.

This change, however, was short-lived in view of India's second detonation of five nuclear devises in two sets of tests on 11 and 13 May 1998. Despite calls from Canada and many other countries for restraint, neighbouring Pakistan retaliated with an alleged six nuclear detonations on 28 and 30 May. The Canadian government rapidly condemned the nuclear tests in South Asia, and placed its political relations with India and Pakistan on hold. Foreign Affairs Minister Axworthy stated that the nuclear tests in South Asia constituted a clear and fundamental threat to the international security regime, and thus, to Canada's security. Canada imposed several measures on India and Pakistan to demonstrate its strong disapproval of their nuclear tests, including temporarily withdrawing the Canadian High Commissioners from New Delhi and Islamabad, banning military exports, suspending non-humanitarian development assistance and restricting official contacts. Bilateral political relations, thus entered into another period of calculated neglect.

Observers, however, feel that 1998 was not 1974. As Ryan Touchey points out that the sanctions were, in the end, more detrimental to Canada than India. Also, as was the case in 1974, the bulk of Canada's allies, particularly in the G8, had either eased their own sanctions or abandoned them in favour of resuming normal relations with India. With Axworthy's retirement from politics in 2000, coupled with India's continued economic rise, Ottawa also started adjusting its approach. Thus, in a major policy reversal, the new minister of foreign affairs, John Manley, announced on 21 March 2001, that Ottawa wished to 'pursue' the broadest political and economic relations with India. Canada will encourage bilateral ministerial visits, resume full CIDA programming in India, including industrial cooperation and provide support to culture and sports. The government still expressed deep concern about the proliferation of nuclear weapons but appeared to be following the American strategy of compartmentalizing the disagreements so that other facts of the bilateral relationship, particularly economic, could be developed and pursued (Touchey 2007).

A key driver for this change is globalization—the explosion and rapid movement across borders of information, technology, people, goods, services and knowledge. The result of these processes is a world that is smaller and more interdependent. In this new world Canada has started feeling that economic, political, technological and demographic forces will intensify, making the world of 2020 dramatically different from the world of today. Yet this changing context also represents a tremendous opportunity for Canada. As a rich and open economy, with a skilled and adaptable population, it is well placed to gain from these global transformations. But Canada can do more than benefit. It can also contribute. A series of positive developments, both at home and abroad, have coalesced to provide Canada with an unprecedented chance to make a difference (Canada 2005a). In addition, Canada also started feeling that trade too can be a valuable tool for development. It can play an important role in generating economic activity, building healthy economies and alleviating poverty. There are many connections between Canada's trade and development strategies. In multilateral and regional trade negotiations, Canada supports taking into account disparities in the participating country's size and level of economic development. Canada is also working to devise new trade rules that take into account the interest of developing countries. Canada extends trade-related technical assistance and capacity building to help developing countries participate in various trade negotiations, facilitate their implementation of trade agreements and better enable them to adjust and diversify their economies. In addition, Canada offers generous market access programmes and liberal rules of origin to facilitate imports from developing countries and least developed countries. With regard to trade specifically the policy statement says:

> The 21st century presents a dramatically different economic landscape for Canadian companies. While our current relationship with major trading partners will remain important, large developing countries are emerging as powers in their own rights, with implication for our own prosperity. These economic opportunities must be better understood today, so that Canadians can benefit from them in the decades ahead.
>
> Emerging economic powers like China, India and Brazil are the key drivers of a new era of global economic growth. As a result, they will have a profound impact on Canada's long-term economic future. While China is poised to become the most important national economy in the 21st century, it still represents only one-tenth of 1 per cent of Canada's direct investment abroad. We will increase the pace of our engagement with these new giants. But we must also recognize their different stage of development. China and Brazil are deeply embedded in regional economies and while India is not yet a major player in supply chains, its knowledge-based industries, size and outward orientation make it an important player. Canadian policy must reflect an intimate knowledge of these dynamics.
>
> India has developed largely on the basis of its own market and the considerable skills of its people. Building on the WTO, we will also pursue particular Canadian needs—such as air links, investment protection and science and technology partnering—that tap into the dynamics of India's information and technology sectors in particular. The new science and technology agreement with India will open the door to accelerate cooperation in this area. (Canada 2005a)

In the above-mentioned framework, since 2003 there has been a steady maturing of the Canada-India relationship from one of engagement towards one of partnership. Throughout 2003 a continuation of high-level visits to India, including the Secretary of State for Asia-Pacific David Kilgour and Foreign Minister Bill Graham, culminated in the 24 October 2003 visit of Prime Minister Jean Chretien, and Prime Minister Atal Behari Vajpayee issuing a joint statement committing their governments to an expanded partnership for the twenty-first century. The statement (Partners for the 21st Century: Joint Statement by India and Canada) is a clear articulation that Canada and India have common interests and lays out a framework to increase trade and investment, address security concerns and leverage civil society linkages.

The Honourable Herb Dhaliwal, member of parliament, on 16 June 2004 came as a special envoy of the Government of Canada and transmitted a letter from Prime Minister Paul Martin and the good wishes of the Canadian prime minister to the prime minister of India. Dr Manmohan Singh, the renowned architect of India's early (1991-6) economic reform programme, had been appointed prime minister a month before this visit. Prime Minister Singh and Dhaliwal agreed that the ties between India and Canada could be strengthened, including in economic relations. Canadian Prime Minister Paul Martin paid a two-day visit to India on 17 January 2005. The prime minister met Dr Manmohan Singh, President Abdul Kalam and Mrs Sonia Gandhi. The prime ministers of India and Canada reviewed the bilateral relations and discussed important international and regional issues. They agreed on initiatives that could strengthen the India-Canada partnership and contribute to addressing global challenges more effectively. Prime Minister Manmohan Singh welcomed Prime Minister Martin's initiative for a meeting of G20 leaders to discuss issues of global concern, such as terrorism, development and global public health. Both agreed to work towards the recommendations of the high-level UN panel on Threats, Challenges and Change and reiterated their commitment towards contributing to a more effective, representative and accountable world body.

The 2005 Canada-India joint statement reaffirmed Canada's and India's commitment to deepen their bilateral dialogue on key global issues and enhance their cooperation in areas of mutual priority, including regional security and counter-terrorism;

science and technology; the environment; bilateral trade and investment; and people-to-people links.

Acknowledging bilateral complementarities in the areas of science and technology (S&T), Canada and India signed a Canada-India Agreement for Scientific and Technological Cooperation in November 2005 which aims to foster greater bilateral S&T collaboration in five priority areas—nanoscience and nanomedicine; information and communications technology; biotechnology and health research and medical devices; sustainable and alternate energy and environmental technologies; and earth sciences and disaster management. In the area of the environment, both countries are actively working towards the creation of a Canada-India Forum for Environmental Collaboration to work more closely on key global environmental issues, including climate change. Canada and India are also exploring avenues for greater cooperation in the energy field, reflecting the importance both countries attach to issues of energy security and bilateral complementarities that exist in this sector.

India's rapidly expanding economy and market reforms are opening the door to international commerce, making India a vital partner for Canada's prosperity agenda. In addition to the potential for mutual financial gain, the growing prosperity in India is a force for regional security and provides the governments with the potential to address development priorities more effectively. A key part of the strategy includes identifying priority sectors and developing targeted action plans for a number of sub-sectors that will lead to increased two-way trade, investment and technology partnerships. Selected priority sectors include agriculture and agri-food, infrastructure, information and communications technologies, extractive industries, life sciences and enabling services. Its potential economic importance to Canada was demonstrated by the fact that Mumbai was the first overseas destination for Canada's new minister for emerging markets. Two-way investment figures are growing although they still remain lower than desired. In 2005, official statistics valued Canadian direct investment into India at $204 million and Indian direct investment into Canada at $145 million; however, it is believed that official investment figures may be highly underestimated due to the fact that significant investment flows through third countries.

People-to-people links are also increasing as Canada and India foster greater links through academic and cultural exchange, including the work of the Shastri Indo-Canadian Institute. This activity and interchange is taking place *in tandem* with a rapidly growing Indo-Canadian community, now estimated to be nearing one million. In 2005, Canada opened nine new visa application centres across India. India is currently the second largest source country of immigrants to Canada and may well become the main source country within the next few years.

Both in India and Canada, a desire and efforts to be closer to each other have been there, irrespective of the party in power. In India, in 2003 it was the NDA government led by BJP's Atal Behari Vajpayee that responded positively to the Chretien led Liberal Party government in Ottawa, leading to a joint statement in October 2003. That statement and process was not only continued but further strengthened by Manmohan Singh's UPA government that came to power in 2004. In Canada, the defeat of the Liberals and coming to power of the Conservatives in 2006 has not reduced the tempo of efforts since 2001 to re-evaluate and expand relations with India. In fact, the Harper government has made India a 'key priority' and through doing so is showing a desire to move further away from the historical spite of the past in setting course for a new foreign and trade policy agenda that seeks to strengthen relations, especially economic, trade and investment relations (Touchey 2007). In April 2008, Harper said, 'Canada simply cannot afford to miss out on India's phenomenal economic growth. That is why our government is putting so much emphasis on improving trade and investment between our countries.'

Canada's intention to end a frosty relationship with India and India's reciprocal move to downplay old grievances seems to have moved well towards more cordial, pragmatic and fruitful partnerships. Close watchers of Canada-India relationships, however still see lack of clarity as far as a comprehensive direction is concerned. Alistair D. Edgar, for instance, points out that the arrow currently points upwards in Canadian relations with India but it remains unclear exactly in what sense, or how (and how far) to advance this potential if it is to be translated into concrete expressions of policy. Is it more better, that is, the quantitative approach to foreign policy seeking more agreements, especially involving trade, science and technology and other economic and educational linkages? Or is it better to focus efforts on moving forward with a small number of the 'higher end' issues of security and stability—a bilateral policy area that for various reasons has been contentious and diverse over the past three decades? (Edgar 2008).

Similarly Ryan Touchey observes that despite deeming India a 'key priority', present signs suggest that the Canadian government has arrived at a crossroads and, in contrast to key allies such as Australia and the United States, is not wholly certain, as to what it wants from India, apart from increased trade linkages. According to Touchey there are two options that the Conservative government can now pursue following the Liberal's decision to abandon the policy of isolating India in 2001 after the 1998 Pokhran nuclear tests. The first option entails Ottawa, along with the provinces and the private sector, emphasizing the primacy of trade and investment links above a broader political relationship. The second option is more ambitious. It will entail Ottawa cultivating a broader political relationship that acknowledges the importance of expanding a complex commercial relationship involving trade, two-way investment, and advanced cooperation in service and technology while developing political and security aspects of a more comprehensive relationship. Touchey finds at this moment, the first option being favoured by Ottawa (Touchey 2007). Edgar, Touchey, Kapur, and many close watchers of India-Canada relations, however, are looking beyond economic and trade relations, and towards strategic and more active political relations. As Edgar points out, trade and business cooperation is already taking shape with new initiatives or proposals about free trade, foreign investment, science technology projects, agriculture, environment and energy. Finding the synergies between these emerging areas of cooperation and bringing greater coherence to them, can also play a role in building closer ties through mutual economic benefits, assuming that the relationship is a two-way street. Edgar in this context suggests some avenues for

Canada-India security policy cooperation, or at least improved mutual understanding and coordination, in these countries' approaches towards fragile states in West Asia—and in particular towards Afghanistan. Edgar points out that both New Delhi and Ottawa do have wider political and security interests that can benefit from improved bilateral cooperation, and that can be negatively effected by a relationship that either remains cool or that takes a step backwards (Edgar 2008). For Touchey (2007) the litmus test that will illustrate to what extent Canada and India have successfully exercised their historical demons rests with whether they can work past their longstanding schism on the NPT file. In this context referring to the US-India civil nuclear cooperation deal, Touchey, points out that while the USA and Australia, two of Ottawas' closest allies had come to terms with India on this matter, Canada had a little different historical baggage. He, however, saw signals that Ottawa also was overcoming its historic allergy in dealing with a nuclear India. Touchey has been proved correct and Canada, not only supported India in the NSG meeting but has also entered into a nuclear energy agreement with India.

The trend, thus, is movement towards a more multilayered relationship. Of course, there are various challenges on the way. But David M. Malone (2008), former High Commissioner to India, points out certain factors that had helped the two countries emerge from the dark, or at least bleak age in the bilateral relationships. These include the Indo-Canadian population, trade relations, investment, education, etc. Fortunately, these factors, at present are stronger then earlier. Indo-Canadian population has grown up to about 3 per cent of the overall Canadian population. It represents a tremendously sturdy bridge between the two countries. Malone, in addition, points towards various structural similarities conducive for better relations. These include largeness of the two countries because of which both countries are in the spotlight more than would otherwise be the case. Then, the British colonial rule which both experienced (although in very different ways) left them with institutions of governance that each recognizes in the other (parliamentary system, judiciary, etc.). Further, Canada and India both as Federal states are constantly struggling with both centrifugal and centralizing forces; making beyond governance. Malone also takes note of the fact that both India and Canada have often been cited as models of pluralistic, multi-ethnic, multi-confessional, multi-cultural societies that, in spite of intercommunal tensions, have succeeded in accommodating the multiple identities of most of their citizens. Along with these both countries also, at present face environment challenges. He, thus sees much scope for cooperation between the two countries. It is becoming quite clear that Canada and India have entered the twenty-first century with a shared vision to promote mutually rewarding economic and hopefully strategic partnership in an increasingly competitive and dynamic globalized world.

Ottawa believes that it shares a number of common or at least similar values with a democratic India. The Indian diaspora in Canada is becoming increasingly politically influential. They represent a hidden advantage for Canada, and are at the same time emerging as an important component of a transnational community, composed of various segments of the Indian diaspora, which will have an important clout in the world at large. India today is dynamic and on the move. However, it still has to consolidate its position. Canada definitely is an important partner for that. Both India and Canada are vibrant democracies, committed to global peace, sustainable development and harmonious coexistence. This commonality in values definitely provides the necessary basis for long-term beneficial diplomatic, strategic and economic relations.

REFERENCES

Asaadi, Muzzaffar, 'Contesting Globalization: Canada and India in Comparative Perspective', *Indian Journal of Canadian Studies*, vol. XII, 2004, pp. 151-3.

Basdeo, Sahadeo, 'Lester Pearson's Participatory Internationalism: Canada-India Relations into the New Millinium', *6th Lester Pearson Lecture*, Centre for Canadian Studies, University of Delhi, 25 April 2000.

———, 'Cultural Understanding in International Relations: The Case of Canada and India during the Pearson Years at the Foreign Ministry', lecture delivered at the XVII International Conference of the Indian

Association for Canadian Studies, University of Calicut, 3 January 2001.

Government of Canada, *Canada's International Policy Statement: A Role of Pride and Influence in the World: Overview,* Ottawa: Department of Foreign Affairs and International Trade, 2005a.

Edgar, Alistair D., 'The Arrow Points Up: A Track-II Perspective on Opportunities for Canada-India Security Politics in Afghanistan', lecture presented at Canada-India Policy Dialogue hosted by Asia-Pacific Foundation and the Centre for Policy Research, New Delhi, 2-3 April 2008.

Hadwen, John G., 'Some of the Realities of the Indo-Canadian Relationship', in J.S. Grewal and Hugh Johnson (eds.), *The India-Canada Relations: Exploring Political, Economic and Cultural Dimensions,* New Delhi: Sage, 1994.

Kapur, Ashok, 'Canada and India', in Arthur G. Rubinoff (ed.), *Canada and South Asia: Issues and Opportunities*, Toronto: Centre for South Asian Studies, 1988.

———, 'Canada-India Diplomatic Relations', paper presented at Shastri Indo-Canadian Institute Conference, Shimla, May 1991.

Malone, David M., 'India and Canada—A Study In Contrasts', Lester B. Pearson Lecture, University of Delhi, 30 April 2008.

Rubinoff, Arthur G., 'Comparing Americans and Canadian Perceptions and Policies towards the Indian Subcontinent', in J.S. Grewal and Hugh Johnson (eds.), *The India Canada Relationship: Exploring the Political, Economic and Cultural Dimensions,* New Delhi: Sage, 1994.

Touchey, Ryan, 'Canada and India at 60', *International Journal*, Autumn 2007.

———, 'A Perspective on Canada-India Higher Education Partnerships: Prospects and Obstacles', paper presented at Canada-India Policy Dialogue, New Delhi, 2-3 April 2008.

CHAPTER 2

Shaping Multilateralism in Canadian Foreign Policy: Implications for India

G. GOPA KUMAR

This essay attempts to examine the basic shifts in the Canadian foreign policy in the twenty-first century by moving more towards multilateralism and at the same time engaging the 'big neighbour' USA in trade, business and issues related to migration and homeland security. The essay also examines the experience of Canada as a middle power beginning from the twentieth century and how the shifting trajectory of Canadian foreign policy can serve as an influential element in shaping India's foreign policy in the twenty-first century. Since there are many commonalities between the two countries, such as liberal and parliamentary democracy, multiculturalism, federalism, human rights, pacifism and minority rights, the study explores how India adapt to the era of globalization without injuring basic goals like social justice and secularism by taking clues from the Canadian experiences in successfully engaging the USA as well as potential developing countries.

The three major pillars of Canadian foreign policy continue to be the three 'd's—defence, development and diplomacy. The peculiar geographic dimension had made the USA and Canada 'neighbours, friends, partners and allies' ever since both countries became independent from colonial rule. At the same time, Canada drifted from the USA to the extent possible once the latter began to show her imperialistic ambitions across the world, particularly after the end of Cold War. Even while joining the North American Free Trade Agreement with the USA and Mexico on 31 December 1998, the Canadian priorities were very clear. Managing the political distance from the big neighbour and at the same time adjusting economic relations with a small economy like Mexico was indeed a difficult balancing act. Again, Canada learned diplomatic lessons from the USA in adapting to the *soft-power* relations. The North American Defence was covered under the NORAD and traditional nuclear relations helped Canada in receiving the security umbrella from the US. But how far these arrangements are valid today? Has Canada become an extended nation of protecting the interests of USA? The Canadian ethos of nationalism and multiculturalism suggests a different picture altogether.

With globalization opening up opportunities for market expansion, Canada found the potentialities of engaging countries not only in Europe but also Asia-Pacific region. Canada could play major roles in other economic forums like G7, EU, AU, etc., besides improving relations with countries like India, China and South Africa. The tradition of Canadian exports in the past was such that more than 80 per cent of her exports were moving towards the USA. Currently, this is slowly shifting, although proximity with the US would continue to influence economic relations. Today, Canada needs to attract huge investments from different parts of the world besides encouraging migration from talented human resources across the world. The current policy of the USA towards migration is very different as seen by the recent moves like Contemporary Immigration Regulation Act (CIRA). The 9/11 developments had heavily shifted the US approach towards migration. At the same time, the Canadian policy on immigration is entirely positive and influenced by her domestic conditions and values.

Another aspect of Canada-US divide can be seen in the practice of human rights, particularly after 11 September 2001. Not only that US has become more suspicious of all kinds of immigrants but also shut down her borders with the needle of suspicion on illegal immigrants entering from Canadian and Mexican borders. Canada's soft policy towards refugees became another issue for the USA. Further, Canadian aid to developing countries has a long history cherished by the Canadian policy towards humanitarian intervention. All these parameters were challenged at least for a while following the domestic scenario in the USA after the terrorist attacks. Canada's refusal to join the Second Gulf War in 2003 (Iraq War) was treated with hostility from the US side while the domestic response to Canada's involvement in the Afghan campaign in 2001 was mixed in nature.

The consistent environment policy of Canada also demanded a shift following America's negative reaction to the Kyoto protocol. Canada's tradition of protecting the environment, initiative against global warming and maritime security in the Arctic region also became irritants in the bi-lateral relations with the US. Altogether, we can notice Canada's compulsion to shape genuine multilateralism in the specific context of globalization, terrorist threats and the neo-imperial policies of the US after the demise of Cold War. The challenges and opportunities of the twenty-first century are so huge which demands Canada to move out of her conventional premises of the foreign policy practiced in the previous century. As an emerging superpower in the twenty-first century, India can certainly learn many lessons from Canada's setbacks and accomplishments. Depending on the *big brother* for majority of imports and exports will not be feasible for Canada in the era of multilateral trade. Expanding and diversifying trade and investment to Asia-Pacific region is benefitting Canada in many ways. Indo-Canadian relations are also entering a new phase after the success of India since 1991 in promoting exports with both developed and developing countries.

MULTILATERALISM AS A VIABLE STRATEGY

Multilateralism is one of the major foundations in the foreign policy structure of Canada. It is a product of Canada's social culture, ideological faith and pressures of geography. With the emergence of a nation-state heavily conditioned by unending flow of immigration initially from the Caucasian region and subsequently from Asia-Pacific region, Canada found the changing social and political values influencing her foreign policy priorities significantly. With firm commitment to international peace, Canada was discovering the potentialities of using multilateral institutions for promoting unity and international peace. This trend evinced soon after Prime Minister Trudeau started abandoning biculturalism in favour of multiculturalism. Indeed, the history of the US influence in the traditional Canadian foreign policy was a product of Canada's geographical proximity and dependence with the US on imports and exports. Later, Canada found the need to develop multilateralism as a strategy to distance herself from the orbit of the extraordinary American influence. Canada, therefore, experimented this strategy during the Cold War period and earned the reputation of a peace loving nation and *soft-state*. With the emergence of middle-size economy and acquiring the status of a middle power, Canada was admitted to various institutions like G8, NATO, NAFTA besides active involvement in most of the auxiliary bodies of the UN.

The unilateral policies of the USA following the disintegration of the Soviet Union in December 1991 and the emergence of a unipolar world soon after the first Gulf War convinced the Canadian strategists to reinvent the potentialities of multilateralism in international politics. We could notice this increasing trend during the last 15 years. The 9/11 incidents once again convinced the Canadian leaders on the necessity of shaping an independent foreign policy. But the concept was fraught with several handicaps. The US pressurized Canada to be extremely vigilant on cross-border terrorism and the problem of terrorists migrating to Canada in the guise of refugees. The US alleged that Al-Qaeda units were opened in many border pockets of Canada without the knowledge of Canadian security forces. The lengthy unmanned US-Canadian boundaries soon became a sensitive component in the foreign policy priorities of both the countries. Patrolling the arctic region became another issue between the two countries.

Interestingly, Canada was an ally of the UN coalition against Afghanistan following 11 September developments. She continued to maintain her defence force for peacekeeping in the region in spite of domestic criticisms. The Canadian priorities in the Iraq War (2003-8) were quite different to that of the Afghanistan campaign. Canada tried to distance from the USA as much as it could on the Iraq war unlike the position adopted by the UK and Australia.

Today, Canada is the 33rd contributor to the UN peacekeeping efforts. She is a part of the 17 UN-led missions including Haiti, Congo, Somalia, Sierra Leone, etc. 'The concept of *peacekeeping* is too deeply ingrained in the public consciousness and too valuable to dismiss. Canada should do much more to live up to its image as a peacekeeping nation, as its citizens expect. . . . A legitimate UN mandate, consent for deployment, impartiality and the minimum use of force are time honoured standards that engender public support.'[1] Many critics notice that Canada had at all times supported the USA in many of her Cold War designs including the support to Israel. Since the 1950s, Canada's military strategy and structure have been shaped in the deliberate synchronization with those of the US through a series of bilateral and multilateral agreements. In fact, the economy is dominated by the American capital. America's direct investment in Canada is high, many of Canada's most profitable industries are owned by US federal corporations.[2] Eighty per cent of Canada's agricultural imports and exports are linked to the US markets.

Normon Hillmer et al. has rightly argued that

> in the continuing predicament of multilateralism, one of the central challenges of global governance is the need to educate governments, generate and disseminate knowledge, and collaborate in finding and executing remedial policies. In the Iraq War (2003) Canada wanted to reinvigorate international debate and discussion about the challenges of humanitarian interaction and help device principles of action that are central around the *responsibility to protect*. Canada can help the UN Secretary General to redefine the agenda of UN by organizing a more effective global response to disease control, hunger, lack of education and environmental destruction.[3]

According to the Canadian Council for International Co-operation, the primary values and interests that drive Canadian foreign policy are global social justice, peace and respect for the planet's ecosystems. The CCIC put forward a 10-point agenda for global action which highlights the values and interests of Canadian foreign policy—creating an equitable global economic order, promoting sustainable development, upholding human rights, achieving gender equity, improving the lives of children, building peace, promoting global food security, promoting individual and social corporate responsibility, reinventing Canada's Foreign Aid Programme and creating new opportunities for citizen participation.[4] Similarly, the basic features of defence policy constitute the following—defending Canada, defending North America and protecting Canada through NORAD, promoting Arctic security, defence cooperation with the US, contributing to international security and participation in full range of multilateral operations through the UN, NATO and other regional organizations and coalitions of like minded countries, supporting humanitarian relief efforts and restoration of conflict-devastated areas; and participating in arms control and other confidence building measures. Canada has thus adopted an international posture and dropped its older style of isolationism.[5] At the same time Canada distanced with the US on many strategic issues. For instance, the Canadian government decided not to participate in the Iraq invasion, citing the lack of UN mandate for the use of force and mindful of the strong public opinion to an unnecessary war. The reluctance of the US to submit to international treaties and agreements is a major concern for Canada since Canada has become more integrated into a North American economy and security arrangements. Lloyd Axworthy, noted scholar and former minister of foreign affairs, Canada, notes that the dilemma is how to pursue independent economic policies on multilateral platforms. The concept of human security emerged as the lens through which Canada could view the international scene.[6]

It appears that Canadian foreign policy combines the features of globalization and globalism. The three d's harmonizes the basic interests of the society. The DFAIT's understanding with developing aid, trade and diplomacy with other countries itself is unique. Canada's faith and commitment to human security is also expressed in terms of liberal approaches in policies towards immigrants and refugees. It was not accidental that Canada has the maximum number of Nobel laureates in the area of promoting peace. Again, militarism has never been a basic principle of Canadian foreign policy. The Royal Canadian Mountain Police (RCMP) has been trained more in the maintenance of domestic law and order and peacekeeping. As a middle power, Canada has been active in numerous multilateral bodies. Its refusal to endorse American interests in Iraq War was fundamentally different to its role in the UN coalition for the Gulf War of 1991.

According to Stev Lee, there exists a 'core set of values' that might be characterized as 'quality of life values' in Canada. These include (1) respect for the environment, (2) commitment to democracy, (3) defence of human rights, (4) a desire to encourage fairness in developing societies (fair labour, business, legal and governance arrangements), (5) a recognition of the importance of tolerance and diversity, and (6) a strong attachment to the ideas of an engaged civil society both at home and abroad.[7] Here multilateralism is a central aspect through which Canada is advancing a vision of collective security that acknowledges international responsibility to balance between security and development. The 11 September developments brought some shift in the defence policy. The Missile Defence Policy was promoted by the USA consequent to 11 September developments and Canada also succumbed to an increasing role of military corporate in the defence industry. The future of Canada as a peacemaker and peacekeeper ultimately depends to a very great extent on the regional and international trends which include both security and economic considerations.[8]

EXPLORING NEW AVENUES IN INDO-CANADIAN RELATIONS

The early phase of Indo-Canadian relations started with a positive note since the Colombo Plan of 1950 provided for a longstanding commitment towards South Asia and the Third World. The Nehru era found a strong potential for shaping Indo-Canadian relationships. Indeed, India was a recipient of Canadian aid during the 1970s and 1980s. But political relationship between the two countries was not developing considerably. India's foreign policy proximity with USSR, suspicion about the USA in helping Pakistan, Canadian position on Kashmir issue and active involvement of India in Non-Aligned movement during the Cold War era did not facilitate new steps in strengthening Indo-Canadian relations. The 1980s period throughout witnessed many strains in bilateral relations. Canada's soft policy towards refugees, especially Sikh militants who allegedly ran an exile Akali government in Vancouver, was a major concern for India. The bombing of Air India flight (Kanishka tragedy) in 1982 by Sikh terrorists settled in Canada and the slow judicial process in Canada in punishing the culprits also raised major issues in Indo-Canadian relations.

By the middle of the 1980s there witnessed a decline in the status of the Canadian High Commissioner in Delhi. Although Shastri Indo-Canadian Institute could fill a growing gap in the nature of bilateral relationship at the educational and cultural level, there was a little emphasis at the political level. Noted biographer of Pt. Jawaharlal Nehru and V.K. Krishna Menon, Michael Brecher, identifies the following reasons for the negative state of affairs—(1) increasing American influence over Canada and conversely India's political distance with the USA and close ties with the USSR during the Cold War period, (2) Canada became more inward looking, and further the UN peacekeeping operation led by Canada was not necessarily linked with India, (3) India's nuclear support from Canada was allegedly misused for Pokhran-I explosion in 1974.[9] This situation has changed especially during the last 10 years and now Canada looks towards India as a major innovating economic power. If, in the past, India was a recipient of Canadian aid, today India is a potential area for investment and business partnership. Michael Brecher predicts that two decades from now Canada certainly will prefer India more than China. Not only that common elements of democracy and diversity bring India to the top of Canadian foreign policy, but also serious economic swings will positively impact on bilateral relationships.[10]

In spite of many commonalities the relations between India and Canada were not strong at least until 2000. The conventional position of India being a leader of Non-Aligned movement and Canada being a member of NATO and further India's close relationship with the USSR (the natural ally principle) and Canada's proximity with the USA (geographically, ideologically and culturally), had further widened the gap between the two countries. In fact, the shift of India's economic policy from the state sponsored public sector to the opening up of the economy for free trade and liberalization of regulations brought a new change in Canadian mindset in considering India as an emerging market as well as a huge reservoir of human resources. The consistent economic performance which began in late 1990s and the booming Information Technology sector had attracted international attention. The West began to look at the emerging India with all seriousness and soon erased the conventional values and images attached towards a post-colonial nation.

It was the new foreign minister of Canada, John Manley, who took the initiatives for 're-engaging India'. The two incidents for which Canada disliked India in the past were India's nuclear explosion in 1974 and 1998 and her refusal to join the NPT and CTBT regimes. On 20 March 2001 John Manley announced that 'Canada would pursue the broadest possible political and economic relationship with India'. The period 2001-2 witnessed a new watershed in bilateral relations. The official visits strengthened the morale of the emerging relationships. The two foreign ministers, Bill Graham and Yashwant Sinha, resolved to intensify political, economic and cultural relationships and expand the existing cooperation on counter terrorism, global and regional security matters. A joint statement entitled 'Partners for the 21st Century' was released in October 2003 which outlined the vision of the two prime ministers, Jean Chretien and A.B. Vajpayee to 'strengthen government, commercial and civil society linkages'. The statement committed the two countries to deepen their engagements, to strengthen international and regional peace and security; prevent proliferation of nuclear weapons; enhance strategic dialogue; upgrade Canadian representation in India; promote cooperation in counter-terrorism; hold dialogue on global issues and high level trade policy consultations.[11]

Similarly, a small shift in the Canadian policy on Jammu & Kashmir can also be seen in this context. In the past Canada supported the need for strengthening dialogue between India and Pakistan while 'protecting the interest of Kashmiri people'. Canada was also a regular participant of the UNMOGIP and felt that the Kashmir issue had the potentiality for a nuclear conflict in South Asia. Canada now shifted slightly towards

India and subscribed to the G8 statement which indirectly criticized Pakistan for sponsoring armed intruders across the Line of Control. She also agreed that resumption of Indo-Pak dialogue in the spirit of the Lahore Declaration as the best immediate measure for maintaining peace.[12]

Following India's economic reforms beginning in 1991 and the financial crises in East Asian economies, Canada recognized the potentiality of an emerging India. The 'Focus India' campaign was started in June 1995 to capitalize on the opportunities presented by the Indian market. In turn, the Confederation of Indian Industry (CII) took the initiative to promote trade cooperation. The Canada-India business Council, Canada Manufacturers Association, FICCI, ASSOCHAM and other associations joined the new trend of developing trade and business cooperation. The CII promoted business delegations in sectors such as oil and gas, environment, mining, etc. Similarly, Canada had shown interest in promoting relations in sectors such as power, telecommunications, mines, etc.[13]

During the last five years there has been a steady growth in the economic relationships between the two countries. The bilateral trade was just C $788.49 million in 1992 while in 2004 it rose up to C $2.4 billion. In 2004, India has become the twentieth largest exporter to Canada with C $1.58 billion (0.45 per cent of Canadian imports) while Canadian exports to India is only C $875 billion (0.26 per cent of Canada's exports). The Indian Foreign Direct Investments (FDI) in Canada C $68 million compared to C $186 million in India. While India's investment in Canada are mainly in areas of IT sector, software, pharmaceutical, metals, petrochemicals, auto-ancillaries, financial services, etc., Canada focuses its investments in areas like banking, insurance, financial services, engineering, telecommunications, environment, energy, mining, etc. Canada has noticed the potential opportunities emerging in India in sectors like oil and gas, hydro-energy, mining, construction, transportation, telecommunication, environment, technologies, agriculture, biotechnology, information technology, etc. Both countries had also noted the scope for third country collaborative projects in Africa, Middle East and South-East Asia.[14]

In addition, the areas of potential Indian investment in Canada include pharmaceuticals, metals and minerals, pulp and paper, petrochemicals, etc. In turn, Canada has targeted a wide range of sectors including agriculture and agri-food, footwear, energy (power generation, oil and gas), mining, aviation and aerospace, transport and medial equipment. The Ministry of External Affairs in India feels that Canada's focus will be on six thrust areas—power and energy, equipment and services, oil and natural gas, environment protection and services, telecommunications and information technology and financial sector including insurance.[15]

The joint statement by India and Canada titled as 'Partners for the 21st Century' laid out a framework to increase trade and investment, address security issues, and develop civil society linkages. The highlights of joint statement included enhancing Canada's diplomatic presence in India, expanding commercial and economic ties through identification of priority areas through routine trade consultations, enhance academic and cultural links, strengthen Joint Working Group on Counter Terrorism, enhance dialogue to strengthen international and regional peace and security and improving Cooperation on Preventing Spread of Weapons of Mass Destruction, encourage civil society ties, etc.[16] Again, during the visit of Prime Minister Paul Martin to New Delhi in January 2005 Prime Minister Manmohan Singh appreciated the initiative for a meeting of G20 leaders to discuss the issues of global concern, such as terrorism, development and global public health.[17]

On 1 March 2004, the South Asian Partnership Canada hosted a round table discussion to examine Canada's evolving relations with India. Here three main problem areas were identified—(1) economic and commercial issues—since India is also a force for regional security and has the potential to address developmental priorities more effectively; (2) humanitarian and social issues—to achieve Millennium Development Goals, Canada must help India's effort in alleviating poverty and thereby address crucial issues on regional stability and security, (3) military and non-military issues (including environmental issues)—since these problems in South Asia are of international concerns and have cross-national implications.[18]

Trade between the two countries has increased manifold in the past decade. Major exports from India include readymade garments, textiles, steel, jewellery, precious stones, leather products, coffee and tea, spices and carpets. India imported newsprint, pulp, lumber, peas, asbestos, iron, copper and other industrial materials from Canada. In 2006, India exported US $9.9 billion worth of goods and imported US $131 billion worth of goods, exceeding US imports valued at $96 billion. The Parliamentary Secretary to the Minister of International Trade, Ted Menzis visited Indian cities from 12-16 March 2007 for developing investment and other trade flows. A new agreement has been formed by Information Technology Association of Canada and National Association of Software and Service Companies (NASSCOM) in India. Similarly, the provinces of Canada like Nova Scotia had started improving trade with India. Nevertheless, Canada's share in the Indian imports is less than 1 per cent.[19] The need to enhance imports to India is certainly obvious in this context.

The balance of trade has remained in India's favour since 1998. The Canadian Export Development Corporation identified India amongst its three 'premium' markets. Canadian presence has increased in areas like banking, insurance, financial services, engineering and consultancy services. While Canada could see India as a gateway to South and South-East Asia, India could use Canada as a gateway to North America. India could export to Canada items like cotton yarn, fabrics, drugs, pharmaceuticals and fine chemicals, metals, gems and jewellery, leather, electronic and computer software, carpets, minerals, engineering goods, etc.[20]

Significantly, in the struggle against globalization by the civil society groups, there witnessed greater links between Canadian civil society groups and Indian social movements. In the process, these groups and movements cut across boundaries of nation/nationality, geography and established anti-global collectives at the international level. The People's Global Action (PGA) is one such international collective. Assadi notes that the PGA brought India and Canada closer together for a scrutiny of globalization. Thus in spite of the different historical trajectories, Indian social movements can negotiate with their counterparts in Canada on common issues produced by the negative effects of globalization.[21]

Indeed, Canada has severe limitations in distancing its relations with the superpower, the USA, considering economic and geographical factors besides the commitments in NAFTA. Yet Canadians have distanced from the USA on issues like the Landmine Treaty, International Criminal Court, the anti-Child Soldier Protocol, the Kyoto Accord, economic sanctions and human rights violations and war in Iraq. Hence, it is argued here that Canada can strive for a more independent foreign policy and enhance free trade with emerging economies like India even while maintaining economic rapport with European Union and the USA.

CONCLUSION

While the new trends in strengthening Indo-Canadian relations offer hope for positive growth in the twenty-first century, it is very clear that only a small portion of the total potential area has been achieved so far. This is in spite of the favourable political and economic situation prevailing in both the countries. India has joined the neo-liberal agenda since 1991 only but Canada has always been following a combination of welfare state principles with the strategy of shaping a middle range economy in a capitalist framework. Especially after 1999, many favourable initiatives had taken place for improving bilateral relationships. But economic relationship, as evinced by statistics, suggests marginal gains only. Given the emerging nature of Indian economy and the large educated middle class, there exists tremendous potentiality for Canada to invest in India as well as accept exports from India. Similarly, India can exchange technical experts on a wide variety of areas besides expanding business in Canada. Both countries can compete with the USA and China in strengthening bilateral relationships. The responsibilities for developing this task rest not merely with DFAIT and MEA, but also with civil society structures and academic bodies in both the countries. The favourable international and domestic political situations could be utilized for expanding this relationship.

Multilateralism has been a basic strength of Canadian foreign policy. It will continue to be so given the Canadian culture and political values. Even today, more than 70 per cent of Canadian imports and exports are directed towards the USA. Again, the US provides a nuclear security umbrella for Canada. At the same time, Canada has tried to retain its independent identity and distanced itself from the US on many spheres. Again, Canadian participation in international and regional political and economic bodies, besides the unique role in peacekeeping, has made it amply clear about the major benefits of using multilateral platforms for national advantage. Being a nation dependent on migration for economic growth and development (estimated at 70 per cent in 2004 and more than 90 per cent in 2011), the Canadian strategy of maintaining good relations with other countries, using diaspora and other means, has been observed as a successful strategy. Thus both multilateralism and multiculturalism have become strong pillars in domestic and foreign policy realms. On the other hand, India's external relationship had witnessed huge changes during the last sixty years. Considering its cherished values against colonialism and imperialism, commitment to international peace, India can also take a few cues from the Canadian strategy of multilateralism. Again India, like Canada, has contributed significantly for peace-keeping in different parts of the world.

Engaging with most of the countries and further strengthening relations with potential economic partners are essential requisites for the successful logistics of the twenty-first-century international relations. Unlike yesteryears, contemporary actors in international scene include, besides the government, non-state forces like NGOs, civil and military corporate, civil society leaders, diaspora groups, refugees, terrorists, etc. The dimensions, art and practice of diplomacy are changing very fast now. Multilateral platforms and strategies, rather than conflict diplomacy, are needed in this context. Both India and Canada have to do a lot of ground work in this regard. The ideological, cultural and economic similarities of these two countries offer sufficient space for improvising multilateral engagements in the coming decades. The welfare state principles of Canada and the social justice concept of India have several areas of convergence rather than conflict.

NOTES

1. W. Walter Dorn, 'Peacekeeping then, Now and Always', *Canadian Military Journal*, vol. 6, no. 4, Winter 2005-6, pp. 105-6.
2. Mark Charlton and Paul Barker (eds.), *Contemporary Political Issues*, Ontario: Thomson Nelson, 2002, p. 5.
3. Normon Hillmer, Fen Osler Hamspon and David Carment, 'Small Power in Canadian Foreign Policy', in David Carment et al., *Canada Among Nations 2004*, Montreal: McGill University Press, 2005, pp. 14-15.
4. CCIC's response to the DFAIT's 'A Dialogue in Foreign Policy', *Canadian Foreign Policy*, vol. 10, no. 3 (Spring 2003), p. 159.
5. Robert J. Jackson and Doren Jackson, *Politics in Canada: Culture, Institutions, Behaviour and Public Policy*, Toronto: Prentice Hall, 2001, pp. 554-60.
6. Lloyd Axworthy, *Navigating a New World: Canada's Global Future*, Toronto: Alfred A. Knopf Canada, 2003, p. 4.
7. Alison Howell, 'Peaceful, Tolerant and Orderly? A Feminist Analysis of Discourses of "Canadian Values" in Canadian Foreign Policy', *Canadian Foreign Policy*, vol. 12, no. 1 (Spring 2005), p. 51.
8. Interview with Aaron Hywarren, Director of Public Policy, National Defence Headquarters, Ottawa on 10 August 2006.
9. Interview with Michael Brecher at McGill University, Montreal, on 2 August 2006.
10. Ibid.
11. http://www/cgitoronto.ca/indiacanada bilateral relations.htm, Ministry of External Affairs, India, accessed on 15.4.2008.
12. Ibid.
13. Ibid.
14. High Commission of India, Ottawa/Consulate General of India, Toronto, *Basic Facts About Canada*.
15. Ministry of External Affairs, India, op. cit.
16. http://www.geo.international/gec/asic/new-delhi (site/canada india bilateral relations - en.asp. accessed on 15.4.2008. also see, http://www.cgitoronto.ca/PMs Joint Statement 24 Oct 03 htm. accessed on 16.4.2008.
17. Ibid.
18. http://www.action.web.ca/home/sap/india_resources.shtml?x=59319 accessed on 15.4.2008.

19. http://www.indiacanada.wordpress.com/2007/03/23/indo-canadian trade-history and recent initiatives accessed on 15-4-2008.
20. http://www.cgitoronto.ca/indiacanada bilateral relations.htm accessed on 15.4.2008
21. Muzzaffar Assadi, 'Contesting Globalization: Canada and India in Comparative Perspective', *Indian Journal of Canadian Studies*, vol. XII, 2004, pp. 151-3.

CHAPTER 3

Indo-Canadian Cooperation on Counter-Terrorism in the New Millennium: A Study

LOPAMUDRA BANDYOPADHYAY

Terrorism is not a new phenomenon. It permeates recorded history in one form or another. Yet, each time it reappears, still very complex, it looms as a new menace. More than a hundred definitions have been offered for the phenomenon called 'terrorism'. One of the earliest attempts was provided by the League of Nations Convention on Terrorism, 1937. Article 1 of this convention defines terrorism as 'all criminal acts directed against a State and intended or calculated to create a state of terror in the minds of particular persons or a group of persons or the general public' (UN website 2008). However, the convention drafted in 1937 never came into existence.

While the United Nations has not yet accepted a definition of terrorism, the UN's 'academic consensus definition', written by terrorism expert A.P. Schmid and widely used by social scientists, runs:

> Terrorism is an anxiety-inspiring method of repeated violent action, employed by (semi-)clandestine individuals group or state actors, for idiosyncratic, criminal or political reasons, whereby—in contrast to assassination—the direct targets of violence are not the main targets. The immediate human victims of violence are generally chosen randomly (targets of opportunity) or selectively (representative or symbolic targets) from a target population, and serve as message generators. Threat- and violence-based communication processes between terrorist (organization), (imperilled) victims, and main targets are used to

manipulate the main target audience(s), turning it into a target of terror, a target of demands, or a target of attention, depending on whether intimidation, coercion, or propaganda is primarily sought. (UN 2008)

The UN short legal definition, also proposed by A.P. Schmid states that an act of terrorism is the 'peacetime equivalent of a war crime'. The UN definition for a convention in 2004, is

any act intended to cause death or serious bodily injury to a civilian, or to any other person not taking an active part in the hostilities in a situation of armed conflict, when the purpose of such act, by its nature or context, is to intimidate a population, or to compel a government or an international organization to do or to abstain from doing any act. (UN 2008)

Walter Laqueur (1986) has stated that 'terrorism is an attempt to destabilize democratic societies'. Elsewhere, he has defined terrorism as

the substate application of violence or the threatened violence intended to sow panic in a society, to weaken and even overthrow the incumbents, and to bring about political change. It shades on occasions into guerilla warfare and even a substitute war between states. In its long history terrorism has appeared in many guises. Today society faces not one terrorism, but many terrorisms. (Laqueur 1996)

In the United States' Department of State publication *Patterns of Global Terrorism* (2003), terrorism is defined as, 'premeditated, politically motivated violence perpetrated against non-combatant targets by subnational groups or clandestine agents, usually intended to influence an audience'. It is also stated that:

The term international terrorism means terrorism involving citizens or the territory of more than one country. The term 'terrorist group' means any group practicing, or that has significant subgroups that practice international terrorism. The US Government has employed this definition of terrorism for statistical and analytical purposes since 1983.

According to the US Department of Defense (2003), terrorism is 'the unlawful use of, or threatened use, of force or violence against individuals or property to coerce and intimidate governments or societies, often to achieve political, religious, or ideological objectives'. The FBI's (Federal Bureau of Investigation) (2003) definition is 'the unlawful use of force or violence against persons or property to intimidate or coerce a government, the civilian population, or any segment thereof, in furtherance of political or social objectives'.

The Indian Government's 'The Prevention of Terrorism Act, 2002' or POTA, defined a terrorist act as one committed by someone

(a) with intent to threaten the unity, integrity, security or sovereignty of India or to strike terror in the people or any section of the people does any act or thing by using bombs, dynamite or other explosive substances or inflammable substances or firearms or other lethal weapons or poisons or noxious gases or other chemicals or by any other substances (whether biological or otherwise) of a hazardous nature or by any other means whatsoever, in such a manner as to cause, or likely to cause, death of, or injuries to any person or persons or loss of, or damage to, or destruction of, property or disruption of any supplies or services essential to the life of the community or cause damage or destruction of any property or equipment used or intended to be used for the defense of India or in connection with any other purposes of the Government of India, any State Government or any of their agencies, or detains any person and threatens to kill or injure such person in order to compel the government or any other person to do or abstain from doing any act;

(b) is or continues to be a member of an association declared unlawful under the Unlawful Activities (Prevention) Act, 1967 (37 of 1967), or voluntarily does an act aiding or promoting in any manner the objects of such association and in either case is in possession of any unlicensed firearms, ammunition, explosive or other instrument or substance capable of causing mass destruction and commits any act resulting in loss of human life or grievous injury to any person or causes significant damage to any property, commits a terrorist act.

But even these working definitions have not found universal acceptance among those studying the subject. Perhaps the only characteristic generally agreed upon is that terrorism always involves violence or the threat of violence. There is thus no one good definition of terrorism. In fact, it might be impossible to define because it is intangible and fluctuates according to historical and geographical contexts. Some forms of it are indistinguishable from crime, revolution, and war. Other forms of it are easily distinguishable. It is of little wonder that thousands of definitions of terrorism have come into being during the course of its long history. There is thus no universally accepted definition of terrorism.

According to Gary Ackerman (2006), discordant, divergent definitions abound and the nature and causes of terrorism are hotly contested. He states that,

> an objective definition of terrorism has proven elusive and the subject has therefore become prone to subjective manipulation by political actors, leading to the aphorism that one person's terrorist is another's freedom fighter. Clearly the word 'terrorist' carries a negative connotation and it continues to be politically expedient to label any opponent as a terrorist, a predilection that can sometimes lead to almost farcical results.

He states that there are certain elements that many commentators agree should be included within any definition of terrorism:

- intentional violence
- a political or ideological (and not purely criminal) motivation
- subnational groups or individuals as perpetrators (some argue for the inclusion of covert government groups)
- non-combatant victims (this refers mainly to civilians)
- some element of symbolism that produces fear in a larger audience than the immediate victims

Unfortunately, these elements are far from universally accepted and may not distinguish terrorism from other forms of political violence (such as guerrilla warfare). They can therefore be taken at most as necessary, but not always sufficient, conditions for applying the term 'terrorism' to a particular act.

Why is it so difficult to find a generally accepted definition? Perhaps, this has been due to the fact that terrorism has had a very long history. Furthermore, there has not been a single form of terrorism, but many, often with few traits in common. What was true of one variety was not necessarily true of another. Today there are more varieties than which existed thirty years ago and many so different from those of the past and from each other that the term 'terrorism' no longer fits some of the erstwhile definitions.

The concept of anti-terrorism emerges from a thorough examining of the concept of terrorism as well as an attempt to understand and articulate what constitutes terrorism in Western terms. It must be remembered that in military contexts, terrorism is a tactic, not an ideology. Terrorism may be a tactic in a war between nation states, in a civil war, or in an insurgency.

Counter-terrorism refers to offensive strategies intended to prevent a belligerent, in a broader conflict, from using the tactic of terrorism. In other words, counter-terrorism is a set of techniques for denying an opponent the use of terrorism-based tactics, just as counter-air is a set of techniques for denying the opponent the use of attack aircraft. Anti-terrorism is defensive, intended to reduce the chance of an attack using terrorist tactics at specific points, or to reduce the vulnerability of possible targets to such tactics.

THE CASE OF CANADA

The 11 September terrorist attacks in the United States had immediate consequences for Canada. Alexander Filipov, a Regina born engineer had switched his reservation at the last minute to be on American Airlines 11. This flight was the first 767 aircraft driven into the massive twin towers of the World Trade Center. Another Canadian, former NHL hockey player, Garnet 'Ace' Bailey, was on United Airlines flight 175 as it crashed into the south tower. Twenty-two other Canadians were among the 2,823 people killed in the subsequent collapse of the two towers (Roach 2003). Although Canada extended ample support towards the United States as a compassionate neighbour, however, the relationship between the two countries has never been at ease. Soon after the attacks, reports surfaced that as many as five of the terrorists had entered the United States through the common border it shared with Canada, quite like the case of Ahmed Ressam, an Al-Qaeda terrorist, who in 1999, entered the United States with a Canadian passport in an attempt to bomb the Los Angeles Airport.

In this volatile international scenario, South Asia as a region has become vital to Canadian interests, which Canadian policy-makers cannot afford to ignore, whether from an economic or a strategic point of view. After an early short prelude of a partnership relationship with India and, to a lesser extent with Pakistan, Canada's foreign policy *vis-à-vis* the South Asian region during the ensuing four decades has ranged from indifference to neglect interrupted by a short-lived period of re-engagement in the mid-1990s, and the current renewed efforts to re-engage.

At present, India's top priority is to control cross-border terrorism and this has become India's major focus in its bilateral and multilateral relationships. In addition, its Ministry of External Affairs has recently set-up a counter-terrorism division to handle the diplomacy involved in the fight against international terrorism. Following the 11 September events, South Asia has been brought back into prominence in Western security and foreign policy. There has emerged a convergence of interests between India and the United States in particular with regard to the control of international terrorism. Consequently, it is particularly timely now that Canada reconsiders its choice of the appropriate trade-off between anti-proliferation on the one hand, and anti-terrorism and economic development in South Asia, on the other.

INTERNATIONAL TERRORIST GROUPS AND CANADA

Canada's threats from South Asian terrorist groups manifest themselves in several different ways. These include funding, extortion, intra-state violence and threats to Canadian international interests. The three genres of terrorist movements primarily engaged in this are the LTTE, the Khalistan Liberation movement and Islamic Fundamentalism. These have been selected for two primary reasons. First, the level of terrorist activity effecting Canada by these three forms of terrorism vary in intensity and purpose. While the LTTE only uses Canada as a fund-raising base, the Khalistan movement is responsible for varying levels of intra-state violence in Canada. The Islamic terrorist movement which cover a gamut of groups use Canada not only as a transit point to the United States, but also as a country for raising funds, seeking safe haven, as well as a place for planning future operations.

Second, a link may be established between these groups because of their intimate relationship to South Asia. India has been fighting various factions of each of these movements for decades. In comparison, Canada's involvement in counter-terrorism measures against these groups has been a recent phenomenon. An in-depth study of the three genres of terrorism has been conducted in the next section.

THE LTTE PROBLEM

The Tamil Liberation movement began in 1970 with the formation of a militant student group fighting with the Sri Lankan government over a lack of access to post-secondary education for the Tamil population. By 1976, as a result of the increasingly oppressive and discriminatory policies of the Sri Lankan government, it gave rise to the current-day LTTE under the leadership of Velupillai Prabhakaran (SATP 2007). Small-scale conflict between the government and the LTTE continued until a 1983 Tamil riot resulted in a massive government crackdown. Over the course of this standoff 90 per cent of Tamil businesses were destroyed, 2,500 Tamils were killed, thousands of refugees went to India, 100,000 people were internally displaced and this event catalyzed the demand for an independent Tamil state (CBC News 2006). Initially, India had a friendly relationship with the Tigers, even providing them with humanitarian aid, military supplies and training. The conflict between India and the LTTE technically began in 1986 when conflict broke out between Indian peacekeepers in Sri Lanka and the LTTE (de Voorde 2005). This exacerbated the most commonly known LTTE terrorist attack—the assassination of Indian Prime Minister Rajiv Gandhi in 1991.

India's relations with the Tamil Tigers have not improved since, as Indian judicial and military responses to the attack have targeted potential LTTE members in retaliation. Further, despite a 2002 ceasefire, there was no halt to the hostilities, partially because of a lack of discipline within the Sri Lankan army, who pursued indiscriminate, shoot-at-sight killings, and partly because of continued military build-up and terrorist attacks by the LTTE (Singh 2007).

Canada's responsibilities towards this conflict are rooted in the large Sri Lankan Tamil diaspora within Canada, most of who arrived as refugees between 1996 and 2001. Within this group, there is estimated to be approximately 8,000 Tamil Tigers currently living in Toronto, Montreal and Vancouver. Also, the large diaspora cover has allowed the LTTE to mask its *several* means of collecting funds, including intimidation, extortion and violence. One, technique used by the LTTE has been solicitation of funds at religious gatherings and social events (Singh 2007).

Second, the Tamil Tigers use the lax Canadian monitoring laws to collect a bulk of their funds through *legal* social, religious and ethnic 'front organizations' CSIS (2008) estimates that there are 8 to 10 such organizations that raise money for the LTTE, including the World Tamil Movement (in Toronto and Montreal), the Tamil Eelam Society of Canada, Federation of Associations of Canadian Tamils, and the Eelam Tamil Associations of BC and Quebec.

The third and the most ominous LTTE activity in Canada is the violent means of extortion that have come from these high financial demands. In 2005, Human Rights Watch released a report focused on Toronto that highlighted the exhortative means of the LTTE. The report notes that often the LTTE threatens individuals with bodily harm in their door-to-door visits. In other cases, with an extensive database of familial connections between Canada and Sri Lanka, they threaten the well-being of family members back home.

Internationally, the activities of the Tamil Tigers consist of several illegal activities. For example, their money laundering, extortion and drug smuggling rings are run through 150 to 200 different informal money trading networks similar and linked to the *hawala* system used by Islamic terrorist organizations. These are funded by a sophisticated network of refugee smuggling, narcotics trafficking, frauds, and extortion rings. Second, the LTTE has a historical relationship with several other terrorist organizations. Throughout its military campaigns and terror training camps, the LTTE invited Palestinian terrorist groups to share arms and train with one another in Sri Lanka. There are also reported arms trading with Islamic and separatist militants in Kashmir, Pakistan and Afghanistan (Singh 2007).

Despite these obvious signs of terrorist activity, the Canadian government has taken little recourse in addressing the threat posed by the LTTE. The Human Rights Watch report (2006) suggests that 'In Canada, the Tamil community forms a powerful voting bloc, and many members of Parliament from ridings (electoral districts) in the Toronto area are dependent on Tamil votes', and therefore, politicians are unwilling to address the LTTE problem.

THE KHALISTAN LIBERATION MOVEMENT

Since 1964, a section of the Sikh community in India has been asking for the creation of an independent Sikh state called Khalistan. India's steadfast secularism rejected partition on the basis of religion. In April 1984, a group of Sikh extremists wanted by the Indian government, led by Jarnail Singh Bhindranwale, took refuge in the Sikh Golden Temple in Amritsar. In response, Prime Minister Indira Gandhi raided the temple compound, killing Bhindranwale, his supporters, and a thousand civilian worshippers. The Sikh community retaliated and a few months later, Indira Gandhi was killed by her two Sikh bodyguards, resulting in an immediate backlash in the general population and anti-Sikh riots occurred across northern India, solidifying the movement (Singh 2007).

Sikhs have been in Canada as early as 1920s to work in British Columbia's natural resource industries and by the 1970s they constituted 70 per cent of Indian immigration to Canada. With the bulk of its operations within the UK and Canada, the major Khalistan organizations include the Babbar Khalsa (BK), Babbar Khalsa International (BKI) and the International Sikh Youth Federation (ISYF) (Jane's 2003). BKI is best known for its patronage to the first-ever Canadian terrorist attack—the June 1985 Air India bombing. Like the LTTE, the Khalistan movement has found Canada suitable for terrorist financing, with most of the proceeds ending up in the hands of Indian extremist groups, including the Khalistan Commando Force, Khalistan Liberation Force, Bhindranwale Tiger Force of Khalistan and the Sikh Students Federation (Singh 2007).

As mentioned, one of the major differences between the LTTE and the Khalistan movement has been the propensity for the latter to use violence against Canadian citizens. The Air India bombing is just one example, but Sikh extremists have also beaten and killed local dissidents. Two notable cases include Tara Singh Hayer, the editor of the *Indo-Canadian News* in Vancouver and an outspoken advocate against Sikh extremism. The 1987 attack on Hayer paralyzed and confined him to a wheelchair, until 1998 when he was eventually assassinated. A more famed example is the 1985 beating of former British Columbia Premier Ujjal Dosanjh, who was targeted for his comments against Sikh extremist actions during the Air India event. More recently, Dosanjh received threats once again for his comments about the glorifying of Air India bombers during a 2007 Vaisakhi parade in BC.

Canada's actions against the BK or any of its affiliates have been minimal. Most worrisome is the lack of general awareness within the political elite of the terrorism-promotion amongst hard-line Sikhs. Also, because of the regional concentration of Sikhs in Canada, they constitute an important voting bloc, which forces knowledgeable politicians to ignore their activities both locally and in India.

ISLAMIC FUNDAMENTALISM AND CANADA

There is a growing body of evidence indicating that Islamic terrorist groups have been operating effectively in Canada by taking advantage of Canada's liberal immigration and political asylum policies and the porous Canadian-American border. Terrorist-related activities in Canada include fund-raising, lobbying through front organizations, providing support for terrorist operations in Canada or abroad, procuring weapons and materiel, coercing and manipulating immigrant communities in Canada, facilitating transit to and from the US and other countries, and other illegal activities.

According to an August 2002 report of the Canadian Security Intelligence Service (CSIS 2002),

> . . . with the possible exception of the United States, there are more international terrorist organizations active in Canada than anywhere in the world. This situation can be attributed to Canada's proximity to the United States which currently is the principal target of terrorist groups operating internationally; and to the fact that Canada, a country built upon immigration, represents a microcosm of the world. It is, therefore, not surprising that the world's extremist elements are represented here, along with peace-loving citizens. Terrorist groups are present here whose origins lie in regional, ethnic and nationalist conflicts, including the Israeli Palestinian one, as well as those in Egypt, Algeria, Sudan, Afghanistan, Lebanon, Northern Ireland, the Punjab, Sri Lanka, Turkey and the former Yugoslavia.

Islamic extremists and their supporters from Al-Qaeda, Hezbollah, Hamas, Islamic Jihad, Armed Islamic Group (GIA), and Egyptian Islamic Jihad are among those suspected of operating in Canada.

Al-Qaeda

A major Al-Qaeda/GIA cell was Ahmed Ressam's Montreal-based terror cell. Among the cell's other members are Fateh Kamel, convicted in Paris in April 2001 for supplying fake passports to Islamic militants; Mokhtar Haouari, sentenced in New York in 2002 to 24 years in prison for providing a fake driver's license and other assistance to Ressam; Samir Ait Mohamed, indicted by US authorities in 2001 on charges of conspiring to commit an act of international terrorism and currently fighting extradition from Canada to the US; and Mourad Ikhlef, accused by Canada of advising Ressam on how to handle explosives and carry out the Los Angeles Airport attack (CSIS 2008).

Egyptian-born long-time Canadian resident Ahmad Sa'id Al-Khadr left Toronto for Pakistan to become the regional coordinator for the Canadian-based Human Concern International, a charity that has allegedly diverted funds to Al-Qaeda. He reportedly became a senior aide to Osama bin Laden.

Al-Khadr was detained by Pakistani authorities for his alleged involvement in the 1995 bombing of the Egyptian Embassy in Islamabad but was later released, reportedly, after the personal intercession of Canadian Prime Minister Jean Chrétien. In October 2001, the US froze his assets and in December 2001, the US placed him on a list of nine Al-Qaeda members most wanted by the US. He is believed to be now in Afghanistan (CSIS 2008).

One of Khadr's sons, Omar Khadr, was arrested in Afghanistan in July 2002 after he allegedly murdered a US army medic with a grenade. He is currently being held in Guantanamo Bay. Another one of his sons, Abdul Rahman Khadr, was captured by Northern Alliance troops in Kabul in November 2001 while allegedly fighting for Al-Qaeda and later sent to Guantanamo. In November 2003, against the background of the US releasing a number of detainees from Guantanamo, Abdul Rahman Khadr was freed. On 30 November 2003, Canadian authorities permitted Khadr to re-enter Canada.

An Al-Qaeda plot to bomb the US Embassy in Paris also had a Canadian element to it. In June 2002, Canadian authorities arrested Algerian-born Montreal resident Adel Tobbichi, a.k.a. Amine Mezbar, who allegedly altered passports and other documents to allow members of the embassy conspiracy cell to travel throughout Europe. He was extradited to the Netherlands in July 2002.

Following the leads of the UN Security Council and the US, Canada shut down the offices of several Islamic charities operating on Canadian soil, with alleged links to Al-Qaeda. These include: Benevolence International Fund, Islamic Relief Organization, Muslim World League and the SAAR Foundation (CSIS 2008).

Hezbollah

Hezbollah is believed to have an active presence in Canada. According to Canadian intelligence, Canada is an important source of Hezbollah fund-raising and recruitment as well as a key component of the group's international network (CSIS 2008).

In June 2002, two members of a North Carolina-based Hezbollah terror cell were convicted of providing material support to the terrorist organization. Their cell was part of a larger Hezbollah network that raised funds and procured dual-use technologies for Hezbollah. The Canadian part of the network was allegedly run by Mohammed Hassan Dbouk and his brother-in-law Ali Adham Amhaz, who allegedly received money from Hezbollah officials in Lebanon and engaged in credit card and banking scams in Canada in order to finance the purchase in Canada and the US of night-vision goggles, global positioning systems, stun guns, laser range finders and other military items which were then smuggled into Lebanon. Amhaz was indicted in North Carolina in March 2001 on charges of providing material support to Hezbollah. In October 2001, Canadian authorities arrested him based on an American arrest warrant calling for his extradition. Amhaz was freed in December 2001 after the US dropped the arrest warrant; the US indictment against him still stands. Dbouk fled to Lebanon.

Also in June 2002, Israeli authorities arrested Lebanese-born Canadian Fawzi Ayoub, who had entered Israel on a fake American passport. He is accused of being a Hezbollah fighter and of training Palestinian militants in the West Bank in Hezbollah bomb-making techniques.

The Canadian government had originally refused to include Hezbollah on its list of banned terrorist organizations claiming that it is also a humanitarian and political organization. After domestic and international pressure, Canada finally banned Hezbollah in December 2002 (CSIS 2008).

Hamas and Islamic Jihad

Both Hamas and Islamic jihad are believed to raise money in Canada. The Hamas-linked Holy Land Foundation has raised hundreds of thousands of dollars in Canada. Both terrorist groups were banned in Canada in November 2002.

In early December 2003, the Israeli government announced that it had arrested in November a Palestinian-born Canadian, Jamal Akkal, who confessed to being recruited and trained by

Hamas' military wing in Gaza. Akkal reportedly had orders to kill Israeli officials and Jews in Canada and the US. According to Israeli authorities, senior Hamas militant Ahmed Wahabe allegedly told Akkal to raise funds among Muslims in Canada ostensibly for the families of suicide bombers, which he would actually use for purchasing weapons and financing his attacks (CSIS 2008).

INDIA AND CANADA'S JOINT WORKING GROUP ON COUNTER-TERRORISM

Canada's bilateral relationship with India to its mutual terror threats has been dismal. Not only did Canadian security authorities ignore investigations over the Air India case for twenty years, efforts to stem terrorist financing within Canada have been addressed with token measures, and counter-terrorism efforts in South Asia have occurred without little consultation with India. In 1987, the two states signed an Extradition Treaty, meant for people involved in terrorist activities in either state. This was a significant gesture from both parties.

The potential for a Canada-India partnership was furthered in 1997 when, in response to the continuing threat of Sikh terrorists, the two countries formed the Joint Working Group (JWG) on counter-terrorism. The first of its kind, the group was formed to strengthen cooperation in the global campaign against terrorism through the bilateral JWG on counter-terrorism. The JWG, set up in 1997, has evolved its agenda over the years to strengthen the India-Canada partnership on counter-terrorism. It had been one of the areas supported by the prime ministers of India and Canada during their meeting in New Delhi on 18 January 2005.

WORKING OF THE JWG ON COUNTER-TERRORISM

India and Canada held the seventh meeting of their JWG on counter-terrorism in New Delhi on 11-12 April 2005. The talks were held by delegations constituted on an inter-agency/inter-departmental basis on both sides, led by Additional Secretary in the Ministry of External Affairs, Meera Shankar and Senior Coordinator for International Crime and Terrorism in the Canadian Department of Foreign Affairs Ruth Archibald (MEA 2005).

This particular meeting included useful discussions on assessments of current terrorist challenges, including in the South Asia region, and ways to strengthen ongoing international action to counter-terrorism, including through regional and international fora like the United Nations. While discussing sources and modalities of terrorist financing and counter-measures, both sides addressed concerns over the *hawala* system and discussed ways to promote the use of legitimate banking channels. Talks have begun on a remittance partnership between the two countries. The delegations discussed the growing link between narco-trafficking and the financing of terrorism, the new challenge of cyber terrorism and the increasing need for further collaboration in aviation and maritime security. Both sides agreed on the need for sharing information on financial transactions meant for diversion to finance terrorist activities made under the cover of charity organizations and NGOs.

First, the JWG has provided a forum for discussion between the two states, where both parties can air their grievances to the other state. For example, during the 7th meeting of the group in April 2005, the parties discussed the matter of terrorist financing, eventually deciding that the two states would share financial information of terrorist groups to better track monetary flows from charity groups and NGOs. This included a discussion and brainstorming sessions for both states to undermine the use of the *hawala* system of monetary exchange. Further, the two states discussed, as a growing relevance to the mission in Afghanistan, the relationship between the drug trade and terror-financing. This session ended with a mutual agreement for intelligence sharing and 'capacity-building'.

Second, another positive outcome of the JWG is its continued potential to develop a relationship between the states. In other words, with the current framework of the JWG, Canada and India have a preexisting forum with which to develop a counter-terrorism structure.

CONCLUSION

In conclusion, it may be stated, that although the impact of terrorism on both the countries is phenomenal, however, certain steps may be taken to ensure that terrorism is effectively stopped. Further, joint counter-terrorism exercises are extremely important with regard to the curtailment of various genres of terrorism as well as fostering the security environment of both nations.

Canada must use the JWG on counter-terrorism as a mutually beneficial step for both countries. Care should be taken with regard to such issues as immigration, secure borders and prevention of any such activities that are detrimental to the security of both nations.

India could step up its counter-terrorism activities in Kashmir. Further, terrorist sentiments within Canada should be curtailed, with special reference to the elevation of terrorists to the position of martyrs as was seen during the 2008 Vaisakhi Day Parade in the city of Surrey near Vancouver.

India must be included in dialogue between NATO countries and Pakistan. As India has had years of negotiation with Pakistan on this issue, it would be beneficial to both parties to consolidate their pressure on Pakistan to control its extremist issues.

Both India and Canada should aim at a joint cooperation with regard to counter-terrorism in the sphere of the emerging catastrophic terrorism.

At the domestic level, Canada needs to build the confidence and capabilities of its judicial and intelligence organizations. Canada and India need to move away from their historic Cold War tensions and reinvent their strategic relationship, especially in the area of counter-terrorism.

Finally, it would strongly benefit both countries to help one another over the threat emanating from the three major terrorist movements that are a common cause of worry for both countries; namely, the LTTE problem, the Khalistan Liberation Movement and Islamic terrorism.

REFERENCES

Ackerman, Gary, 'WMD Terrorism: Distinguishing Hype from Reality', a paper that he sent to the author during mutual correspondence. For details: see http://cns.miis.edu.

Alexander, Yonah, 'Terrorism in the Twenty-First Century: An Overview', in *Terrorism and Medical Responses: US Lessons and Policy Implications*, ed. Yonah Alexander and Stephen Prior, New York: Transnational Publishers, 2001, pp. 5-10.

BBC News, 'Sri Lanka leader gambles on tsunami aid', 2005, accessed electronically at http://news.bbc.co.uk/2/hi/south_asia/4628125.stm.

Canada: Basic Facts About the Country, New Delhi: Ministry of External Affairs Publication, 2005, p. 10, accessed electronically at http://meaindia.nic.in/foreignrelation/canada.pdf

CBC News 'Tamil Tigers: A History' (2006), accessed electronically at http://www.cbc.ca/news/background/srilanka/tamiltigers. html.

Chalk, Peter, 'Liberation Tigers of Tamil Eelam's (LTTE) International Organization and Operations—A Preliminary Analysis', 1999, accessed electronically at *CSIS Commentary No. 70.* http://www.csisscrs.gc.ca/en/publications/commentary/com77.asp.

Council on Foreign Relations, 'Liberation Tigers of Tamil Eelam', 2006, accessed electronically at http://www.cfr.org/publication/9242

CSIS website accessed electronically at http://www.csisscrs.gc.ca/en

Department of Defense, *Dictionary of Military and Associated Terms*, US Department of Defense, accessed electronically at http://www.dtic.mil/doctrine/jel/new_pubs/jp1_02.pdf.

FBI website at http://www.fbi.gov.

Gearson, John, 'The Nature of Modern Terrorism', in *Superterrorism: Policy Responses*, ed. Lawrence Freedman, Oxford: Blackwell Publishing, 2002, pp. 7-23.

Hanratty, Dennis M. and Sandra W. Meditz, *Post-National Front Political Developments, Colombia: A Country Study*, Library of Congress, 1988, accessed electronically at http://countrystudies.us/colombia/89.htm.

Human Rights Watch, 'Funding the Final War—LTTE Intimidation and Extortion in the Tamil Diaspora', 2006, accessed electronically at http://www.hrw.org/.

International Convention for the Suppression of the Financing of Terrorism, 5 May 2004, accessed electronically at http://www.un org.

Jane's Defence Weekly, accessed electronically at http://www.janes.com.

Kupperman, Robert and Darrell M. Trent, *Terrorism, Threat, Reality, Response*, Palo Alto: Hoover Institution Press, 1979.

Laqueur, Walter, 'Reflections on Terrorism', *Foreign Affairs*, New York: vol. 65, no. 1, 1986, p. 87.

——— 'Post Modern Terrorism', *Foreign Affairs*, New York: vol. 75, no. 5, 1996, p. 24.

——— *The New Terrorism: Fanaticism and the Arms of Mass Destruction*, New York: Oxford University Press, 1999, p. 5.

Lia, Brynjar, *Globalisation and the Future of Terrorism: Patterns and Predictions*, London: Routledge, 2005.

Mackenzie Institute 'Overseas Terrorism in Canada', 2003, accessed electronically at http://www.mackenzieinstitute.com/2003/other_peoples_wars3.htm

Metz, Helen Chapin, *The Occupied Territories, Israel: A Country Study*, Library of Congress, 1988, accessed electronically at http://countrystudies.us/israel/32.htm

———, *Patterns of Global Terrorism*, United States Department of State, Washington, DC: U.S. Government Printing Office, 2003, p. xii.

Public Safety Canada, 'Banned Terrorist List', 2007, accessed electronically at http://www.ps-sp.gc.ca/.

———, 'Canada's new government lists the LTTE as a terrorist organization' (2007), accessed electronically at http://www.pssp.gc.ca/media/nr/2006/nr20060410-en.asp

Roach, Kent, *September 11: Consequences for Canada*, Montreal: McGill-Queen's Press, p. 3.

Ross, Jeffrey Ian and Ted Robert Gurr, *Violence in Canada: Sociopolitical Perspectives*, New Jersey: Transaction Publishers, 2004.

'Sikh Separatists', *Jane's World Insurgency and Terrorism* 17, 2003, accessed electronically at www.janes.com.

Singh, Anita, *Engaging India: Canadian Threats and Counter-Terrorism Strategies in South Asia*, 2007, accessed electronically at http://www.cda-cdai.ca/symposia/2007/SINGHAnita.pdf.

South Asian Terrorism Portal, 'International Sikh Youth Federation', 2007, accessed electronically at http://www.satp.org/satporgtp/countries/india/states/punjab/terrorist_outfits/ISYF.htm

———, 'Liberation Tigers of Tamil Eelam', 2007, accessed electronically at http://www.satp.org/satporgtp/countries/shrilanka/terroristoutfits/ltte.html.

The Prevention of Terrorism Act, 2002, Chapter II, accessed electronically at http://www.satp.org/satporgtp/countries/india/document/actandordinances/POTA.htm .

Trembley, Reeta Chowdhari, *Canada and India: Broadening and Deepening Relationship*, Vancouver: Asia Pacific Foundation of Canada, 2003, p. 11, accessed electronically at http://www.asiapacific.ca/analysis/pubs/pdfs/canadaindia4_14oct03.pdf.

UN Expert welcomes Proposed Sri Lanka Commission, United Nations Special Rapporteur on extrajudicial executions, accessed electronically at http://www.unhchr.ch/huricane/huricane.nsf/view01/A4C0BEC5C39CEDACC12571E0005456C3?opendocument.

de Voorde, Cecile Van, 'Sri Lankan Terrorism: Assessing and Responding to the Threat of the Liberation Tigers of Tamil Eelam', *Police Practice and Research*, vol. 6, no. 2, 2005, p. 190.

CHAPTER 4

Track II: Political Euphemism or Tactical Reality: An Indo-Canadian Perspective

SAYANTANI SEN

The art of diplomacy has a long-standing history. It is the practice of verbal discussion with the intent to influence, transmit a position or negotiate on a given issue or situation for a mutually acceptable outcome. It is considered an art because each situation calls for a unique blend of empathy, persuasion, and cajoling. It has traditionally been a method of conducting inter-state relations involving discussions and negotiations between heads of States or their representatives in order to advance national interests. Broadly conceived, diplomacy often involves efforts to keep channels of communication fluid between adversaries with the intention that tension can be diffused and violence averted. Modern diplomacy is in several ways more complicated with the involvement of intergovernmental organizations (IGO) and non-governmental organizations (NGO) punctuated by globalization and the adjoining phenomena of communicability and transportability, along with the induction of new participants opening new vistas for the conduct of diplomacy.

Most conflicts in the contemporary world are not wars between nations but rather intra-state conflicts, conflicts that can be located within national boundaries. In 1987, for instance, only four of the world's major armed conflicts were cross-border wars; 32 of the 36 major armed conflicts (fought in 1987) were civil wars or intra-state wars of independence. Such statistics, coupled with the inability of traditional state-to-state dialogue to resolve intra-state conflicts exemplify and strengthen the case for Track II or informal diplomacy.

Diplomacy is a crucial activity undertaken by actors engaged in peacemaking efforts. Track I diplomacy involves the participation and interaction of state and/or official actors. These diplomats act with authority, on behalf of the state. It utilizes the skills, resources and intentions of official or state actors. Track II diplomacy is more subtle, engaged in activity at the grassroots level resorting to back channel measures (Vasquez 1996: 45).

Opinions and deliberations on the individual roles of Track I and Track II diplomacy have been the crux of persistent polemics. There is a wide range of diversity in views over the respective role played by actors affiliated to either breed of diplomacy in the process of conflict management. The division of actors involved in conflict management into two tracks however, constitutes no more than a procedure of distinguishing between the different parties associated with conflict management (Kumaraswamy and Subrahmanyam 2004: 193).

Track II involves the participation of informal intermediaries, represented by private citizens including experts, former government officials and representatives from non-government organizations (Barash and Webel 2002: 278). Track II affiliates can actually contribute to enhancing or reinforcing mutual understanding between those engaged in conducting Track I processes on either side. More importantly their mediation effort could elevate mutual confidence among their respective leadership, when accompanied by genuine progress accrued through Track I diplomacy. The contemporary vocabulary—ranging from Track II to multitrack and private diplomacy—has become an important jargon, emphasizing on the vitality to find common grounds. Collaboration of actors thus, remains a meaningful and important component in the promotion of peaceful conflict resolution.

The process of unofficial (Track II) diplomacy usually connotes informal interaction with influential actors from the civil society, business or religious groups and local leaders or actors who are believed to be experts in questions pertaining to the moot issue. It involves a process of informal diplomacy, in which non-officials (academic scholars, retired civil and military officials, public figures, and social activists) engage in dialogue to promote the cause of conflict resolution, or confidence-building.

Track II or non-official diplomacy has gained considerable attention in recent years as a mechanism for conflict resolution and peace building among countries. The contemporary conduct of Track II methods however, are neither limited to the narrow domain of conflict resolution nor merely confined to the members of adversary groups or nations. It has been employed and utilized pragmatically to enlarge common grounds between countries.

Track II diplomacy does not constitute an isolated process seeking to replace official Track I diplomacy. It rather seeks to strengthen official channels (involving direct government-to-government interaction at the official level) through the involvement of non-traditional methods, including the facilitation of dialogue mechanisms and meetings that register a convergence between governmental and non-governmental institutions. This mechanism proves particularly helpful in events where both sides want to prevent escalation of tension and are simultaneously wary of third party involvement apprehending the spiraling of the situation beyond control.

Although Track II diplomacy may appear to be less important and influential compared to official Track I diplomacy (that comprises the work of actual diplomats at their embassies), in several occasions it assumes far greater significance. Indeed its informal disposition is often suggestive of the seriousness of its intent.

Track I diplomats or official representatives often suffer from a want of leverage and influence at the site of the conflict. Instances of incompatibility and friction among disputant groups in almost immediate subsequence to a negotiated settlement are not rare. A probable reason behind such a tendency could be traced to the distrust or suspicion among adversaries over the integrity of intention of the 'diplomat' as their true representative, or because they do not acquiesce unto the settlement. Therefore steps must be taken to ensure that adversaries and signatories strike a semblance of communion of views during the peacemaking process.

Track II diplomacy surmises the host of unofficial initiatives undertaken towards the abatement of a conflict situation. The limitations of formal diplomacy, government and politics, about being creative in problem solving . . . the need for unofficial, informal, non-committal initiatives designed to establish dialogue and communication and to mobilize adversaries on both sides on how to solve a problem are not corroborated by formal diplomacy, Track I diplomacy, simply doesn't have those toolkits. Track II, from a standpoint defines 'unofficial people to people diplomacy' or 'citizen diplomacy'. The *New York Times* typically refers to it as 'private foreign policy conference'.

Track II diplomacy is pervasive through the course of the conflict, but has accelerated significance in conflict prevention and peace building where Track II diplomats can monitor the situation 'on the ground'. It is crucial in laying the basis for further negotiations, ensuring the stability of communities and enabling former adversaries to live harmoniously. Citizen initiatives and actions beyond official governmental parameters demonstrate the diverse ways in which Track II diplomacy can benefit conflict resolution.

Lederach conceived a leadership triangle that illustrates the importance of coordination at all levels among actors to arrive at sustainable peace. He classifies actors into three categories: elites, community leaders and grassroots representatives, wherein each group is endowed with a distinct responsibility in the larger process of peace building. The leaders in Track I are dependent on the community leaders, who in turn are dependent on the grassroots actors for successful and sustainable conflict resolution, exemplifying the entwined interaction between Track I and Track II; in the absence of which, the cause of peace suffers (Yaacov 2004: 73).

There is a lot of misconception over the exact meaning and connotation of Track II diplomacy. Any effort to clarify the confusion and approach an approximation should begin with the acknowledge that all non-Track I activities do not fall within the parameters of Track II. Track II construed as diplomatic descent denotes something that remains in close proximity of Track I to justify its relevance and resuscitate its survival. Therefore, people-to-people contact, cultural and student exchanges, which are addressed as Track II initiatives, do not constitute the definitive elements of Track II. Similarly, back channel diplomacy (Niaz Niak and R.K. Mishra negotiations) cannot exactly conform to the requirements of Track II diplomacy due to its secretive *modus operandi*. Track II diplomacy is perceived as a process deployed by countries as a useful tool to augment confidence among nations while exploring prospects of co-operation and enlarge the common space to further relations in an affirmative direction (Kumaraswamy and Subrahmanyam 2004: 199).

In certain circumstances, for instance; direct communication among adversaries seems unlikely to reduce tensions. Instead of creating an optimum ambience for exchange of views and settle on a compromise, direct communication is likely to produce a simple repetition of demands, vindicating the intractability of the conflict. There is also an invincible tendency to paint one's own side in a favourable light to the disadvantage of the other.

Informal diplomacy has found increased importance in addressing and resolving international conflicts in the past fifty years partly due to the enhanced ability of organizations and individuals to visit and participate in other cultures and also because of the elevated interaction among states in the international arena. Track II, owing to its public component thus, opens into a larger and wider scope of movement. As J. Lewis Rasmussen says:

> [They] are largely unencumbered by the political baggage their official counterparts carry and thus can be more effective at times in providing networking capabilities among parts of societies that are 'off limits' to most government personnel. In addition, unofficial actors, serving as neutral parties can help provide a bridge within divided societies; unofficial activities are often the only means through which members of opposing parties or factions can safely meet. (Abu-Nimer 2001: 360)

Track II surmises unofficial, informal interactions among members of contending groups or nations to develop strategies, influence public opinion, and organize human and material resources in ways that might help the resolution of a conflict situation.

It ought to be clarified that Track II diplomacy in no way

seeks to substitute the official, formal Track I, government-to-government or leader-to-leader liaisons. It is rather an activity that is designed to assist official leaders by compensating for the constraints and restrictions confronted in course of official Track I negotiations.

Both formal (Track I) and informal/unofficial (Track II) diplomacy despite their individual breathing spaces and spheres of influence remain two mutually reinforcing processes within the larger context of conflict management. They are like two overlapping circles, sharing common characteristics and responsibilities within conflicts. Each approach has its own effectiveness and irrespective of the similarity in the methods employed by either breeds, the role of either cannot be usurped by the other.

Table 4.1 gives a Comparative study of Track I and Track II diplomacy.

TABLE 4.1: COMPARATIVE STUDY OF TRACK I AND TRACK II DIPLOMACY ALONG BASIC PARAMETERS

	Track I	Track II
Actors	Official representatives, governments, elites, adversarial leaders	Unofficial representatives, non-governmental organizations, regional and local leaders, grassroots groups
Methods	Positive or negative incentives, mediation, political or economic support	Back-channel discussions, education programmes workshops, grassroots reconciliation
Stages of Conflict	Present in all stages but of particular importance during *peacemaking* and *peacekeeping* when official actors determine ceasefires, peace accords and terms to negotiate agreements.	Present in all stages but of particular importance during *conflict prevention* and *peace building* when local and regional actors can detect early warning signs of violence and can help foster personal reconciliation techniques between the adversarial parties.

The two breeds of diplomacy delineate discernible lines of convergence and divergence. In terms of actors, Track I comprises official and governmental representatives or adversarial leaders who participate in their official capacities to broker peace in a conflict situation. Track I involves the participation and interaction of state and/or official actors who act with authority on behalf of the state. The process utilizes the skill, expertise, resources and intentions of official or state actors. In case of Track II, unofficial representatives, members hailing from non-governmental organizations or actors from grassroots groups take up the mantle of conflict resolution. Track II defines a more subtle process, that focuses on activity at the grassroots level through the deployment of back channel communication, etc. (Johnston 2003: 34).

Viewed through the perspective of the methodology employed by either version of diplomacy (Track I/Official or Track II/ Unofficial), there might be an apparent similarity of approaches considering the commonality of the ultimate purpose. In actual practice, however, each resonates a distinct *modus operandi.* While Track I/formal diplomacy employs positive or negative incentives and mediates to secure political and economic support, Track II/informal diplomacy uses processes like back-channel discussions, conducts workshops and educational programmes to approach a reconciliation at the grassroots level.

Both Track I and Track II diplomacy have a loosely designated place in the diplomatic scheme of things. Although it is difficult to exactly demarcate their respective spheres of influence, it is possible to roughly indicate their roles in the broader process of conflict management. Track I as the official process is present through the process of conflict resolution, though it can be more specifically located in the stages of peacemaking and peacekeeping during which official representatives are required to determine ceasefires, negotiate peace accords and terms of agreement. Similarly some semblance of Track II initiatives can be discerned through the course of a conflict but is particularly relevant in conflict prevention and peace building where local and regional actors detect early warning signs of violence and facilitate reconciliation mechanisms among adversarial groups (Vasquez 1996: 50-3).

ADVANTAGES OF TRACK II DIPLOMACY

- *Track II or informal diplomacy provides a vision beyond the conventional paradigms.* Official commitments often restrict formal diplomatic channels to overstep demarcated parameters. Thus, more often than not, Track I limits itself to the conventional diplomatic mandate.
- *Informal/Track II diplomacy allows one to operate beyond official constraints.* Official representatives that man the formal diplomatic mantle of the government bear the onus of transmitting the image of the government's position across nations, internationally. Hence, it is imperative that they cannot overstep the defined official parameters, within which they are expected to function.
- *It makes independent discussion of options possible.* Since Track II representatives are not directly associated with the government, their statements or opinions are not burdened with the onus of official responsibility, making the prospect of independent and free exchange of views possible.
- *Informal or unofficial diplomacy is not laden with judgemental assumptions or preconceived diplomatic perceptions.* Diplomatic offices are often burdened with the historicity of relations among nation-states, in a manner that such preconceived notions tend to impact the contemporary diplomatic manoeuvrings so as to prevent an affirmative course of action.
- *Track II diplomacy often appears to be the best option to break into an impasse or stalemate.* In dealing with deadlocks and stalemates among contending parties or adversarial groups, official channels are more unlikely to be able to tap unconventional means to break the ice.
- *Informal diplomacy is likely to address grievances better.* Track II diplomacy should ideally incorporate members from aggrieved groups as well and thence be more adept in addressing issues since people who are directly affected by issues participate in the negotiating process.
- *Track II initiatives are less likely to steer away from core issues.* Often official representatives choose to avoid overtly sensitive issues and thereby end up neglecting associated focal

problems, while engaging in inconsequential policies that behave as inert components when it comes to the resolution of the actual issue.

- *The engagement of people makes a peace process more viable and durable.* The involvement and participation of people who are themselves affected by a problem or conflict is more likely to produce a solution that is durable enough to stand the test of time.

SIGNIFICANCE OF INFORMAL/TRACK II DIPLOMACY

- *Most conflicts today are intra-state.* In contemporary history, we have seen few inter-state conflicts (in the nature of wars of the yesteryears). They assume the form of civil wars, genocide, etc., elucidated through the likes of situations in places like Sudan and Darfur, the erstwhile Yugoslavia culminating in the sordid state of Bosnia and Herzegovina. There is thus, implicit wisdom in reviewing the concept of Track II (or informal diplomacy) as a possible means of bridge-building.
- *Internal strife makes negotiations somewhat difficult at the level of government.* Within themselves internal conflicts are so complicated that governmental channels find it difficult to deal with them, so much so that they often end up diluting the core issue. In such circumstances, it is more useful and advisable to engage the civil society through the informal linkages of Track II.
- *Unofficial diplomatic endeavours in the form of Track II initiatives do not override diplomatic channels.* They only seek to supplement the formal governmental processes. Although Track II may postulate features that appear to be distinct from the essential means of conventional Track I diplomacy, such mechanisms and processes do not attempt to replace the official first Track. Instead, it supplants the formal course, facilitating a smoother operation of diplomatic processes.
- *It makes dialogue between governmental and non-governmental organs possible.* Since the informal (Track II) process primarily

calls for the involvement of non-governmental representatives, any progress at the end of the day depended on proactive governmental support, thus ensuring a continuity of communication between governmental and non-governmental channels (Vasquez 1996: 49).

- *The vicissitude necessitates changes commensurate with the developments in the international power system.* Significant evolutions have underscored the sphere of international diplomacy, urging for an enhanced role for private citizens in fostering the processes of peacemaking around the world.
- *People-to-people diplomacy, envisioned through Track II offers a potential mechanism to enhance India's soft power, especially in the twenty-first century when the globe is pulsating with multiple power points.* The contemporary international power structure exonerates an optimum climate for countries like India to create a niche for itself. People-to-people diplomacy, capitalizing on India's soft power provides an effective mechanism to strengthen the same.
- *Cultural diplomacy is yet another aspect that can enhance India's global image.* To much of the world, India and Indian culture is like an enigma. *It is still perceived by many to be the land of the yogis, the land of the elephants and snake-charmers.* The export of Indian culture across nations could be influential in transmitting a favourable image of the country worldwide.

INDIA-CANADA RELATIONS

The international environment has witnessed enormous changes through the decade of the 1990s. The end of the Cold War, the collapse of Communism in eastern Europe, the disintegration of the Soviet Union, the end of military alliances, the unification of East and West Germany, the revival of market economy at the global level, the emergence of new trade blocs and diverse centres of power have had different implications on the international political environment as well as on Indo-Canadian relations.

The far-reaching changes have prompted Canada to revisit

its stand *vis-à-vis* India. Emerging markets, growing business and investment opportunities make India an attractive destination for much of the world. Further, India's sustainable economic development, infrastructural and technological advancements and environmental protection hold great promise for the future of India-Canada relations.

The Legacy of Bilateralism

Bilateralism forms the basis on which relations among states are created and nurtured. The legacy of bilateral relations between India and Canada has been historically manoeuvred and politically tempered. From 1947 to 1974, Canada-India relations were mostly cordial and cooperative, though largely uneventful. Escott Reid, a one-time Canadian High Commissioner to India, has characterized this period as one of 'special relationship' (Cooper and Rowlands 2005: 172). India purported close links with Canada through the early years of Independence. The relations between India and Canada sustained despite India's non-aligned ideological position as opposed to Canada's NATO affiliation. Canada remained an important development partner for India throughout the 1950s and 1960s.

The relations between the two countries, however, saw a downward spiral with India's peaceful nuclear explosions in 1974, which froze connections between the two countries for over 20 years. In the consequent years, activities of terrorist groups further soured relations between the two countries. In the 1980s activities of groups like the Babbar Khalsa that was based out of Canada introduced an additional element of strain in Indo-Canadian relations. The relations between the two countries demonstrated an upward swing in the 1990s, but the nuclear tests of 1998 stalled the rapprochement. The visit of Raymond Chan, then Secretary of State for Asia Pacific to India in 1999 restored a measure of normalcy in relations. Trade and economic relations featured back on the bi-lateral agenda with the resumption of ministerial visits. The arrival of the new foreign minister John Manley in 2000 marked a new beginning in Indo-Canada relations with his decision to 're-engage' India.

Canada sought to pursue the broadest possible political and economic relations with India. A spate of high-level visits between 2001 and 2002 at the political and senior officials' level progressively turned around the bi-lateral relations (Malhotra 1999: 1-5). In 2003 the two countries issued a joint statement entitled 'Partners for the twenty-first century' delineating the vision to strengthen governmental, commercial and civil society linkages between India and Canada.

Canada-India Interface

There are several identifiable areas in which Canada and India have demonstrated a tendency to cooperate. Herein, further collaboration along these lines would be likely to enhance the strategic and bi-lateral links between the two countries.

People-to-people Links

People-to-people ties should be the basis of economic and strategic cooperation between the two countries. With an ascending Indian diasporic community in Canada, human linkages between the two countries are sustained through family ties, cultural presence, and travel and business linkages.

Economy

Although the commercial proximity between India and Canada is appreciable, it remains modest compared to the standards that it can attain. There has been some Indian investment in Canada, particularly in the information and technology sector—a development that is expected to rise in the coming years. Both countries need to identify the priority sectors and develop targeted action plans for a number of sub-sectors to facilitate increased two-way trade, investment and technology partnerships. 'Instances of priority sectors would include agriculture and agri-food, infrastructure, information and communication technology, extractive industries, life sciences and enabling sciences' (Bayne and Woolcock 2007: 333-7).

Political and Security Issues

In the past, political and security issues have negatively impacted Indo-Canadian relations (the influence of Babbar Khalsa and similar other terrorist groups based out of Canada). The nuclear tests of 1974 and 1998 created far too many sore points in the relations between the two countries. However, the promotion of dialogue and partnership between India and Canada is in the best interest of both the nations.

Culture

Cultural relations between India and Canada have generally been low-key, with a perceptible Canadian interest in aspects of Indian culture, and only and narrow but informed interest by some Indians in Canadian cultural trends. There is a discernible Canadian interest in promoting increased trade and investment in the Indian cultural industries sector. The first ever cultural and industries trade mission to India was launched in March/April 2004. The global presence of some writers and filmmakers of Indian origin working in Canada further add an interesting dimension to the cultural paradigm of Indo-Canadian relations.

Science and Technology

In the past Canadians and Indians have collaborated to produce and develop research work. There is tremendous potential for collaboration and co-action based on 'mutual interest' in research, science and technology to pool in the respective strengths of both the partners (India and Canada) to yield stronger ties and more attractive economic pay-offs.

Educational Links

While educational links between India and Canada are viable, Canadian educational institutions should expand their student recruitment and faculty exchange capacities with India, in competition with the other countries (which are also favoured student destinations) that aggressively chart such courses.

Environment

With the contemporary awareness environment has come to assume a different level of importance in recent years. The environmental effect of India's growing economy, the relevance of the global environment regimes and the prospect of mutually beneficial cooperation and trade in environmentally sustainable technologies.

Health is yet another area where the two countries would need to work together in close cooperation in the coming years.

CIDA: Canada-India Development Assistance

Developmental cooperation has been one of the most important elements in Indo-Canadian relations over the last five decades. It dates back to 1951, when a grant of about Canadian $1.5 million (comprising mainly food aid, limited project financing and technical assistance) was provided under the Colombo Plan. Since then Canada provided over Canadian $3.4 billion in Official Development Assistance (ODA), making India one of the largest recipients of Canadian development assistance. CIDA's Country Development Framework for India seeks to contribute to poverty reduction and sustainable development through support for economic reform, social development and environmental management (Malhotra 1999: 42-3).

India and Canada in the New Millennium

Civil society links between Canada and India have had a long history. People of India origin have been migrating to Canada for over hundred years, and other linkages through cultural, scientific and academic exchanges and through development assistance have existed since India's Independence. A reviewed Canadian stance should reckon with India's new economic and political realities. An intensive global security dialogue between the two countries should consider India's nuclear position and propose an end to the long estrangement on that front.

An ambitious 'breakthrough on brainpower' between the two countries, with optimum financing should promote collaborations of mutual interest in research, science and technology. A more creative diplomatic approach should among other things aim at engaging Indo-Canadian communities to better harness their strengths. An effective Canadian engagement should be preserved in India's continuing development challenges through a country-programming approach developed by CIDA, erected on the pillars of multilateral contributions, with a more strategic and competitive programme of civil society enlisting the support of the private sector. The new millennium calls for stronger support for priority cooperation India in the budgets of other government departments. The new foreign policy tools should help fill the 'CIDA gap'.

Unless alternative linking mechanisms evolve, Canadian bilateral development cooperation with India is likely to appreciably shrink the availability of opportunities for Canadians and Indians. The reduction in collaborative India-Canada partnerships will primarily affect the institutional and civil society partnerships, some public sector collaboration and the provision of specialized services.

A more visible government role, however, remains essential. Canadian businesses need knowledge about India and Indian business practices, and about possible commercial opportunities that await them. Moreover, as the Indian government devolves economic development and planning matters to lower levels of government, the information needs of Canadian business will increase and become more complex. Since the 1980s, organizations such as the C-IBC, ICCC and the Conference Board of Canada have been urging the Canadian government to engage India in a more concerted manner in order to facilitate Canadian business entry into the Indian markets (Cooper and Rowlands 2005: 177-8).

A study of India-Canada relations over the years reveals that the countries are likely to drift further apart, on their generally cordial but diverging paths, lest they manage to strike major breakthroughs. The review of India-Canada relations vindicates a case of missed opportunities interspersed with sporadic successes that were never fully capitalized on by either side.

Uninspired relations between the two countries must now confront the altered realities of the twenty-first century. Canada's recent initiatives to re-engage India, with a focus on upgrading economic linkages first, hold significant promise for a more sustained relationship.

India-Canada relations however, face several challenges. More than anything else, Ottawa must accept that India is a nuclear power and work with it as an equal partner. Canada now confronts split images in terms of its foreign policy, it also faces split images in its relationship with India (Cooper, Andrew and Rowlands 2005: 181). While recognizing these differences, it is still possible to envision a more sustained and coherent relationship, that skillfully blends the existing political, economic and social linkages into a better focused and more cohesive bilateral policy.

It is advisable to strengthen the existing instruments of co-operation between India and Canada, the likes of the Shastri-Indo-Canadian Institute, the Asia-Pacific Foundation, and the Canada-India Business Council. Such organizations and apparatus of cooperation should be encouraged and sharpened along lines of commonality with the unique Canadian contributions accrued through the South Asia Partnership in Canada.

REFERENCES

Abu-Nimer, Mohammed, *Reconciliation, Coexistence and Justice in Interethnic Conflict: Theory and Practice*, New York: Lexington Books, 2001.

Barash, David P. and Charles Webel, *Peace and Conflict Studies: A Twenty-first Century Perspective,* London: Sage, 2002.

Bayne, Nicholas and Stephen Woolcock, *The New Economic Diplomacy: Decision-making and Negotiation in International Economic Relations,* England Hampshire: Ashgate Publishing, 2007.

Cooper, Andrew Fenton and Dane Rowlands, *Split Images*, Norman Paterson School of International Affairs, Centre for International Governance Innovation, Montreal: McGill-Queen's Press, 2005.

Johnston, Douglas, *Faith-based Diplomacy: Trumping Realpolitik*, New York: Oxford University Press, 2003.

Kumaraswamy, P.R. and K. Subrahmanyam, *Security Beyond Survival: Essays for K. Subramanyam*, New Delhi: Sage, 2004.

Malhotra, Vinay Kumar, *Contemporary Indo-Canadian Relations*, New Delhi: Anmol Publications, 1999.

Vasquez, John A., *Beyond Confrontation: Learning Conflict Resolution in the Post-Cold War Era,* Michigan: University of Michigan, 1996.

Yaacov, Bar-Siman-Tov, *From Conflict Resolution to Reconciliation: Reflections on the Theoretical and Practical Utility of the Term,* New York: Oxford University Press, 2004.

CHAPTER 5

India-Canada Nuclear Cooperation: Options, Opportunities and Constraints

TEJ PRATAP SINGH

Emerging India has been identified as a 'key priority country' by the Conservative government of Prime Minister Stephen Harper (international.gc.ca. 2008a). As Ottawa elevates the importance given to India and as officials, business leaders, and educators display a keen enthusiasm in fostering linkages with their Indian counterparts, they are reversing a historical trend generated mainly by the differences over the nuclear issue that has been more negative than positive for much of the past six decades. In the aftermath of the May 1974 Pokhran nuclear explosions, from 1976 until 2001, neither country was wholly committed to fostering closer ties with the other (Touchey 2007).

Canada and India share several commonalities. Both have adopted British parliamentary democracy and have fused it with the American federal system. The Indian federal system is very similar to the Canadian federal system. Both share common British colonial heritage and are now members of the Commonwealth. Both share common values such as rule of law, independent judiciary, free media, and respect for human rights, secularism and pluralism. Both are multilingual, multi-ethnic, multi-religious and multicultural pluralistic societies. Despite all these commonalities, both did not have cordial relations and their bilateral relations were characterized by huge trust deficit. During the Cold War period, both India and Canada were on the opposite side of the Cold War divide. Canada was an integral part of the Western security system (NATO) led by the US. India, though not a formal member of the Soviet military bloc, was treated as a Soviet ally despite its proclaimed non-aligned foreign policy. This Cold War bi-polar politics was the major reason for mutual distrust and suspicion.

India was peripheral to Canada, despite being home to one-sixth of the humanity and the second largest source of immigrants for Canada after China. Right now around one million Canadians are of Indian origin. However, the Indian diaspora in Canada is different from that in the US. In the US, the Indian Americans are playing a leading role in the formulation of the US policy towards India. American Indians have effectively and successfully lobbied for the Indo-US Civil Nuclear Cooperation Agreement. The Indian diaspora in the US is highly educated and affluent, but Canadian Indians can be divided into two groups. One group is highly educated and affluent while the second group is barely educated and poor. Sikhs are predominant among Canadian Indians and Kashmiris are also in sizeable numbers. Both the communities have separatist and militant groups hostile to India. This has some time led to a deterioration of bilateral relations. India has accused Canada of being soft on Sikh militants hiding in Canada and was also unhappy over Air India plane bombing and its subsequent tardy investigation and eventual acquittal of all the accused.

India-Canada relations have been marred by the nuclear issue too. The Nuclear issue is the major irritant in India-Canada bilateral relations. Canada accused India for breach of trust and betrayal. Till date Canada has not forgiven India for its 1974 Pokhran I explosions. Canada alleged that plutonium used in Pokhran I explosions was obtained from Canadian supplied CIRUS research reactor. The present paper aims at exploring India-Canada relations in the backdrop of India's quest for nuclear energy and deterrent. It examines India-Canada nuclear cooperation and the various problems associated with it. The paper scrutinizes and analyses the various options for reducing and removing the differences and expanding the opportunities in the nuclear field, which will meet the security, energy and commercial interests of both the countries. Indo-Canadian nuclear cooperation is confronted by several challenges and also offers immense opportunities for strengthening bilateral relations. So far, the nuclear issue has been mismanaged by the leadership of both the countries. It has been the major impediment in the bilateral relations. However, if handled skilfully and imaginatively it can be a major source of strength in the bilateral relations. The options, opportunities and constraints of Indo-Canadian nuclear cooperation has been analysed in the context of Indo-US civil nuclear cooperation agreement.

CANADA AND MAKING OF THE ATOMIC BOMB

Canada along with the US and Britain was an active participant in the Manhattan Project, which led to the development of the enriched uranium bomb, nicknamed 'Little Boy', which was dropped on Hiroshima and the plutonium bomb, nicknamed 'Fat Man', which was dropped on Nagasaki in 1945 to terminate the Second World War and as a warning to the Soviet Union. Canada not only provided the natural uranium for Hiroshima and Nagasaki bombs but its enrichment and reprocessing of spent fuel for plutonium was also carried out in the Canadian Chalk River nuclear establishment. In the post-Second World War period, Canada was the main source of uranium for the US and British nuclear weapon programme (Bratt 2002; Edwards 2008). However, Canada itself renounced the nuclear weapons. Despite having the capability, Canada announced that it would never acquire nuclear weapons.

This Canadian behaviour can be explained from both realist and idealist perspectives. The realist approach supports nuclear deterrent for national security and Canada beings close US strategic ally and NATO member enjoyed the extended US nuclear deterrence and hence there was no need of developing its own national nuclear deterrent. The idealist approach supports disarmament, particularly nuclear disarmament. Idealists advocate abolition of weapons of mass destruction and use of nuclear energy only for peaceful purposes. In accordance with the idealist perspective, Canada has renounced nuclear weapons and is committed to the peaceful use of nuclear technology for civil purposes only.

CANADIAN CONTRIBUTION TO INDIA'S NUCLEAR PROGRAMME

India's nuclear programme is one of the oldest in the world, older than even China. It began even before India became independent. The genesis of India's nuclear programme can be traced to the letter written by the architect of India's nuclear programme Homi Jehangir Bhabha to Sir Dorab Ji Tata Trust for financial assistance to set up an atomic research centre to train nuclear scientists, who can take up the task of nuclear research after India gained Independence. The Atomic Research Centre set up by Bhabha is the nucleus of India's nuclear programme, which was appropriately named after Bhabha after his untimely demise in a plane crash.

Canada was among the first countries to extend support to India's nascent nuclear programme. Under the Colombo Plan, Canada offered to India, the Canada India Reactor and the United States (CIRUS) research reactor in 1956. Since heavy water for this research reactor was to be supplied from the US and hence the letters 'US' in CIRUS. Later, Canada supplied 220 MW CANDU (Canada Deuterium and Uranium) reactors in 1964 and in 1969, which is known as RAPS-I and RAPS-II (Rajasthan Atomic Power Station respectively). With the rising proliferation concerns, Canada insisted for IAEA safeguards, which India acceded in the case of RAPS-I and II but declined to put CIRUS reactor under the IAEA safeguards (dfait.maeci.gc.ca/nucchallenge 2008a). Later India developed its own Dhruva research reactors, which obviously was out of IAEA safeguards. India obtained plutonium for its 'Smiling Buddha' Pokhran explosions in May 1974 and May 1998 from these two research reactors.

Despite warning from Canada, India continued its nuclear weapon programme and continued to use Canadian-supplied CIRUS reactor for this purpose. India eventually carried out nuclear explosions in May 1974 and Canada was outraged and felt cheated by India. Canada condemned the explosions in the strongest possible terms and denounced India for violating its promise given to Canada for the use of Canadian nuclear reactor and materiel only for peaceful purposes. Canada held itself responsible for India's nuclear explosions. Had it not been the Canadian CIRUS reactor and American heavy water, there would have been no Indian nuclear explosion and consequently no US and Canadian Nuclear Non-Proliferation Acts, no Nuclear Suppliers Group (NSG), no IAEA full-scope safeguards and elaborate nuclear non-proliferation architecture to prevent further horizontal proliferation. CIRUS holds a very special place in India's nuclear programme, non-proliferation history and the development of global non-proliferation regime (Leventhal 2005). India dismissed Canadian allegations and termed its explosions as peaceful nuclear explosions (PNE), which is permitted even by the NPT, to which India is not a signatory. India also claimed that by conducting Pokhran explosions, it has not violated any international treaty or agreement. Canada terminated all nuclear cooperation with India and till date it has not resumed nuclear cooperation with India.

Frosty India-Canada relations continued till the end of the Cold War. During 1970s and 1980s, India was always in the news for all the wrong reasons in Canada. Apart from nuclear proliferation, abuse of human rights and terrorism were other issues of discord between India and Canada. However, relations improved with the advent of economic reforms in India. Liberalization and privatization of the Indian economy made it attractive for Canadian trade and investment. India's emergence as global leader in the field of information technology compelled the Canadian leaders to take notice of India as an emerging economic power. Not to be left behind, Canada also began wooing India, leaving the nuclear bitterness behind. When Indo-Canadian relations were improving, 'Buddha smiles again' happened in May 1998 and the gradually improving Indo-Canadian relations crashed.

POKHRAN II AND ITS AFTERMATH

In the wake of Pokhran II explosions, Canada was in the forefront condemning India for defying world public opinion and demanded strict action against India. Like other Western nations, Canada imposed economic sanctions against India and urged India to cap and roll back its nuclear weapon programme and join NPT as a non-nuclear weapon state. India dismissed Canadian criticism and justified it in the name of national security and threat perceptions from nuclear China and Pakistan.

India of 1998 was not the India of 1974, which had been ignored for a long time. Rising India ensured that economic sanctions did not last long. The United States, Australia, EU, Japan and other major powers began engaging India, immediately after the Pokhran dust has settled down. The United States led the way. It was the first country in the aftermath of the Pokhran II explosions, which began engaging India. The US Deputy Secretary of State Strobe Talbot and Indian Foreign Minister Jaswant Singh initiated the comprehensive strategic dialogue, which paved the way for gradual dismantling of economic sanctions by the US and eventually highly successful visit of President Clinton to India. This smoothened the way for India-US strategic partnership in the twenty-first century.

After the 1998 nuclear explosions and the subsequent sanctions by the Western powers, countries such as the United States, Australia and Israel quickly undertook to re-engage India. They have been quick to recognize the new realities of India. Canada however, remained stuck to its 'human and soft policy' and neglected to consider India's relevance in the strategic and economic arena. While most Western states undertook to engage India, Canada virtually stood alone in its intransigence. Canada's cooling of its relationship resulted in turn in India in taking Canada of its foreign policy radar. The cooler Canada became to India, the more Indians were inclined to consider Canada, as irrelevant to their foreign policy domain (Tremblay, 2008).

During his tenure as the Foreign Minister, John Manley made serious attempts to engage India economically. Although reiterating Canada's commitment to the NPT and CTBT, Manley sought to pursue a political and economic relationship with India. His visit to India in 2002 brought rapprochement to the Indo-Canadian relations (ibid.).

INDO-US CIVIL NUCLEAR COOPERATION AGREEMENT AND ITS IMPLICATIONS FOR NON-PROLIFERATION REGIME

With the signing of India-US Civil Nuclear Cooperation Agreement in Washington on 10 October 2008, by Minister of External Affairs Pranab Mukherjee and his US counterpart Secretary of State Condoleezza Rice, the process of Nuclear Agreement has been completed. It took three and a half years to finalize the deal and went through several ups and downs and even threatening the very survival of the United Progressive Alliance (UPA) government in India led by Prime Minister Manmohan Singh. It generated high voltage acrimonious debate in the parliament, where right-wing BJP joined hands with the left-wing Communists to oppose the nuclear deal and topple the government. Eventually the government survived and the stalled process of nuclear agreement was expedited and government approached IAEA for India-specific safeguards and NSG for exemption from nuclear materiel export guidelines, which was passed quickly with the active support and persuasion of the US. President Bush was keen to have an agreement signed before the expiry of his term and so Congress approved it in the last Congress session of the Bush administration. Cutting across party lines, both Republicans and Democrats voted overwhelmingly in favour of the deal. Not only for Bush, it is also a significant achievement for Manmohan Singh, whose term was also coming to an end.

Canada surprisingly did not oppose the Indo-US civil nuclear agreement in IAEA and NSG. Opposition to the India-US nuclear deal was led by smaller countries like Austria, Ireland and New Zealand. Canada backed India at both IAEA and NSG. Canada supported the India-specific safeguard agreement in IAEA and waiver from the NSG export guidelines that ended India's thirty-four years of nuclear isolation. Canada is now negotiating a comprehensive atomic deal with India, which will allow India to set up new civilian nuclear power plants. Canadian Foreign Office spokesperson Lisa Monett said, 'India has made substantial non-proliferation and disarmament commitments to achieve the trust of the NSG, which were reiterated in a political statement on September 5, 2008.' It is because of these commitments,

Monett said, but Canada extended its support for India's re-engagement with the broader nuclear-energy community, when it backed the NSG's decision on a waiver to India (*Hindu* 2008a).

The Indo-US Civil Nuclear Cooperation Agreement has attracted global attention. The agreement is the culmination of the growing Indo-US strategic partnership. The nuclear deal has alarmed the global non-proliferation lobby. It has far-reaching consequences for the global nuclear non-proliferation regime. It has strong supporters and equally strong critics. This is one of the most contentious nuclear agreements, which has divided not only the people of concerned nations—India and the United States but the international community as well.

In India, it is being opposed by different political groups on different grounds. The Left is opposed to the deal because of its strategic implications and growing proximity of India to the US which will lead to erosion of its independent foreign policy and resultant loss of national sovereignty. The right-wing BJP is opposed to the deal because it will lead to the compromise of India's strategic autonomy, meaning India will not be able to conduct further nuclear testing for the refinement of 'credible minimum nuclear deterrent' as the agreement will result in *de facto* moratorium on nuclear testing (Advani, 2008; *Hindu*, 2008a). This in reality will cap the Indian nuclear weapon programme, which has been the longstanding demand of the all the nuclear weapon states. Not only the political community but even the scientific community and strategic analysts are also divided over the nuclear deal (Gopalkrishnan, Iyengar and Prasad, 2008).

The proponents of the deal in India argue that it will provide energy security to the country, by expanding the energy basket and will reduce the dependence on fossil fuel; this will also arrest global warming as nuclear energy is clean energy, which does not emit any greenhouse gases. The nuclear deal has ended the 'nuclear apartheid' of India and has enabled India to access nuclear reactor, fuel and dual-use technology, which was denied to India because of its nuclear weapon programme. It has granted legitimacy to India's nuclear programme and ended its thirty-four years of nuclear isolation.

The opponents of the deal in the US and elsewhere argue that India has been rewarded for its continuous defiance of global nuclear non-proliferation regime. The global non-proliferation architecture in the form of Nuclear Suppliers Group (NSG) was erected under the US leadership in response to India's nuclear explosion in 1974. The existing non-proliferation provisions for non-nuclear weapon states were strengthened by upgrading IAEA safeguards to full-scope safeguards. These measures were adopted to plug the loopholes in the global non-proliferation regime to prevent non-nuclear weapon states to carry out nuclear explosions. Ironically, the same United States has led the international community in passing an India-specific safeguard agreement by the IAEA and waiver by the NSG under the Indo-US civil nuclear cooperation agreement. The deal has weakened and undermined international nuclear non-proliferation regime and emboldened countries like Iran and North Korea to go for nuclear weapons. It has also destabilized the region, as Pakistan is demanding the same treatment. It has also enabled India to use its limited indigenous uranium for its nuclear weapon programme, which has led to nuclear arms race in South Asia, destabilizing the whole region.

The supporters of the deal in the US and elsewhere argue that the agreement accepts the nuclear reality of the twenty-first century and tries to bring India into the non-proliferation regime. The deal has brought India into the mainstream of the global non-proliferation regime. India has also accepted voluntary moratorium on nuclear testing and has promised to cooperate for the smooth passage of the Fissile Materiel Cut-off Treaty (FMCT), which is currently being negotiated in the Conference on Disarmament in Geneva. India has been a responsible nuclear power and it has impeccable non-proliferation record and so it has been a rewarded for its responsible behaviour by enabling India to access nuclear technology and materiel.

However, the main reason for this deal is the potential use of India as a counterweight against rising China in the Asia. According to the US neoconservative logic, India is the only power in the Asia, which can counter-balance China. Therefore, India has to be helped to emerge as a global power. To bolster Indian power, the US allies such as Japan and Australia have to be brought together with India in the name of concert of democracy or quadrilateral initiative consisting of Australia, India, Japan and the US.

US FACTOR IN INDIA-CANADA RELATIONS

India-Canada relations have been hostage to India-US relations. Canada usually toes the US line in the foreign policy realm. It is because of this blind following of the US line that Canada has often been accused of not having an independent foreign policy. There are very few global issues where both the US and Canada disagree. Canadian foreign policy makers have become more habituated to the leadership role of the US. The growing strategic partnership between the United States and India reflected in the Indo-US Civil Nuclear Cooperation Agreement has compelled Canadian policy makers to take the note of the changing wind in international politics and bring corresponding change into its attitude and policies *vis-à-vis* India.

The largest democracy India and the strongest democracy US were at loggerheads during the Cold War period. However, their relations improved dramatically in the post-bipolar post-Cold War world. The former US ambassador to India Robert D. Blackwill has termed India a *friend indeed*. He writes, 'While one can argue that no positive bilateral relationship is "permanent" in the very long run, it is safe to say that the alignment between India and the United States is now an enduring part of the international landscape of the 21st century' (Blackwill, 2007: 16). Now both are busy in forging strategic partnership. Several factors have been responsible for this change in the US-India relations. R. Nicholas Burns, US Under Secretary of State identified the end of the Cold War, India's historic economic reforms of the early 1990s, and India's emergence as a global force as three significant developments, which have helped bring about the recent dramatic strengthening of US-India ties (Burns, 2007: 131).

Relations between the US and India are at an all time high, with the two countries enjoying unprecedented levels of co-operation in the economic, strategic, and diplomatic spheres. India-US bonhomie is having a positive impact upon India-Canada relations. All the factors cited by Nicholas Burns in favour of the improved Indo-US relations are equally valid in the case of Indo-Canadian relations too. The end of Cold War has removed the East-West rivalry as the principal focus of the Canadian foreign policy and the reason behind India's non-aligned policy. India's economic reforms initiated by Manmohan Singh, the then finance minister and now prime minister, opened India to the global economy for the first time. Dismantling of the licence-permit raj and abandoning of the import substitution policy opened the Indian market to foreign trade and investment. Liberalization and privatization of the Indian economy has made India an attractive destination for trade and investment which no significant country can afford to be indifferent to. This is the main reason for the renewed global interest in India. India is the world's fourth largest economy in terms of purchasing power parity. India's geographic location puts it at the centre-stage of today's geo-strategic and geo-economic scenarios, dominated by the needs of energy security and terrorism concerns. India's emergence as a global power has moved from the realm of possibility to that of reality (Mehta, 2008).

OPTIONS FOR CANADA

The Indo-US nuclear deal to reopen global nuclear commerce and cooperation with India was concluded on 10 October 2008, with its formal signature in Washington by both India and the US. For Canada, civil nuclear agreement has created a great dilemma. Many non-proliferation advocates in Canada were opposed to India-US civil nuclear deal. India has refused to join either the Nuclear Non-Proliferation Treaty (NPT) or the more recent Comprehensive Nuclear Test Ban Treaty (CTBT). India set off its first nuclear explosion in 1974, conducted a series of nuclear tests in 1998, and has now embraced nuclear deterrence in its security policies. To critics, re-opening nuclear engagement with India *de facto* legitimizes its nuclear-armed status, betraying the many countries that enjoy nuclear trade only as non-nuclear NPT parties and encouraging the nuclear weapons ambitions of other countries, such as Iran (Huntley, 2007).

Canada has been one of the most vociferous critics of India's nuclear programme. It used very harsh words against India's nuclear programme in the wake of the Pokhran explosions in

1974 and then again in 1998. Canada has been accusing India of betraying, cheating and stealing its nuclear technology for its nuclear weapon programme. This Canadian polemics has annoyed India and it has generated a lot of bitterness in India against Canada. After adopting such an intransigent attitude and high moral ground against India's nuclear programme, it became difficult for Canada to support India in the NSG and then enter into profitable nuclear commerce.

After the approval of India specific safeguards by the IAEA Board of Governors, the deal went to the 45-member NSG for its India specific exemption from nuclear export guideline. NSG takes unanimous decision and so every NSG member has veto power. Canada is the founding member of the NSG and has been very vocal in its non-proliferation efforts. Canada faced the tough choice to choose between realism and idealism. Canada preferred realism over the idealism and along with others supported NSG waiver for India. By doing this Canada avoided annoying the powerful neighbour and reliable ally United States and won over rising India. In major foreign policy matters, Canada usually supports US and so it was expected that Canada would not vote against the wishes of the US in the NSG.

If, however, Canada would have adopted a moralistic posture and stuck to its old demand of India surrendering its nuclear weapons and joining NPT as a non-nuclear weapon state, then it would have blocked the passing of the India specific waiver in the NSG and would have brought an end to India-US civil nuclear agreement. This gesture of Canada would have brought laurels from the non-proliferation lobby, which is feeling genuinely concerned with the Indo-US nuclear deal as it will strike a blow to the non-proliferation regime.

Ashok Kapur, Professor Emeritus at the University of Waterloo who specializes in India-Canada relations, expressed the apprehension that Canada might vote against the deal. However, if that happens, Canada has to pay a very heavy price. He observed,

> If Canada votes against the lifting of restrictions, it stands to lose in a variety of ways. While most of the NSG members were initially opposed to the exemption, the main opponents are Pakistan, China and

Canada. Even China is now starting to lean the other way. If China defects, it will be Canada and Pakistan as the sole opponents. And if Canada is seen as obstructionist, there will be a price to pay. Those repercussions won't come solely from India. The American industry is pushing for this because they are the big beneficiaries of this, including the US defence and aerospace industries. It's across the board on the US side. It would be counter-productive for Canadian industries. Non-proliferation efforts are already weak and Canada must look to its own long-term interests when weighing how to vote. (Kapur, 2008)

Canada voted with others in IAEA and NSG and did not create any problems in both the international institutions in the smooth passage of the safeguard agreement and waiver for India.

Policy makers in Ottawa are grappling with the delicate issue of what this deal means for Canada, given its staunch support for the NPT and the need to contain India's nuclear ambition. Ottawa faces a conundrum. It is redeveloping its own historically frosty relationship with India. Supporting the deal can only assist this process and may allow Canada to enjoy the economic advantages of resuming civil nuclear cooperation. Ottawa's current approach to India puts commercial objectives at the forefront as an emerging market. The government has also made much of the fact that India is a democracy and shares many common values with Canada. Yet if Ottawa would have opposed the deal at NSG, Canada would have risked not only recent bilateral gains with India but would have surely alienated the Bush administration which had made the India deal a high priority (Asia Pacific Bulletin, 2007).

OPPORTUNITIES FOR NUCLEAR COOPERATION

The relationship between India and Canada had suffered for over thirty years. This changed in 2003 when 'both governments, again for their own reasons, woke up to the fact that allowing one issue to dominate the relationship was a bad idea, and that we could agree to disagree about what happened in 1974 and move on recognizing that India had not proliferated internationally since it created nuclear weapons,' observed Canada's High Commissioner to India, David M. Malone (*Hindu*, 2008b).

Over the past few years, Canada and India have continued to enhance their dialogue on regional security and global strategic issues of common interest through the annual Canada-India Strategic Issues Dialogue and regular meetings of the Canada-India Joint Working Group on Counter-Terrorism (international.gc.ca. 2008b).

India-US civil nuclear cooperation agreement offers immense opportunities to Indo-Canadian civil nuclear cooperation. India's civil nuclear energy programme is primarily based on Canadian supplied CANDU nuclear reactor technology. India is also member of CANDU Owners Group (COG), which is a Canadian led body for the maintenance and innovation of CANDU reactor. Despite the snapping of all nuclear ties in the wake of Pokhran I explosions, the Canadian government on the request of IAEA allowed Atomic Energy of Canada Limited (AECL), to carry out repairing and maintenance work at RAPS and the leaking tubes of RAPS were replaced by Canadian AECL (ccnr.org/India_pak_coop.). This shows that despite formal termination of nuclear cooperation in 1976, Canada has been assisting India in the maintenance of reactors to prevent a Chernobyl type of nuclear disaster. However, Indo-Canadian nuclear cooperation was confined only to the safety field.

Canada, France and Russia will be the main beneficiary of the nuclear commerce with India and not the United States. The US will get a small slice of nuclear technology and fuel sale to India. After the Three Mile nuclear accident in 1979, US discouraged nuclear energy. Consequently, research and development in civil nuclear energy technology was adversely affected in the US. Moreover, there is only one nuclear plant built by the US General Electrical at Tarapur (TAPS), based on light water reactor technology and fuelled by enriched uranium.

India adopted Pressurised Heavy Water Reactor (PHWR) technology for the first phase of its three phase civil nuclear energy programme. PHWR uses natural uranium as fuel and heavy water as moderator. Spent fuel can be reprocessed and plutonium can be separated. This plutonium can be used as fuel in breeder reactor, which will constitute the second phase of

India's nuclear energy programme. The third phase nuclear reactors will be fuelled by thorium, which is found abundantly in India. The indigenous PHWR technology is based on Canadian CANDU technology. Over the years, India has acquired mastery over this technology despite the termination of Canadian nuclear collaboration and technology control and the denial regime imposed by the NSG against India. Both Atomic Energy Commission (AEC) of India and AECL of Canada can learn and immensely benefit from each other's experiences in running nuclear reactors based on PHWR technology. Indo-Canadian nuclear collaboration will definitely be a mutually beneficial enterprise.

India has very limited source of uranium. According to AEC estimate, indigenous uranium is adequate to generate only 10,000 MW of nuclear power annually. India has fixed the target of generating 20,000 MW of power by 2020. In view of the Indo-US civil nuclear deal, this target has been revised to 40,000 MW by 2030 (Jain, 2006: 92-3; Subramanian, 2006: 90-1). This target can be achieved only by importing uranium from external sources. Because of the shortage of indigenous uranium and non-availability of the fuel from external source, even the existing nuclear plants are not being able to utilize their installed capacity and are generating power far below their capacity. Canada is the second largest producer of uranium in the world after Australia. If the Indo-US nuclear deal goes through, then Canada can be an important source of fuel for Indian nuclear reactors. So far, Canada has maintained silence over the issue, but it is expected that Canada will go along with the US and will supply uranium to Indian nuclear industry.

Indo-US nuclear deal offers enormous opportunity to Canada to gain from nuclear commerce with India. The global non-proliferation regime imposed by the IAEA and NSG and Canadian concerns with nuclear proliferation prevented Canada from cooperating with India. Passing of India-US civil nuclear cooperation agreement has paved the way for India-Canada nuclear cooperation. Canada can now resume nuclear commerce with India. India can be a lucrative market for Canadian nuclear technology and uranium. A Foreign Affairs report tabled in the

Canadian parliament in November 2007 said, 'Canada will pursue nuclear cooperation with India, which would provide substantial commercial opportunities for Canada' (Berthiaume, 2008). Thus, a major beneficiary of the nuclear deal is Canada and not the US. India will also gain from Canadian nuclear collaboration, as India is more familiar with the Canadian technology and most of its indigenous reactors are replicas of Canadian nuclear technology.

In view of Indo-US Civil Nuclear Agreement, Canada has softened its attitude and has agreed to cooperate with India in the civil nuclear energy field. During former foreign minister Natwar Singh's visit to Canada in September 2005, the foreign minister of Canada Pierre Pettigrew, welcomed India's support of international nuclear non-proliferation norms and noted Canadian interest in cooperation with India in civil nuclear energy. To this end both ministers agreed on the following measures:

- agreement by India to Canada's proposal for nuclear safety collaboration and agreement by both governments to develop a mutually beneficial bilateral framework;
- support by both governments for scientific and technical contacts on a broader range of civilian nuclear issues within the public domain;
- agreement by Canada to allow the supply of nuclear-related dual-use items to Indian civilian nuclear facilities under IAEA safeguards, in accordance with the requirements of the Nuclear Suppliers Group's dual-use guidelines; and
- agreement by both governments to pursue further opportunities for the development of the peaceful uses of nuclear energy both bilaterally and through the appropriate international forums, consistent with their international commitments (international.gc.ca. 2008c).

The successful conclusion of the Indo-US Civil Nuclear Cooperation Agreement has cleared the deck for India-Canada civil nuclear cooperation. It will be a mutually beneficial collaboration as the nuclear scientists of both the countries are working on the same PHWR technology.

CONSTRAINTS

The Canadian government is far behind when it comes to truly understanding India. In spite of grand statements, it is consistently patronizing. Canada started off well, with strong relations between Lester Pearson and Jawaharlal Nehru. Canada was even involved with helping to set up India's civilian nuclear programme. But when India (a democracy that had already been attacked by authoritarian neighbours China and Pakistan) conducted nuclear weapons tests in the early 1970s, Canada furiously cut-off relations. When tests were repeated again in 1998, Canada was one of the most vociferous in condemning India. Canada's foreign affairs minister at the time, Lloyd Axworthy, went so far as to say that India would never be considered for the UN Security Council if it continued acting like that. This showed a stunning misunderstanding of geopolitics. One of the reasons India is being taken so seriously in international circles is because it is nuclear capable, and also because it is next door to China. It is seen not only as economically attractive, but also as a potential balancer of regional power (Paskal, 2008).

There are several impediments to India-Canada nuclear cooperation. The major constraint is the non-proliferation concern of Canadian foreign policy. Canada is committed to the peaceful application of nuclear energy.

> Canadian nuclear non-proliferation policy has two major objectives. The first is to ensure that Canadian nuclear exports are used only for peaceful, non-explosive end-uses and that they do not contribute in any way to the development of a nuclear explosive device. The second is to promote an effective and comprehensive international nuclear non-proliferation regime. (dfait.maeci.gc.ca/nucchallenge 2008)

Canadian experience with India has been very bitter over the nuclear issue. In the past Canada has accused India of betraying its faith and violating the solemn commitment given to Canada for the peaceful use of Canadian technology. 'Canada's nuclear non-proliferation policy is the result of decisions made by the Cabinet in 1974 and 1976 following a review of the policy that was undertaken after India detonated a nuclear device in 1974' (ibid.). The non-proliferation lobby in Canada, which is very strong and vocal, is arguing that India cannot be trusted. India will again cheat and so Canada should not resume its nuclear cooperation with India. Canada should not compromise with the basic principles of its foreign policy for the sake of some geopolitical and commercial gain.

Even if Canada enters into nuclear commerce with India, it will not be a cakewalk. Canada has to face stiff competition from other rivals such as France, Russia and the USA to sell nuclear reactors to India. For the supply of natural uranium, Canada has to face competition from Australia, Kazakhstan and others, which are one of the largest producers of uranium. If Canada agrees to export uranium to India then there should not be any problem for Australia, Kazakhstan and others to do the same.

Despite the passing of India-US civil nuclear cooperation agreement, Canada has to overcome several obstacles to enter into normal civil nuclear cooperation with India. The non-proliferation lobby in Canada is very strong and vocal. Public opinion is also divided over the nuclear cooperation with India. Canada being a vibrant democracy, it will be very difficult for the political leadership to brush aside the public opinion and strong objections by the non-proliferation lobby to enter into nuclear cooperation with India.

CONCLUSION

Indo-US civil nuclear cooperation agreement offers various kinds of opportunities to resume, expand and strengthen Indo-Canadian nuclear cooperation. This cooperation will be mutually beneficial for both the countries. Canada desperately needs markets to revive its sick loss-making nuclear industry. India can be an attractive market as it can revive the sagging fortune of the Canadian nuclear industry. Canada also has vast deposits of uranium and it wants markets for it without violating the rules laid down by the global non-proliferation regime. Canada is primarily an exporter of natural resources and natural uranium can be an important resource for export. Uranium trade with India can be highly profitable for Canada.

If Canada wants markets for its nuclear technology and uranium, India desperately needs both for its ambitious nuclear energy programme, to secure energy security and to diversify its energy basket and to reduce its dependence on fossil fuels. There are very few countries who are exporting uranium and so India's options are also very limited. Moreover, Canadian technology is more suited to Indian needs. Thus Indo-Canadian economic interests converge in the nuclear arena and both can gain immensely from their nuclear commerce.

This enhanced nuclear cooperation will also address the Canadian non-proliferation concerns. By practising 'nuclear apartheid' against India, Canada and its allies could not prevent Pokhran II and overt weaponization of India's nuclear programme. By engaging India, probably Canada and its allies can exercise some kind of restraint on further nuclear testing and will have some leverage over India's nuclear weapon programme. It is better to engage an important rising power like India, who is on the way to emerging as a global power, rather than alienating it. It is precisely because of this reason that all the Western powers such as the United States, Australia and others began courting India after imposing economic sanctions in the wake of Pokhran II explosions in May 1998. Canada is the only Western major power, who ignored India for a long time but began engaging India again, when it discovered that it is alone in ignoring India.

India is also annoyed with the hypocritical attitude of Canada. Being a founder member of NATO, Canada enjoys the security provided by the NATO alliance and extended deterrence of the United States. After enjoying the security provided by the nuclear umbrella of the NATO and US, Canada has no moral right to preach India not to have its own nuclear deterrent. Moreover, Canada has no major external or internal security threat and so it does not need any nuclear deterrent. If ever there is any threat to its security, the US will take care of it. For all practical purposes the US is its only neighbour and with it Canada has most cordial relations.

The case of India is entirely different. It has a very precarious national security scenario. It faces grave internal and external threats to its security. It is also surrounded by two hostile and nuclear armed neighbours, viz., China and Pakistan, with whom it has waged several wars in the past and future wars cannot be ruled out. India has border (MacMahon line) and territorial dispute (Kashmir) with nuclear weapon equipped China and Pakistan. Both of them usually hobnob and join each other against India. In this external security scenario, it has become imperative for India to develop nuclear deterrent of its own to protect itself from China and Pakistan. If Canada would have been facing this kind of adverse external security scenario, then Canada definitely would have acquired nuclear deterrent long back.

India's nuclear weapon programme should be viewed from this perspective. Now the Western countries have a better understanding of India's external security scenario and India's credible minimum nuclear deterrent has better international acceptability. The Indo-US civil nuclear cooperation agreement is the result of this better understanding. It has enabled India to access advanced nuclear technology and fuel. The nuclear agreement has ended India's nuclear isolation and eased the technology denial regime created thirty years back by the international community to prevent India from emerging as a nuclear power.

NOTES AND REFERENCES

Former Atomic Energy Commission (AEC) Chairman and Secretary Department of Atomic Energy (DAE) P.K. Iyengar, A. Gopalkrishanan former Chairman Atomic Energy Regulatory Board and A.N. Prasad, former Director, Bhabha Atomic Research Centre (BARC), all eminent nuclear scientists, have written a letter addressed to Prime Minister Manmohan Singh opposing nuclear deal with the US as it will undermine indigenous nuclear research and compromise India's strategic nuclear programme. See A. Gopalkrishnan, A.N. Prasad, P.K. Iyengar, 'Don't Go Ahead with N-Deal: Top Scientists', *Mainstream*, New Delhi, vol. XLVI, no. 29, 11 July 2008.

Advani, L.K., in interview with N. Ram, 'In the Name of Energy Autonomy, You are Surrendering our Strategic Autonomy', *The Hindu*, 11 July 2008.

Asia Pacific Bulletin, 3 October 2007. 'U.S.-India Civil Nuclear Agreement: What Could it Mean for Canada?' accessed from http://www.asiapacificbusiness.ca/apbn/pdfs/bulletin290.pdf

Bilateral Nuclear Cooperation and Canadian Nuclear Non-Proliferation Policy, 2008a. accessed from http://www.dfait.maeci.gc.ca/nucchallenge/menu-en.asp

Bilateral Nuclear Cooperation and Canadian Nuclear Non-Proliferation Policy, 2008b accessed from http://www.dfait.maeci.gc.ca/nucchallenge/menu-en.asp

Blackwill, Robert D., 2007, 'A Friend Indeed', *The National Interest*, May/June, vol. 89, p. 16.

Burns, R. Nicholas, 2007, 'America's Strategic Opportunity with India; The New U.S.-India Partnership', *Foreign Affairs*, November/December, vol. 86, no. 6, p. 131.

Bratt, Duane, 2002, 'Canada's Nuclear Schizophrenia', *Bulletin of the Atomic Scientists,* March/April, vol. 58, no. 02, pp. 44-50.

Canada announces new areas of cooperation with India, 26 September 2005, no. 171, accessed from http://www.international.gc.ca

Canada-India Relations, accessed from http://geo.international.gc.ca/asia/new-delhi/geo/india-bb-en.aspx

Canadian Nuclear Cooperation with India and Pakistan, at www.ccnr.org/india_pak_coop.html

Edwards, Gordon, 2008, 'Canada's Nuclear Industry and the Myth of the Peaceful Atom', accessed from http://www.ccnr.org/myth_1.html

Foreign Affairs Report, 2008, Cited by Lee Berthiaume, 'Mulling a Meltdown of India's Nuke Rules', *Embassy: Canada's Foreign Policy Newsweekly*, 16 January, accessed from http://www.embassymag.ca/2008/january/16/

Harper, Stephen, 2008, accessed from http://international.gc.ca.

Hindu. 2008a, 'Canada, India to hold nuclear talks', *The Hindu*, 16 November.

Hindu, 2008b. 'BJP not against Nuclear Deal', *The Hindu* (Chennai), 4 June.

Huntley,Wade L., 2007, 'The Right Way to End India's 'Nuclear Apartheid', *Embassy: Canada's Foreign Policy Newsweekly*, 19 December, accessed from http://www.embassymag.ca/2007/december/19/

Kapur, Ashok, 2008, Quoted by Lee Berthiaume, 'Mulling a Meltdown of India's Nuke Rules', *Embassy: Canada's Foreign Policy Newsweekly*, 16 January 2008, at http://www.embassymag.ca/2008/january/16/

Jain, S.K., 2006, in interview with T.S. Subramanian, 'Nuclear Power: Working to a Plan', *Frontline*, 16 June, pp. 92-3.

Leventhal, Paul, 'CIRUS Reactor's Role in a US-India Nuclear Agreement', 19 December 2005, accessed from www.nci.org/06nci/04/CIRUS%20Role%20in%20a%20US-India%20Nuclear.htm

Malone, David M., 2008, *The Hindu*, 13 February.

Mehta, Suresh, 2008, 'Maritime Contribution Towards Furtherance of India's Foreign Policy', B.C. Joshi Memorial Lecture at Pune University, 18 January.

Paskal, Cleo, 2008a, 'India Roars, Canada Snores', accessed from http://www.barricades.ca/current/INDIA.htm

Subramanian, T.S., 2006, 'Nuclear Power: Rising Stakes', *Frontline*, 16 June, pp. 90-91.

Touchey, Ryan, 2007, 'Canada and India at 60: Moving Beyond History?', *International Journal*, September.

Tremblay, Reeta Chowdhari, 2008a, 'Canada-India Relations: The Need to Re-engage,' accessed from http://www.asiapacificresearch.ca/caprn/discussion/tremblay_mar03.pdf

CHAPTER 6

Canada-India Research Partnerships in the Fields of Justice, Public Safety and Human Rights

YVON DANDURAND

Given the progress that Panjab University and this author's institution, the University of the Fraser Valley, have already achieved in developing a dual degree programme in police studies and criminal justice, it is particularly fitting for this author to talk about research partnerships in the fields of justice, public safety and human rights. As we are laying the grounds for greater cooperation in teaching in this sector, it is quite timely also to consider some of the very real opportunities which exist for research collaboration, not only for researchers from our two institutions, but also for criminological researchers across India and Canada.

The words 'criminology' and 'criminological research' are being used rather broadly and include under that rubric all aspects of research on crime, offenders, the process of defining and responding to crime, as well as all aspects of our public safety and criminal justice institutions. And, of course, how can one speak about any of these issues without reference to the all important question of the rule of law and human rights protection?

In addition to the School of Criminology and Criminal Justice at the University of the Fraser Valley, there are several other institutions in Canada which are actively engaged in international and comparative research collaboration in the field of criminal justice including some well-known schools of criminology at the University of Montreal, Simon Fraser University, and the University of Ottawa. There are also some very well-known specialized research institutes, including, to name but a few, the Institute for the Prevention of Crime, at the University of Ottawa, the International Centre for Crime Prevention, in Montreal, the Centre for Safe Schools and Communities at University of Fraser Valley, and the International Centre for Criminal Law Reform and Criminal Justice Policy, in Vancouver. They are all very likely to be interested in engaging in various forms of collaboration with Indian scholars and research institutions. Unfortunately, to be honest, it is probably fair to say that at this point Canadian criminologists and researchers are not very aware of the research that is taking place in India and of the fascinating opportunities which exist for collaboration.

There is no need to emphasize on the importance of comparative research in the fields of justice, public safety and human rights. We all know that many of the issues faced today by national justice systems have become global. Crime is increasingly transnational in nature and, in some instances, de-territorialized. Criminal justice institutions and law enforcement agencies are under tremendous pressure to learn to cooperate more effectively with each other at home and across borders. National authorities are expected to work together to counter various forms of transnational threats, whether it is organized crime, fraud, corruption, or terrorism.

There now is a greater sense of urgency with respect to the development of more effective international cooperation in the fields of public safety and criminal justice. That sense of urgency is now mirrored in the academic world's growing interest in comparative analyses and the identification of best practises in this whole sector. In this field of terminology, many of the new research partnerships seem to develop along lines that are often defined by convergent national security and public safety interests.

The strongest research partnerships in this sector are most commonly observed among researchers from countries which share similar security concerns, face similar crime problems or public safety threats, or have similar justice systems or legal traditions. Countries which enjoy broad commercial, social, cultural and economic exchanges also tend to share similar crime problems and safety concerns. One should not be surprised therefore to learn that this is where research collaboration is also the strongest.

A quick look at the relationship between India and Canada reveals that there are many reasons for these two countries to cooperate in the field of justice and public safety: they often face common threats; the level of social, economic and business exchanges between them is fast increasing; the institutional similarities and affinities in the justice area run quite deep, in part because of a similar colonial past; and, in the past decade or so, the two countries have become parties to international treaties which create a mutual cooperation obligation in the fields of crime prevention and criminal justice.

In fact, the extent to which there is academic cooperation in the field of criminal justice and criminological research between the two countries often seems to be a function of how much each country is prepared to invest in improving operational cooperation in the fields of justice and public safety. For that reason, much of the research that results from these efforts tends to be 'instrumental' in the sense that it tends to focus on building the knowledge necessary to improve the capacity of countries to cooperate with and assist each other in facing common public safety and security threats.

One can readily observe a proliferation of that kind of research in many countries and there is no doubt that this is a useful and important work. But on the other hand, there tends to be a noticeable and deplorable lack of critical comparative research in the justice and public safety field.

THE FRAIL HEALTH OF CRIMINOLOGICAL RESEARCH

Why has it become increasingly difficult for criminologists to conduct good, independent and critical research in their field? Let me follow this idea here for a few minutes. We can digress a little here to talk about the health of criminological research in the world.

Criminology is a science which has rarely enjoyed the luxury of basking in the comfort of its own irrelevance. It is a practical science which is close to power, concerned with issues of immediate and pressing public concern, and limited in its ability to assert itself as something separate and apart from the social control apparatus. It is a political science which deals with essentially political issues.

In recent years, public concerns and fears about crime, violence and insecurity have been exacerbated to a dangerous level. We are, after all, at the tail end of the post-9/11 era and we are still feeling the impact of the security panic that followed the dreadful incidents that occurred on that day. The resulting climate of fear has had huge consequences on the ability of researchers to conduct meaningful and impartial research. At least that is the case in North America. In my view, criminological research in Canada (and in many other countries) is not as healthy and strong as it once was.

One can, of course, blame the researchers themselves for that state of affairs. Because of their proximity to power and their dependence on the authorities to gain access to funding and even more importantly to data, many criminologists have been prepared to make unacceptable compromises with their own scientific and ethical principles. For example, it is appalling that some researchers have apparently been prepared to use dubious information supplied by intelligence services sources as if it could be treated as scientifically valid data, ignoring the possibility of disinformation and the nature of the methods used to obtain such information.

This author remembers that some thirty years back one of Canada's early criminologists, used to accuse the whole profession of being little more that a group of 'government-paid obscurantists'. In the course this author's career, it has been noticed how governments and criminal justice agencies have become far better at controlling the funding for criminal justice research and, sometimes even more importantly, at controlling the researchers' access to data.

In Canada as in other countries, some government ministries and law enforcement agencies have managed to develop an in-house research capacity which, in their view, replaces the need for independent research. Some of them may tolerate within their midst what one could call 'imbedded criminologists', but only in a way which seriously curtails the possibility of independent and critical research, only in a way which implicitly or explicitly encourages the selective use of research findings in order to support and defend the agency's policies and practices.

These issues are being emphasized because international research cooperation in that whole area, and in particular comparative research, is a powerful antidote for some of these poisonous trends affecting the health of criminological research. Comparative research, no matter what the subject, intrinsically challenges the notion that there is only one good way to understand a phenomenon, to define a problem—to approach it or to solve it.

At the epistemological level, to use a term which Bertolt Brecht used to describe art, comparative research produces a 'distanciation effect' which immediately forces the researcher to challenge his/her own assumptions. At the political level, it also places a distance between the researcher and a range of phenomena which always falsely impose themselves as inevitable.

This author obviously places a lot of hope in the future and impact of international research collaboration and comparative research in the fields of crime prevention, criminal justice and human rights.

A COMMON RESEARCH AGENDA

Can one identify an agenda for Canada-India research in the fields of crime prevention, criminal justice, public safety and human rights? Answering this question would presuppose that the criminological research collaboration between the two countries is far advanced than it currently is. The current focus of Canadian criminological research and to emphasize some of the possibilities that I see for an interesting and productive collaboration.

In general, some of the main areas upon which criminologists have focused in recent years include: organized crime groups and patterns of organized crime; human trafficking and other forms of transnational crime; terrorism and counter-terrorism measures; crime reduction and prevention strategies; juvenile crime, juvenile gangs and juvenile justice; criminal justice system's inefficiencies; the criminal justice response to mentally ill offenders; drug abuse, the drug trade and the criminal justice response to these problems; sentencing patterns; domestic violence; fear of crime (and the role of the media); or, the waning credibility of the justice system.

With respect to policing, one will find researchers in Canada who have developed a keen interest in the study of: police integrity and police corruption; police performance and police training; police governance and oversight; modern methods of police management; use of force by the police; police response to domestic violence; police treatment of victims and witnesses of crime, particularly children; the use of agents and informants; witness protection programmes and strategies; and, police-community relations, particularly interactions between the police and minority groups (immigrants, aboriginal people).

Other researchers have focused on: police-based crime reduction strategies; the role of the police in maintaining safe schools and communities; the prevention of identity theft, economic fraud, and computer facilitated crime; or preventing domestic violence or the sexual exploitation of children.

Some significant work is also being conducted in Canada in the areas of: the impact of terrorism and counter-terrorism measures on human rights and on communities; modern methods of investigation; international law enforcement cooperation; methods of ensuring the safety of justice officials; the control of drug markets and the control of drug production (mostly marijuana cultivation).

The justice system research in Canada is also yielding some interesting results in the areas of: measures to promote expeditious trials and greater efficiencies within the justice system; research on the role of prosecutors and the capacity of prosecution services to collaborate internationally and to manage major cases and mega trials; the role of the judiciary; the evolving role of the jury in the criminal trial process; sentencing practices (disparities, inefficiencies, public perceptions, etc.); the effectiveness of specialized—problem-solving—courts (drug courts, community courts); diversion; and restorative justice programmes and practices.

In the field of penology and corrections, some interesting research is also taking place relating to: modern methods of prison management; prison overcrowding, prison conditions; prisoners' rights; detention of juvenile offenders; women in prison; conditional release and supervision; the challenges created by gang members in prison; the effectiveness of rehabilitation programmes; and community corrections and alternatives to imprisonment.

In the context of growing public expectations and shrinking resources, the effectiveness of criminal justice and crime prevention programmes and practices is a source of growing attention on the part of Canadian researchers and their government sponsors. Several researchers are involved in measuring the effectiveness, the costs and the cost-effectiveness of various crime prevention and criminal justice programmes. They focus on identifying best practices and supporting evidence-based programming and policy development.

Also, mentioned before, Canada and every other country has had to face the challenges of transnational crime and the need for enhanced international cooperation. Several Canadian researchers including myself, have focused some of our attention on these new challenges. In recent years, the United Nations and other multilateral organizations have produced the main architecture of an international criminal justice cooperation regime for instance treaties such as the United Nations Convention against Transnational Organized Crime (and its protocols on human trafficking, immigrant smuggling, and trafficking in firearms); the United Nations Convention against Corruption; the Rome Statute establishing the International Criminal Court; the global conventions against terrorism; and, various regional conventions such as those adopted by the Organization of American States. The implementation of such a complex cooperation regime certainly call for brand new and much deeper comparative criminal justice research.

As you can tell from this frustratingly quick and superficial enumeration, there are many opportunities for research collaboration between both the countries. It is time to look at how we can actively promote and support Canada-India research partnership in this field?

SOME SUGGESTIONS

The aim of this paper is, not to identify a whole programme of action. However, it would seem that there are few simple steps that we should immediately consider.

First of all an inventory of research centres potentially interested in Canada-India research partnerships should be made. Their current interests and research programmes could be mapped out and this information be made widely available in both countries. Criminal justice institutions in both countries would also find this exercise useful.

A Canada-India conference or research workshop could be organized on current criminal justice research and identify some potential research synergies and some concrete comparative and collaborative research projects.

The graduate students could be encouraged to engage in comparative research relating to the two countries and support them in working with each other.

The Shastri Institute could perhaps sponsor a collection of criminal justice research publications with a focus on Canada-India comparative analyses.

These are just a few obvious suggestions. There could be many more.

CHAPTER 7

Canada, India and Economic Globalization in the New Millennium: Issues and Evidence*

V.K. VASAL

Globalization is a conspicuous feature of the new millennium. Aiming at a brave new world with no barriers, globalization has been manifesting itself through enhanced integration of economies and societies through cross-country flows of information, ideas, technologies, goods, services, capital, finance, and people (Rangarajan 2006a, 2006b). The process of globalization that had begun to dominate the policies of nearly all the major countries during the last couple of decades of the previous century/millennium is continuing with its forward march with the usual vigor during the early years of the new century/millennium.

Broadly, four dimensions of globalization are identified in the established literature. These are economic, political, social, and cultural. Of these, primary focus of the present paper is on the economic dimension of globalization.

RESEARCH OBJECTIVES

It is widely stated that because of their common colonial heritage, Canada and India share the same language of commerce (English), and institutions such as membership in Commonwealth,

* An earlier version of this paper was presented at the 40th Anniversary Seminar 'Canada-India Relations in the New Millennium', organized by the Shastri Indo-Canadian Institute at New Delhi on 23 April 2008.

parliamentary democracy, and legal systems based on common law. Also shared between them are the values of freedom, democracy, human rights and the rule of law (Emerson 2008). Given this shared environment and values between Canada and India, objectives of the present paper are twofold. The first objective is to evaluate the available evidence on the globalization of Canada and India, particularly their economic globalization, with the world, in the new millennium. The second, and undeniably the more important, objective of the paper is to discover the trends and stability in the bilateral economic links between Canada and India during the new millennium. The analysis for the second objective has been performed from the viewpoint of the Canadian economy—Canadian exports of goods and services to India. In order to fully appreciate the findings of the research study, results obtained for the Canada-India economic links have been benchmarked against (i) the results of a comparable time period ending with the previous millennium (year 2000 being the anchor); (ii) the results on, *inter alia*, trends and stability of Canadian merchandise exports to India as discussed in Assanie et al. (2003b) for a period of 15 years ending, appropriately, in 2000; and (iii) the results on Canadian economic integration with select other emerging market economies. Findings of the paper are expected to be useful to the policy makers and others in their designing and pursuing appropriate strategies and action plans for enhancing the Canada-India economic links in the future.

METHOD

For the first objective—evaluating the available evidence on the globalization of Canada and India, particularly their economic globalization, with the world at large—relevant data have been extracted from the findings of the five most recent annual AT Kearney/*Foreign Policy Globalization Index* surveys. Findings of these surveys have been reported in various volumes of *Foreign Policy* during the years 2003 to 2007.[1] Data thus collected have been analysed in this paper by using the descriptive statistics—measures of location (quartiles, deciles and percentiles) as well as techniques of rank and percentage analysis.

For the second objective—discovering the trends and stability in the bilateral economic links between Canada and India during the new millennium—relevant data have been collected from the databases of the *Statistics Canada* (Government of Canada). For benchmarking the results over time, data have been collected not only for the calendar years of the new millennium but also for a comparable time period ending with the previous millennium, with calendar year 2000 being the benchmark.[2] For comparing the results of Canada-India economic links against those for others, data for Canadian links with select other emerging market economies[3] have also been collected for the relevant time periods, as described earlier. Data collected from the aforesaid sources have been analysed in this paper by using both the descriptive and inferential statistics—measures of central tendency, measures of dispersion, rank and percentage analysis, regression analysis, and tests of significance.

ECONOMIC GLOBALIZATION: CANADA, INDIA AND THE WORLD

The first objective of the present paper is to evaluate the available evidence on the globalization of Canada and India, particularly their economic globalization, with the world at large. In this regard, it is pertinent to note that economic integration of the countries can broadly occur with the world economy through three channels. These are trade in goods and services; movement of capital; and flow of finance (Rangarajan 2006a). The following paragraph gives a synoptic view of the economic relevance of each of the three channels of the economic integration in a modern economy.

Economic importance of international trade, first channel of economic integration, to a modern economy is evident from the fact that, recognizing that trade in goods and services is generally beneficial for the economic growth, many economies (particularly the developing ones) which had earlier pursued the growth model of import substitution have now begun to adopt a policy of outward orientation and international trade. Further, it is agreed that foreign direct investment, the second channel of economic links, enables total savings of the world to be distributed among the countries according to their investment potential. Hence, insufficiency of domestic savings, ideally, should no more be a constraint in enhancement of a country's production base and the consequent improvements in her (and global) rate of economic growth. The third channel of economic globalization, flow of finance, refers to the integration of the national financial markets—foreign exchange, debt, equity, derivatives, and others—with the global financial market. Economic globalization in terms of integrated financial markets, however, is often viewed as a mixed blessing. While integrated financial markets enable cross-country transfer of resources with ease, speed, and efficiency; they also transfer the risks of defaults and volatility from one economy to the others, thus, creating panic and painful situations on a wider scale. The adverse effects of ongoing subprime mortgage loans crisis (with its origin in the United States) being felt in the financial markets worldwide is an appropriate illustration in this context.

Of the aforesaid three channels of economic globalization, literature on business and economics (both popular and academic) has predominantly focused on the first two channels—international trade in goods and services, and capital mobility. This is evident from the fact that some widely accepted metrics have been devised in the established literature for comparing economic globalization of the countries in terms of the said two channels. Besides helping in cross-country comparisons, these metrics supply inputs in the computation of some composite metrics. The annual ranking of the world's most globalized nations in terms of the AT Kearney/*Foreign Policy Globalization Index* (a composite metric), for example, is an illustration in this regard. In the following paragraphs, globalization of Canada and India, particularly their economic globalization, has been evaluated by using the information generated by the said 'Globalization Index'.

Devised and implemented jointly by an international consultancy and research firm AT Kearney, along with her partner *Foreign Policy* magazine, since the beginning of the new millennium, the 'Globalization Index', as already stated, is a composite of a number of metrics relating to four dimensions of the globalization including the economic one (Laudicina and

Janet 2007).[4] Economic dimension of globalization is currently measured in the index in terms of two metrics—one each for total trade, and total foreign direct investment (FDI) flows.[5] Extracts of the findings of the 'Globalization Index' surveys (particularly those for the economic dimension) concerning both Canada and India for the five most recent surveys are presented in Table 7.1.

An analysis of results on ranks (a positional statistical measure) has shown the following for the period of analysis, 2003-7. Whereas Canada has consistently occupied a position at and around the outer domain of the first (top) decile (1-10 per cent), India has consistently occupied a position in the domain of last (bottom) decile (91-100 per cent), among the sample countries. Further, there is some evidence on the worsening of India's position in terms of the 'Globalization Index' over the period of analysis. These findings of the analysis are in agreement with the statement 'whereas Canada is a highly globalized country, India is not'.

In the backdrop of the above findings on the status of overall globalization of Canada and India, an important aspect of the analysis, in terms of the objectives of this paper, is the evaluation of the economic integration of Canada and India over the period of analysis, 2003-7. Results presented in Table 7.1 for the trends in economic integration of Canada and India with the world economy have revealed that Canada has occupied a position in the domain of the second quartile (26-50 per cent) during the period of analysis, a *position significantly worse* than that occupied by her in terms of the overall 'Globalization Index'. Noticeably, there is some evidence on the *worsening of the Canadian 'economic integration' with the world economy over the period of analysis*. This tendency of gradual worsening of Canadian 'economic integration' is *particularly obvious in terms of the first metric—total trade as a percentage of GDP* (systematically declining from 39 percentile position to 59 percentile position). In terms of the second metric, the sum of FDI inflows and outflows as a percentage of gross domestic product (GDP), the observed rank for the Canadian economy, has been unstable over the period of surveys—oscillating between the domain of the first (2003, 2004 and 2006) and second quartiles

TABLE 7.1: GLOBALIZATION INDEX AND ECONOMIC INTEGRATION RANKINGS, CANADA AND INDIA: 2003-7

	Metric	2007		2006		2005		2004		2003	
		Canada-rank	India-rank	Canada-rank	India-rank	Canada-rank	India-rank	Canada-rank	India-rank	Canada-rank	India-rank
Number of countries surveyed		72	72	62	62	62	62	62	62	62	62
Globalization Index—Overall		8	71	6	61	6	61	6	61	7	56
Gross Domestic Product	Gross Domestic Product	8	12	9	12	8	12	8	12	8	12
ECONOMIC INTEGRATION		34	66	23	59	27	59	18	61	17	61
(i) Total International Trade	Total trade as a % of GDP	42	62	30	58	26	59	25	59	24	58
(ii) Foreign Direct Investment	Sum of FDI inflows and outflows as a % of GDP	25	67	12	49	23	51	12	55	10	55

Source: AT Kearney and *Foreign Policy*, various issues.

(2005 and 2007). On the other hand, India has consistently ranked in the domain of the last (bottom) decile (91-100 per cent) in terms of her 'economic integration' with the world (a finding parallel to the one found for India's integration with the world in terms of her overall 'Globalization Index'). However, there is *some evidence on the consistent improvement, though slight, in the 'economic integration' of India with the world* over the period of analysis. This improvement is particularly evident *in terms of the first metric—total trade as a percentage of GDP—for the more recent years.* In terms of the second metric—the sum of FDI inflows and outflows as a percentage of GDP—the observed position of India, like that of Canada, has been unstable over the period of analysis.

An interesting finding based on a *comparison of the observed ranks for 'Globalization Index' and 'economic integration'* is that whereas the *rank of the former is consistently higher than that of the latter for Canada*, the *rank of the latter is mostly higher than that for the former in case of India.* This implies that whereas Canada has performed relatively better on globalization dimensions other than the economic, India has performed better in terms of the economic dimension as against others. Also, amongst the metrics summarized in Table 7.1, *observed distance between the ranks secured by Canada and India is least in terms of the first metric of 'economic integration'—total trade as a percentage of GDP.* This finding of gradual decline of the Canadian ranks and slight improvement of the Indian ranks provides a useful context for appreciation of the research findings of this paper concerning 'economic integration' between Canada and India during the new millennium.

To sum up, the above findings on trend analysis of ranks have shown that Canada has maintained its high position as a globalized economy despite slight worsening of her economic integration in terms of total trade as a percentage of GDP. On the other hand, India has continued to remain near the lowest position of the globalized economies despite improvements in her economic integration with the world. Coalesced, these results have the following two implications. First, whereas 'better than the rest' improvement in dimensions other than 'economic integration' has enabled Canada to maintain her overall position in terms of the overall Globalization Index, 'worse' performance by India on dimensions other than the 'economic integration' has not allowed India to exhibit an improvement in her overall 'Globalization Index'. Second, with improving economic integration of India and observed systematic decline of Canadian position in terms of the first metric of economic integration—total trade as a percentage of GDP, it should be interesting to discover the trends in the trade linkages between Canada and India in the new millennium. In other words, the above findings have provided a useful perspective for interpreting the results of the second objective of the present study.

CANADIAN EXPORTS OF GOODS AND INDIA

The second objective of the present paper is to discover the trends and stability in the bilateral economic links between Canada and India during the new millennium. As already stated, the present paper aims at discovering the facts for the second objective from the viewpoint of the Canadian economy. Accordingly, this section discusses the first part of the research findings relating to the second objective of the paper. That is, Canadian merchandise exports to India. The study has laid a particular focus on the trends in Canadian merchandise exports to India during the period of 2001-7 (termed 'new millennium'). As per research design, these results are benchmarked against (1) the results of a comparable time period of 7 years ending with the previous millennium, that is 1994-2000 (termed 'old millennium'); (2) the results on trends and stability of Canadian merchandise exports to India, as discussed in Assanie et al. (2003b); and (3) the results on Canadian trade in goods with select group of emerging market economies. Accordingly, research findings of the paper in terms of rank analysis, percentage share analysis, and average annual growth for Canadian exports of goods are presented in Table 7.2a through Table 7.2c.

Results on rank analysis presented in Table 7.2a have revealed that India has occupied a rank between 13 and 30 as a trade partner for Canada during the sample period, 1994-2007, with an average of 22nd rank.[6] Over this time period, among the G18 + India and O5 countries, India has ranked 6th and 4th

TABLE 7.2a: CANADIAN MERCHANDISE EXPORTS: RANK ANALYSIS

Countries	Overall sample period (1994-2007)	Old millennium (1994-2000)	New millennium (2001-7)	Maximum (1994-2007)	Minimum (1994-2007)
India	21.50	26.14	16.86	13	30
Argentina	45.50	35.29	55.71	29	70
Brazil	14.64	12.57	16.71	9	17
China	4.29	4.71	3.86	3	6
Colombia	29.29	28.14	30.43	22	36
Egypt	43.71	45.43	42.00	37	48
Indonesia	20.00	18.43	21.57	16	23
Malaysia	26.14	23.71	28.57	20	37
Mexico	8.71	12.00	5.43	5	15
Philippines	32.57	32.29	32.86	27	38
Poland	46.93	47.57	46.29	43	56
Russia	33.00	37.29	28.71	20	45
South Africa	33.43	34.14	32.71	24	46
Thailand	25.43	26.14	24.71	20	33
Turkey	35.93	37.29	34.57	27	47
Venezuela	21.07	18.43	23.71	16	35
Czech Republic	58.57	60.14	57.00	49	66
Hungary	64.50	63.14	65.86	56	76
Peru	45.50	45.00	46.00	38	50
United States	1.00	1.00	1.00	1	1

respectively. An exami nation of results by splitting the time period into two sub-samples of 7 years each has shown the following. During the old-millennium (1994-2000), India had occupied the 7th and 4th positions, respectively, as an export destination for Canada among the G18 + India and O5 countries. During the new millennium, however, India has improved her rank of engagement with Canada to 4th, both amongst the G18 + India and O5 groups of countries.' That is, Canadian engagement with India has grown *vis-à-vis* other emerging market economies, and Canadian exports of merchandise to India in the new millennium are higher than those with Indonesia, Malaysia, and Venezuela. It is noteworthy that among the O5

TABLE 7.2b: CANADIAN MERCHANDISE EXPORTS: PERCENTAGE SHARE

Countries	Overall sample period (1994-2007) (%)	Old millen-nium (1994-2000) (%)	New millen-nium (2001-7) (%)	Maximum (1994-2007) (%)	Minimum (1994-2007) (%)
India	0.20	0.14	0.25	0.39	0.13
Argentina	0.06	0.09	0.03	0.14	0.01
Brazil	0.34	0.43	0.25	0.57	0.19
China	1.22	0.95	1.49	2.06	0.75
Colombia	0.12	0.14	0.10	0.20	0.07
Egypt	0.06	0.05	0.07	0.10	0.04
Indonesia	0.19	0.22	0.15	0.35	0.12
Malaysia	0.14	0.16	0.11	0.23	0.09
Mexico	0.62	0.46	0.78	1.10	0.43
Philippines	0.10	0.10	0.09	0.14	0.08
Poland	0.05	0.05	0.05	0.07	0.03
Russia	0.11	0.09	0.13	0.25	0.05
South Africa	0.10	0.10	0.10	0.17	0.05
Thailand	0.14	0.15	0.12	0.22	0.09
Turkey	0.09	0.08	0.09	0.15	0.04
Venezuela	0.19	0.24	0.15	0.32	0.08
Czech Republic	0.03	0.02	0.03	0.05	0.01
Hungary	0.02	0.02	0.02	0.05	0.01
Peru	0.06	0.06	0.05	0.10	0.04
United States	83.60	83.08	84.12	87.13	79.03
G18	3.64	3.43	3.85	5.35	2.60
O5-I	2.29	1.94	2.63	3.68	1.58

countries, India continues to hold the 4th rank in the new millennium, very much like in the old millennium. Significantly, the only O5 country to which Canadian exports are lower than those to India is South Africa. Incidentally, United States has been the top export destination for Canadian exports of merchandise during all the sample years.

Results on percentage (market share) analysis presented in Table 7.2b have revealed that Canadian exports of goods to India have averaged 0.20 per cent over the sample period of

14 years, 1994-2007 with minimum and maximum values of 0.13 and 0.39 per cent. The average value is 4th highest amongst the G18 + India and O5 countries (the only O5 country to which Canadian exports were lower than those to India is South Africa). The results have shown that whereas Canadian exports of goods to India had averaged 0.14 per cent during the old millennium, the average value of Canadian exports has gone up to a quarter of 1 per cent during the new millennium. An examination of results by splitting the time period into two sub-samples 'old-millennium' (1994-2000) and 'new millennium' (2001-7) has shown that while India's position in terms of market share was joint-8th (with Colombia) and 4th among the G18 + India and O5 countries, respectively, in the 'old millennium' (seven of the G18 countries ahead of India/Colombia, in order, being China, Mexico, Brazil, Venezuela, Indonesia, Malaysia, and Thailand), India held joint-3rd position (with Brazil) both among the G18 + India and O5 countries in the new millennium. Seemingly encouraging in terms of enhanced Canadian economic links with India, the results (on average) have demonstrated a very low level of Canadian economy's engagement with India (0.25 per cent), G18 (3.85 per cent) and O5-I (2.63 per cent) even in the 'new millennium'. This is in sharp contrast to the Canadian exports to its top ranked destination—the United States—where it has exported 84.12 per cent of its merchandise in the 'new millennium', more than one percentage point (that is, four times India's percentage share in the new millennium) higher than 83.08 per cent in the 'old millennium'. This is a clear case of Canada's economic globalization in terms of trade in merchandise resting heavily on its economic linkages with only a single economy, the United States (accounting for more than 8 out of 10 dollars of Canadian exports of goods). Small scale of Canadian economic integration with the emerging market economies is evident from the fact that Canada did not export more than 2.06 per cent of its goods to a G18 + India group economy (China in this case) in any of the sample years, 1994-2007.

Results on annual average growth rate presented in Table 7.2c have revealed that Canadian exports of goods to India

TABLE 7.2c: CANADIAN MERCHANDISE EXPORTS—ANNUAL AVERAGE GROWTH RATE

(in per cent)

Countries	Overall Period (1994-2007)	Old Mil. (1994-2000)	New Mil. (2001-7)	Std. Dev. (1994-2007)	Maxi-mum (1994-2007)	Mini-mum (1994-2007)
India	15.9	13.0	18.9	22.1	54.1	-19.9
Argentina	15.0	14.6	15.5	48.0	100.2	-67.1
Brazil	6.5	7.3	5.7	18.2	33.9	-21.9
China	14.8	14.8	14.8	21.0	50.4	-20.1
Colombia	11.6	10.7	12.4	31.3	91.6	-45.9
Egypt	10.7	7.3	14.1	24.5	55.9	-17.5
Indonesia	8.7	9.7	7.7	26.1	46.9	-33.9
Malaysia	11.0	14.9	7.0	32.2	95.4	-31.1
Mexico	14.7	14.2	15.2	15.9	40.0	-12.2
Philippines	9.3	15.3	3.2	26.5	65.8	-38.2
Poland	15.6	19.8	11.4	48.6	172.1	-24.2
Russia	13.1	-4.1	30.4	35.4	58.5	-57.0
South Africa	15.9	11.6	20.3	32.2	79.0	-29.8
Thailand	5.0	2.9	7.2	19.0	41.4	-34.9
Turkey	15.2	12.9	17.5	34.6	97.4	-33.5
Venezuela	7.1	5.2	9.0	33.8	64.0	-43.2
Czech Republic	17.8	12.8	22.8	26.7	67.3	-21.8
Hungary	23.5	11.8	35.2	44.6	90.5	-47.5
Peru	13.8	18.0	9.6	34.2	77.7	-39.7
United States	6.6	13.3	-0.1	8.2	21.7	-5.4
G18	10.5	9.0	12.0	14.6	36.7	-13.1
O5-I	12.9	12.2	13.5	15.6	35.9	-7.2
Total (All Countries)	6.7	12.1	1.3	7.4	20.4	-3.9

increased (on average) at 15.9 per cent over the sample period of 14 years, 1994-2007. This rate of growth in exports to India is 3rd highest amongst the G18 + India countries and means that India shares the 1st rank (with South Africa) amongst O5 countries over the sample period. An examination of results by splitting the time period into 'old-millennium' and 'new millennium' has shown that while the growth rate of Canadian exports to India had averaged 13.0 per cent giving India 8th and 3rd highest rank among the G18 + India and O5 countries, respectively, in the 'old millennium'; the observed growth rate of 18.9 per cent in the new millennium implies that India occupies 5th and 2nd ranks among the G18 + India and O5 (after South Africa) countries.

Table 7.2c shows that the growth rate of Canadian export of goods to India has varied within a minimum and maximum values of (19.9 per cent) and 54.1 per cent with the value of standard deviation at 22.1 per cent. Value of standard deviation for Canadian exports to India is found higher than those observed for G18 and O5-I groups (and also against the Canadian exports to the world at large, and its top ranked trading partner, the United States), yet again highlighting the issue of high degree of volatility in the merchandise trade relations between Canada and India (Assanie et al. 2003b). However, unlike Assanie et al. (2003b), not only the observed growth rate in Canadian exports to India is much higher at 15.9 per cent (against 6.2 per cent found in Assanie et al. 2003b) in the present study, but the observed rank of standard deviation at 5th lowest among G18 + India countries (and 4th lowest among O5 countries) also appears quite reasonable over the sample period. Notably, an improvement in the overall ranking of India as a trade partner of Canada (as shown in Table 7.2b in terms of increased percentage share of Canadian merchandise exports to India) and a ranking in terms of long-term average annual growth rate (3rd highest amongst the G18 + India) over the sample period, as against 8th and 5th highest recorded in the sub-samples of old and new millennium, has implied more consistent growth of Canadian exports to India *vis-à-vis* several other G18 countries. In other word, a significant part of high value of observed volatility in the trade relations between Canada and India should, rightly, be attributable to the relatively higher growth rate in Canadian merchandise exports to India over the sample period, and may perhaps not be interpreted as a matter of serious concern.

CANADIAN EXPORTS OF SERVICES AND INDIA

Aiming at discovering the trends and stability in the bilateral economic links between Canada and India during the new millennium from the viewpoint of the Canadian economy, this

TABLE 7.2d: CANADIAN EXPORT OF SERVICES: RANK ANALYSIS

Countries	Overall sample period (1996-2005)	Old millennium (1996-2000)	New millennium (2001-5)	Maximum (1996-2005)	Minimum (1996-2005
India	21.90	23.33	21.20	25	20
Brazil	17.20	15.83	19.20	20	13
China	8.40	8.67	8.60	10	6
Mexico	15.40	18.17	12.60	20	10
South Africa	30.80	30.33	30.80	35	23
United States	1.00	1.00	1.00	1	1

section discusses the second part of the research findings concerning the second objective of the present paper. These findings focus on the trends of Canadian export of services to India during the period 2001-5 (termed 'new millennium'). As per research design, these results are benchmarked against (i) the results of a comparable time period of 5 years ending with the previous millennium, i.e. 1996-2000 (termed 'old millennium'); and (ii) the results on Canadian trade in services with select group of emerging market economies. Accordingly, research findings of the Canadian exports of services to India for rank analysis, percentage share analysis, and average annual growth are presented in Table 7.2d through Table 7.2f.

Results on rank analysis presented in Table 7.2d have revealed that Canadian exports of services to India have occupied position between 20th and 25th ranks during the sample period 1996-2005, with an average of 22nd rank. Over the overall sample period, India has ranked 4th amongst the O5 countries. An examination of results by splitting the time period into two sub-samples of five years each have yielded the results similar between the 'old millennium' (1996-2000) and the 'new millennium' (2001-5). However, higher value of average rank in the new millennium has indicated a relative improvement in the Canadian exports of services to India *vis-à-vis* few other countries. Significantly, the only O5 country to which Canadian exports are lower than those to India, like the findings on Canadian exports of merchandise, is South Africa. Incidentally,

TABLE 2e: CANADIAN EXPORTS OF SERVICES: PERCENTAGE SHARE

(*in per cent*)

Countries	Overall Sample Period (1996-2005)	Old Millennium (1996-2000)	New Millennium (2001-5)	Maximum (1996-2005)	Minimum (1996-2005)
India	0.43	0.39	0.46	0.49	0.33
Brazil	0.69	0.76	0.58	0.91	0.55
China	1.26	1.15	1.36	1.45	1.09
Mexico	0.84	0.65	1.02	1.18	0.57
South Africa	0.25	0.27	0.25	0.32	0.19
World	100.00	100.00	100.00	100.00	100.00
United States	58.32	58.36	57.88	61.33	55.95
O5-I	3.05	2.83	3.21	3.31	2.75

United States has been the top export destination for Canadian exports of services in all the sample years.

Results on percentage (market share) analysis presented in Table 7.2e have revealed that Canadian exports of services to India have averaged 0.43 per cent over the sample period of 10 years, 1996-2005 with minimum and maximum values of 0.33 and 0.49 per cent. This average value is 4th highest amongst the O5 countries (the only O5 country to which Canadian exports of services were lower than those to India is South Africa). Table 7.2e shows that whereas Canadian exports of services had averaged 0.39 per cent during the 'old millennium', the average value of Canadian exports has gone up to a little above two-fifths of 1 per cent during the new millennium. An examination of results by splitting the time period into two sub-samples 'old millennium' (1996-2000) and 'new millennium' (2001-5) has shown that India's position in terms of market share has been steady at rank 4 among the O5 countries, in both the sub-periods. The seemingly little change in the proportion of Canadian export of services to India is not in agreement with the objective of enhancing Canadian economic linkage with India (a priority country). Specifically, results have demonstrated (on average) the low level of Canadian economy's engagement with India (0.43 per cent), and O5-I (3.05 per cent) even in the new millennium. This is again in sharp contrast to the Canadian exports to its top ranked destination—the United States—where it has exported 57.88 per cent of its services in the new millennium, about half a percentage point (about the size of India's share in the new millennium) less than 58.36 per cent in the old millennium. This shows Canada's heavy economic integration with the US, with a little less than three-fifths of Canadian exports of services attributable to the United States. This level of economic integration is, however, much less than that found for the Canadian exports of goods. As against the US, small scale of Canadian economic integration with the emerging market economies is evident from the fact that Canada did not export more than 1.45 per cent of its services to an O5 group economy (China in this case) in any of the sample years, 1996-2005.

Results on annual average growth rate presented in Table 7.2f have revealed that Canadian exports of services to India increased (on average) at 11.4 per cent over the sample period of 10 years, 1996-2005. This rate of growth in exports to India is 3rd highest amongst the O5 countries over the sample period. An examination of results by splitting the time period into two sub-periods—'old-millennium' and 'new millennium'—has

TABLE 7.2f: CANADIAN EXPORTS OF SERVICES: ANNUAL AVERAGE GROWTH RATE

(*in per cent*)

Countries	Overall Period (1996-2005)	Old Mil. (1996-2000)	New Mil. (2001-5)	Std. Dev. (1996-2005)	Maximum (1996-2005)	Minimum (1996-2005)
India	11.4	17.2	6.7	16.9	38.4	-14.3
Brazil	10.8	39.4	-0.9	32.2	95.7	-19.1
China	9.5	12.6	5.8	6.3	19.8	-1.3
Mexico	14.4	16.1	10.3	21.5	47.3	-11.3
South Africa	2.8	3.7	-0.6	18.1	32.7	-20.9
World	6.6	10.6	2.4	5.4	14.8	-2.7
United States	6.6	11.8	0.6	7.2	17.5	-4.5
O5-I	9.5	15.0	4.5	11.3	35.4	-5.8

shown that while the growth rate of Canadian exports to India had averaged 17.2 per cent giving India 2nd highest rank among the O5 countries in the 'old millennium'; a deceleration in average annual growth rate to 6.7 per cent in the 'new millennium' has still permitted India to occupy 2nd rank among the O5 countries, particularly when the average annual growth rates of Canadian exports of services to both Brazil and South Africa have been negative.

Table 7.2f also shows that the growth rate of Canadian exports of services to India has varied within a minimum and maximum values of (14.3 per cent) and 38.4 per cent with the value of standard deviation at 16.9 per cent. Value of standard deviation for Canadian exports to India has been found lowest (except for China) amongst the O5 countries (though higher than the Canadian exports of services to the world at large, the United States and 'total Canadian exports of services to O5 as a whole').

GROWTH AND VOLATILITY: FURTHER STATISTICAL ANALYSIS

For further examining the issues of trends in growth and volatility of Canadian exports of both goods and services to India, particularly in the new millennium, some further statistical analysis has been performed in this section of the paper. The analysis performed in this section has focused on testing the following four null hypotheses:

- H_1: there is no difference between the average annual growth rates of Canadian exports to India *vis-à-vis* each of the O5-I,
- H_2: there is no difference in the variability of growth rates of Canadian exports to India *vis-à-vis* each of the O5-I country,
- H_3: there is no difference between the average annual growth rates in Canadian exports to India during the old millennium *vis-à-vis* the new millennium,
- H_4: there is no difference between the percentage share of Canadian exports to India during the old millennium *versus* the new millennium.

It may be noted here that, firstly, pair-wise *t*-test and *F*-test have been performed in this section of the paper for Canadian exports to India *vis-à-vis* O5-I countries for the overall sample period. This is in contrast to the analysis performed in Assanie et al. (2003b) wherein Canadian merchandise exports to India had been compared against G18 as a group. Secondly, *t*-test and *F*-test values have been found by making a comparison of Canadian exports of both goods and services to India across two sub-sample periods—the 'old millennium' and the 'new millennium'. Values of the test statistics found for the first two hypotheses are presented in Table 7.3.

Results of *t*-statistics (assuming both equal and unequal means) presented in Table 7.3 have shown that the *first null hypotheses*

TABLE 7.3: CANADIAN EXPORTS TO: TESTS OF SIGNIFICANCE

Countries- Canadian exports to India *vs*.-	Brazil	China	Mexico	South Africa
Merchandise				
t-test: Assuming Equal Variances	1.24	0.14	0.17	0.00
[*P*(*T*<= Critical two-tail) in parentheses]	(0.23)	(0.89)	(0.87)	(0.99)
t-Test: Assuming Unequal Variances	1.24	0.14	0.17	0.00
[*P*(*T*<= Critical two-tail) in parentheses]	(0.23)	(0.89)	(0.87)	(0.99)
F-test two-sample for variances	1.48	1.12	1.93	0.47
[*P*(*F*<=*f*) one-tail in parentheses]	(0.24)	(0.42)	(0.12)	(0.10
Services				
t-test: Assuming equal variances	0.05	0.33	-0.35	1.10
[*P*(*T*<= Critical two-tail) in parentheses]	(0.96)	(0.74)	(0.73)	(0.28)
t-Test: Assuming Unequal Variances	0.05	0.33	-0.35	1.10
[*P*(*T*<= critical two-tail) in parentheses]	(0.96)	(0.74)	(0.73)	(0.28)
F-Test two-sample for variances	0.28	7.25	0.67	0.87
[*P*(*F*<=*f*) one-tail in parentheses]	(0.03)	(0.00)*	(0.24)	(0.42)

Note: *Significant at 1 per cent level of significance

of no difference between the average annual growth rates of Canadian exports to India *vis-à-vis* Canadian exports to each of the O5-I country cannot be rejected at 5 per cent level of significance for both Canadian exports of merchandise as well as Canadian exports of services. On other hand, for the *second null hypothesis* of no difference in the stability of the Canadian exports to India *vis-à-vis* Canadian exports to each of the O5-I country, results of *F*-statistic consistently support the null hypothesis for the Canadian exports of merchandise. However, for Canadian exports of services, the null hypothesis of no difference in the instability of average annual growth rates between India and China has been rejected at 1 per cent level of significance for the overall sample period. Thus, results presented in Table 7.3 have shown that except for volatility of growth rate of Canadian exports of services to China *vis-à-vis* that to India, the average annual long-term growth rates of Canadian exports to each of the other O5-I countries are not significantly different from those for India (pair-wise).

For the *third null hypothesis* of no difference between the *average annual growth rates* in Canadian exports to India during the two sub-periods—'old millennium' *versus* the 'new millennium'—the following results have been found. First, *F*-statistic values at 2.26 and 1.69 for Canadian exports of merchandise, and Canadian exports of services, respectively, with *P*(*F*<= Critical one-tail) being 0.17 and 0.31 have suggested that *volatility (standard deviation) of Canadian exports to India during the 'old millennium' is statistically not different from the volatility in the 'new millennium'*. Second, values of *t*-statistic (assuming equal variance) for Canadian exports of merchandise and Canadian exports of services are observed at 0.48 and 0.87, respectively, with *P*(*T*<= Critical two-tail) being 0.64 and 0.41 respectively. These results, on the whole, have implied that the average annual growth rates of Canadian exports to India, both merchandise as well as services, in the 'new millennium' are statistically not different from their counterparts in the 'old millennium'.

For the *fourth null hypothesis* of no difference between the *percentage share* of Canadian exports to India during the 'old millennium' and the 'new millennium', the following results have been obtained. First, values of *F*-statistic at 0.03 and 1.42 with P(F<= Critical one-tail) being 0.00 and 0.37 have implied that *volatility (standard deviation) of percentage share of Canadian exports to India during the 'old millennium' is statistically not different from the volatility in the 'new millennium'*. Second, values of *t*-statistic (assuming equal variance) are observed at 3.04 with P(T<= Critical two-tail) being 0.01 for percentage share of Canadian exports of merchandise to India, and at 2.22 with P(T<= Critical two-tail) being 0.06 for percentage share of Canadian exports of services to India for the two sub-periods. These research findings have implied that the null hypothesis of no difference in the percentage share of Canadian exports to India during the 'old millennium' *versus* the 'new millennium' is rejected at 5 per cent and 10 per cent levels of significance, respectively, for Canadian exports of merchandise, and Canadian exports of services, to India.

Given the foregoing, it is proposed to examine the following research question. Does the improvement in the percentage share of Canadian exports to India in the new millennium represent a significant net change of the effects of time trend? For answering this question, a multivariate analytical framework has been used in the paper. In operational terms, the following regression model has been designed and tested in this paper for the aforesaid limited objective:

$$Y_t = a_0 + b_1X_1 + b_2X_2 + e$$

where

Y_t—Percentage share of Canadian exports to India in year t,

X_1—time trend, and

X_2—dummy variable for old/new millennium (1 for old millennium).

The above regression model has been applied to the empirical data for the period, 1994-2007 pertaining to Canadian exports of goods, and 1996-2005 for Canadian exports of services, to India. Based on discussions above, a statistically significant coefficient for X_2 would imply that percentage share of Canadian exports to India in the 'old millennium' has been significantly different from the 'new millennium'. The empirical results obtained by using the method of ordinary least squares (OLS) for the regression model designed above are as given below (*t*-values in parentheses).

Merchandise Trade

$$Y_t = 0.000367 + 0.000196X_1 + 0.000275X_2 + e$$
$$(0.44) \quad (2.67)^{**} \quad (0.46)$$

$R^2 = 0.66$ Adjusted $R^2 = 0.60$
(** significant at 5 per cent level of significance)

Trade in Services

$$Y_t = 0.004684 - 0.000014X_1 - 0.000645X_2 + e$$
$$(5.86) \quad (0.15) \quad (1.16)$$

$R^2 = 0.38$ Adjusted $R^2 = 0.21$

Non-significance of the coefficients of X_2 variable in both the estimated regression equations have indicated that, net of the effects of time trend, the percentage share of Canadian exports to India in the 'new millennium' is statistically not different from the 'old millennium', both for Canadian exports of goods as well as Canadian export of services to India. However, positive and statistically significant coefficient of variable X_1 in estimated regression equation for Canadian merchandise exports to India is in agreement with the view that market share of Canadian exports of goods to India is directly changing with time. Though, no such inference can be drawn for Canadian exports of services to India. On the whole, results of the regression analysis have implications for pursuing strategies and action plans by the Canadian policy makers and businesses for increasing the Canada's economic linkages with India in near future. This alone should make a difference from the low levels of economic integration that Canada has shared with India during, at least, past one decade and a half spanning over both the old as well as the new millennium.

IMPLICATIONS AND CONCLUSIONS

This research paper has discussed, first, some empirical evidence on the current status of globalization of Canadian and Indian economies and, second, trends and volatility in the trade relationships between Canada and India. Importantly, the study has highlighted the very low level of economic integration of Canada with India in particular, and other major emerging market economies in general. Though, some improvement in Canadian exports of goods and services to India has been observed during the new millennium, the percentage share of trade at a quarter of 1 per cent (merchandise) and two-fifths of 1 per cent (services) are indicative of a very low level of economic integration by the Canadian economy with a potentially vital economy in the world, i.e. India.

To put the above inference in perspective, it is noted that several authoritative studies and international surveys have underlined the importance of economic engagement with countries like India as a key aspect of the modern globalized era. For instance, it has been predicted by Wilson and Purushothaman (2003) that the Brazil, Russia, India and China (BRIC) economies have the potential to become a much larger force in the world by the middle of the current century. They have predicted that, out of the benchmark G6 developed economies (G8 *minus* Canada and Russia),[7] only the US and Japan may be among the six largest economies (in US dollar terms) in 2050. That is, the list of world's ten largest economies by GDP may look quite different in 2050.[8] In terms of GDP, *China and India have been forecast by the authors to be the 1st and 3rd largest economies in the world by 2050.*[9]

In a more recent and enlarged study,[10] O'Neill et al. (2005) predicted that BRICs can realize the 'dream' of overtaking many of the G7 (G8 *minus* Russia) economies more quickly than that forecast by Wilson and Purushothaman (2003). They have *forecast that India and Canada would be the 3rd and 15th largest economies respectively in the world by 2050*[11] (incidentally, Canada has been predicted to be the smallest of the current G8 economies by the year 2050). This study too, like many others, has unambiguously advocated a case for economic engagement with countries like India as a key aspect of global policy making in the modern globalized era.

Coalesced, findings of the present paper have some implication for the Canadian policy makers. Undoubtedly, strategies followed by Canada have enabled it to be ranked as one of the most globalized economies till date. The analysis of results and discussions above, however, have shown that during the past one-and-a-half decades, the demonstrated spirit of globalization by Canada has brought only marginal change in her economic engagement with a country like India, a country whose economic integration with the world has been on an upswing during this time-frame, and in any case an economy widely recognized as a significant economic power of the future. Notably, Canada's economic engagement, like India, has been limited with various other similarly placed major emerging market economies of the world, in the recent past. Considering these facts, it is of paramount importance that Canadian policy makers and businesses should be devising more pragmatic and, perhaps, more aggressive strategies for broadening and deepening the economic linkages with India (and other major economic players of the future). Such initiatives may provide Canada with the strategic gains in the form of, for instance, being less vulnerable to the adverse economic changes in one or a handful of economies. With economic integration of more than eight-tenths/three-fifths of trade with a single economy, as at present, avoidance of the ill effects of such risky situations is, however, highly improbable.

NOTES

1. While findings of the surveys were reported during the years 2003 to 2007, an investigation into the methodology and databases used in these surveys has revealed that the latest data used for ranking of the countries, particularly the economic globalization (of prime interest to this study), in the successive surveys have corresponded to the years 2001 to 2005.
2. Latest year for which data on trade in goods and trade in services (first channel of economic globalization, as described below) were available are 2007 and 2005, respectively. Since data for trade in goods are available for 7 years further into the new millennium (calendar year 2000 being the benchmark), for measuring annual growth trends in relevant economic variables, data have been collected for a time period of 7 years prior to the benchmark year 2000 in the previous millennium. This has implied collecting long-term time series data for a maximum period of 15 years (1993-2007) that has been split into two equal-term sub-samples of 7 years each, 1994-2000 (termed 'old millennium' sample) and 2001-7 (termed 'new millennium' sample). However, since

data for trade in services are available for only 5 years further into the new millennium (calendar year 2000 being the benchmark), data have been collected for a comparable time period of 5 years in the previous millennium, that is prior to the benchmark year 2000. This has implied long-term time series data for 11 years (1995-2005) consisting of two medium term sub-samples of 5 years each, 1996-2000 (termed 'old millennium' sample) and 2001-5 (termed 'new millennium' sample). In short, data used in the study for Canadian exports of goods, and Canadian exports of services are for 15 and 11 years, respectively.

3. For evaluating Canadian export of goods to India, like Assanie et al. (2003a, 2003b), the benchmark group of countries consists of 18 emerging market economies (termed G18): Argentina, Brazil, China, Colombia, Czech Republic, Egypt, Hungary, Indonesia, Malaysia, Mexico, Peru, Philippines, Poland, Russia, South Africa, Thailand, Turkey, and Venezuela. However, for benchmarking the results in general, the paper has recognized the following two facts: first, that *The Economist* (all editions) has discontinued, as of now, the practice of publishing the list of 'Emerging Market Economies' (basis for selection of the benchmark group in Assanie et al. [2003a, 2003b]) as an independent section in the weekly newsmagazine, and second, that the erstwhile G7 had formally inducted Russia as a full member into the prestigious International Forum for Governments of developed industrialized countries in 1997, and has expanded the Forum by including five big developing economies—Brazil, India, China, Mexico and South Africa (termed 'outreach five' (O5))—since 2005. Hence, in the present paper, the research findings for India have been benchmarked against a contemporary (hence, more relevant) politico-economic group of four countries—'outreach five except India (termed O5-I)'. Thus, Canadian export of goods to India have been benchmarked against two groups—'G18' and 'O5-I'. Canadian export of services to India have been, however, benchmarked against 'O5-I' only.
4. AT Kearney/*Foreign Policy Globalization Index* tracks and assesses changes in four key dimensions of global integration—economic integration, personal contact, technological connectivity, and political engagement.
5. Besides, trade and foreign direct investment (FDI), economic dimension of globalization had included the following metrics during the 2003 and 2004 surveys—portfolio capital flows (in both 2003 and 2004), income payments and receipts (including compensation of non-resident employees and income earned and paid on assets held abroad) (in 2003), and investment income payments and receipts (in 2004). So far as these additional metrics had influenced the cross-country rankings of economic integration in the years 2003 and 2004, results of the

surveys relating to these two years are, strictly speaking, not comparable against those presented for the years 2005 to 2007.

6. For rank analysis for all economic variables, ranks have been assigned year-wise to all the countries with economic relations with Canada. Average rank is measured as simple arithmetic mean of ranks assigned to individual years.
7. The following had constituted the G6—France, Germany, Italy, Japan, the UK, and the US. The authors had noted that adding of Canada and other larger developed economies would not have materially changed their conclusions.
8. It is clarified that the largest economies in the world by GDP may no longer be the richest in terms of the per capita income. In fact, it is predicted that in 2050, individuals in the BRICs economies, with the exception of Russia, are likely to be poorer than individuals in the benchmark G6 economies.
9. The predicted order (largest to smallest) of the 10 economies in 2050 is as follows—China, the US, India, Japan, Brazil, Russia, the UK, Germany, France and Italy.
10. Besides including Canada, a country omitted in the earlier study by Wilson and Purushothaman (2003), O'Neill et al. (2005) have included a group of 11 additional developing countries, termed the 'Next Eleven (N-11)'. N-11 group represents the following countries: Bangladesh, Egypt, Indonesia, Iran, Korea, Mexico, Nigeria, Pakistan, the Philippines, Turkey, and Vietnam.
11. The predicted order (largest to smallest) of the 22 economies in 2050 is as follows, top 10—China, the US, India, Japan, Brazil, Mexico, Russia, Germany, the UK, and France; followed by the other 12—Indonesia, Nigeria, Korea, Italy, Canada, Vietnam, Turkey, the Philippines, Egypt, Pakistan, Iran, and Bangladesh. As in Wilson and Purushothaman (2003), Russia still emerges as the wealthiest BRIC nation in terms of GDP per capita.

REFERENCES

Assanie, N. et al., *Emerging India: Canadian Business Perceptions on Trade and Investment,* Vancouver: Asia Pacific Foundation of Canada (APFC), May 2003.

———, *Canada-India Trade: Retrospect and Prospects,* Vancouver: Asia Pacific Foundation of Canada (APFC), and National Council of Applied Economic Research (NCAER), New Delhi, September 2003.

AT Kearney and Foreign Policy, 'Measuring Globalization: Who's Up, Who's Down?,' *Foreign Policy*, January-February 2003, pp. 60-72.

———, 'Measuring Globalization: Economic Reversals, Forward Momentum', *Foreign Policy*, March-April 2004, pp. 54-69.

———, 'Measuring Globalization', *Foreign Policy*, May-June 2005, pp. 52-60.

———, 'The Globalization Index', *Foreign Policy*, November-December 2006, pp. 74-81.

———, 'The Globalization Index', *Foreign Policy*, November-December 2007.

Dobson, Wendy, *The Indian Elephant Sheds its Past: The Implications for Canada*, Toronto: C.D. Howe Institute, no. 235, June 2006.

Emerson, David (Minister of Foreign Affairs, Government of Canada), Letter to the Editor, 'India Deserves our Support on Nuke Deal', *Toronto Star*, Ottawa, 8 August 2008.

Laudicina, Paul A. and Pau Janet, *The 2007 AT Kearney Foreign Direct Investment Confidence Index: New Concerns in an Uncertain World*, Virginia: AT Kearney, Inc., 2007.

O'Neill, Jim et al., *How Solid are the BRICs? (Global Economics Paper No. 134)*, Goldman Sachs Group, Inc., USA, 2005.

Rangarajan, C., 'Meeting the Challenges of Globalization', *Fourteenth Convocation Address at Dr. B.R. Ambedkar Open University*, Hyderabad, 24 January 2006.

———, 'Responding to Globalization: India's Answer', *Fourth Ramanbhai Patel Memorial Lecture on Excellence in Education*, Ahmedabad, 25 February 2006.

Statistics Canada, Government of Canada, Ottawa.

Wilson, Dominic and Roopa Purushothaman, 'Dreaming With BRICs: The Path to 2050' (Global Economics Paper No. 99), Goldman Sachs Group, Inc., USA, 2003.

CHAPTER 8

Situating Bilateral Trade of India and Canada within the World Trade Scenario

ARTI NANAVATI

Bilateral merchandise trade relationship of India and Canada is an important, though still an underutilized element of their economic relationship despite India making all efforts in the last two decades to integrate herself with the world economy. The potentials on this front was more in case of India and Canada, since both the countries were already in a relationship of 'aid and migration', which is complemented by politico-economic factors such as their being members of Commonwealth countries with parliamentary system and federal set-up. Of recent the two countries have embarked on a process of strengthening bilateral ties initiated at the level of governments. The Canadian government's policy is to 're-engage' India mainly due to her emerging role in the past few years in the global economic system. The institutional efforts both at the level of government and at business community levels might take some time to mature; it is of interest and importance to analyse the prospects of Canada-India trade in the context of world trade scenario.

The bilateral trade between any two nations gets impacted by the forces of multilateralism represented by WTO and regionalism in the form of regional trading blocks over and above factors like distance, elasticity of demand for export and import, economic growth and also some non-'economic' factors which might be both exogenous and indigenous. The intent of the present paper is not to identify the factors for relatively meager bilateral trade flow of Canada-India as it is beyond the scope of this paper, but to situate it in the context of global trading relations of both the countries. It might also be too premature an issue for analysis as it is only in the last few years that India is recognized as a player in the world economic system. The paper attempts to situate Canada-India trade in the context of changing pattern of world trade in general and that of Canada-India trade flow in particular so as to indicate the potentials of their trade relationship. For this the two main sections of the paper discuss world trade scenario including that of NAFTA and trade relationship between Canada and India and its prospects in the context of Canada's trading relationship with China. Based on these the paper concludes in the third section.

I

WORLD TRADE SCENARIO

Merchandise Trade

During the first six years (2000-6) of this millennium, the annual percentage change in world merchandise exports was 5.5 per cent, which exceeded world merchandise production of 2.5 per cent and world GDP annual percentage change of 3.0 per cent. In case of all the three major sectors, agriculture, mining, and manufacturing the world merchandise exports respectively, 4 per cent, 3 per cent, 6 per cent were double to world merchandise production indicating a much higher element of interdependency in world economy.

The regional trade flow in world merchandise export (Table 8.1) in 2006 was dominated by Europe (42 per cent), Asia (28 per cent) and North America (14.2 per cent), however, the flow was mainly intra region as it was 38 per cent in case of North America, 71 per cent in case of Europe and 58 per cent in case of Asia. The flow of exports from Asia to North America (30 per cent) was much higher than North America to Asia (11 per cent) indicating higher dependency of Asia to North American markets than vice versa.

TABLE 8.1: PERCENTAGE SHARE OF REGIONAL TRADE IN WORLD MERCHANDISE EXPORT, 2006

Origin/ Destination	World	North America	South & Central America	Europe	CIS	Africa	Middle East	Asia
World	100.0	100.0	100.0	100.0	100.0	100.0	100.0	100.0
North America	14.2	38.4	28.4	5.5	2.8	7.7	11.0	11.1
South & Central America	3.6	5.7	29.5	1.7	2.1	4.0	2.1	2.2
Europe	42.1	18.3	17.6	71.3	48.7	42.6	33.8	12.9
CIS	3.6	1.0	2.0	4.8	27.7	2.0	3.5	1.6
Africa	3.1	3.4	3.0	2.9	0.5	11.6	1.7	2.6
Middle East	5.5	3.0	1.2	2.0	1.0	7.4	18.8	12.0
Asia	27.8	30.1	18.4	11.8	17.1	24.7	29.2	57.7

Note: All the tables, except specified are from *International Trade Statistics*, 2006, WTO.

Table 8.2 provides information about the changing pattern of merchandise trade from 1948-2006. In 1948 the share of North America in exports was 28 per cent and in imports 19 per cent, whereas the share of Asia was 14 per cent in both exports and imports. By 2006, things reversed. North America had the share of 14 per cent and that of Asia 28 per cent. In imports share of North America increased to 21 per cent and of Asia 25 per cent. Thus Asia emerged as an important trading region in the world economy.

In world exports and imports Canada has a share of around 3 per cent and ranks 9 (Table 8.3). India with 1 per cent share ranks 28 in exports and 17 in imports, and China with 8 per cent share in exports and 6.5 per cent share in imports ranks 3 in 2006. Thus China is a big player in world merchandise trade.

TABLE 8.2: WORLD MERCHANDISE EXPORTS AND IMPORTS BY COUNTRIES/REGION

Year	World Value (billion US $)	% Share of				
		Canada	India	China	North America	Asia
1948	58	5.5	2.2	0.9	27.1	14.0
	62	4.4	2.3	0.6	18.5	13.9
1953	84	5.2	1.3	1.2	24.1	13.4
	85	5.5	1.4	1.6	20.5	15.1
1963	157	4.3	1.0	1.3	19.2	12.4
	164	3.9	1.5	0.9	16.1	14.1
1973	579	4.6	0.5	1.0	16.9	14.9
	595	4.2	0.5	0.9	17.2	14.9
1983	1,838	4.2	0.5	1.2	16.8	19.1
	1,882	3.4	0.7	1.1	18.5	18.5
1993	3,675	4.0	0.6	2.5	18.0	26.1
	3,770	3.7	0.6	2.8	21.5	23.3
2003	7,369	3.7	0.8	5.9	15.8	26.1
	7,650	3.2	0.9	5.4	22.6	23.1
2005	10,159	3.5	0.9	–	14.5	27.4
2006	11,783	3.3	1.0	8.2	14.2	27.8
	12,113	3.0	1.4	6.5	21.0	25.0

Note: Figures in the second row are imports.

TABLE 8.3: LEADING EXPORTERS AND IMPORTERS IN WORLD MERCHANDISE TRADE, 2006

Rank	Exporters	Value (billion US $)	Share (%)	Rank	Importers	Value (billion US $)	Share (%)
1	Germany	1112.0	9.2	1	USA	119.4	15.5
2	USA	1038.3	8.6	2	Germany	908.6	7.3
3	China	968.9	8.0	3	China	791.5	6.4
4	Japan	649.9	5.4	4	UK	619.4	5.0
5	France	490.4	4.1	5	Japan	579.6	4.7
6	The Netherlands	462.4	3.8	6	France	534.9	4.3
7	UK	448.3	3.7	7	Italy	437.4	3.5
8	Italy	410.6	3.4	8	The Netherlands	416.4	3.4
9	Canada	389.5	3.2	9	Canada	357.7	2.9
10	Belgium	369.2	3.1	10	Belgium	353.7	2.9
28	India	120.3	1.0	17	India	174.8	1.4
	World	12,083.0	100.0		World	12,413.0	100.0

Table 8.4 shows merchandise exports of NAFTA by destination. It can be seen from the table that in 2005, the trade within NAFTA was 55.8 per cent and with all other countries it was 44 per cent. In case of Canada, with all other countries the

TABLE 8.4: MERCHANDISE EXPORTS OF NAFTA COUNTRIES BY DESTINATION, 1990-5 (BILLION US $ & PERCENTAGE)

Origin	Year	US	Canada	Mexico	NAFTA	All other countries	World
Value							
US	1990	–	83.0	28.3	111.3	282.3	393.6
	2000	–	176.4	111.7	288.1	493.8	781.9
	2003	–	169.5	97.5	266.9	457.9	724.8
	2004	–	189.1	110.8	299.9	518.9	818.8
	2005	–	211.4	120.0	331.5	572.9	904.4
Canada	1990	95.2	–	0.5	95.7	31.9	127.6
	2000	241.6	–	1.4	243.0	33.7	276.6
	2003	233.4	–	1.6	235.0	37.8	272.7
	2004	267.9	–	2.3	270.1	46.4	316.5
	2005	302.2	–	2.7	304.9	54.5	359.4
Mexico	1990	32.3	0.2	–	32.5	8.2	40.7
	2000	147.2	3.3	–	150.5	15.9	166.4
	2003	147	2.8	–	149.9	15.5	165.4
	2004	166.5	2.8	–	169.3	18.7	188.0
	2005	183.3	4.2	–	187.6	26.2	213.7
NAFTA	1990	127.5	83.2	28.8	239.5	322.4	561.9
	2000	388.8	179.7	113.1	681.6	543.4	1224.9
	2003	380.4	172.3	99.0	651.7	511.2	1162.9
	2004	434.4	191.9	113.1	739.3	584.0	1323.3
	2005	485.5	215.6	122.7	823.9	653.6	1477.5
Share							
USA	2005	–	14.3	8.1	22.4	38.8	61.2
Canada	2000	19.7	–	0.1	19.8	2.7	22.6
	2005	20.5	–	0.2	20.6	3.7	24.3
Mexico	2000	12.0	0.3	–	12.3	1.3	13.6
	2005	12.4	0.3	–	12.7	1.8	14.5
NAFTA	2000	31.7	14.7	9.2	55.6	44.4	100.0
	2005	32.9	14.6	8.3	55.8	44.2	100.0

percentage share was 3.7 per cent. The US had the share of 38.8 per cent. Thus, in Canada's international trade it is the US, which is a dominant partner.

Trade in Services

In 2006 (Table 8.5) world exports of services was 2,755 billion US $ and imports 2,650 billion US $, which was 19 per cent and 18 per cent respectively of the total international trade. The United States ranked one in exports of services with 14 per cent share; China ranked 8 (3.3 per cent share), India 10 (2.7 per cent share) and Canada 14 (2.1 per cent share). In imports the US having the share of 11.6 per cent ranked number one, China ranked 6 (3.8 per cent share), Canada 11 (2.7 per cent share) and India 13 (2.4 per cent share). Thus China emerges an important trader in services and India as ahead of Canada in exports of services.

Table 8.6 shows the trend in the export of services by regions during 1996-2006. It can be seen from the table that the share of North America, which was 20 per cent in 1996, declined to 18.85 per cent in 2006. The share of Canada fell from 2.25 per cent to 2.35 per cent in the same period. The share of China increased from 1.62 per cent to 3.72 per cent, and that of India from 0.57 per cent to 3.01 per cent. The growth rate continuous compound was 6.7 per cent in case of Canada, 14.7 per cent for China and 21.5 per cent for India. This shows that India had an impressive performance in export of services as compared to China and Canada.

Table 8.7 showing the import in services, indicates that Canada's share has declined and was 2.71 per cent in 2006 and that of China 3.79 per cent and of India 2.41 per cent. In case of import of services also the highest growth rate was that of India with 26.9 per cent China 14.8 per cent and Canada 6.8 per cent. Thus in terms of growth rate of imports, India is fast emerging to be a major global player.

In order to analyse the nature of trading relationship of NAFTA (Table 8.8), one finds that during 1996-2006 the intra exports increased from 46.9 to 53.8 per cent and extra exports declined from 53 to 46 per cent. Intra imports declined from

TABLE 8.5: LEADING EXPORTERS AND IMPORTERS IN WORLD TRADE IN COMMERCIAL SERVICES, 2006

Rank	Exporters	Value (billion US $)	Share (%)	Rank	Importers	Value (billion US $)	Share (%)
1	USA	388.8	14.1	1	USA	307.8	11.6
2	UK	227.5	8.3	2	Germany	219.1	8.3
3	Germany	168.8	6.1	3	UK	172.0	6.5
4	Japan	122.5	4.4	4	Japan	144.0	5.4
5	France	114.5	4.2	5	France	108.8	4.1
6	Spain	105.5	3.8	6	China	100.3	3.8
7	Italy	97.5	3.5	7	Italy	98.4	3.7
8	China	91.4	3.3	8	Ireland	78.4	3.0
9	The Netherlands	82.5	3.0	9	The Netherlands	78.1	2.9
10	India	73.8	2.7	10	Spain	77.9	2.9
11	Hong Kong, China	72.7	2.6	11	Canada	71.7	2.7
12	Ireland	68.0	2.5	12	Korea, Republic of	69.8	2.6
13	Austria	58.9	2.1	13	India	63.7	2.4
14	Canada	57.7	2.1	14	Singapore	60.8	2.3
	World	2,755.0	100.0		World	2,650.0	100.0

TABLE 8.6: PERCENTAGE EXPORTS OF COMMERCIAL SERVICES BY REGION AND SELECTED ECONOMY, 1996-2006

	Growth rate continuous compound	1996	1997	1998	1999	2000	2001	2002	2003	2004	2005	2006
World	7.2	100.00	100.00	100.00	100.00	100.00	100.00	100.00	100.00	100.00	100.00	100.00
North America	5.3	20.13	20.8	20.95	21.75	22.15	21.16	20.22	18.38	17.37	17.25	18.85
Canada	6.7	2.25	2.33	2.44	2.5	2.63	2.53	2.46	2.34	2.19	2.19	2.35
Mexico	4.0	0.83	0.83	0.85	0.83	0.91	0.84	0.78	0.68	0.63	0.65	0.67
United States	5.1	17.05	17.64	17.65	18.42	18.62	17.79	16.99	15.36	14.54	14.4	15.83
South & Central America	6.5	2.81	2.92	3.1	3.05	3.15	3.06	2.77	2.69	2.58	2.73	3.09
Europe	8.3	49.53	48.53	50.97	50.07	48.48	49.8	50.71	52.9	52.87	51.98	57.58
Commonwealth		0.00	0.00	0.00	0.00	0.00	0.00	0.00	0.00	0.00	0.00	0.00
Independent States (CIS)	10.8	–	1.69	1.46	1.16	1.18	1.32	1.44	1.46	1.56	1.68	2.06
Africa	8.7	2.21	2.14	2.08	2.17	2.11	2.15	2.14	2.31	2.32	2.34	2.61
Middle East	10.6	–	1.86	2.00	2.13	2.24	2.17	2.14	2.35	2.27	2.32	2.65
Asia	8.0	22.01	22.05	19.44	19.67	20.68	20.35	20.57	19.91	21.04	21.69	25.36
China	14.7	1.62	1.86	1.77	1.86	2.02	2.2	2.45	2.52	2.8	3.01	3.72
India	21.5	0.57	0.68	0.82	1.00	1.07	1.12	1.19	1.25	1.68	2.21	3.01

TABLE 8.7: PERCENTAGE IMPORTS OF COMMERCIAL SERVICES BY REGION AND SELECTED ECONOMY, 1996-2006

	Growth rate continuous compound	1996	1997	1998	1999	2000	2001	2002	2003	2004	2005	2006
World	7.4	100.00	100.00	100.00	100.00	100.00	100.00	100.00	100.00	100.00	100.00	100.00
North America	7.3	14.58	15.46	16.25	17.12	18.15	17.66	17.11	16.15	15.63	15.40	15.19
Canada	6.8	2.80	2.88	2.83	2.89	2.95	2.89	2.81	2.87	2.71	2.71	2.71
Mexico	7.4	0.79	0.91	0.94	1.01	1.13	1.10	1.08	0.97	0.90	0.88	0.86
USA	7.4	11.00	11.67	12.48	13.23	14.07	13.67	13.23	12.31	12.01	11.81	11.62
South & Central America	3.9	3.63	3.89	4.00	3.63	3.70	3.67	3.08	2.83	2.72	2.96	3.04
Europe	7.9	46.16	45.06	48.16	47.65	45.69	46.59	47.62	49.57	48.79	47.88	47.16
Commonwealth		0.00	0.00	0.00	0.00	0.00	0.00	0.00	0.00	0.00	0.00	0.00
Independent States (CIS)	13.2	–	2.02	1.74	1.44	1.63	1.98	2.15	2.19	2.36	2.54	2.65
Africa	8.0	2.82	2.83	2.81	2.59	2.54	2.66	2.64	2.64	2.75	3.00	3.04
Middle East	9.2	–	3.69	3.21	3.16	3.30	3.13	3.22	3.35	3.45	3.71	3.87
Asia	6.5	27.45	27.04	23.84	24.40	24.98	24.30	24.18	23.27	24.31	24.50	25.05
China	14.8	1.77	2.13	1.99	2.23	2.43	2.61	2.91	3.04	3.34	3.49	3.79
India	26.9	0.09	0.94	1.07	1.23	1.28	1.32	1.31	1.41	1.70	2.07	2.41

TABLE 8.8: TRADE IN COMMERCIAL SERVICES OF NAFTA, 1990-2006

	1996	1997	1998	1999	2000	2001	2002	2003	2004	2005	2006	Growth rate compound
NAFTA												
Toral exports	923	1014	1014	1071	1225	1148	1106	1163	1324	1479	1678	4.9
Intra-export	433	495	520	580	682	637	626	652	739	824	902	6.3
% to total export	46.9	48.8	51.3	54.2	55.7	55.5	56.6	56.1	55.8	55.7	53.8	
Extra-export	489	519	494	491	543	510	480	511	585	655	776	3.4
% to total export	53.0	51.2	48.7	45.8	44.3	44.4	43.4	43.9	44.2	44.3	46.2	
Total Import	1082	1208	1271	1421	1679	1570	1591	1715	1996	2271	2525	7.7
Intra-import	422	482	512	574	664	620	609	632	705	782	855	5.9
% to total import	39.0	39.9	40.3	40.4	39.5	39.5	38.3	36.9	35.3	34.4	33.9	
Extra-import	660	726	759	847	1014	950	982	1083	1291	1489	1670	8.7
% to total import	60.9	60.0	59.7	59.6	60.0	60.5	61.7	63.1	64.7	65.6	66.0	

39 to 34 per cent whereas extra imports increased from 60.8 to 66 per cent. Thus one finds that in case of services the trade in terms of imports increased with the rest of the world whereas in terms of exports there was an intra region increase. Thus there is an element of potential increase in trading relationship in services from regional framework to multilateral framework. This gets also confirmed from Table 8.9, which shows Canada's international trade in services. The US remains the major partner. It exports 1.5 per cent of total service exports to China and 0.5 per cent to India and imports 1 per cent of total imports from China and 0.4 per cent of total imports from India. Hence there is a scope for further increase in trading relationship with these two countries, especially India, as it is below China in its trading relationship with Canada.

II

BILATERAL TRADE: CANADA-INDIA

In the context of world trade scenario it is of interest to situate India-Canada trade. Though India is not a significant trader in merchandise exports, the growing realization to integrate much further in global economy and Canada's reengagement with

TABLE 8.9: TRADE IN COMMERCIAL SERVICES OF CANADA, 2005

	Exports (billion US $)		Imports (billion US $)
World (billion US $)	5,3938.0	World	6,4496.0
USA	57.5	USA	60.2
EU (25)	18.2	EU (25)	16.7
Bermuda	2.4	Japan	3.0
Japan	2.3	Hong Kong, China	2.3
Barbados	1.7	Bermuda	1.9
Above 5	4,4279.0	Above 5	5,4226.0
	(82.1)		(84.1)
China	1.0	China	1.5
India	0.5	India	0.4

India due to the latter's impressive growth rate, call for exploring the potentials.

The trade openness of India in 2004-5 (export and import as per cent of GDP) was 30 per cent (exports as a per cent of GDP, 13 per cent and imports 17 per cent) (*Economic Survey*, 2006-7), and of Canada during 2004-6, 70 per cent (exports as a per cent of GDP 36.4 per cent, and imports 33.8 per cent) (IMF, *International Finance Statistics*, 2007). Thus Canada is a much more export-oriented economy than India.

The bilateral trade relationship between India and Canada is relatively recent in origin. India is still not a major trading partner of Canada and the fact is that despite government level efforts Canada's share in India's trade has come down from 1.07 per cent in 2002 to 0.82 per cent in 2006. India's share in Canada's trade however has increased from 0.28 per cent in 2002 to 0.43 per cent in 2006 (Asia Pacific Foundation of Canada). India has a trade balance with Canada since 1993. With fluctuations, it increased from 87.44 (US million $) in 1998-9 to 259.40 in 2000-1 and was 113.64 in 2005-6 (Economic Survey). Thus India exports much more than what it imports from Canada.

The chief commodities of import from India in 2006 to Canada were knitted or crocheted apparel, woven clothing and apparel, etc., organic chemicals, pearls, stones, boilers, mechanical appliances, electrical machinery, mineral fuels and articles of iron steel. These ten commodities constituted 64.2 per cent of Canadian import from India in 2006. The top 10 merchandise exports to India were paper, paper board, edible vegetables roots, fertilizer, wood pulp, mechanical appliances, electrical machinery, iron and mineral steel, ores, optical equipment, salt, sulphur, etc. These commodities constituted 87.4 per cent of total exports to India. The first three items of Canada's imports from India constitute 32.1 per cent of the total ten whereas Canada's exports to India of the first three commodities constituted 49.3 per cent of the total top ten. Thus still both the countries rely on few commodities for bilateral trade. Share of India in Canadian imports was 0.47 per cent whereas share of India in Canadian exports were 0.25 per cent indicating a weak trading relationship.

TABLE 8.10: CANADA'S MERCHANDISE TRADE WITH INDIA 2006

Rank	Canadian Imports from India Merchandise Classification	(%)	Canadian Export to India Merchandise Classification	(%)
1	Knitted or crocheted apparel	11.4	Paper and paperboard	19.2
2	Woven clothing and apparel	10.7	Edible vegetables, roots & tubers	16.5
3	Organic chemicals, etc.	10.0	Fertilizers	13.6
4	Pearls, precious stones/metals, etc.	7.8	Wood pulp and other pulp	7.8
5	Boilers, mechanical appliances, etc.	6.6	Boilers, mechanical appliances, etc.	6.9
6	Other textile articles	4.6	Electrical machinery and parts	6.8
7	Articles of iron or steel	4.0	Iron and steel	5.0
8	Mineral fuels, oils and waxes, etc.	3.5	Ores, salt and ash	4.8
9	Electrical machinery and parts	2.9	Optical/photographic equipment, etc.	3.7
10	Carpets, other textile floor coverings	2.7	Salt, Sulphur, earths, limestone, etc.	3.0
	Top 10 as % of total from India	64.2	Top 10 as % of total to India	87.4
	Indian imports as % of Cdn total	0.47	Indian exports as % of Cdn total	0.25

In order to examine whether India's exports to and import from Canada have become more diversified over a period of time the Herfindahl Hirschman Index (HHI) was calculated (Table 8.11). The table shows that the index pertaining to exports to Canada decreased during 2001-2 to 2004-5 from 886 to 663. The index pertaining to imports decreased during the same period from 1465 to 954. Thus both India's exports to Canada and imports from Canada are getting diversified. In 2006 the HHI index of imports from Canada was much higher than the exports to Canada implying relatively more concentration in the former than the latter. Canada thus not only has the

TABLE 8.11: HERFINDAHL HIRSCHMAN INDEX OF EXPORT TO AND IMPORT FROM CANADA

Year	Export	Import
2001-2	886.13	1,465.38
2002-3	895.92	1,130.42
2003-4	764.48	1,180.86
2004-5	730.21	1,023.95
2005-6	663.15	954.16

potential to increase her exports to India but it has also the potential to diversify them also. On the basis of HHI it can be deduced that India's exports to Canada are much more defined, as they are concentrated in a few commodities compared to imports from Canada. Thus trade performance of India improved in terms of increasing volume of exports rather than in terms of diversifying the export basket.

In order to indicate the areas where Canada can exploit the potentials of trade with India, it is imperative to know the composition of India's export/import with the world. The latest report of Indian *Economic Survey* (2006-7) reveals that the largest single item of imports is POL (29.5 per cent) in 2005-6 followed by capital goods (15 per cent). Others constitute 55.5 per cent, wherein the largest share was of electric goods followed by pearls, precious and semi-precious stones and chemicals. Exports are dominated by manufactured goods. Within these, engineering goods has 20.7 per cent, gems and jewellery 15.1 per cent and readymade garments 14.5 per cent share in the total. Agricultural products constitute around 15.4 per cent of the exports. In 2000-1 agricultural products, gems and jewellery, readymade garments and cotton yarn accounted for about 50 per cent of total exports, the composition changed in favour of engineering exports in 2004-5.

The growth and composition of trade is mainly linked to a country's capability to produce the commodity in question at a lower cost than its competitors. In order to examine this, Revealed Comparative Advantage (RCA) is calculated (Table 8.12). RCA of value 1 indicates normal export performance in the given product whereas a value greater than 1 indicates competitive strength in that product. An increase in the value of RCA over a period of time indicates increase in the competitiveness in that product. It can be seen for the table that India has a competitive advantage (RCAs greater than 1) in natural resource-based products like fish, cereals, vegetable, sugar, coffee, feeding stuff or animals, leather, articles of apparel and clothing accessories. However the disturbing thing is that in all these traditional strong items RCA has declined, especially in between 1998 and 2003. Over and above it is observed that all such products in general have low-income elasticity of demand.

The major exports of Canada are machinery and equipment and automotive products. Their respective percentage shares in 1997 were 22.6 and 23.3. Industrial goods and material and

TABLE 8.12: REVEALED COMPARATIVE ADVANTAGE: INDIA

Division sr. no.	Commodities	1990	1998	2003
1	Meat and meat preparations	0.411	0.715	0.775
3	Fish, crustaceans & molluses & preparations	2.888	4.010	2.621
4	Cereals & cereal preparations	1.145	2.371	2.849
5	Vegetables & fruits	1.450	1.651	1.238
6	Sugar, sugar preparations & honey	0.269	6.207	1.925
7	Coffee, tea, cocoa, spices & manufactures	7.255	5.358	2.738
8	Feeding stuff for animals	3.921	6.014	3.303
12	Tobacco & tobacco manufactures	1.478	1.479	0.921
22	Oilseeds & oleaginous fruit	1.442	2.342	2.013
28	Metalliferous ores and metal scrap	3.837	2.113	2.886
51	Organic chemicals	0.597	1.477	1.603
52	Inorganic chemicals	0.412	5.705	0.398
53	Dyeing, tanning & colouring materials	2.126	2.198	1.916
54	Medical & pharmaceutical products	2.185	1.774	1.177
55	Essential oils & perfume materials soaps, etc.	2.078	0.737	0.657
57	Explosives & pyrotechnic products	0.255	1.135	0.537
58	Artificial resins, plastic materials & others	0.080	0.171	0.764
59	Chemical materials & products n.e.s.	0.414	1.053	0.866
61	Lather, leather manufactures & dressed fur skins	11.454	4.430	3.577

65	Textile yarn, fabrics, made-up articles	3.775	5.160	4.308
66	Pearls precious and semi-precious stones	17.894	16.583	16.269
67	Iron & steel	0.485	1.345	1.994
69	Manufactures of metals n.e.s.	0.940	0.970	1.231
71	Power-generating machinery & equipment	0.281	0.276	0.292
72	machinery specialized for particular industries	0.362	0.311	0.417
73	Metal-working machinery	0.340	0.352	0.610
74	General industrial machinery & equipment	0.182	0.182	0.373
75	Office machinery & ADP equipment	0.162	0.147	0.130
76	Telecommunication & sound recording, etc.	0.515	0.085	0.000
77	Electrical machinery apparatus & appliances	0.237	0.146	0.244
78	Road vehicles	0.200	0.250	0.271
79	Other transport equipments	0.028	0.084	0.000
84	Articles of apparel & clothing accessories	4.257	3.675	3.303
	Other exports	0.456	0.464	–

Note: RCA is calculated as the share of a country's export of product x in total world exports of product x divided by the share of the country's total exports in world total exports.

Source: Calculated from the information contained in *Economic Survey*, Government of India, various issues.

forestry products followed these. Within forestry products, newsprint constituted 34 per cent of the total. The major imports of Canada were machinery equipment and automotive products, followed by Industrial goods and materials. The nature of exports and imports indicate that there is an element of intra-industry trade.

Table 8.13 shows the RCA of Canada. It can be seen from the table that Canada has a comparative advantage in agriculture raw material, fuel, and machinery and transport equipment. In case of major groups like mining products, manufacturers, machine and transport equipment, RCA is around one. This indicates normal export performance. It does not have comparative advantage in the export of textiles and other consumer

TABLE 8.13: REVEALED COMPARATIVE ADVANTAGE: CANADA

	1997	1999	2005
Agriculture	1.4480	1.3732	1.3800
Food	0.9472	0.8701	–
Raw material	3.3866	3.4235	–
Mining products	1.3869	1.2726	–
Ores & other minerals	1.7712	1.3840	–
Fuels	1.1962	1.1570	1.5110
Non-ferrous metals	1.9794	1.6685	–
Manufacturers	0.8402	0.8707	0.8050
Iron & steel	0.5353	0.5261	–
Chemicals	0.6312	0.5615	–
Other semi-manufacturers	1.2623	1.3294	–
Machinery & transport equipment	0.9816	1.0160	0.8770
Office & telecommunication equipment	0.4776	0.4182	–
Automotive products	2.3918	2.5249	–
Other machinery & transport equipment	0.6065	0.7061	1.7100
Textiles	0.2916	0.3148	0.3457
Clothing	0.2032	0.2315	1.191
Other consumer goods	0.5838	0.6363	0.6540

goods. Thus Canada, will have to improve its comparative advantage in the products such as machinery and manufacturing in general, where the demand from developing countries, including India, has increased.

Direction of Trade

Another significant indicator apart from the structure of treaded goods and services is the direction of trade of both the countries. In case of India, the *Economic Survey* 2006-7 reports that the single largest trading partner of India has been the USA, though with a declining trend. China has increased its share almost threefold and is the second largest trading partner of India. Regionwise, Asia and ASEAN countries have emerged as major export destinations. India's exports to these regions, including Africa have posted a strong growth, while exports to Europe and America registered moderate growth. This confirms the world trade scenario discussed earlier that intra-region trade plays a dominant role in the geographical pattern of trade. Thus there is in general a move away, though moderate, from West to East.

The merchandise trade of NAFTA, as shown in Table 8.4, reveals that exports from the USA to Canada declined marginally from 14.4 to 14.3 per cent during 2000-5, whereas exports from Canada to the USA increased from 19.7 to 20.5 per cent. Exports to all other countries increased from 2.7 to 3.7 per cent. Thus there is some indication of Canada to initiate its trading relationship with the rest of the world. However as discussed earlier, despite such a move, Canada's trading relationship with India has not picked up; on the contrary there is a relative decline in its exports to India. India's neighbour China's trade relationship with Canada thus becomes of interest to us.

Canada's total merchandise trade with China has soared in the last decade, reaching $42.1 billion in 2006 and accounting for 5 per cent of Canada's world trade. In 1997, China was Canada's fourth largest trading partner, and by 2003, China emerged as Canada's second largest trading partner surpassing the UK and Japan. Imports from China were five times higher in 2006 than in 1997 while exports to the country tripled (Khondaker). Tables 8.14-8.17 show the bilateral trade in 1997 and 2006. In 1997, 34.3 per cent of Canada's exports to and 37.6 per cent of imports from China involved two-way trade within the same commodity groups. By 2006 the two-way trade was 45 per cent of the exports and 57 per cent of the imports. Leading commodities in the two-way trade include org/inorganic chemicals, plastic and rubber materials, iron and steel including articles made thereof, industrial and agriculture machinery and equipment, electronics, automotive and other equipment, wood products, paperboard and fish products. Apart from these, Canada experienced over the last decade a rapid growth in the exports of nickel articles, copper and metal ores. Imports from China of furniture, apparel, etc., and aluminium articles also increased significantly. The commodity mix has changed little between 1997 and 2006 except wheat, which was the major commodity of exports from Canada to China, declined in its

TABLE 8.14: LEADING CANADIAN EXPORTS TO CHINA, 1997

Rank	Commodity group	Share of total exports to China (%)
1	Wheat	18.9
2	Electrical machinery & equipment	13.0
3	Wood pulp	10.9
4	Fertilizers	10.7
5	Machinery; reactors, boilers	5.1
6	Synthetic fibers & fabrics	4.4
7	Metal ores	4.2
8	Fats, oils, etc.	3.6
9	Paper, paperboard & articles	3.5
10	Plastic & articles made of plastic	3.0
	Total (top ten)	77.5
	Total exports	2,407.5
	Total exports	7,661.3

TABLE 8.15: LEADING CANADIAN IMPORTS FROM CHINA, 1997

Rank	Commodity group	Share of total exports to China (%)
1	Electronic sound equipment, etc.	14.9
2	Toys, games & sports equipment	13.7
3	Footwear, etc.	8.8
4	Machinery; reactors boilers	8.7
5	Apparel articles & accessories not knitted	8.2
6	Leather articles, including handbags	6
7	Furniture; bedding, etc.	4.6
8	Plastic & articles of plastic	3.7
9	Apparel articles & accessories knit or crochet	2.8
10	Optic, photo, etc., medical or surgical instruments, etc.	2.5
	Total (top ten)	74.0
	Total exports	6,341.4

TABLE 8.16: LEADING CANADIAN EXPORTS TO CHINA, 2006

Rank	Commodity group	Share of total exports to China (%)
1	Wood pulp	14.8
2	Organic chemicals	11.5
3	Nickel articles	8.4
4	Metal ores	7.3
5	Machinery; reactors, boilers	6.8
6	Electrical machinery & equipment	5.6
7	Vehicles, except railway or tramway and parts, etc.	5.4
8	Plastic & articles made of plastic	4.3
9	Fish and seafood	3.5
10	Fertilizers	3.2
	Total (top ten)	70.8
	Total exports	7,661.3

TABLE 8.17: LEADING CANADIAN IMPORTS FROM CHINA, 2006

Rank	Commodity group	Share of total exports to China (%)
1	Machinery; reactors boilers	20.8
2	Electronic sound equipment, etc.	19.7
3	Toys, games & sports equipment	7.0
4	Furniture; bedding, etc.	6.6
5	Apparel articles & accessories not knitted	5.3
6	Apparel articles & accessories knit or crochet	4.6
7	Articles of iron and steel	3.9
8	Footwear, etc.	3.3
9	Plastic & articles of plastic	2.8
10	Optic, photo, etc., medical or surgical instruments, etc.	2.3
	Total (top ten)	76.3
	Total exports	3,4486.3

TABLE 8.18: CANADA'S TRADE BALANCE WITH CHINA, 1997-2006

(*in billions US $*)

Year	Export	Imports	Trade balance
1997	2.4	6.3	-3.9
1998	2.5	7.7	-5.2
1999	2.7	9.0	-6.3
2000	3.7	11.3	-7.6
2001	4.3	12.7	-8.5
2002	4.1	16.0	-11.9
2003	4.8	18.6	-13.8
2004	6.8	24.1	-17.3
2005	7.1	29.5	-22.4
2006	7.7	34.5	-26.8

Source: For the Tables 8.14-8.18, Jafar Khondaker, *Canada's Trade with China: 1997 to 2006*, Statistics Canada, 2007.

importance during 1997 to 2006. China's importance as an exporter of machinery and equipment has significantly increased from 1.8 per cent share in total imports of Canada from the world to 13.6 per cent in 2006. Dominant items are computers, computer parts, auto parts, cellphones, TV, audio and video equipment, hand tools and household appliances.

Comparing India's and China's trade with Canada, it is clear that China in comparison to India is a major trading partner of Canada and its exports are more diversified than India. The top ten commodities account for 71 per cent of the total exports in 2006, whereas in case of India the top ten commodities accounted for 87 per cent of the total. In case of imports, top ten China's exports to Canada constituted 76 per cent, whereas Indian exports top ten commodities was 64 per cent of total implying more diversified India's exports to Canada. Like India, China's trade balance with Canada is positive. Table 8.18 shows that Canada's trade deficit with China increased from 3.9 to 26.8 billion dollars in 2006.

CONCLUSION

The above analysis shows that despite Government of India's effort in terms of reducing the tariffs and non-tariff barriers, exchange rate reforms, arresting inflationary pressures, lowering of interest rates and policies to attract foreign direct investment, current account convertibility, the trade relations with other countries in general, and with Canada in particular has not increased substantially. On the contrary one finds some deceleration in the bilateral trade in recent years. Thus there is a need to enhance the trade relations between the two countries both in terms of volume and the number of commodities. In the light of these facts and the nature of both the economies being dominated by the service sector, possibilities of increasing trade in services should be explored.

Increasing trade relations among the regional groups has also accentuated the problems for countries like India, which is not a member of any regional group. Though intra, NAFTA trade relations are indicative of the phenomena that the strengths of regional trading are gradually diluting, especially in terms of imports, it will take some time to strengthen Canada-India trade relations. It has still a long way to go!

REFERENCES

Canadian Service Coalition, *Canada & India, Trade and Investment Opportunities in the Service Sector*, March 2007.

Canada's International Trade in Services, Catalogue no. 67-203-XIE.

IMF, *International Trade Statistics*, 2006, www.wto.org.

Khondaker, Jafar, *Canada's Trade with China: 1997 to 2006*, Statistics, Canada, 2007, Report on World Trade Statistics, 2006, www.wto.org.

CHAPTER 9

Globalization and Indo-Canada Trade Relations: Issues and Challenges

KRISHAN K. KAUSHIK

INTRODUCTION

The world economy is in the midst of a profound transformation. The term 'globalization' is used both in a descriptive and normative sense. It describes a process of internationalization and growing interdependencies where national boundaries become less and less important in decisions to be taken by economic agents. The normative perspective assumes that the full liberalization of market forces through open trade and foreign investment regimes will stimulate sustained growth and greatercon-vergence of income per capita throughout the world.

Globalization involves the diffusion of ideas, practices and technologies. It is something more than internationalization and universalization. It isn't simply modernization or Westernization. It certainly isn't just the liberalization of markets. Giddens (1990) has described globalization as 'the intensification of worldwide social relations which link distant localities in such a way that local happenings are shaped by events occurring many miles away and vice versa. The rise of the so-called 'knowledge economy' has meant that economists have been challenged to look beyond labour and capital as the central factors of production.

There is no agreed theory of globalization. A fourfold taxonomy of globalization is provided by Bowles (2005). (1) Globalization is a technologically-driven process that strengthens markets while weakening nation states: 1970s witnessed the start of a 'revolution in the means of production' with the revolution being grounded in the development of 'computers' (Teeple 2000). The role of nation states has changed. The first bourgeois revolution represented the political consolidation of capitalism by creating nation state, and the 'second' bourgeois revolution is the globalization of national regimes of accumulation. When capitalism underwent processes of regionalization in the 1980s, capitalism became more like Marx's vision of a 'self-organizing process' with a more limited role of the state (Desai 2004). (2) Globalization is a myth as the national basis of economic activity has not weakened much: Globalization is one of the biggest myths of our time. Integration implies true mobility of all factors of production including people, absence of restrictions on trade, and the absence of any kind of cartels. (3) Globalization as imperialism, and (4) Globalization is inadequate as a descriptor of the process underway in the contemporary period and the terms 'regionalization' and/or 'regionalism' are more accurate descriptors.

There are three main dimensions of globalization: Economic, political and social. Economic globalization is characterized as long distance flows of goods, capital and services, as well as information and perception that accompany market exchanges. Political globalization is characterized by a diffusion of government policies that involves creation of a world government which regulates the relationships among nations and guarantees the rights arising from social and economic globalization. Social globalization is expressed as the speed of ideas, information, images and people. The aspects of globalization that are hardest to pin down relate to the flow of information and ideas.

An integrating world economy can be seen from the data that between 1990 and 2006, the percentage of trade in goods to world GDP increased from 32.5 to 45.3 per cent, gross capital formation increased from 10.1 per cent world GDP to 24.1 per cent and gross direct foreign investment from 2.7 per cent to more than 7 per cent of world GDP (World Bank 2006).

With this background the aim of this paper is to analyse globalization and Indo-Canada trade relations: Issues and challenges in the new economic environment. The contribution begins with theoretical issues of concept and ramifications of globalization. We then discuss how far Indian and Canadian economies are integrated with the world economy? Main features of Canadian and Indian economy with special reference to bilateral trade have been further analysed. This is followed by conclusions and policy implications.

HOW FAR INDIAN AND CANADIAN ECONOMIES ARE INTEGRATED WITH THE WORLD ECONOMY?

An overall indicator of integration is the extent of international trade in the domestic economy as measured by the share of exports and imports in GDP and in the global economy, as measured by the share of a country's exports and imports in global exports and imports. In this age of globalization the size of the market you offer for other countries' (actual or potential) effect your command over them. It requires least effort to switch most imports from one nation to another than to shift exports from an established buyer/country to others. Hence, the size of a country's imports is a better measure of its economic power that wields over others than the size of its exports.

After the Second World War, there has been a phenomenal expansion in international flows; world exports increased from $6.1 billion in 1950 to $11.76 trillion in 2006. The strong global macro-situation in 2006 provided a favourable framework for the expansion of international trade. In 2006, world merchandise exports grew in real terms (i.e. at constant prices) by 8.0 per cent compared to 6.5 per cent in the preceding year. The expansion of real trade exceeded global output growth by more than 4 percentage points. Developing countries' share of world merchandise exports reached an all time record of 36 per cent (WTO 2007). India's exports as well as import have shown remarkable progress during 2006-7 showing 25.24 per cent increase in export and 30.6 per cent in imports in terms of rupee value compared to previous year. In dollar terms the achievement was 22.5 and 27.7 per cent respectively. India emerged as the world's 12th largest importer of commercial services and 17th largest importer of goods. India's trade position marginally varied during 2006. Goods export is just 1 per cent and in goods import a mere 1.4 per cent, in services, the country has 2.7 per cent share in both exports and imports during 2006 in world trade (CMIE 2006-7).

To what extent a nation state or culture is globalized in a particular year has until most recently been measured employing simple proxies like flow of trade, migration, or FDI, as mentioned earlier. As globalization is not only an economic phenomenon. Recent index calculated by the Swiss think-tank (KOF) at Zurich making use of a multivariate approach found that the world's most globalized country is neither United States nor Canada, rather it is Belgium, followed by Austria, Sweden, the UK and the Netherlands. This index is based on multivariate approach making use of 23 variables, into three sub-indexes, for 122 countries taking 30 years period into account from 1970-2000. According to another 2006 index (based on three years data), Singapore, Ireland, Switzerland, and the US, the Netherlands, Canada and Denmark are the most globalized, while Egypt, Indonesia, India and Iran are the least globalized among countries listed.

Trade openness is an important measure of globalization. It is defined as the combined weight of tradable—imports and exports in a country's economy. During the last decade of the twentieth century, there has been a considerable increase in the share of merchandise trade in as a percentage of GDP in most of the countries. Nearly 60 per cent of GDP of most countries (with the exception of the US, France, India and Japan) is now directly affected by international price and demand changes (Table 9.1).

China, UK, Germany, Sri Lanka and India recorded great expansion in trade in services. India and China registered maximum percentage point growth in real trade less growth in real GDP. The expansion in FDI inflows has been quite impressive in the case of China and India. Outward investment also simultaneously showed signs of a pick up with domestic companies making deeper forays for acquisitions abroad. FDI inflows were mainly in the form of equity accounting for about 75.2 per cent of the total FDI to India during 2005-6. FDI abroad (outward

TABLE 9.1: INTEGRATION WITH THE WORLD ECONOMY

Country	Merchandise trade % of GDP			Trade in services % of GDP			Growth in real trade less growth in real GDP % points	Gross capital inflows as % of GDP		
	1990	2004	2006	1990	2004	2006	1990-2004	1990	2004	2006
Canada	43.7	61.0	59.31	8.3	10.7	9.10	3.3	8.1	14.0	28.3
China	32.5	59.8	2.9	7.0	5.7	2.50	10.1			
France	36.4	44.7	11.1	10.2	4.2	20.20	26.1			
Germany	45.5	45.5	8.7	12.2	4.3	9.40	27.4			
India	13.1	25.0	33.39	3.4	8.2	13.11	6.8	0.8	6.9	6.21
Japan	17.2	22.1	4.1	5.0	2.7	5.40	14.4			
Sri Lanka	57.3	68.5	13.4	17.1	2.5	13.10	5.2			
UK	41.2	38.1	10.6	15.4	3.4	35.30	91.7			
US	15.8	20.0	4.6	5.4	4.0	5.60	20.0			

Source: World Development Indicators, 2006. Table 6.1.

investment) grew sharply to reach US $3.2 billion in 2005-6 (GOI 2006-7).

In terms of investment, Canadian companies have a modest presence in India. They have grown considerably in five major areas: power and energy, equipment; oil and gas; environment products and services; telecommunications and information technology; and the financial sector, including insurance. On the investment front, recently there has been a rapid increase in FDI in Canada by Indian software companies with the intent to establish software development centres in Canada. Indian companies include Tata Consultancy Services, Wipro, Infosys and Satyam. Areas of Indian investment also include pharmaceuticals, metals, petro-chemicals, auto ancillaries, financial services, etc. SBI, Canada has four branches in the country and ICICI has recently started operations. Canada has a modest presence in India in terms of investment.

Canadian FDI in India during 2006 is valued at $327 million, while India's FDI in Canada is currently estimated at $210 million. However, India's rapidly expanding economy and the government's continued commitment to totalling its investment regime will provide significant opportunities for Canadian investors in a variety of sectors including financial services, infrastructure, information technologies, life sciences and natural resources. Brazil, Russia, India and China (BRIC) are now generally considered as emerging economies. The Canadian government is paying special attention to development of its economic relations with China, India, Mexico and Brazil (Table 9.2).

India is the world's largest manufacturing centre of cut and polished diamonds. More than 20 Indian companies have offices

TABLE 9.2: CUMULATIVE FOREIGN DIRECT INVESTMENT (FDI) DATA

Figures in C $ (2006)	2006 (end of year)	% change over previous year
Canadian FDI in India ($ million)	327	+4.14
Indian FDI in Canada ($ million)	210	+48.9

in Canada. A.V. Birla Group took over the Alholiville Pulp Mill in NB, Canada in a joint venture partnership with Tembec Inc., a US $1.4 billion Canadian Forest Product Company. India has three marketing offices and one development centre in Canada with more than 200 professionals, likely to grow into more than 500 in the coming years. India has major R&D interaction with leading universities in Canada. Rosy Blue acquired Canada's largest diamond cutting factory in Yellow Knife. The Canadian Export Development Corporation (EDC) has identified India amongst its three 'premium' markets and is actively seeking more business. Canadian presence has increased in Indian banking; insurance and financial services sectors as also in engineering and consultancy services.

Global Competitiveness

The World Economic Forum's Global Competitiveness Index, evolved over the last three decades into the world's most comprehensive assessment of countries' competitiveness, offering invaluable insights into the policies, institutions, and factors driving productivity and, thus, enabling sustained economic growth and long-term prosperity. A record 131 economies, accounting for more than 98 per cent of the world's GDP have been taken into account for measuring national competitiveness. The microeconomic and macroeconomic foundations of national competitiveness are covered and data displaying the relative rankings of more than 100 variables is provided. The productivity level also determines the rates of return obtained by investments in an economy. India's rank is 31, whereas Canada ranks 14 in global competitiveness (Table 9.3).

GROWTH OF INDO-CANADA TRADE—AN OVERVIEW

Canada and India have long-standing ties, built upon shared values of democracy and pluralism and on strong people-to-people links. Bilateral relations have grown significantly in many spheres for periods of years, but also went through periods of decline because of disagreements between the Canadian and Indian governments over substantive issues. Indo-Canadian

TABLE 9.3: GLOBAL COMPETITIVENESS INDEX 2007-8

	Rank (out of 131) countries/ economies		Score (out of 7)	
	Canada	India	Canada	India
	13	48	5.34	4.33
Sub-index A: Basic requirements	11	74	5.73	4.22
1st pillar: Institutions	17	48	5.26	4.32
2nd pillar: Infrastructure	8	67	6.05	3.45
3rd pillar: Macroeconomic stability	42	108	5.26	4.21
4th pillar: Health and primary education	8	101	6.37	4.92
Sub-index B: Efficiency enhancers	5	31	5.39	4.52
5th pillar: Higher education and training	13	55	5.49	4.13
6th pillar: Goods market efficiency	15	36	5.26	4.66
7th pillar: Labour market efficiency	8	96	5.24	4.07
8th pillar: Financial market sophistication	13	37	5.64	4.93
9th pillar: Technological readiness	13	62	5.34	3.17
10th pillar: Market size	14	3	5.34	6.13
Sub-index C: Innovation and sophistication factors	17	26	5.01	4.36
11th pillar: Business sophistication	20	26	5.12	4.81
12th pillar: Innovation	12	28	4.90	3.90
Rank (out of 131) countries/economies Business Competitiveness Index 2007-8			14	31

relations deteriorated in the wake of India's 'peaceful' nuclear explosion of May 1974. Canada severed bilateral nuclear co-operation with both India and Pakistan in 1976. New opportunities to improve the Canada-India relationship arose when India instituted major reforms of its economy in the early to mid-1990s. India's economic transformation attracted sufficient attention from the Canadian government and business community that the prime minister of Canada, Jean Chrétien, led a Team Canada mission to India in January 1996 comprising two cabinet ministers, seven provincial premiers and 300 business persons. India surprised the international community when it announced the detonation of five nuclear devices in two sets of tests on 11 and 13 May 1998. The Canadian government rapidly condemned the nuclear tests in South Asia, and placed its political relations with India and Pakistan on hold.

Despite the disagreement over India's nuclear policy, Indo-Canadian relations grew in some areas of mutual interest during 1999 and 2000. Canada's commercial relationship with India has been enhanced through various mechanisms: the signing of an S&T Cooperation Agreement, the negotiation of a FIPA, and the resolution of a number of sanitary and phyto-sanitary issues relating to plant products. In 2006, Canada and India also signed MoUs on biotechnology—one related to research and the other to agriculture. As well, Canada and India concluded a plant health MoU and agreed to extend an interim arrangement for pulse imports for an additional year. India also agreed to temporary access improvements on wheat and accepted Canada's certificates for the export of pine wood lumber and horses.

The Canadian economy continues to perform well. The year 2006 saw the country's fifteenth consecutive year of economic growth with solid real gross domestic product (GDP) growth of 2.7 per cent. Canada's unemployment rates continue to reach lows not seen in 30 years. Canada is expected to be one of only a few developed countries to have posted a fiscal surplus in 2006. It was the only country in the G7 to do so. Trade plays a key role in an increasingly interconnected and interdependent world, and it makes up a large part of the global economy. An integrating world economy can be seen from the data that between 1990 and 2004, the percentage of trade in goods to world GDP increased from 32.5 to 45.3 per cent, gross capital formation increased from 10.1 per cent world GDP to 24.1 per cent and gross direct foreign investment from 2.7 per cent to more than 7 per cent of world GDP (World Bank 2006). With the merchandise trade, export and import, of the country currently valued at $400 billion, it accounts for about 1.5 per cent of the world trade. Since liberalization in the 1990s, India's exports have been consistently rising, covering 66.28 per cent of its imports in 2006-7, up from 66.2 per cent in 1990-1. India's exports stood at a little over $63 billion in 2004 and more than doubled in 2007-8 registering an average cumulative annual growth rate (CAGR) of 23 per cent (*Economic Times* 12 April 2008).

India's major trading partners are China, the US, the UAE, the UK, Japan and the EU. The exports during April 2007 were $12.31 billion up by 16 per cent and import were $17.68 billion with an increase of 18.06 per cent over the previous year. Although India is still a net importer, since 1996-7, its overall balance of payments (i.e. including the capital account), has been positive, largely on account of increased FDI and deposits from non-resident Indians; until this time, the overall balance was only occasionally positive on account of external assistance and commercial borrowings. As a result, India's foreign currency reserves stood at $285 billion in 2008 (*Economic Survey* 2007-8).

Import-export relations between India and Canada have steadily increased over the years. India presents a good business opportunity for Canadian companies. Canada can leverage on the growth of infrastructure related sectors in India. In South Asia, India is the largest trading partner for Canada. India is capitalizing on its large numbers of well-educated people skilled in the English language to become a major exporter of software services and software workers. Software services exports has led to creation of knowledge intensive jobs in India.

GROWTH TRENDS

Total Canada-India merchandise trade in 2006 was $3.6 billion. In 2006, India became Canada's 14th-largest export market, up from 18th the previous year. Growth in two-way trade is expected to continue, and significant commercial opportunities in India will continue to emerge with rising consumerism and infrastructure development in India. The recent data released by trade data on line industry shows that Canada's exports to India have increased from C $529 million in 1992 to C $1,680 million in 2006 registering a growth of 13.52 per cent per annum. Despite this growth, the $1.7 billion of merchandise exported to India in 2006 amounted to less than 1 per cent of Canada's exports, with imports accounting for a similarly small percentage. During

TABLE 9.4: MAIN ECONOMIC INDICATORS CANADA AND INDIA

	Canada	India
Area	9,984,670 sq km	3,287,590 sq km
Population	33,212,696 (July 2008 est.)	1,147,995,898 (July 2008 est.)
GDP (purchasing power parity	$1.274 trillion (2007 est.)	$2.965 trillion (2007 est.)
GDP—per capita (PPP)	$38,200 (2007 est.)	$2,700 (2007 est.)
GDP (official exchange rate)	$1.406 trillion (2007 est.)	$1.09 trillion (2007 est.)
GDP—real growth rate	2.7% (2007 est.)	8.5% (2007 est.)
GDP—composition by sector	Agriculture: 2.1% Industry: 28.8% Services: 69.1% (2007 est.)	Agriculture: 16.6% Industry: 28.4% Services: 55% (2007 est.)
Exports	3.2% of world exports $440.1 billion f.o.b. (2007 est.) Rank: 9th	1.0% of world exports $140.8 billion f.o.b. (2007 est.) Rank: 28th
Imports	2.9% of world imports $394.4 billion f.o.b. (2007 est) Rank: 8th	0.8% of world imports $224.1 billion f.o.b. (2007 est.) Rank: 7th
Commercial services	Canada ranks 15th in exp. and 11th in imports	India ranks 10th in exp. and 12th in imports
Stock of direct foreign investment—at home	$398.4 billion (2006 est.)	$67.72 billion (2006 est.)
Stock of direct foreign investment—abroad	$458.1 billion (2006 est.)	$21.11 billion (2006 est.)
Exchange rates	Canadian dollars per US dollar 1.0724 (2007), 1.1334 (2006), 1.2118 (2005), 1.301 (2004), 1.4011 (2003)	Indian rupees per US dollar 41.487 (2007), 45.3 (2006), 44.101 (2005), 45.317 (2004), 46.583 (2003)
Reserves of foreign exchange and gold	$39.31 billion (2007 est.)	239.4 billion (2007 est.)

the same period Canada's imports from India registered a growth of 9.21 per cent per annum. During January-May 2007, Canada's exports to India registered an increase of 46.01 per cent and imports from India showed a decline of 3.30 per cent. Canada is emerging as a strategic trading partner for India.

Canada is also a source of supplies for critical imports including important raw materials and investment goods. In commercial services, where India is reputed to be particularly strong, Canada's imports did rise 188.60 per cent over 1999-2006, but the share India takes of Canada's total commercial services trade again remains considerably below 1 per cent. While Canada's trade with India has been increasing, it remains only a small fraction of Canada's total commerce. Canada's top exports to India in 2006 were cereals, paper and paperboard, ores, slag and ash. Much of the 2006 export growth was propelled by a sharp increase in wheat sales, totalling over $240 million. Canada's top imports from India in 2006 consisted primarily of knit apparel, precious stones and metals, and organic chemicals. India offers many opportunities for Canadian firms, including in the areas of manufacturing, construction and engineering. In 2005, Canada and India signed an agreement for Scientific and Technological Cooperation that will enhance future trade and investment through the commercialization of research.

Canada's international trade performance remains robust in the face of a number of challenges, most notably a more than 35 per cent increase in the value of the dollar over the past four years. Canadian goods and services exports increased 1.1 per cent in 2006 to reach $523.7 billion. Imports were also up 4.2 per cent to $486.5 billion propelled by the strong Canadian economy and lower import prices due to the appreciating dollar. Canada's trade with Asia (17 major economies) registered a growth of 11.6 per cent during first five months of 2007 over the same period in 2006. Japan and China are the main destinations of Canada's exports. China continues to be Canada's top import supplier followed by Japan and Korea.

Although India's exports to Canada have grown steadily over the past five years, its total exports worldwide have grown at a much faster rate. Consequently, Canada has not been one of the more dynamic destinations for Indian exports over this period. However, between 2001 and 2006, the value of Indian imports into Canada grew 66 per cent while imports from other countries increased only 11 per cent. Canada's trade partnership with India is greatly affected by the presence of numerous immigrants from India in many of its provinces. One of the effects of the high-number of immigrants from India to Canada is the considerable expansion of education services in Canada tailored to the requirements of Indo-Canadian students. Commodity exports to India from Canada surpassed the billion dollar mark for the first time in 2005, while in 2003 (latest data available), Canada exported $254 million in services to India.

India exports a wide range of commodities to Canada. However, only 16 of 29 product categories contributed as much as 90 per cent or more to Indian exports (Appendix 9.1). Furthermore, five top product categories alone contributed

TABLE 9.5: INDIA-CANADA BILATERAL TRADE, 1992–2006

Year	Canada's total imports (in C $ million)	Imports from India (in C $ million)	% change over previous	% share
1992	1,48,018	280	16.66	0.19
1993	1,69,953	358	27.86	0.21
1994	2,02,736	459	28.21	0.23
1995	2,25,553	541	18.12	0.24
1996	2,32,566	604	11.65	0.26
1997	2,72,946	743	23.01	0.27
1998	2,98,386	899	21.00	0.30
1999	3,20,409	1018	13.24	0.32
2000	3,56,862	1232	21.02	0.35
2001	3,43,076	1155	(-)6.25	0.34
2002	3,48,672	1326	14.81	0.38
2003	3,09,023	1,423	7.31	0.43
2004	3,58,181	1,576	10.75	0.44
2005	3,88,281	1,787	13.38	0.46
2006	4,04,394	1,920	7.44	0.47
2007	4,15,608	–	–	–

Source: Consulate-General of India, Toronto.

TABLE 9.6: INDIA-CANADA BILATERAL TRADE, 1992-2006

Year	Canada's total Exports (in C $ million)	Exports (in C $ million)	% Changeover previous year	% share
1992	1,62,827	529	81.16	0.32
1993	1,87,515	282	(-)46.69	0.15
1994	2,25,678	286	1.42	0.13
1995	2,65,334	440	53.85	0.17
1996	2,80,079	353	(-)19.77	0.13
1997	3,01,544	491	39.09	0.16
1998	3,18,444	420	(-)14.46	0.13
1999	3,55,420	481	14.52	0.14
2000	4,13,195	559	16.22	0.14
2001	4,03,972	675	20.75	0.17
2002	4,14,038	674	(-)0.15	0.17
2003	3,99,122	658	(-)2.37	0.19
2004	4,29,067	858	30.39	0.20
2005	4,51,783	1,087	26.68	0.24
2006	4,55,696	1,680	54.55	0.36
2007	4,64,993	–	–	–

Source: Consulate-General of India, Toronto.

50 per cent or more. Among the top five, only textiles continued to claim an increasingly large share in Indian exports to Canada. Canada's merchandise exports to India consist primarily of raw materials and basic manufactures. In 2006, wood and paper and ores and metals accounted for 41 per cent of total Canadian merchandise exports to India while 34 per cent of merchandise imports from India consisted of clothing and textiles. But, India's imports of finished products from Canada are increasing, with the share of imports of electronics and machinery doubling over 1999-2006.

The growth rates and instability indices of various product categories have been computed by fitting an exponential time trend to the annual export earnings for the period (1991-7) and (1997-2003). The equation of the exponential trend is $Y_t = ae^{bt}u_t$ where Y_t is the value of export earnings and (t) represents time. OLS is then used to estimate the equation. Export instability index is calculated as coefficient of unexplained variations.

$$I \times E \times P = \frac{100}{\log \overline{Y}}\left[\sum_{t=1}^{n} \frac{\sum(\log_t Y - \log \hat{Y}_t)^2}{n-2}\right]^{\frac{1}{2}}$$

Among the main commodities, the growth rate was maximum in the export earnings of electronic goods (75.38 per cent), followed by coffee (53.35 per cent), woolen yarn fab. made-up (45.17 per cent), gems and jewellery (41.30 per cent) and machinery and instruments during 1991-7. Export earning from primary and semi-finished I&S registered high growth (43.15 per cent) and high instability (37.16). Paints recorded maximum instability. During 1997-2003, the growth rate was maximum in the export earnings of woolen yarn fab, makeup's (31.51 per cent) followed by marine products (25.49 per cent), primary and semi-finished I&S (23.79 per cent), cashew (23, 27 per cent). The above-mentioned commodities have emerged as exportable goods particularly after recent adjustments in the exchange rate and convertibility of rupee on trade account.

Our analysis shows that the instability was maximum in the Indian export earnings of primary and semi-finished I&S (96.9 per cent) followed by paints/enamels/varnishes (90.9 per cent) during 1996-2003. These products are highly volatile and their exports should be discouraged. Drugs and pharmaceuticals, manufactured metals, marine products and processed minerals turned out to be star performers with high growth and low instability in the case of Indian exports to Canada, and their exports should be actively promoted, whereas in the case of Indian imports from Canada, synthetic rubber, electrical machinery and fertilizer manufactured fall under this category (Sharma 2003 and see Appendix 9.1).

AN ASSESSMENT

Several supply- and demand-side factors influence exports, viz., deceleration in output growth, sluggish global demand, Asian crisis, and restricted trade policies adopted by industrialized countries. Over the past decade, Canada has been importing more commodities from India than it has shipped to that country, such that Canada has had a commodity trade deficit with India since 1993. The trade deficit has also been increasing steadily as rising imports and little growth in exports tipped the scales to over $240 million in India's favour in 2006. Conversely, Canada's trade balance with India in services has been in surplus over the last few years of available data. In 2003, Canada exported $254 million in services to India and imported a similar value ($244).

This left the trade balance of services at a mere $10 million, down from $81 million in 2000. Although at just under $500 million the two-way trade in services between India and Canada remains relatively insignificant at this time, it is beginning to show interesting dynamism, increasing almost 125 per cent between 1994 and 2003. Though investment in India has increased slightly over the past few years, according to *Statistics Canada*, Canadian direct investment in India amounted to a rather small $251 million in 2004. Indian investment in Canada was even less significant ($62 million). Globally, however, FDI in India is on the rise, poised to set new records in 2006.

Canadian FDI in India has shown volatility over the past decade. Canada's new government is committed to making Canada an international investment destination of choice. Canada has several assets that make it an ideal investment location: low taxes, a skilled workforce, a healthy business environment, and the most generous R&D tax incentives in the world. In 2005, the cumulative stock of Canadian direct investment abroad increased by 3 per cent to $465.1 billion. FDI into Canada increased by 9.1 per cent in 2005 to reach $415.6 billion.

Bilateral investment relations have been on the rise in recent years as Canada, along with other countries, has warmed up to India subsequent to the volatility and wariness that followed the 1998 nuclear explosions at Pokhran. However, along with these positive developments, there do remain areas of concern that continue to pose challenges for Canadian business and investment prospects in India. A country of India's size and multiplicity is not only full of prospects but can also be potentially precarious. As it stands, even the slightest slip in India-Pakistan relations could impact business and investment climates negatively.

As economic reforms accelerate in India, continued optimism exists for its economic growth prospects. The forecasted annual economic growth rate of 8.2 per cent over the next 20 years would likely place India as one of the most powerful economies in the world. This growth offers Canada-wide firms opportunity to expand trade and tap into some existing markets as well as establish new ones. Given the reality of the markets, the overall growth in trade between India and Canada has been reasonable. However, trade improvement has generally been below the optimistic objectives set in recent round table discussions and trade missions. Canada is still actively engaged in multilateral trade negotiations with India in hopes of addressing some of the trade barriers such as import duties, high tariffs and taxes and the protection of intellectual property rights that impede faster growth in the trade partnership between the two countries.

CHALLENGES AHEAD

If current growth rates continue, India will surpass China as the most populous country in the world around 2030. India's average annual gross domestic product growth rate of 9.5 per cent over the past five years (2003-7) nearly equals China's, which began economic reform initiatives much earlier. If India can continue reforming, it has the potential to grow even more quickly, but faces many challenges in doing so. These challenges include the poor state of infrastructure, restrictive labour laws, and excessive regulation. Inflexible labour laws, which provide disincentives for companies to expand employment, result in less efficient allocation of labour. India's infrastructure is in poor condition, with inefficient ports and unproductive railways. A decrepit road network has resulted in few goods being transported by it.

- India ranks 134th out of 175 countries for ease of doing business
- Inflexible labour laws
- 90 per cent of workers are in the informal sector
- Excessive bureaucracy 10 documents and 27 days on an average to process an export
- Infrastructure is poor
- Energy market needs reforms

- Infrastructure gap holding back growth by 1.5 or 2 per cent annually

The old concept of international assistance is emerging into a new concept as 'trade not aid'. In this changed context in the world, it is challenging to strengthen the balance of payment for external stability and promoting trade getting integrated gradually and taking maximum advantage of broad market and its potentials.

Membership of World Trade Organization (WTO) is also a means to promote and develop the modern management, use new skills, utilize advanced technology, enhance technical skill and entrepreneurship in order to take comparative advantage. The export trade of India seems narrow, both in country and product-wise. Minimizing the cost of production and enhancing competitive capacity of the Indian industries is a must for making the export business sustainable and competitive.

The dynamic export products (textiles, leather, etc.) of India face numerous trade barriers in the form of tariff, non-tariff barriers (NTB) and trade restrictions in potential export destinations. India is supposed to be one of the significant places in the world for possessing different types of high breed and rare herbs. But, most of the herbs have not been identified so far, due to the lack of necessary study and research. Herbs, that are already identified, are also not been utilized properly. Lack of research and development, new and dynamic products are not explored properly. Poor infrastructure is one of the major problems in identifying and developing of new and dynamic products. Thousand tons of green vegetables and fruits rot every year because of the lack of cold house facilities.

CONCLUSION AND POLICY IMPLICATIONS

Major economic reforms were brought about in the early 1990s and India began growing its economy, increasing its visibility and impact on the global economy. Canada realized the need to expand its presence to Asian countries and identified India as a major market with abundant scope for commercialism. In the late 1990s, Canada initiated the move to improve bi-lateral relations. There have been a number of bilateral visits at the political level since thus moving forward the trade growth. Trade between India and Canada has increased many folds in the past decade. Major exports from India to Canada include readymade garments, textiles, steel, jewellery, precious stones, leather products, coffee and tea, spices and carpets. India imported newsprint, pulp, lumber, peas, asbestos, iron, copper and other industrial materials from Canada.

The recent data released by trade data on line industry shows that Canada's exports to India have increased from C $529 million in 1992 to C $1,680 million in 2006 registering a growth of 13.52 per cent per annum. During the same period Canada's imports from India registered a growth of 9.21 per cent per annum. Top ten commodities of exports from India to Canada account for 64.4 per cent and to India 83.9 per cent of total exports. The export of primary and semi-finished I&S and paints/enamels/varnishes should be discouraged as the export earnings of these products are the most volatile. Drugs and pharmaceuticals, manufactured metals, marine products and processed minerals turned out to be star performers with high growth and low instability in the case of Indian exports to Canada, and their exports should be actively promoted. Though investment in India has increased slightly over the past few years, according to *Statistics Canada*, Canadian direct investment in India amounted to a rather small percentage.

There has been major increase in India's export revenue in the past few years. The recent figures show that India exported to Canada 1.92 billion (C $) worth of goods in the year 2006. $1.68 billion worth of goods were imported in the year of 2006 which exceeds the Canada imports valued at 0.24 billion (C $). Imports to India have grown 32 per cent with an annual growth rate of 25 per cent. India has a better balance of trade today than the US. Canada's share in the Indian imports is less than 1 per cent. Canada is engaged in talks with India to initiate a Free Trade Agreement (FTA) between the countries. Currently India holds FTA with Thailand and Sri Lanka. Agreements between China and Singapore are ongoing. FTA locks the relationships between the countries and they are free to trade irrespective of the governments and other factors in place in both countries.

Indo-Canada relations are at threshold stage as both countries are committed to boost trade and investment, cooperation in the field of science and technology, including environmental friendly technologies. India and Canada's economic engagement, both in terms of trade and investment, has a huge untapped potential, even though Canada has done well in exporting various goods to India. Canada's exports to India have increased close to 21 per cent last year than the previous year. Canada must continue to learn the Indian market, understand it, and then create the necessary business and government contacts on both ends to see this economic/ bilateral trade relationship reach its full potential.

REFERENCES

Bowles, Paul, 'Globalization and Neoliberalism: A Taxonomy and Some Implications for Anti-Globalization', *Canadian Journal of Development Studies*, vol. XXVI, no. 1, 2005, pp. 67-87.

Consulate-General of India, Toronto, 'India-Canada Bilateral Relations', Foreign Affairs: Ministry of External Affairs: January 2004, CMIE Report 2007-8.

Desai, Meghanand, *Marx's Revenge: The Resurgence of Capitalism and the Death of Statist Socialism*, London: Verso Development Administration, 2004.

Economic Times, 12 April 2008.

Giddens, Anthony, *The Consequences of Modernity*, Stanford: Stanford University Press, 1990.

Government of India, *Economic Survey*, New Delhi: Ministry of Finance, 2006-7.

Sharma, Pooja, 'Indo-Canadian Trade Relations in the New Economic Environment: A Statistical Verification', unpublished M. Phil dissertation, Himachal Pradesh University, Shimla, 2003.

Teeple, Gary, 'What is Globalization?', in Stephen McBride and John Wiseman (eds.), *Globalization and its Discontents*, Basingstoke: Macmillan, 2000, pp. 9-23.

World Bank, *World Development Report 2006:* Washington, DC: The World Bank, 2006.

——, *World Development Indicators 2007*, Washington, DC: The World Bank, 2006.

World Trade Organization, 'Risks Lie Ahead Following Stronger Trade in 2006', WTO: Appendix, Table 5, 2007.

APPENDIX 9.1: COMPOUND GROWTH RATES AND INSTABILITY INDICES OF INDIAN EXPORTS TO CANADA, 1991 TO 1997 AND 1997 TO 2003

Commodities	1991 to 1997			1997 to 2003		
	g	IXEP	% share X	g	IXEP	% share X
RMG cotton	25.30	2.17	27.03	11.01	1.48	29.45
Cotton yarn fab. made-ups	2.36	1.72	12.75	5.91	2.04	9.87
Gems and jewellery	41.30	2.50	6.58	5.03	8.57	4.03
RMG manmade fibres	4.93	3.85	64.25	9.25	4.73	3.88
Drugs and pharmaceuticals	26.23	2.56	3.96	22.20	4.01	7.17
Manufactures of metals	19.67	4.06	3.50	15.42	2.82	4.75
Handicrafts exel. carpets	18.41	2.86	2.87	11.23	6.83	2.36
Spices	2.51	1.66	2.80	-1.71	10.04	1.40
Electronic goods	75.38	13.30	2.03	-1.70	14.59	0.84
Carpet handmade	-1.32	2.36	1.90	-1.82	3.68	0.97
Basmati rice	14.36	5.17	1.89	5.01	37.15	1.00
Woollen yarn fab. made-ups	45.17	13.10	1.83	31.51	32.07	0.63
Manmade yarn fab. made-ups	23.09	3.33	1.69	13.45	9.37	1.91
Machinery and Instruments	40.21	7.37	1.57	13.49	5.12	1.78
Marine products	1.20	11.12	1.55	25.49	6.23	2.81
Leather goods	-4.37	2.72	1.44	0.23	5,65	1.00
Coffee	53.35	25.61	1.38	–	–	–
RMG of other textile material	12.79	4.75	1.30	8.33	10.95	0.97
Dyes and Intermediates	26.00	4.67	1.20	5.50	6.86	1.13
Natural silk yarn fab. made-ups	0.90	6.10	1.17	2.94	15.80	0.69
Footwear of leather	0.92	5.05	1.15	5.99	9.32	1.31
Leather garments	–	–	–	14.59	19.03	0.70
Paints /enamels/varnishes	13.35	120.33	0.88	16.62	90.89	0.52
Processed minerals	13.68	9.89	0.75	17.71	6.01	1.24
Transport equipment	28.43	8.66	0.69	16.97	26.61	1.60
Cashew	3.65	17.81	0.58	23.27	28.24	0.83

Primary and semi-finished I&S	43.15	37.16	0.59	23.79	96.85	0.56
Leather footwear component	–	–	–	–	–	–
RMG silk	-3.52	5.04	0.52	–	–	–
All commodities	20.74	0.66	100.00	11.09	1.43	100.00

Source: Foreign Trade, CMIE, 1998, 2003.
Note: X = Total Exports and M = Total Imports.

COMPOUND GROWTH RATES AND INSTABILITY INDICES OF INDIA'S IMPORTS FROM CANADA, 1991 TO 1997 AND 1997 TO 2003

Commodities	1991-1997			1997-2003		
	g	IXEP	% share M	g	IXEP	% share M
Newsprint	47.60	5.35	25.74	-5.83	6.32	8.97
Metal ferrous ores & scrap	16.98	10.76	9.95	2.8	15.80	5.22
Non-ferrous metals	25.83	2.42	9.39	-5.10	7.53	3.72
Pulp and waste paper	7.32	6.05	7.07	13.97	5.31	11.17
Non-electric machinery	15.45	3.98	6.18	6.50	8.59	4.63
Iron and Steel	-14.63	32.60	5.02	-11.55	10.17	1.14
Pulses	-30.49	8.98	4.23	-0.79	5.87	2.25
Other crude minerals	-3.06	2.88	4.02	7.14	32.95	1.06
Professional Instruments	51.18	8.44	3.08	-10.98	27.53	0.39
Artificial resin and plastic Material	-10.40	11.57	2.19	11.34	26.98	6.57
Project goods	-30.81	6.95	1.61	-22.11	45.86	0.53
Organic chemicals	48.49	23.91	1.53	48.57	-99.034	0.41
Synthetic & reclaimed rubber	39.18	20.00	1.36	35.28	41.37	2.68
Electric machinery	-15.81	17.47	1.05	1.59	11.75	0.57
Woolen and cotton rags	71.75	14.41	0.35	-8.41	83.01	0.24
Wood & wood products	133.99	29.44	0.51	46.50	29.45	3.63
Fertilizers manufactured	-38.60	17.97	0.40	22.26	45.66	1.06
Other commodities	-14.39	10.78	4.95	37.31	-359.50	0.30
All commodities	3.15	2.72	100.00	8.45	1.91	100.00

Source: Foreign Trade, CMIE, 1998, 2003.
Note: X = Total Exports and M = Total Imports.

FOREIGN TRADE OF INDIA—2002-3 TO 2006-7

(*Rs. Crores*)

Year	Exports	Export % to GDP	Imports	Import % to GDP	Trade Balance
2002-3	2,55,137	10.38	2,97,206	12.09	-42,069
2003-4	2,93,367	10.61	3,59,108	12.99	-65,741
2004-5	3,75,340	12 00	5,01,065	16.03	-1,25,725
2005-6	4,56,418	12.79	6,60,409	18.51	-2,03,991
2006-7	5,71,642	13.86	8,62,302	20.9	-2,90,660

Source: CMIE, 2007-8.

CHAPTER 10

The Diasporic Dimension of India's Bilateral Economic Relations

K.R.G. NAIR

There exists a view that even in this age of electronic convergence, people-to-people contacts can help strengthen economic ties between countries.[1] The fact that 60 per cent of foreign direct investment (FDI) in China between 1978 and 1999 came from three ethnically Chinese economies—Hong Kong, Macao and Taiwan, having 95 per cent or more of people of Chinese origin in their respective populations, is often quoted as empirical evidence to prove the point. Additional analytical arguments are emerging in support of such a view with the stress on the importance of network and reputational capital in international economic relations.[2] India has opened up her economy in a major way at least from the 1990s. There are 48 non-SAARC countries of the world in which 10,000 or more of persons are present or former Indian citizens or their descendents.[3]

It would hence be interesting to enquire into the extent to which this Indian presence in select countries is having an impact on the concerned country's bilateral economic relations with India, particularly since overt measures are being increasingly taken to tap this source for the promotion to India's benefit of bilateral economic relations. There are many aspects of international economic relations and only two of these—trade and FDI—are taken up for analysis here. Three countries of the developed world—Canada, USA and UK—are chosen for the purpose of this study which is divided into four sections. Section 1 poses the issue. Section 2 gives the details of the manner in which India's bilateral trade relations with these three countries have undergone change since the 1990s. Section 3 goes on to analyse changes in this regard in FDI inflows and outflows between India and these three countries. Section 4 examines certain relevant aspects relating to the Indian diaspora in these three countries. The concluding part puts together the main findings of this study and draws some policy inferences.

POSING THE ISSUE

Diaspora can be defined as 'communities of migrants, living or settled permanently in other countries, aware of its origins and identity and maintaining varying degrees of linkages with the mother country'. According to this definition, the Indian diaspora would include non-resident Indians (NRI) who are Indian citizens holding Indian passports, but are staying abroad for an indefinite period whether for employment or for carrying on any business or vocation or for any other purpose. It would also consist of persons of Indian origin (PIO) who or whose spouse, parents, grandparents, or great grandparents were once citizens of India. In the year 2001, the Indian diaspora defined in this manner numbered around 20 million and were scattered in more than 110 countries all over the world.

Some relevant details about the top seven countries of the world in terms of the number of Indian diaspora are given in Table 10.1. It is apparent from the table that the USA, Canada and the UK are the more developed of these seven countries in terms of per capita income. While the USA ranks number one in terms of the number of Indian diaspora among these three countries, it ranks the lowest not only among these three countries but also in the table as a whole if we consider the percentage of Indian diaspora in the total population. As regards Canada, it is true that it occupies the lowest position in the table in terms of the number of Indian diaspora. But it occupies the highest rank in terms of the percentage of Indian diaspora if we consider the three more developed nations in the table, beating even the UK which had ruled over India for around a century and a half and to which country Indians had started moving as early as in 1690 when Canada in the modern sense of the term was not even born.[4] In fact, Canada occupies a higher rank in this regard in the entire table than even South

TABLE 10.1: SOME RELEVANT DETAILS ABOUT THE FIRST SEVEN COUNTRIES IN TERMS OF THE NUMBER OF INDIAN DIASPORA*

S. no.	Country	Indians number (000)	Diaspora as % population	Per capita income 2001 in US $
1.	Myanmar	2,902	6.00	745
2.	USA	1,679	0.59	34,280
3.	Malaysia	1,665	7.02	7,910
4.	Saudi Arabia	1,500	7.01	13,290
5.	UK	1,200	2.27	24,340
6.	South Africa	1,000	2.31	10,910
7.	Canada	851	2.74	26,530

Source: *Singhvi Committee Report and the World Bank.

Africa to which country also Indians had started moving very much earlier.[5]

An earlier study confined mostly to the year 2000-1 and focused mainly on Canada and did not indicate any clear relationship between percentage Indian diaspora in a country's population and its relative importance in FDI in India or in India's foreign trade.[6] The study worked out the total trade of India with each of these seven countries as the percentage of India's total trade with the world as a whole. The value was highest at 12.96 for the USA which has the least percentage Indian diaspora in its total population among the seven countries in the table.[7] The second lowest value in this regard was 1.11 for Canada which has the highest percentage Indian diaspora in its total population if we consider the three more developed countries of the table. The study then went on to focus on Canada, found the relative importance of Canada in India's foreign trade and FDI approvals very low and hence inferred that there is unrealized potential for trade and business relations between India and Canada.

The analysis here explores all this much further and in greater detail for all the three countries—Canada, the UK and the USA. Instead of taking total trade, exports and imports are studied separately. Further, since there is often a big slip between the cup and the lip, instead of approvals, actual accruals of FDI into India are taken up for examination. Moreover since the

Indian elephant is slowly raising its trunk in a big way in FDI abroad, this aspect is also enquired into.

BILATERAL TRADE RELATIONS

This section attempts to analyse the trends, if any, in the relative importance in bilateral trade of India with each of these countries and of each of these countries with India. The data used are the ones brought out by the UNCTAD and the period covered is between 1991 and 2004. First and second degree trend equations are tried with RI the relative importance, as the dependent variable and time *T* as the independent variable. Table 10.2 presents the results of this exercise in cases where there appears to be a significant trend, with significance being tested on the basis of the two-tailed *t*-statistic at 5 per cent level.[8]

As regards Indo-Canadian bilateral trade relations, the trends seem decipherable except in the case of the relative importance of exports to India in Canada's total exports. The relative importance of Canada in exports from India seems to be experiencing an increasing trend, though there are some indications that this may not sustain for long. The relative importance of India in Canadian imports seems, in slight contrast, is more definitely set for an increase over time. If we consider the relative importance of Canada in imports to India, there seems to be a declining trend, though there are some indications that this may be reversed over time.

If we consider Indo-British trade relations, there is no trend decipherable in India's relative importance to the UK, irrespective of whether we consider imports in, or exports from, the UK. There are, however, definite declining trends in the relative importance of the UK in imports to or exports from India. It is true that in the case of Indo-US trade relations also, there is no decipherable trend if we consider the relative importance of India in exports from the USA. There is also similarity between trends in Indo-British and Indo-US trade relations in the sense that the relative importance of the USA in Indian imports is undergoing a definite decline over time.[9] Further there are also clear indications that the relative importance of the US in India's

TABLE 10.2: TRENDS IN RELATIVE IMPORTANCE IN BILATERAL TRADE RELATIONS

Description	Trend equation	R^2
RI of Canada in*		
India's exports	RI = 0.818 + 0.109T** −0.006T^2 (0.151) (0.046) (0.003) [5.404] [2.338] [−1.846]	0.447
India's imports	RI = 1.654 − 0.156T** + 0.008T^2 (0.203) (0.062) (0.004) [8.150] [-2.493] [1.874]	0.519
RI of India in		
Canada's imports	RI = 0.159 + 0.018 T** (0.011) (0.001) [15.058][14.439]	0.946
RI of UK in		
India's exports	RI = 7.106 − 0.172 T** (0.135) (0.016) [52.712] [-10.852]	0.908
India's imports	RI = 0.668 − 0.015 T** (0.035) (0.004) [19.325][-3.640]	0.525
RI of USA in		
India's exports	RI = 15.769 + 1.271T**−0.076T^2** (1.373) (0.421) (0.027) [11.482] [3.018] [-2.791]	0.463
India's imports	RI = 1.135 − 0.036 T** (0.062) (0.007) [18.435][-4.923]	0.669
RI of India in		
USA's imports	RI = 0.678 + 0.026 T** (0.025) (0.003) [27.379][9.071]	0.873

Notes: * RI stands for percentage relative importance in terms of value and T for time.

** Indicates significance as defined in the text.

Figures in round and square brackets are standard errors and t-values. Sources of data are as mentioned in the text.

exports will ultimately be experiencing a decline over time. The Indo-US trade relations appear, however, to tread a completely different path over time on one count. In striking contrast with the trend in Indo-British trade relations, if we consider the relative importance of India in US imports, there is a definite increasing trend over time.

The results here cannot, however, be considered indicative of a clear and positive relationship between the per cent of Indian diaspora in a country and bilateral trade relations between India and the country in question. The rising trend in the relative importance of India in Canadian imports is of course somewhat suggestive of the existence of such a relationship. The fact that there is a similar trend in the relative importance of India in the US imports, despite the percentage Indian diaspora in US population being the lowest among all the seven countries in Table 10.1 and the absence of any such trend in the case of UK which ranks number two among the three more developed countries in Table 10.1 with regard to the relative importance of Indian diaspora in total population, implies that much more detailed studies are required before more definite inferences in this regard can be drawn.

FOREIGN DIRECT INVESTMENT

Table 10.3 gives the total actual inflow into India of FDI from 1991 to 2007 for the three countries considered here. On the face of it and from the table it appears as if there is an inverse

TABLE 10.3: FDI INFLOWS TO INDIA: 1991-2007*

S. no.	Country	Total inflow (in million as % inflow) US $	From all countries
1	Canada	132.6	0.22
2	UK	4060.1	6.48
3	USA	6352.0	9.79

Source: Data as brought out by the Secretariat of Industrial Assistance of the Ministry of Commerce and Industry of the Government of India.

TABLE 10.4: TRENDS IN RI_{FDI}, RELATIVE IMPORTANCE OF DIFFERENT COUNTRIES IN FDI INFLOWS INTO INDIA, 1991-2007*

Country	Trend equation	R^2
Canada	$RI_{fdi} = 0.094 + 0.021\ T^{**}$ (0.070) (0.008) [1.346][2.772]	0.372
UK	$RI_{fdi} = 17.579 - 3.451\ T^{**} + 0.207\ T^{2**}$ (3.398) (0.977) (0.059) [5.173] [-3.531] [3.492]	0.511
USA	No trend decipherable	

Notes: * RI_{fdi} stands for percentage relative importance in terms of FDI inflows and T, for time.
** Indicates significance as defined in the text.
Figures in round and square brackets are standard errors and t-values. Sources of data are as mentioned in the text.

relationship between the percentage Indian diaspora in population and the percentage share of the concerned country in FDI in India. But an analysis of the trends in RI_{fdi} the relative percentage shares of these three countries in FDI in India, given in Table 10.4 indicates that the picture on closer look is somewhat different. As regards the USA with the smallest percentage Indian diaspora in its population, there does not seem to be any trend in the relative importance of the country in India's FDI. UK with the second largest percentage Indian diaspora in population is experiencing an initial decline in relative importance in FDI, but seems to have a tendency over a longer period of time to have a larger percentage share in India's FDI inflows. There are indications of an increase over time of the relative importance in inflows of FDI to India in the case of Canada, which has the largest percentage share of Indian diaspora in its population among the three countries.

A similar picture regarding the possible impact of the diasporic element emerges also if we consider the changes over time in Indian FDI in these three countries. This is apparent if we consider Table 10.5, which gives the Indian FDI approvals in

TABLE 10.5: APPROVALS OF FDI FROM INDIA, 1996-2007

(*in US $ million*)

Country	Approvals of FDI from India	
	1996-2002	2002-7
Canada	5.58	405.12
UK	410.62	1,739.00
USA	1,540.83	1,227.47

Source: Secretariat for Industrial Assistance, Department of Commerce and Industry, Government of India.

these three countries. In the first sub-period, the USA with least percentage Indian diaspora in population ranks number one, but this rank is occupied by the UK in the second sub-period. Actually while approvals of FDI from India increased in the case of both Canada and the UK between the two sub-periods, they underwent a decline in the case of USA. The increase is actually the maximum—more than seventyfold—in the case of Canada while it is only around fourfold for UK.

CERTAIN OTHER RELEVANT ASPECTS

It has, however, to be borne in mind that the impact that the Indian diaspora can have on the concerned country's bilateral economic relations with India depends on a number of other relevant factors besides just relative importance in terms of its percentage in the concerned country's total population. These include the historical aspects, the extent of proven urge to maintain relations with India and the institutional framework available for this purpose. On all these counts there appear to be considerable differences between the three countries.

From the historical angle, there are many noticeable points in this regard. Indian immigrants seem to have arrived in the UK around the year 1700, while in the other two countries it happened two centuries later—in 1898 in USA and 1903 in Canada. There were, till 1948, no special restrictions on the entry of Indians to the UK since India was one of its subjects, while this was not so in the case of the other two countries. Possibly as a result also of this, there was in the UK no overt movement like the Asiatic Exclusion League of the US in around

1910 or like the *Kamagata Maru* incident of 1914 in Canada.[10] Further, before Indian Independence, while the flow of migrants from India to the UK consisted mostly of two groups—the workers looking for better employment and the elites going for higher education—it was mainly the former group which migrated to the USA and more particularly to Canada. After Indian Independence, this distinction between the UK and the other two countries considered here disappeared and to all the three countries selective migration was allowed of more trained persons—particularly of doctors to the UK and to some extent to the USA and IT professionals to all the three countries—in recent years. There was also a stream of multiple migrants or migrants who had moved from India earlier to another country and then moved to one of these three countries later. The most noticeable in this regard was the movement to the UK of migrant Indians from Uganda in the early 1970s. As a result, there are considerable differences in the composition of the Indian diaspora in these three countries. Another noticeable feature is that while in the USA, the Indian diaspora has spread to most parts of the country, the same does not hold true in regard to the UK and particularly to Canada.[11]

There are some indications that possibly as a result of this the degree of the diasporic urge in the Indian diaspora is different in these three countries. This is clearly reflected in the extent to which the Indian diaspora from these countries participate in the Pravasi Bharatiya Divas, organized annually in India since 2003 to facilitate the continuance of the links of these diaspora with India. Table 10.6 gives the number of registered delegates from these three countries per million Indian diaspora in them. The maximum value in all the six years is of the USA indicating the most diasporic urge. The minimum value in four of the six cases is that of Canada.

Canada has, however, stolen a march over the USA and the UK in having evolved a unique institution—the Shastri Indo-Canadian Institute (SICI)—which is of immense help in building bridges between the two countries—India and Canada. The SICI was conceived by Prof. Michael Brecher of McGill University in the early 1960s to overcome the total information gap and the utter lack of economic and cultural contacts between India

TABLE 10.6: NUMBER OF REGISTERED DELEGATES FROM DIFFERENT COUNTRIES AT PRAVASI BHARATIYA DIVAS, 2003-8*

S. no.	Country	Registered delegates per million Indian diaspora					
		2003	2004	2005	2006	2007	2008
1.	Canada	121	46	94	14	41	38
2.	UK	125	76	94	25	28	22
3.	USA	300	247	351	179	105	89

Note: * The data on the number of Indian Diaspora relate to the year 2001 as given in the Singhvi Committee Report.

and Canada.[12] The governments of India and Canada signed a Memorandum of Understanding on 28 November 1968 in this regard and the SICI was set up on that basis as a registered non-profit charitable organization in Canada with four Canadian institutions as its founding members, with the basic aim originally of promoting Indian studies in the fields of humanities and social sciences in Canada.

The SICI has, in its four-decade long life span so far, indeed come a long way from these modest beginnings. Its office in Canada, is located since 1 June 1990 at the premises provided free by a member university—the University of Calgary. Its India office in New Delhi set up on 1 January 1969, moved on 13 May 1991 into its own very impressive premises built with funds from the Canadian government on land donated by the Government of India. Besides these improvements in physical infrastructure, there also took place over time major changes in its perspective. Since the late 1980s, SICI has started also to promote Canadian studies in India.[13] From late 1990s SICI began encouraging collaborative development studies under the Shastri Applied Policy Research Project (SHARP).[14] All this meant that while SICI was originally set up to promote studies in art, literature, culture and social sciences, its mandate now incorporates a rich diversity of topical disciplines like law, information management, and science and technology. There was also considerable expansion in its membership which rose from 4 Canadian institutions in 1968 to 23 in 2004. Addendum IX of the MoU signed on 3 August 2006 brought another major qualitative change by enabling Indian institutions to become members of SICI. As a result, by 2007, while SICI had 32 Canadian institutions, including 4 from Francophone Canada, as members, there were 42 Indian institutions including prestigious ones like Indian Institutes of Technology and Indian Institutes of Management as members. The SICI has thus, in fact, emerged as a truly bilateral organization tailor-made to build bridges between India and Canada in this globalized and competitive world scenario.

It is, of course, true that SICI was not the direct brainchild of the Indian diaspora. But to the extent that the desire to learn about India was aroused partly also by the presence of the Indian diaspora, it can be attributed to its indirect impact. It has also been recognized that there has been a natural and progressive change of Canadians of Indian origin getting more and more involved in SICI.[15] Such a view gets substantiated by the fact that in 36 years, out of the 26 incumbents who had occupied the post of Resident Director to head the India office of the SICI and be in India for at least a year on that count, 14 have been members of the Indian diaspora. In fact, one of the Canadian institutional members of SICI for the past few years has been University College of the Fraser Valley in British Columbia where the involvement of the Indian diaspora is overt and strong.

There is, however, a feeling that the full potential of SICI is yet to be realized and that the organization can soar to even greater heights in building bridges between Canada and India. It has been stressed that to facilitate this, even greater involvement and support of the Indian diaspora in Canada both individually and collectively are called for.[16] An area in which it can easily intervene is in providing support for Indian interns going to Canada in terms of funding to the India office to coordinate this and also of provision of internship amenities in organizations in Canada, particularly since in regard to interns, there has been only one-way traffic from Canada to India. One also wonders whether the blank that exists on information in India about Francophone Canada and a similar vacuum about India in Francophone Canada and in particular Quebec can at least be reduced by SICI making special efforts in this direction including also steps to increase its membership from Francophone Canada. Without upsetting the beautiful apple cart that SICI has emerged as, it should be possible to continue its path of evolution to make it more sustainable and appropriate to the changing world scenario in terms of accepting private funds, of not being the baby of just one government department and of retaining and providing career prospects and opportunities to most competent personnel.[17]

INFERENCES

On the basis of the Singhvi Committee Report (2001), the study here finds that the USA, the UK and Canada are three of the more developed countries which are among the top seven in the world in terms of the number of Indian diaspora. Of these three, Canada ranks the highest in terms of the percentage Indian diaspora in its population and the USA, the lowest. But it appears at first sight that contrary to the views of the protagonists of the concepts of social and reputational capital, the economic relations in terms of relative importance in trade as well as flows of FDI between India and these three countries, are not directly related to the relative importance of the Indian diaspora in these. But a closer look, particularly of the trends in these in recent years, seems to suggest that this is not entirely so. More in-depth and detailed studies are needed before more definite inferences in this regard can be drawn. In such studies, it has also to be borne in mind that the historical roots of the Indian diaspora, the composition of the diaspora and the extent of diasporic urge as reflected in participation in PBD are different in these three countries. The fact that institutions like the SICI have emerged has also to be considered in such analysis. There are already some indications in the study that the diasporic advantage that Canada has, is gradually having its impact on economic relations between Canada and India. With unique institutions already in place like the SICI, tailor-made to build bridges including economic ones between the two countries, even cosmetic changes along the lines suggested here can have a sustained and deep positive influence on Indo-Canadian business and economic relations.

ACKNOWLEDGEMENTS

The author, an Honorary Research Professor at the Centre for Policy Research, New Delhi, wishes to thank Mrs. Gouri Singh and Mr. S.L. Dave of the Ministry of Commerce and Industry and Mr. T. Mohammad of the Ministry of Overseas Indian Affairs of the Government of India, Mr. K.T. Chacko of the Indian Institute of Foreign Trade, Mr. Earl Cholden, Ms. Sarmishta Roy and Ms. Anita Dennis of the SICI, Mr. Sanjay Grover of the CII and Mr. Chetan Bijesure of the FICCI for useful discussions and help in collecting data for the preparation of this paper. The usual disclaimers apply.

NOTES

1. As pointed out by Field (2003) such a view that relationships matter underlies the growing literature on Social Capital. See among others also Nair (2005).
2. For detailed discussions in this regard see Kapur (2007) and Nayyar (2007).
3. See Singhvi Committee Report (2001).
4. For detail, please see among others, Kalra (2007).
5. It was around 1860 that Indians moved in sufficiently large numbers as indentured labour to South Africa, while the first outflow of Indians to Canada took place much later around 1903. Please see among others Bhana and Vahed (2007) and Naidoo and Leslie (2007) for details.
6. See Nair (2005).
7. The corresponding value for UK was 5.75.
8. Throughout this study, the same simple format to estimate time trend is being followed.
9. In the case of exports from India, though the sign of the coefficient of T is positive and significant, the coefficient of T^2 is also significant, but it is negative
10. Asiatic Exclusion League was an organization formed in the US to prevent migration of Indians to the US. *Kamagata Maru* was the ship carrying 376 Indian immigrants non-stop from Hong Kong to Vancouver in British Columbia to satisfy legal stipulations, but was disallowed from offloading its passengers there.
11. Most Indians are concentrated along highways M1 and M6 and in Canada in Toronto and Vancouver, with very few in the Maritimes or in Quebec.

12. See in this regard Lynette Lefsrud, *The SICI Celebrates Its 35 Year History*, first published in Indian High Commission Special Edition for Republic Day, Ottawa, 2004.
13. According to a recent SICI report over 800 fellowships have so far been awarded to Canadian faculty researchers and students to further their study of India and Indian languages, over 5 lakh Indian books and journals have been sent to Canadian libraries. 94 distinguished Indians have gone on lecture tours to Canada and 47 international internships for young Canadians to work with Indian research institutions, businesses and NGOs. To promote Canadian studies in India, the SICI has awarded 289 scholarships to support Indian researchers in Canada, funded lecture tours of 19 Canadian academics to India and got 9,000 resource materials on Canada sent to India.
14. Under SHARP, whose aim is to contribute to poverty reduction and sustainable development in India through support for bi-national collaborative policy research projects, in response to public policy priorities identified by government agencies, civil society and private organizations, 40 projects have been sponsored so far. 19 projects are now on in three areas—economic reforms (impact of globalization, liberalization and private sector development on poverty and basic need), environmental management (balancing growth and environmental sustainability) and social development (health sector reforms and capacity building at the local level).
15. Stephen Inglis has made a statement to this effect in Lefsrud (2004).
16. See in this regard the views of Flora McDonald as expressed in Lefsrud (2004).
17. See in this regard the review of the working of the Indian Council of Social Science Research contained in Vaidyanathan (2007) and also the views of Flora McDonald as expressed in Lefsrud (2004).

REFERENCES

Bhana, Surendra and Goolam Vahed, 'South Africa', in Brij V. Lal (ed.), *The Encyclopedia of the Indian Diaspora*, New Delhi: Oxford University Press, 2007, pp. 242-53.

Field, John, *Social Capital*, New York: Routledge, 2003.

Kalra, Virinder S., 'United Kingdom', in Brij V. Lal (ed.), *The Encyclopedia of the Indian Diaspora*, New Delhi: Oxford University Press, 2007, pp. 336-45.

Kapur, Devesh, 'International Migration from India: Economic Impact', in Kaushik Basu (ed.), *The Oxford Companion to Economics in India*, New Delhi: Oxford University Press, 2007, pp. 309-12.

Lal, Brij V. (ed.), *The Encyclopedia of the Indian Diaspora*, New Delhi: Oxford University Press, 2007.

Lefsrud, Lynette, '*The SICI Celebrates Its 35 Year History*', Special Edition for Republic Day, Indian High Commission, Ottawa, 2004.

Naidoo, Josephine C. and James D. Leslie, 'Canada', in Brij V. Lal (ed.), *The Encyclopedia of the Indian Diaspora*, New Delhi: Oxford University Press, pp. 326-35.

Nair, K.R.G., 'Canada-India Economic Relations: Tapping Unrealized Potential', in C.D Wadhva and Y.P. Woo (eds.), *Asian Regionalism: Canadian and Indian Perspectives*, New Delhi: APH Publishing Corporation, 2005, pp. 225-36.

Nayyar, Deepak, 'International Migration', in Kaushik Basu (ed.), *The Oxford Companion to Economics in India*, New Delhi: Oxford University Press, 2007, pp. 305-9.

Singhvi Committee Report, *Report of the High Level Committee on the Indian Diaspora*, New Delhi: Indian Council of World Affairs, 2001.

Vaidyanathan, A., 'An Overview: Fourth Review of ICSSR', *Economic and Political Weekly*, vol. XLIII, no. 5, 2007, pp. 21-5.

CHAPTER 11

Financial Sector Reforms in India: Some Lessons from Canada

JYOTIRMAYEE KAR

FINANCIAL SECTOR REFORMS IN INDIA

India has started reformation of its financial sector since more than a decade. The process of reforms has been marked by gradualism, with reform measures across sectors and within sectors being planned to reinforce each other. The chief objective of the early phase, known as the first generation of reforms, was to create an efficient, productive and profitable financial service industry operating in an environment of operational flexibility and functional autonomy. The second generation of reforms started from the second half of the 1990s aimed at global integration of financial services by strengthening the financial system and introducing structural improvements.

IMPACT OF REFORMS ON THE BANKING SECTOR

The reforms process has succeeded in strengthening the health of the financial intermediaries, deepening the financial markets and enhancing the instruments available in the financial system. There has also been a remarkable improvement in the competitiveness, efficiency and productivity of the Indian financial system. Various measures initiated in the reforms process have significantly strengthened the commercial banking sector in terms of profitability, asset quality and capital position.

1. Asset quality of the Indian Banking System has improved significantly over the past decade. NPAs of all SCBs which

stood at 15.70 per cent of the gross advances and 7 per cent of the total assets in 1995-6, has declined to 3.30 per cent of the gross advances and 1.90 per cent of the total assets in 2005-6 (Table 11.1).

2. Impact of greater competition improved efficiency of the Indian Banking System. The operating profit to asset ratio of the SCBs, which was 1.69 in 1995-6, increased to 2.03 in 2005-6. This is also visible in the significant reduction in the ratio of interest spread to asset, from 3.13 in 1995-6 to 2.78 in 2005-6 (Table 11.2).
3. There has been a decline in the share of the public sector banks in the total income, expenditure and assets, since 1995-6 to 2005-6. Share of the new private sector banks has increased substantially (Table 11.3).
4. Cross-country comparison of several balance sheet and profitability indicators like return on assets, regulatory capital to risk-weighted assets and non-performing loans suggest that the Indian Banking Sector indicators are moving towards global benchmark (Table 11.4).

The reforms process initially focused on the commercial banks. After significant progress in this sector, it was extended to encompass regional rural banks, cooperative banks, all-India

TABLE 11.1: GROSS AND NET NPA OF SCHEDULED COMMERCIAL BANKS

Year (end-March)	Non-performing assets			
	Gross		Net	
	As percentage of gross advances	As percentage of total assets	As percentage of net advances	As percentage of total assets
1996-97	15.7	7.0	8.1	3.3
1999-00	12.7	5.5	6.8	2.7
2002-3	8.8	4.0	4.4	1.9
2005-6	3.3	1.9	1.2	0.7

Source: *Handbook of Statistics on the Indian Economy 2005-6.*

TABLE 11.2: IMPORTANT FINANCIAL INDICATORS—SCBs

Year	Operating profit to assets	Net profit to assets	Income to assets	Expenditure to assets	Operating expenses to assets	Provisions and contingencies to assets	Spread (NII) to assets
1995-6	1.69	0.68	–	–	2.94	1.54	3.13
1999-0	1.66	0.66	10.40	9.74	2.50	1.00	2.73
2002-3	2.39	1.01	10.14	9.14	2.24	1.39	2.77
2005-6	2.03	0.88	7.97	7.09	2.11	1.15	2.78

Source: *Report on Trend and Progress of Banking in India*, RBI, various issues.

TABLE 11.3: BANK GROUP-WISE SHARES: SELECT INDICATORS

(*per cent*)

	1995-6	1999-2000	2002-3	2005-6
Public Sector Banks				
Income	82.5	78.8	74.5	72.4
Expenditure	84.2	79.4	74.8	73.1
Total Assets	84.4	80.2	75.7	72.3
Net Profit	–39.1	70.0	64.8	67.3
Gross Profit	74.3	70.9	76.6	69.2
Private Sector Banks				
Income	8.2	12.3	18.5	19.7
Expenditure	7.4	12.0	18.6	19.7
Total Assets	7.7	12.3	17.5	20.5
Net Profit	59.3	16.8	15.6	20.3
Gross Profit	10.1	14.5	18.7	19.0
Foreign Banks				
Income	9.4	9.0	7.0	7.8
Expenditure	8.3	8.7	6.6	7.3
Total Assets	7.9	7.5	6.9	7.2
Net Profit	79.8	13.2	19.6	12.5
Gross Profit	15.6	14.6	4.7	11.8

Source: *Report on Trend and Progress of Banking in India*, RBI, various issues.

TABLE 11.4: SELECT BANKING INDICATORS: CROSS-COUNTRY

(*End-March*)

Country	Return on assets		Regulatory capital to risk-weighted assets		Non-performing loans to total loans	
	2005	2006	2005	2006	2005	2006
Emerging Markets						
Argentina	0.9	1.9	–	–	5.2	4.7
Brazil	2.1	2.3	17.4	–	4.4	–
Mexico	2.4	2.4	14.3	16.0	1.8	1.7
Korea	1.2	1.3	12.8	13.1	1.2	1.2
South Africa	1.1	–	12.3	12.6	1.5	1.3
Developed Countries						
US	1.3	1.4	13.0	13.1	0.7	0.7
UK	0.8	–	12.8	–	1.0	–
Japan	0.5	–	–	–	1.8	–
Canada	0.7	–	12.9	13.0	0.5	–
Australia	1.8	–	10.3	–	0.2	–
Memo						
India	0.9	0.9	12.8	12.4	5.2	3.3

Notes: '–' denotes not available.
Data relating to Brazil, UK and Australia relate to the end-December 2005 and 2006.

Source: Global Financial Stability Report (GFSR), September 2006.

financial institutions and non-banking financial companies. All these institutions play a major role in financial inclusion and deepening of the financial sector, particularly in the rural areas. The cooperative credit institutions both in urban and rural areas are now placed on a path of revival through a consultative method of policy formulation. This strategy has started showing results which is crucial for sustaining the role of financial intermediation among the rural and urban poor and small savers.

The financial landscape has witnessed

1. Entry of some bigger banks into other financial segments like merchant banking, insurance, etc., which has made them financial conglomerates.

2. Emergence of several new players with diversified presence across major segments.
3. Possibility of some of the non-banking institutions in the financial sector acquiring large enough proportions to have a systematic impact.

RBI has urged the banks to review their existing practices with a view to assess the objective of financial inclusion. All banks were asked to make a provision of 'no-frills' account, with either nil or very low minimum balances as well as charges, that would make such accounts accessible to vast sections of population. Procedure for opening up of small accounts was simplified. Banks were allowed to use the services of NGOs, SHGs, MFIs as business facilitators or correspondents in providing financial and banking services.

SOME GREY AREAS

Yet these achievements are far from satisfactory, *vis-à-vis* that experienced by many emerging market economies. Recent move towards ensuring capital account convertibility underlined some of the flaws in the Indian financial system and recommended that it should be ensured only after the system is strengthened, inflation is controlled, and fiscal discipline has been ensured. Moreover, a recent survey has observed that the Indian banking sector is not ready to practise the norms chalked out in Basel II. Despite decline, NPAs of the banking system continue to be a cause of concern. This speaks of little improvement in the legal arrangements and inefficient risk management practices by the banks. Reduction of transaction cost and improvement of the credit delivery system are the major areas inviting focused attention.

To add to this, at a recent conference on microfinance, P. Chidambaram, the then finance minister of India, acknowledged that almost 60 to 80 per cent of the enterprises and individuals in the country lack access even to basic financial services like savings and credit. This figure works out to around 500 millions of un-banked people. Even after a decade of microfinance, India has been able to cumulatively disburse barely Rs. 39 billion against an annual estimated demand of Rs. 450 billion. In comparison, success of Brazil and South Africa, which started much later, is more laudable. Inadequate risk management practices have constrained the banks to channellize funds to the much needed sector. The nascent Credit Information Bureau is not operating successfully in providing proper credit history of the borrowers so as to facilitate easy credit delivery at a lower transaction cost to the needy small borrowers. Other factors like lack of good quality issuers, institutional investors, supporting infrastructure and high cost of issuance, market fragmentation are the major reasons of lack of depth in the corporate debt market in India.

The Committee on Financial Sector Reforms, headed by Prof. Raghuram Rajan, which delivered its report to India's Planning Commission on April 2008, observed that:

- The financial sector is not providing adequate services to the majority of Indian retail customers, small and medium-sized enterprises, farmers and least to speak of daily wage earners and the very poor.
- Government ownership of 70 per cent of the banking system and hindrances to the development of the corporate debt and derivatives markets have stunted financial development.
- The financial sector, if properly regulated, but unleashed from government securities, has the potential to generate millions of needed jobs and have an enormous multiplier effect on growth.
- In these uncertain times, financial stability is more important than ever to keep growth from being derailed by external and internal shocks.
- Banks have no incentive to expand 'priority sector' lending as price of small loans are fixed by the government.

A financial system cannot function fruitfully if most people do not have access to it. Nearly three quarters of farm households have no access to formal sources of credit, leaving the rural people vulnerable to moneylenders. The committee's analysis shows that nearly half of the loans taken by those in the bottom quarter of the income distribution are from informal money-lenders at an interest rate above 36 per cent a year, much above the rate fixed by the banks, which is less than half of the level.

Moreover, all banks must lend to priority sector like agriculture. Their operation is restricted by imposition of ceiling on the interest rate chargeable to this sector. This also restricts access of the priority sector borrowers to institutional finance. Banks lose the incentive to extend credit support when price of the small loans are fixed by the government. Competition between the formal and informal financial institutions, with reduced restriction on the former could be a better alternative.

The present exercise is a comparative study of the financial sector reforms India with that of Canada. In the process it has highlighted the areas of concern and suggests appropriate policy measures to improve the functioning of the Indian system. It has also attempted to throw light upon recent researches on the entry of foreign banks and removal of regulatory rigidities undertaken in Canada. It also covers how far these outcomes will be compatible with major economic objective of poverty reduction in India.

PROGRESS OF THE CANADIAN ECONOMY

Since the early 1990s the world economy has undergone a structural transformation. It has also experienced shocks like the East Asian crisis and 9/11 economic crash. Still many economies have succeeded in managing well their home front in the face of these external adversities and have marched ahead. The Canadian economy is one such. Achievements of this economy has won accolades from the IMF.

The statement of the IMF Mission (2003) has observed,

> The Canadian economy proved exceptionally resilient in the face of the global downturn and is well-positioned to cope with recent challenges. Growth in recent years exceeded that in most other industrial countries by substantial margins and, despite a series of adverse shocks and a weakening of activity this year, most indicators point to recovery. This performance owes much to the skilful implementation of the authorities' monetary and fiscal policy framework, as well as the structural reforms introduced since the early 1990s, which have laid a solid foundation for growth and increased Canada's capacity to respond flexibly to changing circumstances.

The Canadian financial system has remained resilient in the face of the recent slowdown and spillovers from US accounting scandals. In the banking sector, loan losses have fallen, revenues have strengthened, and credit quality has improved, reflecting progress made by banks in raising operating efficiency and strengthening internal risk management systems. The authorities have also responded effectively to increased global concerns regarding corporate accounting and governance standards by increasing the stringency of disclosure requirements, introducing a new Public Accountability Board to improve the quality of the audit process, developing new corporate governance guidelines, and strengthening enforcement of securities market regulations.

Canada has devoted considerable effort in promoting the efficiency and stability of the financial system, which does not refer exclusively to banks and markets, but rather to all financial institutions, their legal and regulatory framework, and their infrastructures, such as the payment, clearing, and settlement systems. The financial system is functioning well because it has met the two conditions: First, agents have access to the information they need to allocate capital to the most productive investment projects, and second, risk is managed in such a way that it is assumed by those who are most prepared to do so. This type of financial system also contributes to reducing volatility in consumption and investment. It buffers the real economy from harmful shocks, making growth less volatile.

Efficiency of the Canadian financial system has been increased by acting on three complementary paths. The first is by fostering competition in domestic and international markets. Competition stimulates innovation and efficiency. The second path adopted is reduced informational asymmetries through the adoption of certain transparency requirements. Here, the focus is not only on the quantity of the information revealed, but also on its relevance, which, in turn, depends on the specific nature of the market and the preponderance of benefits over costs. For example, the optimal degree of transparency could differ between the bond and the stock markets. Finally, efficiency is bolstered by promoting financial stability in general. When well-designed rules give rise to systemic stability, resources are freed up that can then be devoted to more productive ends. To a large extent, this is the purpose of the international standards in Basel II, which sets banks' regulatory capital requirements as a function of the individual risks assumed. And Canada has succeeded in adopting it.

In Canada, the Porter Commission, in 1964, on banking and finance recommended increasing competition, liberalizing markets, and creating a regulatory framework conducive to greater efficiency. The banks reacted to the new competitive environment by innovating and improving their efficiency. Canadian institutions became global leaders while foreign banks lagged, bound by more restrictive and less efficient regulatory regimes. For full thirty years, Canada maintained its lead in the world stage. Subsequent revisions to the law allowed greater competition between traditional pillars of finance, i.e. banking, insurance, brokerage, and trusts, thus driving down costs and increasing efficiency.

Efforts have focused on improving prudential regulation, which seeks to stabilize institutions and the financial system as a whole. The federal government created the office of the Superintendent of Financial Institutions and the Financial Institutions Supervisory Committee. The purpose of the latter is to facilitate the exchange of information between various federal bodies involved with financial stability, including the Bank of Canada.

Canada has introduced Large Value Transfer System (LVTS), an electronic system launched in 1999, and operated by the Canadian Payments Association. It meets or exceeds the highest international standards in matters of risk management, and does so at a fraction of the cost. In addition, the design of the LVTS minimizes the amount of collateral that each institution needs to pledge to the system, compared with the gross settlement systems used in other countries. This reduction in collateral frees up resources that can then be put to more efficient uses elsewhere.

Overall, there are significant benefits for consumers. They will have more choices in deciding who fulfils their financial needs. The reforms encourage new competitors in the marketplace, increased competition among existing institutions, and more innovative products and services. There are stronger accountability requirements for financial institutions, with a newly created body, the Financial Consumer Agency of Canada (FCAC), dedicated to consumer protection and education. The FCAC promotes consumer awareness of financial issues and ensures that financial institutions comply with federal consumer protection measures. The reforms also increase transparency and public awareness. Financial institutions are required to provide consumers with certain information when they purchase services or make investments, and must give sufficient notice when closing a branch. In other matters, the restructuring of Canadian stock exchanges at the end of the 1990s allowed specialization and solidified the market position. Since that time, the Montréal and Toronto stock exchanges, and the TSX Venture Exchange have experienced remarkable expansion.

The competitive capacity of the Canadian economy depends largely on the ability of its financial sector to compete on the world stage. The Canadian economy has ensured that the rules, and their implementation, are adapted to domestic requirements and reflect the diversity in size and complexity of the publicly traded companies. Therefore, it has regulated the behaviour of market operators who are to be monitored and that violators be prosecuted and appropriately punished. A regulatory framework that ensures strict application of the law and which punishes dishonest players will reinforce the credibility of markets and investor confidence.

In sum, Canada has succeeded in ensuring efficiency of the financial system by ensuring: trust and transparency. With trust in place, social capital is earned and out of this the list of economic benefits for Canada is long indeed. Less time, energy, and money is being spent on protecting oneself against inflation. Labour and financial contracts have lengthened, while the amount of time lost to strikes and lockouts has dropped. The Bank of Canada has dramatically increased the number of opportunities for updating Canadians on the economic outlook. It shares the thinking on the economy. It wants Canadians to have a good grasp of what the goals are and of the framework they use to achieve those goals. This transparency enhances the Bank's accountability and reinforces the trust.

MONETARY POLICY IN CANADA

To ensure efficient functioning of the financial system, role of monetary policy is important. In a narrow sense, monetary policy is a user of the financial system. At the same time, solid monetary policy reduces costs and volatility in credit markets. More generally, a good monetary policy, like an efficient financial system, yields considerable benefits to a country's economy. In short, the Bank of Canada believes that by keeping inflation low, stable, and predictable, it maximizes its contribution to the well-being of Canadians.

The adoption of an inflation-targeting regime in 1991 stabilized inflation at approximately 2 per cent and provided an anchor for medium- and long-term expectations. Together with the restoration of fiscal health, this stability permitted a decline in both the level and the volatility of interest rates. Over the past 15 years or so, Canada has witnessed a sharp drop in short- and long-term interest rates, at times to levels lower than US rates.

The reduced uncertainty of all economic agents has paved the way for loans with longer terms to maturity. The ratio of long-term debt to total business debt has risen from 45 per cent in 1981 to over 70 per cent in 2003. Also, the benefits extend far beyond financial markets. The manner in which monetary policy responds to fluctuations in the business cycle also promotes greater stability in the economy, which then runs closer to its full capacity. For example, if a negative demand shock drives inflation below the 2 per cent target, interest rates are cut or held at lower levels than they would otherwise be, so as to bring economic activity back to production potential. Naturally, the bank's actions are symmetric, and interest rates will typically rise when an overheating economy threatens to drive inflation above target.

Having a credible monetary policy also makes it possible to abstain from reacting to most relative price shocks. For example, if a sudden jump in the world price of oil translates into a greater-than-expected rise in the CPI, the fact that Canada is focusing on inflation 18 to 24 months down the road means that she can ignore this effect, since it will likely to have no impact on inflation expectations.

Finally, a sound monetary policy facilitates the structural adjustments of the Canadian economy in two ways. First, high and variable inflation masks the strong economic signals conveyed by changes in relative prices. With inflation under control in Canada, firms and individuals are better able to understand what rising energy prices and the appreciating Canadian dollar mean for them, and in this way, they can make better-informed decisions. Second, resources released by sunset industries more easily migrate to growth sectors when the economy is running at full capacity.

Canadian rules and their application are tailored to the domestic needs and reflect domestic realities. The tension between domestic and international considerations leads to some challenges for Canadian policy makers. A case in point is the Sarbanes-Oxley law. Canadian policy makers embrace the general principles behind this legislation in terms of promoting good governance and financial practices. But the extreme level of detail in the application of its rules, as well as its focus on process instead of outcomes, creates costs for many of the firms and this may exceed the benefits to the system. Large Canadian corporations that want access to US capital markets have no choice—they must follow both the spirit and the letter of Sarbanes-Oxley. But Canadian regulators are right to take a made-in-Canada approach that accommodates the needs of Canadian issuers and investors. A framework with strong monitoring, prosecution, and application of penalties provides the incentives for firms to follow the rules, and this adds to the framework's credibility. When everyone is playing by the rules—and everyone is confident that others have the incentives to do the same—then markets operate with greater efficiency. And Canada has succeeded.

To sum up, because the economy is very open to world trade and finance, it is able to recognize today's global economic realities and to have the flexibility to adjust accordingly. Second, sound economic policies have a critical role to play in facilitating the necessary adjustments. Such policies include, importantly, a monetary policy aimed at keeping inflation low, stable, and predictable—to which the Bank of Canada is fully committed. Third, based on the history, there is every reason to believe that Canadian businesses and workers, facilitated by a well-reformed financial sector have risen to the current challenges and make the necessary adjustments to take advantage of the opportunities presented by an evolving and expanding global economy. Fourth, basic legal concepts, such as property rights, the rule of law, and the honouring of contracts, are in place in order for market forces to work and to generate wealth.

OTHER STEPS

A number of issues are also being considered to improve the existing financial system of Canada. The economy has been active in terms of research and commentary on developments aimed at improving efficiency. It has worked alongside the private sector to improve the safety and efficiency of clearing, payment, and settlement systems. For example, it has recently worked with various groups to make sure that participants are continuing to pursue more robust business-continuity plans, especially from a system-wide perspective. By increasing the degree of certainty that critical systems will be operational in times of disruption, the development of appropriate business-continuity plans can improve the overall efficiency of the financial system.

The economy is promoting innovations such as electronic trading systems, because they provide opportunities to reduce transactions costs and increase transparency to appropriate levels. This will increase liquidity and lead to better-functioning markets. And through research, commentary, and direct involvement, rules and codes of conduct are designed that improve the functioning of both fixed-income and foreign exchange markets.

Of course, one ongoing issue in the financial system is the question of consolidation among financial institutions. Canada is facing a difficult policy challenge as she tries to keep up with other countries that have enthusiastically adopted the competition-based regulatory philosophy espoused by the Porter Commission. She needs to strive for a policy framework that continues to provide incentives for innovation and efficiency by encouraging competition. At the same time, she has to consider how to allow the financial institutions the scope to improve efficiency through economies of scale.

Another issue that is being hotly debated relates to the ideal structure for securities regulators in Canada. Efficiency dictates that Canada should have uniform securities laws and regulations based on principles that apply to everyone. The key point is that, the application of rules needs to take into account the size and complexity of firms.

For example, one tier could apply to large, complex firms that want access to international capital markets. Rules for these firms would be similar to those that are applied in New York or London. At the other end of the spectrum, another tier could apply to small, speculative resource firms that have historically relied on Canadian equity markets for financing. A third tier in the middle could apply to the bulk of Canadian 'mid-cap' firms, which choose to access only Canadian capital markets, and which very often are smaller and less complex than US 'mid-cap' firms.

True, the Canadian financial sector has reformed up to the mark. What inhibits India? Which factors are responsible for the slow and sluggish growth of the Indian financial sector? Are the Canadian success stories worth emulating in the Indian context? Then, which intricacies should be taken care of so that the effort will not run futile?

CONCLUDING REMARKS

The Canadian experience underlines that opening of the financial system induces competition and ensures efficiency. The Canadian system works on the market philosophy and allows the economy and the population to adjust to the incentives and signals provided by the market. Still the system has stressed on research and commentary, innovations such as use of electronic trading system, so as to reduce transaction cost, improve transparency and allow the financial institutions the scope to improve efficiency through economies of scale. The whole process is consumer oriented, demand driven. To be specific, the system has stressed on efficiency, competition, consumer and flexibility.

Could these be emulated by the Indian financial system? Certainly, but it should be remodelled keeping in view the socio-economic peculiarities of the Indian system. The supply driven financial system of India has to broaden its outreach to encompass small saving masses. Here the formal financial institutions have to out-compete the informal ones. For this the banking procedure should be made simple, playing fields of the banks and the non-banking financial bodies have to be levelled and government intervention should be reduced. Reduced restriction on the foreign players could improve financial infrastructure of the system. A separate policy initiative for the small savers is called for. A system of consumer protection and consumer education could enrich confidence of the consumers in the financial system.

India has a lot to learn from Canada. What Canada has done is visible. But how it has done it, how far India could adopt the procedure and with what type of changes are worth observation.

SCOPE FOR FURTHER RESEARCH

There is a lot of scope for further research. There should be a comparative analysis of the financial sector reforms in India *vis-à-vis* Canada and to suggest measures for improvement in the performance of the Indian financial sector in the light of that in Canada. In-depth research could be taken up:

- to examine the intricacies of successful implementation of the reforms process of the Canadian economy and to assess whether these are worth emulating in the Indian context.
- to assess if the consumer-oriented approach of the Canadian process of reforms would succeed in India. If so, what steps are necessary in implementing such a process?
- to observe if India can adopt the flexibility and adaptability

to change by implementing sound macro-economic policies and structural reforms, as done by the Canadian economy. What structural bottlenecks are to be removed in ensuring such measures?

- to measure if India could go for the choice of a monetary policy framework, including an exchange rate system that will best serve the needs over the longer term as the economy become more and more integrated into the world economy.
- to study how adjustments in the Indian economy will also require a focus on social policies aimed at sharing the gains from global integration across income groups so as to strike a balance between the home front and external integration.
- to suggest how the Indian financial sector could improve its ability to assess the risk involved and then put the right price on that risk. And when concentrations of risk become too high for individual investors and lenders, how could the financial system be flexible enough to allow them to shift their risks and rebalance their loan and investment portfolios.
- to observe in which areas research should be taken up so that Indian financial sector could also come up to the mark.

REFERENCES

Global Financial Stability Report (GFSR), Washington DC., IMF, September 2006.

Reserve Bank of India, *Handbook of Statistics on the Indian Economy*, Mumbai: Reserve Bank of India, 2006.

Reserve Bank of India Bulletin, various issues.

Report on Trend and Progress of Banking in India, RBI, various issues.

Rajan, R. and E. Prasad, 'Fixing India's Financial System', *The Wall Street Journal*, 2008. www.livemint.com

Information about Canadian economy was obtained from different websites.

CHAPTER 12

Museums and Communities: The National and the Nations

STEPHEN INGLIS

When I began my career in museums as an undergraduate student of anthropology in British Columbia, a natural reaction to a proposal from a First Nation was to do what the white people did in Hollywood Westerns, circle the wagons, and get ready for a fight. When I wrote an article for the National Museum Association journal advocating the sharing of collections (Inglis 1979), a leading museum director suggested that I was a traitor to my tribe. When I asked him what tribe that was, he answered 'the museum tribe'. Much has changed since then.

I will discuss the participation of aboriginal people in museum activity, based on my experience working with the Canadian Museum of Civilization (CMC) located in the National Capital Region of Canada. I hope this will also be relevant to issues that museums are dealing with in many parts of the world.

The 'nations' in my title refers to the hundreds of political entities of aboriginal peoples in Canada, consisting of communities of First Peoples and their lands. People of First Nations have also been referred to as Indians, aboriginal, indigenous, or native people in Canada and most often as 'Natives Americans' in the United States. Indians or Native Indians are terms still in popular use.

*I wish to thank Calcutta University for hosting this lecture and particularly Prof. Somnath Bhattacharya, Dr. Dilip Roy and Dr. Atul Bhomick, teachers from my graduate studies as a Shastri scholar thirty years ago.

Canada has often been described as a nation made up of nations, and these refer to ethnic communities, who retain their cultural autonomy more vigorously than in many other culturally diverse countries, language communities, for example French-speaking people of Quebec, and those of First Nations, who are known by scientific evidence to have lived on this land for at least 10,000 and perhaps 20,000 years, been in contact with European visitors for 1,000 years and experienced setters from other places for about 400 years.

The 'national' of my title refers to national museums, which often make an attempt to represent a country and its peoples as a whole and make symbolic statements about sovereignty, territory and citizenship, while at the same time attempting to show respect for the aspirations and identities of particular groups (for an Indian discussion of this issue, see Singh 2003). Saloni Mathur has called for a new kind of critical training addressing the relationship between institutions like museums and communities on a global scale (Mathur 2005).

Wherever the location, the interests of First Nations and national museums inevitably involve tensions, occasionally outright disagreement and also often protracted negotiations, so it is always a pleasure to relate stories of successful events along the way. At the opening of the museum's major permanent exhibition on First Nations, in Spring 2003, one of the project consultants, Gloria Webster, a Kwakwakiwak from Alert Bay, B.C. came to the podium. Her first words were, 'Welcome to my museum'.

What are some of the issues and strategies for resolving them by which it was possible that a member of a First Nation would make common cause with a national museum?

The first issue is collections, or rather the physical or intellectual access to collections. These are the primary resource of the museum and in the case of CMC, include over 50,000 ethnological objects and some 2 million archaeological specimens. Collections also include narratives, songs (25,000 hours in the case of CMC) and photographic images as well as objects and in the case of audio-visual material from First Nations, many of these are 'owned', much like objects are owned in the Euro-American tradition. How does a museum provide access to people in small communities throughout the country as well as to scholars who traditionally had access? How are collections made relevant within the evolving realities of identity and citizenship (Laforet 2006).

One way is through negotiating loans, making copies, and using new technologies like digitization to expand and distribute on a larger scale than ever before. This sometimes means arranging special partnerships with Native Cultural Centres, who can host and distribute information on the local level.

Another is through involving First Nations in the ongoing documentation and description of the collections, by hosting groups, often elders, who have experiential knowledge of kinds of objects and how they are (were) made and used.

This has been extended in several cases to the ritual care of collections held by the museum, that is, arrangements for the periodic blessing of sacred objects, by, for example, offering prayers, and burning tobacco or sweetgrass. This requires special access to the storage areas by specialists and some imaginative decisions with respect to fire codes and other kinds of regulations.

Yet another is by involving First Nations in the development of collections, for example by recruiting and training field assistants in local communities for archaeological excavation and analysis, or for documentation of community events and traditional knowledge. First Peoples who carry on traditional skills of making objects also become involved in the museum collections through commissions to create pieces that augment the historical collections.

A much more dramatic and controversial means of providing access to collections is through what we call repatriation . . . the legal transfer of objects and collections to First Nations. We now regularly return thousands of human remains each year to the descendants of the dead, as well as the burial goods associated with them. These were collected early in the twentieth century, and is a kind of archaeology no longer pursued here.

We also periodically return objects of special sacred power. These are almost always based on a specific request and a bilateral negotiation.

But we don't just open the doors to museum storage. Most

of the collections were purchased legally and most were made for sale to outsiders by entrepreneurial artists, right back to the Cook voyages of the late eighteenth century. Most of what is now on display in ethnological museums throughout the world was made for sale to outsiders, although the long-term attempt to render ethnological value through notions of authenticity has obscured this. Much of this material is difficult to link to a modern community . . . sellers were not always owners, owners not always makers.

The CMC is currently involved in treaty negotiations with over 80 First Nations, all involving artefacts, and our first responsibility under the act that brought our institution into being is to retain and preserve our collections.

One of the first repatriations made by our museum and one of the first in Canada was the return of a collection of ceremonial objects to Alert Bay, the home of Gloria Webster, who I mentioned before. In this case, the objects had been confiscated under duress by government officials in pursuit of a law that made traditional ceremonies among her people illegal. These objects became the core of a museum/cultural centre in her village. In the ways I've described, we have made a special effort to make the collections accessible, particularly to communities in which they originated.

A second issue by which it has been possible to work most closely with First Nations is a change in the attitude toward interpretation. The representation of peoples in exhibitions and other forms of museum communication and education is another fundamental of museum work, and one that has traditionally been carefully and exclusively maintained within the institution. The 'discourse about others' is now a subject of discussion everywhere (Pieterse 2005). At CMC, all exhibitions, websites, publications and other ways in which information about First Peoples is passed from the museum to the public is now done collaboratively. Specialists from 'cultures of origin' and 'cultures of experience' now contribute to the museums productions as elders, consultants, knowledge bearers, advisors, co-curators, and curators. Gloria Webster was for over 10 years a member of the consultative committee of the First Peoples Hall.

Museum curators are advocates on behalf of the wider

participation of community specialists, but we don't encourage that they abandon their role by simply becoming facilitators of community viewpoints that are often diverse and contradictory. Rather, we have found ways of encouraging members of First Nations to develop curatorial skills. These include the establishment of an Aboriginal Training Programme, a one-year subsidized museum training programme for members of First Nations, a programme that has now graduated over 60 people. Another is the facilitation of the hiring and promotion of First Peoples in the curatorial area of the museum's activities, something that has resulted in an ethnology staff at CMC in which 4 of 8 curators are of native origin and work on projects much wider than their own communities.

The 'voice' in which the museum exhibitions 'speak' is now multivocal and can incorporate multiple points of view on a single issue. One example is the treatment of the peopling of North America in our First Peoples Hall. There, side by side, are presented an archaeological perspective involving maps of migration from what is now Asia and evidence from early encampments as well as stories documenting the origin of ancestors according to mythology and oral history.

Another development is the incorporation of First Nations contemporary art into ethnological contexts so that living people are commenting critically and in the first person on issues relating to their past and present (Phillips 2007). The leader and prophet of the Metis people, Louis Riel, who was hanged by the Canadian government for treason in 1885 was quoted as saying, 'My people will sleep for a hundred years, and when they awake, it will be the artists who give them back their spirit.' Although as late as the middle of the twentieth century almost no one would have considered this plausible, this is exactly what has happened.

Why does it matter? One reason is that museums are more popular than ever, and there has been a huge growth in audience. As a result, museums deliver more public information than ever before. Given the stake that both communities and museums have in the preservation of their cultural heritage and the role that they play in national life, it only makes sense that the custodians of a great deal of that information partner with communities in the maintenance and delivery of that information. Once mausoleums of the past, museums are now more often asking themselves about their relevance for the future.

Now that models for access to collections and for developing collaborative exhibitions are in full swing, there is much to refine and carry forward. There are also a whole range of new challenges to face. In closing, I'll discuss just one.

It is how national museums will integrate a more diverse and participatory view of First Nations cultures with the larger narratives of settlement and civilization. How do the rituals of place and community co-exist with the ritual of citizenship?

These narratives are often parallel or contradictory and now must now be faced with a new urgency and vitality. At CMC, we have approached this by presenting different versions of national history on different floors, overlapping in some ways but thematically separate. The First Peoples Hall uses the word 'we' in its texts to emphasize the vital presence of native cultures, and 'an encounter with strangers' to describe the arrival of Europeans. The Canada Hall begins with the arrival of the first Europeans and describes the successive waves of immigration, encounter with the environment and the original inhabitants as part of the challenge of 'nation building'.

History is a matter of fierce public debate in Canada, and one of the key points of contention, as it is in the other 'settler countries', is what happened between First Nations and settler governments. Also controversial is HOW to know what happened, that is how indigenous pasts related in oral histories can be reconciled with dominant historiographies based on written documents. This is a critical theoretical consideration in the abstract but also a practical one for courts and tribunals at which rights and benefits are being negotiated. There is currently no consensus about whether indigenous rights pre-existed the settler states, were extinguished and should now be restored, whether rights previously granted by the State, through treaties, etc., were ignored or withdrawn and should now be reinstated, or whether new rights based on a liberal democratic reading of fairness and history should now be established. There is also, of course, a sector of public sentiment that feels strongly that historical hindsight or reconciliation is nonsense.

Museums and other national institutions are directly implicated in how indigenous local histories are transformed into public history. They are in the forefront of revealing different versions of the past, often versions not included in dominant national histories. This will be a long-term challenge of bringing together the Nations and the National in public museums.

REFERENCES

Inglis, S., 'Cultural Readjustment: A Canadian Case Study', *Museum*, (Canadian Museums Association), Summer 1979.

Laforet, A., 'Good Intentions and the Public Good: Intangible Cultural Heritage in a National Memory Institution', paper presented at the conference on 'The Politics of Intangible Cultural Heritage', Harvard University, May 2006.

Mathur, S., 'Museums and Globalization', *Anthropological Quarterly*, Summer 2005, pp. 697-708.

Phillips, R., 'The Museum of Art-thropology: Twenty-first Century Imbroglios', *RES 57*, Autumn 2007, pp. 9-19.

Pieterse, J.N., 'Multiculturalism and Museums: Discourse about Others in the Age of Globalization', in Gerald Corsane (ed.), *Heritage, Museums and Galleries*, New York: Routledge, 2005, pp. 163-99.

Singh, K., 'The Museum as National', in Geeti Sen (ed.), *IIC Quarterly, India: A National Culture*, New Delhi: Sage, Summer 2003, pp. 176-96.

CHAPTER 13

The Value of Cultural and Academic Diversity: Observations about Hinduism in Canada*

PATRICIA DOLD

This paper draws upon perspectives on Hinduism from this author's experiences as a Professor of Religious Studies at secular universities in Canada since 1990 to highlight the differences betwee n secular scholarly and religious perspectives on religions generally and on Hinduism specifically. It offers a description of one Canadian Hindu community—the Hindu temple community of St. John's Newfoundland—to highlight the many activities of this community and outline some of its concerns and goals.[1] This essay aims to demonstrate that although the goals and methods of the secular study of religion differ considerably from those of a religious community, there are contexts in which these differences can complement rather than conflict. This complementarity underscores the value of preserving a variety of perspectives on Hinduism within academia. While one would not argue that such complementarity is only possible in Canadian contexts, certain Canadian cultural ideals create an environment conducive to mutual respect and cooperation within a diverse community.

*An earlier draft of this paper was presented at Banaras Hindu University on 28 February 2008 in celebration of the Shastri Institute's 40th Anniversary. At that time, I was a faculty research fellow of the Shastri Institute, conducting research on the Śākta *Mahābhāgavata Purāṇa* in Varanasi and also at Kāmākhyā Mandir in Assam. I thank the Institute for its support of my work and also thank Dr. Jha of BHU for organizing the lecture.

I begin, therefore, with general observations about Canadian cultural ideals. Canada sees itself as a secular nation, multicultural and religiously plural. I must emphasize that these are ideals rather than actualities. Not all Canadians share the ideals and even where the ideals of secularism, multiculturalism, and religious pluralism are held, they are complicated in practice.[2] Christianity and European culture characterize the identity of a majority,[3] and 'secular' public institutions, while insisting they honour all cultures and religions, continue to privilege Christianity. For example, government and educational institutions observe Christianity's holy days at Easter and Christmas as 'holidays', but there is no such recognition for holy days of any other religion. On the other hand, officials representing the municipal, provincial, and federal levels of (secular) government actively recognize the diverse religious communities of the nation and often do so in the name of multiculturalism.

For example, on 22 July 2007, Prime Minister Stephen Harper, Federal Liberal leader Stephane Dion, Ontario Premier Dalton McGuinty, and David Millar, Mayor of Toronto attended the opening of a new Swaminarayan complex in Toronto, Ontario. Speaking on behalf of the Government of Canada, the prime minister declared the new temple open with words that express the ideal of cultural diversity: 'Located in the country's most ethnically diverse city, the facility stands as a testament to Canada and India's proud traditions of pluralism.'[4] The Swaminarayan temple is part of a larger complex that also includes the Canadian Museum of Cultural Heritage of Indo-Canadians. As described in the same Government of Canada press release quoted above, this museum is seen to embody the ideal of multiculturalism:

> While the Mandir will provide an additional place of worship for local Hindus, the museum will inspire visitors to appreciate how the spiritually diverse, multi-ethnic, multi-linguistic heritage of Indo-Canadians has contributed to the fields of arts, architecture, science, democracy, education, and pluralism.

This is the multicultural ideal: that each cultural group forms its own part of the Canadian mosaic, maintaining a distinctive identity while contributing to the nation as a whole. And so, as the press release also reports:

> The Prime Minister also thanked His Divine Holiness Pramukh Swami Maharaj, the Inspirer [*sic*] of the Swaminarayan Complex, saying that he has given a great and wonderful gift to the people of Canada.

'This awe-inspiring work of architectural brilliance will serve as a source of pride for not just Indo-Canadians, but indeed all Canadians,' said Prime Minister Harper.

The national ideals of multiculturalism and religious pluralism have an impact on the place of religion and instruction on and about religion in Canadian schools. At all levels of education in Canada, both religious and secular educational institutions exist. For most of Canadian history, for example, the Roman Catholic Church has run its own schools. This author was educated in the Separate School System in Calgary, Alberta, a system supported financially by the tax dollars of Roman Catholics while the public school system's funding is drawn from non-Catholic and non-Christian tax contributions. In the province of Newfoundland and Labrador, schools became secular only in 1994. Prior to this, almost all schools in Newfoundland were run by Christian churches.

Nevertheless, and regardless of a school's religious or secular character, all schools must satisfy requirements set by (provincial) governments to receive public funding and accreditation. World religions are taught in schools, both public and private/religious. In many cases, the high school curriculum offers a course introducing the major religions of the world and instruction is also offered in some education systems for early school years. One of the very active members of the St. John's Indian and Hindu communities, Dr Smita Joshi, served as a manager of curriculum development in the Education Department of the provincial government of Newfoundland and Labrador. Part of her work was the development a World Religions curriculum for the early school years and these curriculum materials have attracted international attention.[5] The Newfoundland and Labrador Department of Education curriculum guide for

Religious Studies at the High School level echoes the national multicultural ideal as it asserts the need for education on religion:

> In a world that is truly multi-cultural and multi-faith it is important that each person can value and celebrate his/her own faith (religious heritage or commitment). However, with accurate information about other religions the individual should recognize that others have religious beliefs that they value and celebrate as well. Religious and denominational intolerance will be eliminated only when people are more understanding of the intrinsic worth of religious views and traditions that are not their own. An effective religious education program should give accurate information and demonstrate respect for all world faiths. (*Religious Education, World Religions 3101/3106: A Curriculum Guide*, 7)[6]

For adult students, religion is taught in both secular academic universities and traditional religious contexts such as Christian seminaries and Bible colleges, and many of the latter maintain connections to secular institutions. At Memorial, for example, Queens Theological College is housed on the campus, shares the university library, and occasionally shares teaching resources with Memorial's Department of Religious Studies.

However, the study of religion within secular, publicly funded education systems cannot promote or otherwise favour any one religion over others. At the same time, university professors are often expected to contribute to the community beyond the boundaries of campus, to use and apply our academic work for practical, social, or general cultural goals.[7] As a professor specializing in Hindu religious traditions, I have a professional responsibility to be of service to the local Hindu community in St. John's. To do so means I must bring my expertise as a secular scholar of religion into a non-secular context, a context where my stance of religious neutrality will likely conflict with the religious stance(s) of members of the community.

It was, therefore, with some anxiety that, in April 2007, I delivered my first presentation at the Hindu temple in St. John's about my role as a Professor of Religious Studies at a secular, publicly funded university. I began by emphasizing the need for religious neutrality in the secular contexts of my courses, my teaching, and my research. In other words, I began by underlining the differences between my methods and goals as a secular academic and the assumed methods and goals of a religious community.

In my academic work, I must be impartial towards all religions collectively. I cannot say that any one is true or that its practices are effective for reaching the goals of practice as taught by the tradition, whereas others are false or ineffective. Like many of my colleagues in religious studies, I understand that the ideal of my discipline lies in the suspension of belief and disbelief. As much as possible, I must set aside judgements about religious truth. Religious studies as a secular academic discipline must not privilege any one religion over another, nor can it accept any one religious authority's claim to speak for the entire religion. As much as humanly possible, I must conduct research and teaching from a neutral stance, and analyse using religiously neutral standards. Like many in the contemporary practice of Religious Studies (and academia generally), I recognize that in our work we must continually scrutinize our assumptions, stance, and methods of analysis to ensure maximum neutrality.

The demands of secular academia can and do conflict with broader social realities, including religious realities, even within the supposedly secular context of the university. On the one hand, in Canada we live and work in a 'multi-culture' that is religiously plural. Therefore, the curriculum of secular educational institutions must include the study of the religions of the world. Christianity in particular cannot be privileged over any other religion or religions precisely because of its massive historical influence in Canadian society and in the work of even secular academics. On the other hand, Christianity's prominence in Canadian history and contemporary Canadian culture creates another imperative for education: according to some, the study of Christianity should be an essential part of the curriculum if our programmes are to properly prepare students to function in our own culture. My own department has faced this particular tension: should our programme require the study of Christianity without imposing the same level of requirement for the study of every other religion? Would a special requirement to study Christianity represent a breach of religious neutrality or merely a response to objective fact?

Religious Studies as a secular academic discipline also must confront the still common assumption that one can only study religion religiously: by accepting a religion as true while seeking to fulfil or achieve its goals. I have been either student or professor at four different universities in Canada, and have encountered this view among professors of other disciplines: 'I didn't think it was possible to study religion in a non-theological way', they say. As a Department of Religious Studies at Memorial, we still find we must explain ourselves to colleagues and administrators. And moreover: we find we must justify our discipline as one that belongs in a secular academic institution.[8]

But religious studies, as a secular academic discipline, holds that much can be learned about human being by studying religion in a non-confessional manner: there is much to be understood about religions while leaving aside judgements about religious truth, and while setting aside one's own beliefs as much as humanly possible. Of course, this approach also means there is much we do not know as secular scholars: we cannot know what is means to be an active member in another religion. We cannot experience directly what it is to belong to each tradition we study.

Like many of my colleagues, I often begin my courses by explaining to my students that we will be learning about religions, not learning religion; that I do not teach a religion, I teach about religions. I understand my own teaching method to be the presentation of a variety of perspectives; secular academic and traditional religious—and there is variety and diversity in each of these broad categories. Not only do secular scholars disagree frequently in their interpretation of data, their methods often draw from different disciplines: history, textual criticism, anthropology, psychology, philosophy, linguistics and more. Traditional religious perspectives include those of established authorities—who often offer different if not conflicting perspectives—but also the words and actions of religious people in day-to-day life—who also often have unique perspectives. I often juxtapose different perspectives and frequently I juxtapose a religious perspective with that of secular historical scholarship. I warn students that a first encounter with a secular academic perspective on one's own religious tradition can be quite shocking. It is not unusual to have difficulty recognizing one's own tradition in secular academic treatments of it. I assure them that the secular study of religion in which we engage in the classroom does not seek to dismantle, replace, or dictate personal religious belief.

Although I expect my students to learn about all the perspectives we study, the simple fact that we are in a secular institution means that the secular academic perspective is privileged over religious perspectives. And more: the simple fact that my own discipline developed in the Christian West means that its fundamental assumptions are more Western than they are Asian and more Christian than they are Hindu.

According to the ideals of academia, I should be prompted to acknowledge this imbalance through an ongoing process of self-examination inherent in my discipline; through 'the well-established but often neglected practice of examining hermeneutic prejudice' (Patton et al. 2006: 292). However, the critique that inspires me here came from Hindu academics in the United States who charge that the secular study of Hinduism by scholars in the West is fundamentally Western; that it distorts Hinduism beyond recognition through the imposition of outsider categories and values, which are not religiously or culturally neutral (Tilak 2006). These charges have led to a number of different responses and developments, including serious re-examination of the discipline by Hindu and non-Hindu scholars.[9]

Recognizing that the imposition upon Hinduism of Western philosophical categories and Western academic methods is unacceptable, several scholars are encouraging re-examinations of Hindu and Indian thought for alternate categories and methods.[10] Further, the Gandhian principle of *satyagraha* has been proposed as a tool for resolving the conflict between the present critics and defenders of Hindu Studies in the American academy (Tilak 2006: 283-5; Patton et al. 2006: 288).

I will make a small contribution here to this kind of effort, though I would point out that this strategy is not entirely new, that many scholars prior to the early 1990s structured their scholarship and teaching around Hindu categories and methods.

My teaching in religious studies and also my research on

Hindu traditions involves presentation of many *darśanas*, many perspectives on any one religious phenomenon. The six *darśanas*, once they were grouped as such were traditionally understood to represent orthodox perspectives on the Vedas and Vedic truth. In other words, they represent multiple perspectives on the Vedas. Furthermore, certain of these *darśanas* come to be seen as compatible or complementary, not opposed. Sāṃkhya and Yoga, Mīmāṃsā and Vedānta, Nyāya and Vaiśeṣika came to be paired with each other and in these pairings, each offered a comprehensive religious vision (Flood 1996: 230-2; Lipner 1994 154-60). To a degree, each *darśana* is true within its own framework or context although certain *darśanas*, Vedānta, for example, emphasized the superiority of their own school even as they acknowledged a lesser place to others.

Similarly, the secular academic and traditional religious perspectives on any religious phenomenon studied in a university course might be compatible, complementary, conflicting, or opposed, and very often each perspective can be seen to express truth within a particular framework. Though conflict is perhaps strongest and most frequent between secular and religious perspectives, it also occurs between different secular academic perspectives: historians see historical change where literary analysts see creative juxtaposition of style or philosophers find philosophical debate or exploration, for example.

I realize that multiple *darśanas* are not always maintained in individual Hindu traditions and that one cannot simply equate Hinduism or even orthodox Vedic schools[11] with the six *darśanas* or with a multi-perspectival stance. As well, I recognize there are differences between my approach to a plurality of perspectives and the attitudes one finds within and among Hindu traditions including the six *darśanas*. The parallel I propose is merely a starting point.[12]

A multi-*darśana* approach is not easy for students. They often complain about having to learn five different perspectives as well as a concept itself. I do not expect students to learn any one perspective—secular or religious—as the whole sole truth and I emphasize that our work in the course does not concern what they should personally believe to be truth. I do, however, expect them to know accurately the content of different perspectives. In other words, though I cannot change the secular nature of the context of my work, or the history of Western academia, I do attempt to treat all perspectives—religious and non-religious as equally valuable in their own context.

Goals of multi-*darśana* study include cultivating a quality that Hinduism possesses, the ability to hold multiple perspectives simultaneously. Julius Lipner (1996) calls this 'polycentrism' and proposes it as a chief mark of 'Hinduness'. As discussed in their interlogue, Patton, Ram-Prasad and Acharya (2006) see this ability as a prerequisite for meaningful exchange and conflict resolution in the American academy.

This polycentric ability is not only a kind of expansion of one's mind; it is also to engage in cultivating knowledge and understanding of oneself and another, while suspending judgement. In almost 18 years of teaching, I have often been told by students that they find religious studies gives them a respect for others' cultures and religions and also, in many cases, a new respect for their own. At the University of Alberta in Edmonton especially, I had many students of Indian and Hindu backgrounds, sometimes more than 50 per cent of students in a class of 50 to 60 students. Many of these students were second or third generation Hindu/Indo-Canadians who, as young adults had a thirst for knowledge about Indian cultural heritage and Hindu religious traditions. After or even during course work on Hindu traditions, some students would take their course learning and their further questions back to their Indian and Hindu communities and families, often to the delight of parents and temple associations. This effect is also experienced by non-Hindu students engaged in the secular academic study of their religious traditions. In Newfoundland, for example, where Christianity is more dominant than in many other parts of the country and where the primary and secondary school systems were governed by Christian churches until 1994, many students do not know the narratives of the Bible, let alone its theological contents. Some of these students too, are receptive to learning about religion in a secular context whereas they resist learning from their parents and/or church authorities. Religious studies as a secular discipline sometimes opens doors (the temple, the church, even the home) that might otherwise remain closed. In a context dominated by secular values and a scientific world-view, young adults are often pulled in contradictory directions and perhaps for some, a multi-perspectival approach to religion provides an opportunity to resolve some of the contradictions between tradition and modernity.

In my research on the Śākta *Mahābhāgavata Purāṇa* also, I have found the notion of multi-perspectivalism useful. This text, like other Śākta texts, insists that the goddess herself is the subtle, formless *brahman* and that *brahman* is only *śakti*.[13] Yet, the text celebrates the goddess's physical forms and portrays Śiva as her greatest devotee who, though he constantly meditates on her formless essence, longs to keep her feet on his heart (Dold 2005: 108-19; *Mahābhāgavata Purāṇa* 20.25-38 & 23.1-28). For a long time, I probed this text to try to find a clear ranking of the physical *versus* non-physical natures of the goddess. Unable to find a consistent hierarchy in the text's theology, I considered the possibility that the text wishes to emphasize the supremacy of both the physical forms and the non-physical *brahman* that is *śakti* (Dold 2005: 220-1). This text's insistence on both positions might reflect the text's connection to the Śākta pilgrimage site of Kāmarūpa (now called Kāmākhyā, which is also the name of its presiding goddess). Texts that avoid identifying only one absolute truth, or one orthodox position, might help preserve the broad appeal of a pilgrimage site. However, Julius Lipner's discussion of Hindu polycentrism (1996) suggests that the *Mahābhāgavata's* stance is characteristic of Hinduism.

Lipner finds several examples of polycentrism within the theology of Rāmānuja. For example, not only does Rāmānuja acknowledge both a transcendent and an immanent aspect of *brahman*, but also the theological importance of the complementarity of these apparently opposed aspects (1996: 113-16). Lipner further develops his exploration of polycentrism as the chief mark of 'Hinduness' with examples from Śaiva Siddhānta—its recognition of multiple authoritative Vedas is a 'multicentrism of scriptural authority' (1996: 118)—and in the multiple considerations entailed by the 'subtlety of dharma' in the *Mahābhārata* (1996: 121). Against the background of

Lipner's discussion of polycentrism, the *Mahābhāgavata's* Śākta stance becomes a narrative theological polycentrism.

Diversity and a deliberate cultivation of multiple perspectives also characterize the Hindu community in St. John's, presently centered at a Kṛṣṇa temple the community built in 1995. The Hindu community, like the larger Indian community in St. John's, is culturally and linguistically diverse with significant number of Tamil, Telugu, Gujarati, Bengali and Hindi members. As a whole, the community is highly professionalized and highly knowledgeable in Hindu traditions and Indian arts; its membership includes several classically trained musicians and singers, a practicing Ayurvedic specialist who has clients from eastern and central Canada as well as the United States. Some members are trained in Vedic recitation, several have studied as well as memorized the Upaniṣads, the *Bhagavadgītā*, and/or a repertoire of *bhajans*. Many are excellent cooks who regularly provide communal meals after worship at the temple. The community is small[14]—perhaps 100 families—but the community is so productive that one has the impression it is much larger.

The temple association has produced a publication to facilitate temple worship called *Prayers and Bhajans*, an impressive collection of hymns from a wide range of Sanskrit and vernacular sources, as well as other texts, such as the Chinmaya Mission pledge that emphasizes belief in God as creator and sustainer of life and a promise to worship and serve family, community, and nation.[15] The volume is amply and variously illustrated with photographs, line drawings, and images from popular and classical art. Many of the hymns and other texts are presented in the original language and script as well as in transliteration and English translation.

Though the temple is dedicated to Kṛṣṇa and the permanent *mūrti* reflects this focus, the temple celebrates ritual and festival for many different deities, and often does so in a manner that represents traditions specific to particular regions of India. Durgā Pūjā, for example, is celebrated in Bengali style with a Durgā Mahiṣamārdinī *mūrti* set up at one side of the main hall by Bengali members, while a south Indian style of worship is represented in a multi-level *mūrti* tableau of *mūrtis* and dolls set up on the other side of the hall. The temple's major *pūjā* service,[16] held Sunday mornings, often beginning at 10:30 sharp, includes congregational *bhajan* singing and typically features a talk given by members of the community or guests and is often followed by a communal meal. There is variety in these talks, as illustrated by the following sampling of titles from 2007: 'Dashavataram—The Ten Incarnations', 'Jiva is Shiva', 'Panca-bhramas from the *Annapurna Upanishad*'. 'Wisdom and Stability of Mind as Explained in the *Geeta*', 'The Messages of Shri Basaveshvar: A Great Social Reformer of the Twelfth Century and a Pioneer in the Evolution of Veerashaiva Dharma', and 'The Chanting of the *Rigveda*: The First Hymn and its Explanation'. Sometimes the presentation is a group effort: in December of 2007, there was a discussion panel presenting different views on the proposition that 'ritual is an obstacle in religious practice'. Following a week-long visitation in 2007 from Swami Tatvavidanand from the Chinmaya Center in Saylorsburg PA, members of the community were invited to present and discuss their experiences of his lectures.

The community works hard to preserve Hindu traditions. But like any Hindu community outside India, the St. John's community adapts its religious practices to its diaspora home. *Visarjan* of festival *mūrtis* like that used for Ganeśa Caturthī takes place at Middle Cove, a short drive from the temple, but the *mūrti* is retrieved for use again in next year's celebration. *Pūjā* takes place daily, but the largest number of worshippers attend the Sunday morning *pūjā*. Worship typically is a group effort and often takes a congregational form. Since the temple has no priest in any formal sense, it relies on the expertise of different individual members for leadership. Every year, the community sponsors visit(s) from a Swami of the Chinmaya association and plays host to the Swami who gives lectures, the opportunity for *darśana*, and instruction on meditation. For most of the year though, the community relies on individual members to volunteer to conduct meditation sessions, conduct *pūjā* and lead the singing of *bhajans*, give talks and other performances, and prepare the meals served following Sunday *pūjā*.

The St. John's Hindu Temple community is proactive in asserting its place within the Canadian society and is involved in local charity work and social activism. The temple contributes financially to such causes and sponsors presentations on poverty in Newfoundland to encourage members to work with various local agencies as they combat poverty and lobby politicians to address social issues.

The temple community also participates in local St. John's events. For example, Regatta Day, the first Wednesday in August is the most important civic holiday in St. John's. Most businesses are closed so that all may gather at Quidi Vidi lake to watch the rowing competitions and eat food from the various pavilions including that of the Hindu community, which prepares and sells hundreds of *samosas*, raising funds for local charities. The temple community also develops Hindu celebrations for Canadian holidays and so, for example, it has created a Hindu Canada Day event to mark the nation's celebration of its birth on 1 July Members of the St. John's community begin their celebration with a sunrise meditation and yoga practice at Cape Spear. The most easterly point in North America, Cape Spear is a cool, wind swept, 'head' of land featuring the rocky shores so characteristic of the island of Newfoundland. I suspect that the landscape of Newfoundland helps inspire such creativity, but the inspiration itself and the religious practice developed are clearly Hindu.

The Hindu temple in St. John's opens its doors to the larger community in several ways. *Pūjā* is open to all and on Sundays, newcomers are invited to introduce themselves and to stay on for the meal. In early autumn, numerous sites in St. John's including the Hindu temple offer tours of their facilities to the public during the 'Doors Open' weekend. But perhaps the biggest open event at the temple is a Saturday evening cultural programme and dinner, followed by fireworks, during the celebration of Diwali. The dinner is prepared and served by members of the temple community. The event draws its audience from all over the island and though the majority of the guests are Hindu and/or Indian Canadians, some are white, Anglo-European Canadians. Typically, the temple invites a few special guests: local and provincial politicians and also representatives of local charities. The evening's programme includes speeches from members and guests, the presentation of the temple community's donations to local charities, performances of classical, folk, and modern styles of Indian music and dance, and a Rām Līlā.

In 2008, the Rām Līlā involved approximately thirty actors, children and young adults, in the creation of several tableaus: Rama as a child, Rāma and Lakṣmaṇa departing with Viśvāmitra, Sītā's *svayamvara*, the announcement of Rāma's exile, and the kidnapping of Sītā. Actors for each scene took their positions on stage to the left, right or centre, and, as the lights went up on their part of the stage, used gesture and expression rather than dialogue to tell the story. The arrival of Hanumān, the defeat of Rāvaṇa, and the reunion of Rāma and Sītā were performed through dance and gesture accompanied by the song 'Pal Pal Hai Bhari', from *Swadesh* (Ashutosh Gowariker, 2004).

Five of the actors this year were university students—white Anglo-European students from my classes at the university, and four of them from a course I teach on the *Rāmāyaṇa* as a literary and performance tradition. All five students, cast as Daśaratha, Kauśalyā, Kaikeyī, Mantharā, and Hanumān, participated with great enthusiasm and gratitude for the opportunity to *experience* some part of the Hindu traditions they were studying. The organizers of the Līlā also were pleased to be able to present such a diverse cast of actors for the temple event and impressed that outsiders would volunteer with such dedication and energy.

The entire Līlā delighted the audience but I think most in attendance would agree that the loudest cheers went to Hanumān during his acrobatic and devotion filled performance of Shahrukh Khan's role (as Mohan Bhargava) in the 'Pal Pal Hai Bhari' segment. In the Līlā, Hanumān leapt and did flips across the stage as he confronted demons and finally, at the end, revealed the image of Rāma and Sītā in his heart (a paper print glued to the actor's chest and revealed when he ripped open his T-shirt). At this, the audience applauded and cheered most enthusiastically and later a fellow cast-member declared that this was 'the best white Hanumān ever!'

Audience members noted all of the students' contributions with approval and appreciation. One person, recognizing the students' understanding of the *Rāmāyaṇa*, told me, 'You could tell by their expressions that they knew what they were doing; they understood their role in the Līlā.' Another commented directly on the mutually beneficial nature of the event: saying, that these students' participation was the 'best example of academia in the community.'

The participation of these white, Anglo-European students could not have happened in the absence of mutual trust and respect between the secular academic community on the one hand and the Hindu community on the other. I am convinced that the students' respect for and knowledge of Hinduism made them welcome as participants in the production of the Līlā. The Hindu community's respect for and knowledge of my academic work in my teaching on Hindu traditions helped create an atmosphere in which people of diverse religious and cultural background could come together to create an experience that satisfied individual and collective needs.

But the broader context here surely has an impact as well. The particular struggles and determination of the St. John's Hindu community as a minority Canadian community and as a Hindu diaspora community, the multicultural ideals of Canadian society, and also the multi-perspectival character of Hindu traditions—all of these contribute to an atmosphere in which the secular academic and the religious perspectives can complement even as they differ. Indeed, it is precisely their differences that make their respectful encounter, profound.

NOTES

1. There are many studies of the global Hindu diaspora and of Hindu diaspora communities in Britain, Canada and the United States. See, for example, Vertovec (2000); Coward et al. (2000); Wahorne (2004); Varma and Seshan (2005); and Brown (2006).
2. For an overview of issues pertaining to religion and government policy in Canada, see Bramadat (2008).
3. According to the 2001 census, 22,851,825 Canadians (77.1 per cent of the total responses) identified as Christian see 'Population by Religion, by Province and Territory (2001 Census)' at <http://www40.statcan.gc.ca/l01/cst01/demo30a-eng.htm?sdi=religion>. Source: *Statistics Canada, Census of Population*. Retrieved 18 February 2008). On ethnicity, see 'Population by selected ethnic origins, by province and

territory (2001 Census)' at <http://www40.statcan.gc.ca/l01/cst01/demo26a-eng.htm> Retrieved 18 February 2008 and 'Canada's Ethnocultural Mosaic, 2006 Census: Highlights.' *Statistics Canada. 2006 Census: Analysis Series.* <http://www12.statcan.ca/english/census06/analysis/ethnicorigin/highlights.cfm> Retrieved 20 December 2008.

4. 'Prime Minister Stephen Harper officially opens BAPS Swaminarayan Complex' Office of the Prime Minister, Press Release, 22 July 2007, Toronto. <http://www.pm.gc.ca/eng/media.asp?category=1&id=1768> 10 February 2008.
5. Numerous curriculum documents are available at the Government of Newfoundland and Labrador website: www.ed.gov.nl.ca/edu/sp/rel_edu.htm. My thanks to Dr Joshi for drawing my attention to these programmes and materials.
6. <www.ed.gov.nl.ca/edu/sp/rel_edu.htm> (17 February 2008).
7. Donald Wiebe (2006) argues that the academic study of religion should not promote religion or religions collectively in any way. To pursue such social or cultural goals implies a positive bias in favour of religion and makes the discipline of Religious Studies into an 'intellectual practice of religion'.
8. Donald Wiebe (2006) argues that although Religious Studies in Canada has successfully distanced itself from sectarian, denominational, and/or Christian religious practice, it continues to insist on Religious Studies's unique character as an academic discipline in that it should engage religious questions and contribute to the religious life of its students and of society. If Wiebe is correct in concluding that Religious Studies in Canada has become 'the learned practice of religion', then we should not be surprised by colleagues' questions about Religious Studies as a secular discipline.
9. See for example, Caldwell and Smith (2000), who introduce several articles on the question 'Who speaks for Hinduism?' For brief overviews of the critique and ensuing developments, see Dhand (2005: 274-86) and Hawley and Narayanan (2006: 25-6).
10. See, for example, Patton et al. 2006. White (2003: 3-7) proposes Tantra as a potential subaltern category through which Indian religious history might be reinterpreted in order to correct and replace the distorted histories of colonial and elitist scholarship. He does not, it should be noted, link this proposal to the critique of scholarship under discussion here. Rather, the proposal is presented as a next logical step in the history of scholarship on Indian religious history.
11. Śaiva Siddhāntā, as noted by Lipner (1994: 159), is one of several schools omitted from the traditional list yet deserving to be included.
12. Indeed, my multiple-*darśana* approach echoes Lipner's discussion of

polycentrism (1996 and see below, pp. 14-15) as a chief mark of 'hinduness' (*hindutva*) and also several of the 'metavalues' identified by L. Patton, C. Ram-Prasad and K. Acharya (2006). These metavalues are academic values identifiable also with the values of specific Indic traditions. First is the value attached to accurate presentation of all available opinion on a matter of philosophical debate in Vedic commentarial tradition and in debate between Advaita and Nyāya philosophers. This value, the authors take as an essential pre-condition for interlogue (*samvada*); for real transformative exchange (p. 292). Similarly, such accurate representation must characterize my presentation of multiple perspectives if the exercise is to be genuine. Likewise with their metavalues of multiplicity (in Yaska's recognition of multiple schools of Vedic interpretation) (p. 295), of contextuality of both text and individual (in Jaimini's commentaries of *Mīmāṃsā Sūtras*) (p. 296), of incrementalism in learning (*upāya*) culminating in the requirement to read many scholarly interpretations in areas of controversy (pp. 296-7), of building community (by choosing battles carefully as Kṛṣṇa does in the *Mahābhārata* always in the interest of dharma) (p. 297), and of reflexivity (in the commentarial traditions of the *darśanas* where sages of the past are honoured but freedom exists for contemporary adaptation) (p. 298).

13. See, for example, *Mahābhāgavata Purāṇa* 1.25-37, and especially 1.35-36 [translated in Dold, 2005: 229-32). The Sanskrit edition used is Kumar (1983)].
14. According to the 2001 Canadian census, 405 people (out of 508,080 total) in the province of Newfoundland and Labrador identified as Hindus, see 'Population by religion, by province and territory 2001 Census)' at http://www40.statcan.gc.ca/l01/cst01/demo30a-eng.htm?sdi=religion. Source: *Statistics Canada, Census of Population.* Retrieved, 18 February 2008).
15. Available at <www.chinmayamission.com/cm-pledge.php?PHPSESSID=92b2e48250a09a0efaba4dd66b279165> (3 January 2009).
16. There is daily *pūjā* at the temple as well, but only the Sunday *pūjā* includes group *bhajan* singing and a talk.

REFERENCES

Bramadat, Paul, 'Religion and Public Policy in Canada: An Itinerary', *Studies in Religion*, vol. 37, no. 1, 2008, pp. 121-43.

Brown, Judith M., *Global South Asians: Introducing the Modern Diaspora*, Cambridge: Cambridge University Press, 2006.

Caldwell, Sarah and Brian K. Smith, 'Introduction: Who Speaks for Hinduism', *Journal of the American Academy of Religion*, vol. 68, no. 4, pp. 705-10.

Coward, Harold, John R. Hinnells and Raymond Brady Williams (eds.), *The South Asian Religious Diaspora in Britain, Canada, and the United States*, Albany: State University of New York Press, 2000.

Dhand, Arti, 'Hinduism to Hindus in the Western Diaspora', in *Method and Theory in the Study of Religion*, vol. 17, 2005, pp. 274-86.

Dold, Patricia, 'The Religious Vision of the Śākta *Mahābhāgavata Purāṇa*', Ph.D. dissertation, McMaster University, 2005.

Flood, Gavin, *An Introduction to Hinduism*, Cambridge: Cambridge University Press, 1996.

Hawley, John Stratton and Vasudha Narayanan, 'Introduction', *The Life of Hinduism*, Berkeley: University of California Press, 2006, pp. 1-29.

Hindu Temple (St. John's) Association, *Prayers and Bhajans*, 3rd edn., St. John's, NL: Hindu Temple (St. John's) Association, 2006.

Kumar, Pushpendra, *The Mahābhāgavata Purāṇa: Ancient Treatise on Śakti Cult*, Delhi: Eastern Book Linkers, 1983.

Lipner, Julius, 1994, *Hindus: Their Religious Beliefs and Practices*, London: Routledge.

——, 1996, 'Ancient Banyan: An Inquiry into the Meaning of "Hinduness'", *Religious Studies* 32, 1: 109-26.

Office of the Prime Minister, 2007, 'Prime Minister Stephen Harper Officially Opens BAPS Swaminarayan Complex', Press Release, 22 July 2007, Toronto. <http://www.pm.gc.ca/eng/media.asp?category=1&id=1768> 10 February 2008.

Patton, Laurie L., Chakravarthi Ram-Prasad and Kala Acharya, 2006, 'Hinduism with Others: Interlogue', in John Stratton Hawley and Vasudha Narayanan (eds.), *The Life of Hinduism*, Berkeley: University of California Press, pp. 288-99.

Religious Education, World Religions 3101/3106: A Curriculum Guide, 2005, Division of Program Development, Department of Education, Government of Newfoundland and Labrador. Download available at <www.ed.gov.nl.ca/edu/sp/rel_edu.htm>. Accessed 17 February 2008.

Statistics Canada, 2006, 'Canada's Ethnocultural Mosaic, 2006 Census: Highlights', *Statistics Canada, 2006 Census: Analysis Series*. <http://www12.statcan.ca/english/census06/analysis/ethnicorigin/highlights.cfm>. Accessed 20 December 2008.

——, 2001, 'Population by Religion, by Province and Territory (2001 Census)', *Statistics Canada, Census of Population*. <http://www40.statcan.gc.ca/l01/cst01/demo30a-eng.htm?sdi=religion>. Accessed 18 February 2008.

——, 'Population by Selected Ethnic Origins, by Province and Territory (2001 Census)', *Statistics Canada, Census of Population*. <http://

www40.statcan.gc.ca/l01/cst01/demo26a-eng.htm>. Accessed on 18 February 2008.

Tilak, Shrinivas, 'Hinduism for Hindus: Taking Back Hindu Studies', in John Stratton Hawley and Vasudha Narayanan (eds.), *The Life of Hinduism*, Berkeley: University of California Press, 2006, pp. 271-87.

Varma, Sushma J. and Radhika Seshan (eds.), *Fractured Identity: The Indian Diaspora in Canada*, New Delhi: Rawat Publications, 2005.

Vertovec, Steven, *The Hindu Diaspora: Comparative Patterns*, London, New York: Routledge, 2000.

Wahorne, Joanne Punzo, *Diaspora of the Gods: Modern Hindu Temples in an Urban Middle-class World*, New York: Oxford University Press, 2000.

Weibe, Donald, 'The Learned Practice of Religion: A Review of the History of Religious Studies in Canada and its Portent for the Future', *Studies in Religion*, vol. 35, pp. 3-4 (*Special Issue: Religious Studies in Canada: Past, Present, and Future*), pp. 475-501.

White, David Gordon, *Kiss of the Yoginī: 'Tantric Sex' in its South Asian Contexts*, Chicago: University of Chicago Press, 2003.

CHAPTER 14

Re-Ethnization of Ethnic Groups: The Canadian Experience

G. KARUNANITHI

Canada's ethno-cultural composition has been shaped over the decades by the inflow of immigrants and their descendents. In the past century, over 13.4 million immigrants settled in Canada and a large number of them arrived during the 1990s (Ethnic Diversity Survey 2003: 6). This trend has made Canada one of the most ethnically and culturally diverse society in the world.

Since the mid-1970s, Canada has been experiencing an increasing number of immigrants, especially from West Europe, South-East Asia, China, Latin America, Africa and the Caribbean. There are two distinct streams of immigrants in terms of their economic status: (1) the entrepreneurs and professionals, who got direct access to the middle and upper economic strata of the Canadian social structure, settled comfortably in the suburbs and affluent neighbourhoods of central cities and (2) the refugees and labour class immigrants who are in lower economic strata and who occupied low-rent apartments. Most of the immigrants settled particularly in Toronto, Vancouver, and Montreal, the three metropolitan centres of Canada's modern economy. In 2001, these three areas accommodated one-third (34 per cent) of the total Canadian population of 31 million (Qadeer 2003).

As reported in the *Ethnic Diversity Survey* (2003: 6), of the 5.3 million people in the first generation, nearly one-half (46 per cent) or 2.4 million of them were non-European. Of the 3.9 million people in the second generation in the age group of 15 and above, over one-third (36 per cent) or 1.4 million of them had an European ethnic ancestry. Of the 13 million people in the age group of 15 and above in the third generation or more, close to two-thirds (63 per cent) or 8.3 million of them were reported British, French and/or Canadian origins alone.

Toronto city in Canada has a mixture of over 135 nationalities. They are visibly identifiable by their colour, racial features, language, religion and culture. In 1971, the members of non-European ethno-racial groups accounted for 5 per cent of the Toronto Census Metropolitan Area (CMA) population of about 2.6 million compared to nearly 40 per cent of the population of 4.6 million in 2001. In 2001, the immigrant ethnic groups in Toronto city comprised Jews (10.6 per cent), Chinese (10.1 per cent), Portuguese (10.6 per cent), Italians (13.4 per cent), East Indian, Punjabis and Sri Lankans (13.4 per cent), West Indians, Jamaicans and Africans (17.2 per cent) and English-Anglos (24.7 per cent). Among them, the first four groups individually constitute over 10 per cent of the total population of Toronto city, whereas the black and brown groups individually constitute a relatively less proportion of the total population (Qadeer: 2003).

The Indian population of the Toronto CMA grew from 88,440 to 142,380 between 1986 and 1991, then to 212,755 in 1996 and to 295,050 in 2001. In combination, the Sri Lankan groups numbered about 3,000 in 1986, rising dramatically to 14,180 by 1991, then increasing to 32,350 in 1996 and to 42,715 in 2001. In the recent census, there were 23,575 Sri Lankan and Sinhalese, and 19,130 Tamilians (Ornstein 2006). Harney observes that Toronto and other cities in Canada have a long history of Blacks, Jews, Italians and Chinese who concentrate in their respective neighbourhoods. Later they were followed by the Polish and Portuguese communities. In course of time, they formed private 'little homelands' as a result of their cumulative individual as well as group initiatives (Harney 1985). Regent Park, the oldest public housing complex of Canada situated in the Downtown, has Jamaicans, Pakistanis, Anglo-Canadians, Tamilians and Somalis in large numbers along with a moderate distribution of several other nationalities.

During 1996-2001, the Arabic and West Asian ethno-racial and the South Asian groups grew rapidly, each by 7.3 per cent per year, compared to 5 per cent for the African groups, 4.5 per cent for the East Asian groups, 4 per cent for the South and Central American groups, 2.9 per cent for the Caribbean groups, and 2.8 per cent for the Aboriginal groups. Everyone of these groups is growing more rapidly than the European ethno-racial groups, whose Toronto CMA population got increased by a mere 0.1 per cent per year during this period (Ornstein 2006).

After the mid-1980s, Toronto became a prominent place for ethnic and racial diversity. Since that time, it has been drawing a large number of immigrants (about 43 per cent) across the world (Lo et al. 2000). For instance, between 1991 and 1996, an overwhelming (4,50,000) immigrants settled in this region (Bourne 2000: 2). Generally the immigrants are from about 169 different origins and belong to 48 ethnic groups settled in the Toronto area. Of them, about 30 per cent of the immigrants are from visible minority groups (Siemiatyeki et al. 2001). Toronto's landscape is spotted with China towns, Indian bazaars, Portuguese villages and Jewish neighbourhoods. There is a concentration of Somalis, Russians and Tamilians in tall apartment buildings across the city. The residential segregation of various ethnic groups in the Toronto region is mainly because of the immigrants' job, their housing opportunities and also their preference to live in close proximity to the people of similar backgrounds. Moreover, within each region, national, political and economic conditions also influence the residential preferences of individual ethno-racial groups.

Normally, the concentration of an ethnic group in a particular area is mainly due to its choice of housing or housing-market transactions determined by their socio-economic position. Obvious acts of discrimination, such as refusal to rent out or sell houses or apartments based on someone's ethnicity, religion or race are offences subject to prosecution according to an act related to the immigration policy of Canada. Poverty and uncertain income are the common bases for refusal to rent or sell houses and apartments to particular individuals and families. Yet, in the Toronto region, undoubtedly there are incidences of ethnic and racial discrimination in buying, selling and renting of houses or apartments. Most commonly, such incidences occur in the rental sector. Some of these institutional practices may be used to favour either covertly or discriminate against particular ethnic groups. Thus, the ethnic concentration in certain places is an outcome of two intersecting factors: the immigrants' house search behaviour and the structure of the local housing market.

One may presume that in the present scenario, the process of 'de-ethnization' is taking place in developed and culturally diversified societies. On the contrary, it is observed that the level of ethnic consciousness is increasing among various ethnic groups settled in those societies and thereby entering into the process of 're-ethnization' by transforming from 'ethnicity-in-itself' to 'ethnicity-for-itself'. The former is that the members of an ethnic group understand themselves and their position in the society objectively, whereas the latter refers to the subjective understanding of their position in relation to the position of other ethnic groups in the same society and thereby organizing themselves to move from an insecure to a secured position. For instance, when the members of an ethnic group want to cherish or retain their cultural practices and values amidst mixed ethnic groups in order to make them distinct from those groups, they readily prepare to organize associations, clubs, congregational worship, cultural programmes and the like. Such endeavours would bring them together and remind them of their ethnic consciousness, identity and solidarity.

OBJECTIVE

The main objective of this paper is to study the 're-ethnization' of certain ethnic groups in Toronto city by using the concepts 'ethnicity-in-itself' and 'ethnicity-for-itself' in the line of Marxist phraseology pertaining to the concept of class. It also attempts to study their strategies to facilitate the process of 're-ethnization'.

METHODOLOGY

The study is primarily based on secondary data collected from available literature related to the proposed area of study. The analysis is mostly done by making use of these data besides some qualitative data obtained by observation and focus group discussion.

INSTITUTIONAL RACISM AND WHITE PRIVILEGE

Racism in contemporary Canada is not clearly pronounced as it was in the late 1980s. Overt racism would cause problems to an individual or a group of individuals from a racial group, whereas covert racism would be detrimental to the extent of causing heavy damage to a racial group as such. Dhruvarajan (2003) argues that racism in the Canadian society was built into institutional structures, and gets manifested though social practices. According to him, this is mainly due to the colonialism and the practices of imperialism. While conducting a focus groups interview with a group of Tamil-Canadian youth, they disclosed that their non-white skin is considered as a main criterion by the majority mainstream racial community to legitimize their racial consciousness and discriminatory behaviour. In order to overcome this discrimination by improving their economic status, the members of minority racial communities work hard by taking two or three jobs a day. He also suggests that an attempt by youth to overcome racism in the Canadian society would turn to be a successful one by educational achievements.

The Tamil immigrants are, after 1983, considered as 'colored' individuals seeking refuge in Canada. In spite of their positive attitudes towards Canada and Canadians, their strong feeling of belonging to the Canadian society as a whole is not much pronounced. This is perhaps due to their strong affiliation to their minority Tamil community to which they identify themselves in different walks of life. Their identity and affiliation seem to be powerful when they happen to experience racial discrimination and social exclusion. The discriminations at schools in terms of the differences between the children of native Canadians and the children of immigrants of various racial groups and the bias of the teachers to the latter category of children and not recognizing the credentials of foreign students are evident across the Toronto area. Many students of Tamil immigrants experience racism, exclusion and discrimination. Moreover the present school system would often magnify these problems when the administrators and educators attempt to stigmatize the non-whites by referring to their ethnicity, culture and English accent. Especially the Punjabi-Sikh families hold high value for education and treat it as means to overcome barriers that prevent their development.

According to the *Ethnic Diversity Survey* (2003: 16-21), sometimes more visible minorities than others were uncomfortable or out of place in Canada because of their ethnicity, culture, race, skin colour, language, accent or religion. Sometimes or often, over a majority (56 per cent) of them had experienced discrimination or unfair treatment, especially at workplace or while applying for work. The other places where perceived discrimination or unfair treatment occurred were stores, banks and restaurants. Over one-third of them (35 per cent) had often or some time had such experience in those places.

From the perspective of Human Capital Theory, discrimination arises out of limitations of the labour market because the employers erroneously underestimate the merits of the employees by referring to some of their characteristic features. On the other hand, from the perspective of immigration and settlement, discrimination is often seen in terms of social capital and the exclusion of immigrants from the networks providing job contacts, information about housing and other important local knowledge (Ornstein 2006).

PROCESS OF ETHNIZATION AND RE-ETHNIZATION

The *Ethnic Diversity Survey* (2003: 8) reports that in Canada, half the population in the age group of 15 and above had a strong sense of belonging to their ethnic group. In this regard, the first generation had a higher proportion (about 57 per cent) than the second generation (47 per cent) and the third generation more (48 per cent) than the second. They have a strong desire to maintain the customs and traditions of their ancestors. Mostly the families and friends of the same ethnic group play a vital role in setting the new immigrants besides assisting them in finding jobs. Sometimes, ethnic or immigrant organizations also provide settlement services to immigrants and account for their higher participation in these organizations.

According to the Survey (2003: 10) nearly two-thirds (63 percent) of them say that maintaining the customs and traditions of their ethnic groups is imperative. However, the first generation of them was more likely than other generations to maintain the view that the ethnic customs and traditions are vital. It is important to note that, in some ethnic groups, irrespective of the number of generations in Canada, a high proportion of people rated their ancestry high and also rated their customs and traditions as essential values. For instance, 92 per cent of Punjabis, 81 per cent of Greeks, 79 per cent of Filipinos and 76 per cent of Jamaicans fall in this category.

The *Survey* (2003: 11) reports that Canadian and provincial or regional identities increased with the number of generations a person's family lived in Canada. For instance, in 2002, 40 per cent of the first generation have a Canadian or a provincial or a regional identity as compared to 78 per cent of those in the second generation and 80 per cent of those in the third generation or more.

For instance, after arriving in Toronto, an immigrant normally contacts friends, relatives, or acquaintances for help in searching a place to live. Initially he or she stays temporarily with any one of these persons while searching for a permanent house. Refugees in the beginning get accommodation in shelters. However, while searching for permanent housing, they get in touch with their settled sponsors, relatives or friends from their ethnic group for information and guidance for locating quarters and guarantors required by house/apartment owners who are willing to rent out their basements or certain portions of their apartment to the new immigrants. Thus, this network proves to be a potential source to help the immigrants to settle in residential areas of their ethnic groups. That is how the centres of ethnic neighbourhoods are established. These ethnic enclaves are not organized along racial lines, but they are rather tied together by bonds of national origin, culture, language and religion. Undoubtedly familial ethnic socialization is also playing a significant role in the process of the formation of ethnic identity. This is, in one way or other, the process of ethnization.

When the population of a particular ethnic group in an area increases substantially to the extent of making its presence visible, it would in course of time turn to be a prominent ethnic community. The expansion of an ethnic group to an extent of ethnic community would facilitate the development of organizations and associations in order to promote socio-cultural and religious activities by organizing and integrating the members of that ethnic community. They would also establish provisional stores, grocery shops, restaurants, video shops and the like to cater to the needs of their members. In the course of time, they would also form ethnic or immigrant associations to cater to the need of their people. In this regard, especially the first generation has a higher rate of participation. For instance, in 2002, about 6 per cent of the first generation participated in ethnic or immigrant associations as compared to 2 per cent of second generation and 1 per cent of third-plus-generation of Canadians.

The immigrants in Canada, particularly the racial minorities, tend to concentrate in racial minority ethnic enclaves (Hou and Picot 2003). The immigrants tend to associate with people who share the same ethnicity. Close to one-third of them (31 per cent report that none of their friends share their identity. For instance, the Toronto area is characterized by the ethnic residential enclaves. For instance, Bathurst and Lawrence West form the main Jewish enclave. Dundas West is dominated by the Portuguese community. The Crescent Town apartment complex and the Victoria Park (north of Danforth Avenue) accommodate mostly Bangladeshis and South Asians. The apartment buildings in a few blocks in east along Dawes Road lodge mostly the Serbs and the Russians. A majority of the Sri Lankan Tamilians inhabit the suburban Scarborough. The Sikh enclaves are found in Malton close to the airport and also in Brampton, an expanding municipality on the north-western periphery of the Canada Metropolitan Area. Thus, the segregated ethnic enclaves make Toronto city as a significant multicultural metropolis. They form spatial bases for community organizations, cultural and religious associations and economic enterprises for particular ethnic communities.

Over a period of time, the immigrants may like to identify themselves with their host nation. As regards this, the factors like duration of time since migration, citizenship status, visible minority status, political participation, language use, religion and the proportion of friends who share the same ethnic identity play a major role in determining whether the immigrants adopt the identity of their host society. Nevertheless the indicators of economic success do not contribute to the ethnic identity of immigrants.

Mohammad A. Qadeer (2003) points out that the Toronto area has almost become a segmented (sub)housing market sustained by proliferating estate agents, businessmen, lawyers, doctors, dentists, and community and religious leaders. They act as 'gate keepers' to facilitate the movement of ethnic households in and around their community. They could also sustain the continuity of their community and stand for the attainment of a sophisticated level of institutional completeness. Though their population is increasing, their ethnic characteristic features and tradition continue to exist. Especially, in the formation of ethnic communities in the Toronto area, the role of religion seems to be an important binding force for communities of the Jewish, Muslim, Sikh, and Orthodox Christian faiths. The affluent Chinese, Italians, Jews, Sikhs, pious Muslims and Eastern Europeans have, 'by choice', reconstituted their neighbourhoods with the help of their language.

Myle (2002) finds that in Toronto, Chinese immigrants, by and large, have moved to Chinese neighbourhoods and retained their ethnic affiliations. He underlines the fact that the members of some ethnic groups choose to live amidst those from their ethnic groups, though their income is rather viable to live elsewhere in the Toronto region. The house owners in certain parts of Markham, Mississauga and North York have lodged the members of distinct ethnic identities. Thus, to Myle, territorialization of ethnic communities may not be a momentary phase of settlement of immigrants; it appears to have become a mode of spatial organization for ethnic-communities in the Toronto region.

In Toronto, the development of ethnic enclaves appears to be the expression of preferences, common values and interests, social networks and the cultural and religious needs of their residents. They provide familiarity and security to the new immigrants and also serve as the basis for their integration into the Canadian economy and society. They are especially helpful to women, children and seniors who may not be fluent in English. The discussion in this section shows the process of re-ethnization of various ethnic communities for obvious reasons in Toronto.

CONCLUSION

The immigrant ethnic groups elsewhere in the world societies initially got into the process of ethnization for their identities and consolidation of their ethnic communities. In the recent decade, they started realizing the need to reconsolidate their communities to face challenges in terms of racial discrimination and marginalization. Various ethnic communities in the Greater Toronto Area have already entered into the process of 're-ethnization' with a sense of involvement. A sizeable proportion of immigrants and refugees from various ethnic groups are confronting difficulties to get access to houses or apartments owing to their economic instability and discriminatory practices of some landlords and the staff of shelters and inns. The educational credentials of young graduates are not recognized by the educational institutions in Canada and therefore, they remain in a state of unemployment or underemployment. Despite their rich experience in particular jobs available in the job market, they face hardships to get work permit.

After experiencing such hardships in the initial period, they started realizing the importance of their ethnic identity and consolidation of their community by getting into the process of 're-ethnization'. One may notice this process in some immigrant ethnic communities settled in the Toronto area. This process has resulted in the formation of associations and organizations, housing markets, commercial markets, various types of stores and shops, restaurants and the like. For instance, such establishments of an ethnic community promote the identity and unity of its members and thereby enabling them to preserve their tradition in different walks of their life. Therefore, the proposed study focuses on 're-ethnization' of ethnic communities in Canada. Moreover, this process has become a global trend in contemporary times, prevailing across the world societies.

NOTE

This author was undertaking a short-term research on refugee issues in the Centre for Refugee Studies (CRS), York University, and Toronto, Canada during May–June 2007 with the Shastri Indo-Canadian fellowship. This essay is based on secondary data collected from relevant literature available in the host Centre and University. I am thankful to my affiliating Professor Paul Anisef in CRS, who helped me to get access to those available resources in the Centre.

REFERENCES

Berry, John, 'Immigration, Acculturation, and Adaptation', *Applied Psychology: An International Review*, vol. 46, no. 1, 1997, pp. 5-34.

Bourne, Larry, *People and Places: A Portrait of the Evolving Social Character of the Greater Toronto Region*, Toronto: NEPTIS Foundation, 2000.

Desai, S. and S. Subramanian, *Colour, Culture and Dual Consciousness: Issues Identified by South Asian Immigrant Youth in the Greater Toronto Area*, Toronto: Council of Agencies Serving South Asians and the South Asian Women's Centre, 2000.

Dhruvarajan, V., 'Second-Generation Indo-Canadians: Change, Resistance, and Adaptation', in Sushma J. Varma and Radhika Seshan (eds.), *Fractured Identity: The Indian Diaspora in Canada*, New Delhi: Rawat Publications, 2003.

Ethnic Diversity Survey: Portrait of a Multicultural Society, Statistics Canada, Ministry of Industry, 2003.

Gill, Rajesh, 'Cities and Ethnic Identities: A Case of De-ethnization or Re-ethnization?' *Sociological Bulletin*, vol. 49, September 2000, pp. 211-28.

Harney, Robert, 'Ethnicity and Neighbourhood', in Robert Harney (ed.), *Gathering Places: Peoples and Neighbourhoods of Toronto, 1843-1945*, Toronto: Multicultural History Society of Ontario, 1985.

Halli, Shiva and Leo Driedger (eds.), *Immigrant Canada*, Toronto: University of Toronto Press, 1999.

Hou, F. and G. Picot, 'Visible Minority Neighbourhood Enclaves and the Labour Market Outcomes of Immigrants', in C. Beach, A. Green and J. Reitz (eds.), *Canadian Immigration Policy for the 21st Century*, McGill-Queen's University Press.

Kalbach, Madeline A. and Warren E. Kalbach, 'Becoming Canadian: Problems of an Emerging Identity', *Canadian Ethnic Studies*, vol. 31, no. 2, 1999, pp. 1-16.

Kalbach, Madeline A. and Warren E. Kalbach (eds.), *Perspectives on Ethnicity in Canada*, Toronto: Harcourt Canada, 2000.

Kazemipur, Abdolmohammed and Shiva S. Halli, 'The Colour of Poverty: A Study of the Poverty of Ethnic and Immigrant Groups in Canada', *International Migration*, vol. 38, no. 1, 2000, pp. 69-87.

Lacroix, Marie, 'Canadian Refugee Policy and the Social Construction of the Refugee Claimant Subjectivity: Understanding Refugeeness', *Journal of Refugee Studies*, vol. 17, no. 2, 2004, pp. 147-66.

Lo, Lucia et al., *Immigrants' Economic Status in Toronto: Rethinking Settlement and Integration Strategies, 2000*, CERIS Working Paper No. 15, Toronto: Joint Centre of Excellence for Research on Immigration and Settlement, 2000.

Myles, John, *Residential Segregation and Neighbourhood Attainment Among Toronto's Visible Minorities*, Toronto: Department of Sociology, University of Toronto, Mimeographed, 2002.

Ornstein, Michael, *Report on Ethno Racial Groups in Toronto, 1971-2001: A Demographic and Socio-Economic Profile*, York University: Institute of Social Research, 2006.

Qadeer, A. Mohammad, *Working Paper on Ethnic Segregation in a Multicultural City: The Case of Toronto, Canada*, Toronto: Joint Centre of Excellence for Research on Immigrants and Settlement, 2003.

Satzewich, V. (ed.), *Racism and Social Inequality in Canada: Concepts, Controversies and Strategies of Resistance*, Toronto: Thompson Educational Publishing, 1998.

Siemiatycki, Myer, Tim Rees, Ng Roxana and Rahi Khan, *Integrating Community Diversity in Toronto: On Whose Terms?*, CERIS Working Paper No. 14, Toronto: Joint Centre of Excellence for Research on Immigration and Settlement, 2001.

CHAPTER 15

Energy, Climate Change and Global Justice: India and Canada

GARY VAN LOON

The complex triangular connection between energy, economic development and environment define issues that are central to every nation and, indeed, to the world as a whole. Energy makes essential contributions to all aspects of life, and consumption of commercial energy is the key component of modern development. While essential in its contribution to the quality of life, use of carbon-based energy sources is widely recognized as being the major contributor to global climate change as well as to local atmospheric pollution problems.

Adding to a growing collection of high-powered reports, the United Nations Intergovernmental Panel on Climate Change states that there is 'unequivocal' evidence pointing to human activities as the major contributor to global warming. The report shows that substantial climate change is already underway and predicts that further warming will lead to multiple major environmental disasters around the world.

Canada and the US are two of the world's heaviest users of energy and, as a consequence, contribute more than their share to the global burden of greenhouse gas emissions. In spite of this, uptil now these two countries have taken only limited steps toward reduction in the *intensity* of their energy consumption. As a result, the absolute amount of emissions continues to increase. The Kyoto Protocol baseline year was 1991, a year in which Canadians released 450 million tonnes of carbon dioxide into the atmosphere. By 2007, the annual rate had increased to 640 million tonnes. North American leaders often repeat the idea that emissions negotiations must include the participation of all the 'big polluters', pointedly referring to India and China. Repeated emphasis underlines a widely-held view that emissions of greenhouse gases from thinly populated countries like Canada are small compared to those from the heavily populated energy consumers. That may be true if one speaks in absolute terms, but energy statistics clearly point to a gaping imbalance in per person energy consumption. And this means an imbalance in who receives the benefits of energy and who contributes to the associated problems.

The 2007 British Petroleum *Review of Energy*, considered to be the authoritative source of data on commercial energy consumption, reports that the total commercial energy consumption in India was 16.5 exajoules (billion billion joules) in 2006, i.e. only 30 per cent greater than Canada's 12.6 exajoules. These large numbers become more meaningful when compared on *per capita* basis, where India's consumption works out to be 15 billion joules *per capita* each year, a rate that is less than 5 per cent of that in North America—300 billion joules in the USA and 389 billion joules in Canada.[1]

How much energy is required to provide a 'good standard of living' in the twenty-first century? This depends on many factors including country size and climate, and the industrial and agricultural situation.

Canada is a large and cold country and it is to be expected that there will be substantial energy requirements for transportation and space heating. Compared, however, to the equally cold and expansive European continent, much greater amounts of energy are used in Canada for these purposes because of its sprawling urban design features and the widely-held aspirations for personal transportation and for very spacious personal living accommodation. Then too, Canada's resource-based economy is often cited as a reason for its near first-place standing as an energy consumer. The massive oil sands deposits in Northern Alberta and Saskatchewan tar sand deposits are the most prominent examples. But, an estimate based on the reported production of 440 million barrels of oil in 2007 is that 0.47 exajoules of energy are consumed in this activity,[2] only about 3.7 per cent of the total energy used in Canada. Clearly, energy use in Canada goes beyond providing the essentials of domestic life and industrial development.

India too is a large country and one would expect that movement of persons and goods for business and recreation across the more than 2,000 km from north to south or east to west would occur just as frequently as over similar distances in North America. Until recently transportation policies wisely focused on trains and buses and other means of public transport. The explosion of personal automobile use in the past decade is, however, changing this picture, at least for a growing middle class. Because of India's warm climate, space heating is a non-issue in most parts of the country, but not so for air-conditioning. Many places in India experience average daytime temperatures well over 35 °C for at least three months in a year. Provision of more energy to support these 'convenience issues' is rapidly occurring.

More important is the Indian imperative to support the major development initiatives, including those in the large rural agricultural sector where there is no other choice but to increase commercial energy consumption in order to improve the meager livelihoods that characterizes a large part of the population there. In this sense, energy should be considered as an essential input to development and can be thought of as a *fundamental right*.

Taking all this into account, some estimates are that a fourfold increase (to around 50 to 70 billion joules of energy *per capita*) should be expected in the next decade in India—energy consumption for building up industrial and agricultural capacity, improved infrastructure and services, and for household amenities.

What does this mean for India and the North American countries? On the Indian side, participation in efforts directed toward emission control is of the highest importance. But for reasons of international social justice the rest of the world should expect, and indeed support, the kind of development that will lead to *increased* energy consumption. Such an increase is in fact now occurring at a rate of about 6 per cent per year. Emphasis on large-scale, clean, renewable energy initiatives is then paramount. India is already fourth in the world in installed wind energy capacity, and is active in pursuing other non-greenhouse gas emitting sources. Expansion of wind-generated electricity as well as solar, nuclear and hydro is therefore an important component of India's energy strategy. On top of this, there will be a need for larger quantities of the convenient liquid and gas based fuels—gasoline, diesel, LPG, propane and natural gas. India has limited reserves of petroleum and natural gas and the development of strategies to supplement these by growing biomass for fuel production is a hot topic, just as it is in North America. Critical for India is the need to ensure that agriculture first focuses on providing food security for the 1.1 billion population. There is, however, hope that carefully designed integrated food/energy agricultural systems can have the potential to provide feedstock for production of at least a small proportion of future fuel needs.

It is encouraging to see that India is not in a blind rush to create wealth and is aware of concerns about global climate change. Among her leaders there is growing recognition of potential climate-connected problems that would adversely impact food production, cause inundation of heavily populated coastal areas by seawater and increase the frequency of cyclones. What is most troubling is that these impacts will fall disproportionately on the poor who are already under severe stress from drought and floods, water scarcity and poor quality, land degradation and desertification.

With all this, India's commercial and industrial development will continue to grow at an accelerated pace and this will inevitably mean accelerated energy use. At present, on a *per capita* basis India is a surprisingly small contributor to global emissions of carbon dioxide compared to many Western countries, but her contribution is certain to become much larger.

This means that profligate energy users like USA/Canada, where so much goes to personal convenience and comfort and to never-ending leisure consumption, must make even greater emission cuts if acceptable global targets are to be reached.

In the global policy deliberations that are urgently required, it is imperative that all countries work within the Framework Convention on Climate Change (FCCC) developed at the Earth Summit in Rio de Janeiro in June 1992. The Convention adopted the notion of *common but differentiated responsibility.* Here it was recognized that global climate is a common resource and a common responsibility. In ensuring that climate remains hospitable to life everywhere on the planet, there are clear asymmetries between countries in terms of both the past and present contributions to the problem as well as the resources to respond to it.

NOTES

1. Some estimates, use barrels of oil equivalent as an energy unit. One barrel of petroleum provides energy equivalent to 5.8 billion joules. Therefore the annual per capita consumption of energy in India is equivalent to 2.6 barrels of oil, while that in Canada is 67 barrels.
2. This is based on an assumption that 1.1 billion joules of energy are required to produce a barrel of oil, approximately 19 per cent of the energy produced.

CHAPTER 16

India and Canada: Shared Visions of Nature and Conservation

ABHIK GUPTA

INTRODUCTION

This paper attempts to probe into the societal attitudes towards nature and the images of man-nature relationships in Indian and Canadian—or more generally speaking—Western societies. There is ample room for skepticisms and doubts about the utility of exercises of this type. After all, we can protect the environment by acquiring progressively 'greener' bio- and even nanotechnologies, enact stiff legislations and sign more international treaties, conventions and protocols outlining concrete, action-based programmes. In this arena of positivist, problem-solving approaches, any hermeneutic emphasis is likely to be branded as one shrouded in an aura of romanticism and mysticism, and consequently of little practical value. However, it can be argued that besides the 'romantic utopia', we also nurture a 'scientific-technological-legal utopia' that leads us to lay our unflinching trust in the omnipotence of technological and legislative tools in solving all our problems, including those arising out of the looming environmental crisis. Are mere scientific and technological interventions, bolstered by stiff legislation, enough to resolve the environmental crisis confronting mankind today? Or is it perhaps the human mind that harbours attitudes—individual or collective-societal—that holds the key to the survival and flourishing of the biosphere or its possible destruction? It is in this context that the images of nature perceived by the humans and the visions of man-nature relationship in different cultures assume great significance. Cairns (1993) noted that the customary scientific approach is unable to check the present rate of habitat destruction, while it may be possible to achieve this on ethical grounds. Leopold (1990) also suggested that unless our legislations and policies are underlaid with a set of ethos or guiding beliefs with regard to biodiversity and the environment as a whole, protection of natural systems or the healing of those which are damaged may remain an unachievable goal. The continued survival of nature—to which the survival of mankind is intricately linked—will depend on the extent to which he (human) can travel with her (nature) along the road of harmony, and the point at which he would desert her to turn from a friend and a partner to a master. The Dutch environmental philosopher Wim Zweers recognized six possible positions that humans could adopt towards nature: despot, enlightened ruler, steward, partner, participant and union with nature (Zweers 1989—cited in van den Born 2007; Zweers 1995). This was condensed to four essential positions—master, steward, partner and participant by Petran Kockelkoren (Kockelkoren 1993, cited in van den Born 2007). Kellert (1989) attempted to translate these essentially hermeneutic perceptions of the human mind into quantifiable, empirical values, and subsequently several scales have been developed, for instance, the New Environmental Paradigm (NEP), Scale of Dunlap et al. (2000) and the Human and Nature (HaN) scale (de Groot and van den Born 2007). In a survey conducted in Victoria, British Columbia (Canada), among the five distinct communities, viz., Christians, Muslims, Buddhists, Native Americans, and secularists to find out about the dominant images of nature in the minds of these groups (de Groot and van den Born 2007), it was found that the master position that envisages an exploitative tyranny over nature was rejected by all the groups. The Buddhists and Native Americans espoused the participant image of nature, while most Christians and Muslims adhered more to the steward image, thereby revealing the role of religion and culture in shaping man-nature relationships.

MAN-NATURE RELATIONSHIPS IN INDIA AND CANADA: A HISTORICAL PERSPECTIVE

All human relationships are guided by values. Humans can assign two types of values to other entities, including nature or other human beings: extrinsic or instrumental value that derives from the objective properties of that entity that has use for humans; and intrinsic or inherent value, which is a value in itself regardless of its utility for others. For example, we are taught to believe that other human beings have a value in themselves as conscious intelligent beings regardless of their value for others (Martell 1994). Recognizing a given type of value in others is in turn guided by the world-view (German: *weltanschauung*) of an individual or the dominant collective world-view that is prevalent in a given place at a given time. World-views may be defined as the overall perspective, from which one sees and interprets the world, or in other words, it could represent a collection of beliefs about life and the universe held by an individual or a group. The world-views and the value system engendered by them determine to a large extent the societal attitudes, i.e. the evaluative responses (Holland 2003—cited in van den Born 2007) towards others.

At least since the sixteenth and seventeenth centuries, the dominant world-view in Western societies, including that in the United States and Canada, was profoundly influenced by a strongly anthropocentric (human-centred) ethic, propounded by philosophers like Descartes, Bacon and Leibniz. Descartes put forward his famous 'mind-body dualism' that postulated that only humans had minds, while all the other components of nature were mere bodies or 'machines'. Even earlier, fifteenth-century renaissance thinkers like Erasmus and Montaigne professed anthropocentric humanism. This trend was carried forward into the nineteenth and the twentieth centuries by Marx, Dewey and Sartre, among others (Sessions 1995). When the Europeans established their first permanent settlements in Canada in the seventeenth century, their attitude towards nature was guided by the predominant European philosophical and scientific traditions that at that time upheld mastery over nature. Till the middle or later part of the nineteenth century, the forest and other natural resource management policies in Canada were largely revenue-oriented, with emphasis on maximizing timber supply and unbridled resource extraction. The pioneers were guided by an exploitative 'frontier attitude' that looked upon land, forests, wildlife, minerals, etc., as infinite and 'kept' there for human use. The prevalent interpretation of the biblical human 'dominion over nature' lent religious and ethical sanctions to such anthropocentric views of man-nature relationship where humans were considered as masters over nature.

In India, British annexation beginning in the mid-eighteenth century led to increased government control over forests and other resources, and similar revenue-oriented, overtly anthropocentric policies were pursued by the new rulers, first represented by the East India Company and then by the British government. Admittedly, many colonial scientists and administrators could foresee the dangerous consequences of such an approach and tried to influence the government to take more ecological and conservation measures, albeit with little success (Grove 1995). The forest policy and practices were also guided by an anthropocentric philosophy. If we view the outlook of Dietrich Brandis, the founder of scientific forestry in India, we find that he could well recognize both economic and ecological utilities of forests. The first ever *Manual of Forestry* by William Schlich also recognized that along with generation of profit, the forests regulated soil and air temperature regimes, climate, water supply and rainfall, and prevented land slips, avalanches, siltation of rivers and wind erosion. Paradoxically, Brandis also was a firm believer in the German forestry principle of 'minimum diversity' that encouraged the conservation, scientific extraction and planting of commercially valuable species like teak (*Tectona grandis*) and *sal* (*Shorea robusta*). He deliberately ignored the other trees, creepers and epiphytes that contributed to the rich diversity of tropical forests as 'arbitrary details of nature' and advocated their replacement with economically important species, wherever possible (Rajan 1998). Hunting was seen as 'the sport' for the royalty and the aristocracy, and wildlife parts and products like fur, ivory, pelts and other items served as a lucrative source of commerce and trade. Thus the European foresters and natural resource managers in both India and Canada were guided by the Cartesian-Baconian world-view of improving over nature and utilizing it for human benefits. Humans were the masters, nature a subservient slave.

From Master to Steward

While the philosophy of mastery over nature continued to hold sway in the Western societies and in the colonies administered by them, and nature was being 'conquered', manipulated, and 'improved upon', dissenting voices espousing a largely ecocentric (nature-centred) ethic that recognized the intrinsic value of nature, also tried to make their presence felt. Such voices included the seventeenth-century Dutch philosopher Baruch Spinoza, the romantic poets Wordsworth, Keats, Shelley, Blake, Coleridge, Goethe (late eighteenth and early nineteenth centuries) and others, followed by nineteenth-century transcendental thinkers like Thoreau, and conservationists like Muir, who could perceive a spiritual value in nature. At the same time, a realization was gradually dawning in the minds of the managers and policy makers about the unsustainable nature of the resource extraction practices. The Canadian perceptions about nature and resource use were also greatly influenced by the ecocentric writings of the romantic poets, by that of 'Grey Owl' (A.S. Belaney), an Englishman who had settled in Canada, and by the American 'preservationist' thinkers like Emerson and Thoreau. The establishment of the Sierra Club by John Muir in 1892 and the efforts of Gifford Pinchot, who initiated the American conservation movement, were also instrumental in shaping Canadian environmental thoughts. Nevertheless, when the first National Parks were being established in Canada—for instance, BANFF in 1885, and YOHO and GLACIER in 1886—the main underlying objective was revenue generation from timber and tourist visits. However, in 1916 the US passed the National Park Service Act, which stated that parks were to be 'unimpaired for the enjoyment of future generations'. This wording was not used in the Canadian National Parks Act until 1930. In this respect, 1930 is a kind of turning point in Canadian conservation thought. The emphasis on setting aside areas of pure wilderness rather than on resource use or recreation gained increasing ground in both the USA and Canada since the 1960s (http://www.thecanadianencyclopedia.com/index.cfm?PgNm=TCE&Params=A1ARTA0000646). Meanwhile, the publication of a series of books such as Aldo Leopold's *Land Ethic* in 1949, Rachel Carson's *Silent Spring* in 1962, Barry Commoner's *The Closing Circle* in 1971 and many others served as eye-openers to the devastating effects of man on nature. The chain of events leading to increased research on and a heightened awareness of the impact of environmental pollution, habitat destruction and biodiversity loss, the UN conference on Human Environment at Stockholm in 1972, the publication of the Bruntland Report in 1987, the Earth Summit at Rio de Janeiro in 2002 (and numerous similar intergovernmental meetings and conventions), brought to the fore the concept of sustainable development and the environmental responsibility of the present generation towards the future progeny. The 'cutting edges' of anthropocentrism were somewhat rounded off, and the idea of man as a 'steward' of nature rather than a 'master' gained ground. The biblical reference to dominion over nature was reinterpreted as that of man's role as a steward and not a domineering master. Nevertheless, it must be emphasized that the concept of steward remains an essentially reformist approach guided by human survival instinct, emanating from the realization that pollution control and biodiversity conservation are necessary for the continued existence and thriving of the human civilization. That stewardship was deemed to be the dominant expression of man-nature relationship was evident in 1897 when John Muir's eco-centric, 'preservationist' ideals that unequivocally opposed commercialization of nature and upheld nature's spiritual and uplifting values, were overtaken at the policy making level by Gifford Pinchot's anthropocentric, stewardship principles that saw conservation as a means of sustainable management of earth's natural resources for wise human use. Thus a reformist, weakly anthropocentric world-view that attempted to strike a balance between exploitation and conservation came to hold sway in the Western societies, including that of Canada.

In India, the commercially-oriented, anthropocentric view of man-nature relationship introduced by the British colonialists continued for about two decades after Independence. Subsequently, India's participation in the 1972 Stockholm UN conference paved the way for more pro-active conservationist measures in terms of enactment of several laws protecting wildlife, air, water and the environment in general during the 1970s and 1980s. Environmental education and awareness became an integral component of curricula at various levels. India also became a signatory of a number of international conventions and protocols to save the environment. Nevertheless, the urban elite who played a dominant role in law- and policy-framing largely subscribed to a benign anthropocentric outlook with a spirit of stewardship of nature. Although the ecocentric traditions nurtured over centuries by the Indian society were not denied outright, these were not considered practical enough to be incorporated into the positivist, 'action-oriented' programmes.

INDIA AND CANADA: SHARED ECOCENTRIC VISIONS

The expressions of ecocentric culture, religion and lifestyle were manifest in many indigenous societies the world over, for example in the aboriginal communities (First Nations) of Canada and the USA, among tribal communities in India, in Buddhist and Shinto traditions, and in certain practices and beliefs of many Eastern religions like Hinduism. These world-views visualize humans as 'partners' or 'participants' in nature rather than as master or even steward.

The aboriginal people of Canada, who are often referred to as the First Nations, developed a unique spiritual belief system for thousands of years before the advent of the Europeans. At least 56 distinct native religious traditions exist in Canada today, including that of the Inuits of its northern parts. A common feature of these myriad religious traditions is the inherent respect for animals, plants, and entire ecosystems like rivers, lakes, rocks and mountains, and the recognition of spirits or 'souls' in these entities. Thus it is a non-dualistic world-view that permeates deep into the psyche of the aboriginal communities. A few major common aspects of belief or behaviour include the following precepts:

- The Earth is understood to have intrinsic value, and humans must care for it as its custodian.
- All living things and objects have a spirit.
- When taking the life of a plant or animal of the Earth, a person must pay respect to the spirit of that plant or animal.
- All individual spiritual beliefs should be respected. (http://www.mdn.ca/hr/ religions/engraph/religions23_e.asp)

Recognition of intrinsic or inherent value in both living and non-living non-humans is also a characteristic feature of indigenous or 'tribal' religious and spiritual belief systems throughout India. Nature worship and offering protection to nature through creation and maintenance of sacred groves, taboos on hunting, and other mechanisms of prudent resource use are the characteristic features of such communities (Gadgil and Guha 1992; Gadgil and Vartak 1994; Gadgil 1995; Gupta and Guha 2002; Singh et al. 2003). It has often been suggested that ecosystem people such as tribes maintain sacred groves and exhibit other mechanisms of protection of nature mainly because they tend to be prudent in their resource use. Consequently, they sacrifice some of their immediate benefits to ensure greater benefits to accrue at a later date. Such behaviours are, therefore, believed to signify the society's recognition of the 'bequest value' of the elements of biodiversity or nature as a whole (Gadgil and Guha 1992; Gadgil 1995). In the language of normative ethics, therefore, the actors displaying such prudence assign only instrumental value to non-humans, and consequently, are governed by the principles of direct or indirect reciprocity. However, people worshipping nature in sacred groves or through tree or animal worship, cannot be said to assign only extrinsic value to the objects they revere, and therefore, there is something more in this relationship than mere expectation of some reward at a later date (Gupta 2006). Kellert (1996) has suggested that altruistic acts towards non-humans in many indigenous cultures are often motivated by 'sentiments of affinity' and not calculated empiricism. Deb and Malhotra (2001) have shown that the tribals of West Bengal, India, hold as sacred a tree (*Adina cordifolia*) and a shrub (*Euphorbia neriifolia*), which have no direct use values. Similarly, the sparrow, the jackal, the tiger, various species of songbirds, and various species of snakes are held sacred in many indigenous cultures of Assam, Manipur and Tripura (Gupta and Guha 2002). Such sentiments and beliefs could perhaps be explained by the concept of 'biophilia', a term originally proposed by Fromm (1973) as love for all living beings. It has been subsequently defined as 'the innately emotional affiliation of human beings to other living organisms' (Kellert and Wilson 1993). Many cultures, exemplified by the Meiteis of Manipur and Assam, north-east India, go beyond biophilia to 'ecophilia' or 'cosmophilia' through the practice of 'Chingoiron'—the worship of hills—and 'Nungoiron'—the worship of rocks (Singh et al. 2003). In Korean shamanism, deities could exist, besides other places, in the trees, the ground, the rocks, the spring, the river, and the sea (Rhi 1993).

Thus the tribal mind is capable of non-dualistic patterns of behaviour by virtue of which they can recognize non-humans as kin or ancestors or as the possessor of a spirit or soul. Besides their rituals and lifestyle, this is also revealed by their myths and folklores. An analysis of these myths and folklores enables us to delve into the aboriginal mind, or in other words, into the minds of early human societies that lived in small groups as hunter-gatherers. These myths reveal to us that the aboriginal mind was devoid of any distinction among god, man, plants, animals and even inanimate natural objects. The creatures themselves played an important role in the creation and construction of the world. Man's origin could be traced to plants, animals and inanimate objects, and there was kinship between humans and these entities. The aboriginal myths also deny the uniqueness of humans in the possession of knowledge, as non-humans frequently handed over vital knowledge to him (Saraswati 1993). A few examples from the tribal creation myths and folklores from Arunachal Pradesh in north-east India, may illustrate these points further. Several myths describe the important role of non-humans in creation and construction. The Hill Miris of Arunachal Pradesh believe that in the beginning, there was water everywhere, with only a gigantic tree raising its head above. A worm gnawed at its wood and the dust fell all around to form the earth. Finally the tree fell to the ground, and the bark on its lower side became the skin of the earth, that on the upper side the sky, the trunk rocks and the branches became mountains. Again, a Gallong myth says that the prawn collected a great pile of rubbish on the surface and the crab dug a hole to drain the water, and thus the land emerged. A number of myths also trace the non-human ancestry and kinship of man, such as from frogs (Dhammai Miji myth), or from a flower (Khampti myth). The great primeval spirits had three children, one a human, another a rock and yet another a gourd. When the rock-child broke open the gourd, the first humans emerged (Singpho tale). In another story (Taraon Mishmi), the first men and women came out of the tusk of an elephant (Elwin 1958). There are many stories of the marriage and sexual union of humans with gods, spirits, real animals (and not humans in animal disguise) like snakes, monkeys, tigers, etc., and even leaves, trees and fire. In these myths, man is not even unique in the possession of knowledge, which more than often came to him from animals. Thus the birds (Hill Miri myth) or flowers and bees (Bugun myth) taught the first man and woman the art of reproduction; the spiders taught a girl how to weave (Singpho); and the rat the technique of cultivation (Saraswati 1993). In another story (Idu Mishmi), the sparrow taught cultivation to man (Elwin 1958). These myths reveal to us the ability of the tribes to recognize intrinsic values and spirituality in non-human components of nature (Gupta 2006).

Interestingly enough, the creation myths of many First Nations of Canada bear striking resemblances to the north-east Indian myths. For instance, the Iroquois believe that the first human being, the sky woman, was rescued by two swans from drowning and put on the back of the turtle. Later, a female toad succeeded in digging up the magical soil that finally formed the earth, and a turtle created the sun and moon from lightning. All the other animals also played important roles in the creation of earth which the sky woman and her progeny gradually populated. In a similar creation myth of the Blackfoot, the credit of diving into the water to bring up a mud ball that finally became the earth goes to the muskrat. The creator—Napi—made the earth from this primordial mud ball. This vital primordial mud ball was brought up by a turtle in a Blood creation myth. The Haida believe that it was the raven that stole the sun and made the moon and the stars from it, created lakes, filled the land with trees and put animals in the forest. It then released the first human being hiding in a giant clamshell and gave him the secret of fire (http://www.ucalgary.ca/applied_history/tutor/firstnations/myths.html). It is possible that these convergences in the world-views of the First Nations and the north-east Indian communities that are widely separated in space originate from their living close to nature and in harmony with it.

A SHIFT IN PARADIGM?

The changing global perception in man-nature relationship where humans have increasingly started to think of themselves as stewards and not masters of nature has indeed contributed significantly towards putting a halt to the unbridled destruction of nature. Nevertheless, it is perhaps necessary to honestly acknowledge that the concept of stewardship is in its essence a duty-bound obligation to nature that has to be carried out in order to save the present and future generations of human beings. Such a world-view has its limitations and is far inferior to an ethic that emerges from love of nature with humans conceived as partners or participants.

Various governmental agencies and other institutions in Canada have started recognizing the relevance of the aboriginal ecocentric world-views and incorporating them in natural resource management programmes and even general policy-framing and judicial reforms. For instance, the Canadian Human Rights Commission recognizes that 'Aboriginal world-views have something to offer, both to Aboriginal people and all people in Canada'. It opposes the oppression and devaluation of the indigenous world-views, and asserts that 'there are Aboriginal ways of doing things that are extremely relevant today, especially because they are rooted in ancient relations to the world'. The commission emphasizes that it is 'first important to recognize and acknowledge the differences and, secondly, to understand and accept them'. There has to be a shift from the idea of 'colonial systems doing things *to* Aboriginal peoples, to doing things *for* Aboriginal peoples, and finally, to the imperative of doing things *with* Aboriginal peoples' (http://www.chrc-ccdp.ca/research_program_recherche/adr_red/page3-en.asp).

> No matter how dominant a worldview is, there are always other ways of interpreting the world. Different ways of interpreting the world are manifest through different cultures, which are often in opposition to one another. One of the problems with colonialism is that it tries to maintain a singular social order by means of force and law, suppressing the diversity of human world-views. The underlying differences between Aboriginal and Eurocentric world-views make this a tenuous proposition at best. Typically, this proposition creates oppression and discrimination. (Little Bear 2000)

> Perhaps one of the most deleterious effects of colonization is the manner in which indigenous cultures and worldviews have been misunderstood and oppressed. Indigenous societies were studied according to 'one-dimensional Euro-centric approximations which held consumer societies, the market economy and the alleged intrinsic goodness of modern (Western) social organization' as superior. Therefore, any culture not in line with the Western Judeo-Christian paradigm was deemed to be 'backward', 'obsolete', 'inferior' and if at all, of 'negligible' value. (Martinez 1992)

The growing willingness to incorporate indigenous world-views and traditional knowledge into natural management systems is illustrated by the concept and science of 'Aboriginal forestry' where 'aboriginal people are becoming increasingly involved as stakeholder, partner, manager, owner and worker. With this increased participation people are bringing their values and beliefs to the management paradigm that is resulting in a shift in sustainable forest management in Canada, from an industrial consultative process to a community-driven manage-ment plan development process.' Aboriginal forestry stems from cumulative observations from which the Aboriginal world-view and value system have evolved over time in a given ecosystem or homeland and passed forward orally from generation to generation. The Aboriginal world-view is ecocentric, i.e. the biotic (organisms, including humans) and abiotic (non-living entities) have equal value (Parsons and Prest 2003). It is often said that Aboriginal people do not manage the forest; they manage their relationship with the forest (Brubacher et al. 2002).

In India, the enactment of the Scheduled Tribes and Other Traditional Forest Dwellers (Recognition of Forest Rights) Act, 2006, is also an attempt to recognize the right of the indigenous communities to forest and its resources. The Act recognizes that 'the tribal people are inseparable with the ecosystem, including wildlife, and cannot survive in isolation'. However, the Act has been hotly debated over between champions of tribal rights and conservationists and remains a controversial issue. The sharing of experiences between India and Canada in this regard could perhaps be rewarding to both the countries.

WORSHIPPING NATURE?

There is skepticism and resistance to the acceptance of ecocentric indigenous world-views that entail recognition of 'rights' of non-humans, and perceive nature as kin, ancestor or God, as they go against rational, scientific and even secular ideals and is often seen as tantamount to superstition. In my view the reluctance arises from interpreting the words 'right' or 'worship' in a literal sense and failing to look beyond in a figurative manner. After all, we have no such hesitation when we are told to 'worship' our country, or a noble ideal, or great minds, as the word 'worship' is perceived in a metaphorical sense. Similarly, we think it natural to try to understand what our country or nation 'wants' from us. This happens because consciously or subconsciously, we tend to assign intrinsic value to our country or nation or ethnic or religious group, but feel indignant or amused when another culture recognizes similar values in plants, animals or entire ecosystems.

While the Western societies and their anthropocentric value systems have been held responsible for the environmental crisis, there is growing evidence of a new 'longing' for nature and for preserving nature for its own sake. Numerous studies conducted in Europe and the USA (reviewed in van den Born 2007) reveals that 78-92 per cent of the respondents were of the opinion that the intrinsic value of nature, irrespective of its use or bequest value was important enough for ensuring its conservation. In yet another study (de Groot and van den Born 2007) conducted among five distinct populations—Christians, Muslims, Buddhists, Native Americans and Secular (non-religious)—in Victoria, British Columbia (Canada), it was found that all respondents, irrespective of their religious affiliation, unequivocally rejected the image of man as master, and dubbed it in terms such as 'arrogant', 'old-fashioned', 'destructive' and 'immoral'. Most Christians and Muslims were enthusiastic about the image of man as a steward, although they were not averse to the idea of man being a participant in nature as well. The participant image found ready acceptance among the Buddhists and Native Americans, and among the female secular respondents as well. Even the most hardnosed male secular respondents agreed that nature evoked a feeling of 'awe' or an 'emotional feeling' in them. Thus nurturing an ecocentric ethic that recognized intrinsic value in nature did not appear to come into conflict with the religious or rational makeup of their personalities.

Thus the 'wave' of biophilia can be said to be gradually inundating human societies worldwide. This wave is albeit a gentle one, and like a tide entering a coastal ecosystem and providing energy subsidy to enrich its diversity and productivity (Odum 1983), this wave could perhaps provide the much needed emotional subsidy for protecting the environment. India and Canada, with their rich ecocentric traditions, could play important roles in constructing this new vision of nature. I would like to conclude this paper by presenting a poem each of a Canadian poet—Achibald Lampman—and the Nobel Laureate poet from India, Rabindranath Tagore.

Morning on the Lievre
Archibald Lampman (1861-99)

Far above us where a jay
Screams his matins to the day,
Capped with gold and amethyst,
Like a vapour from the forge
Of a giant somewhere hid,

Out of hearing of the clang
Of his hammer, skirts of mist
Slowly up the woody gorge
Lift and hang.

Softly as a cloud we go,
Sky above and sky below,
Down the river; and the dip
Of the paddles scarcely breaks,
With the little silvery drip
Of the water as it shakes
From the blades, the crystal deep

Of the silence of the morn,
Of the forest yet asleep;
And the river reaches borne
In a mirror, purple gray,
Sheer away
To the misty line of light,
Where the forest and the stream
In the shadow meet and plight,
Like a dream.

From amid a stretch of reeds,
Where the lazy river sucks
All the water as it bleeds
From a little curling creek,
And the muskrats peer and sneak
In around the sunken wrecks
Of a tree that swept the skies
Long ago,
On a sudden seven ducks
With a splashy rustle rise,
Stretching out their seven necks,
One before, and two behind,
And the others all arow,
And as steady as the wind
With a swivelling whistle go,
Through the purple shadow led,
Till we only hear their whir
In behind a rocky spur,
Just ahead.

A STAR-FILLED SKY AND THE SUN
Rabindranath Tagore (1861-1941)

A star-filled sky and the sun,
The world teeming with life;
In the midst of these, I have found my place,
So in wonder, my songs come alive.

The surge of boundless time,
That rocks the world in ebb and flow;
In the blood racing through my veins,
I can feel its pull all the way;
So in wonder, my songs come alive.

I have trod on tender grass,
In my ramblings through the woods;
Smitten by the aroma of flowers,
My mind is stirred up high;
Gifts of joy are spread all around;
So in wonder, my songs come alive.

I have lent my ears; opened my eyes;
Poured my heart out on the bosom of the earth;
In the familiar, I have sought
the unknown; So in wonder, my songs come alive.

(*Translated from the Bengali original by Abhik Gupta*)

India-Canada relations are expected to flourish in myriad areas such as counter terrorism, science and technology, trade, education and so on. It is hoped that their shared vision of nature also blooms like a wildflower, inconspicuous yet poignant, frail yet redeeming.

REFERENCES

Brubacher, D., J.P. Gladu and H. Bombay, 'First Nations Governance and Forest Management: A Discussion Paper', Ottawa: National Aboriginal Forestry Association, 2002.

Cairns, J. Jr., 'The Zen of Ecological Restoration: Eight Steps on the Path Toward Enlightenment', *Annals of Earth*, no. XI, 1993, pp. 13-15.

Deb, D. and K.C. Malhotra, 'Conservation Ethos in Local Traditions: The West Bengal Heritage', *Society and Natural Resources*, no. 14, 2001, pp. 711-24.

de Groot, M. and R.J.G. van den Born, 'Humans, Nature and God: Exploring Images of their Interrelationships in Victoria, Canada', *Worldviews*, no. 11, 2007, pp. 324-51.

Dunlap, R.E. et al., 'Measuring Endorsement of the New Environmental Paradigm: A Revised NEP Scale', *Journal of Social Issues*, no. 56, 2000, pp. 425-42.

Elwin, V., *Myths of the North East Frontier of India*, Shillong: North East Frontier Agency.

Fromm, E., *The Anatomy of Human Destructiveness*, New York: Holt, Rinehart and Winston, 1973.

Gadgil, M., 'Prudence and Profligacy: A Human Ecological Perspective', in *The Economics and Ecology of Biodiversity Decline: The Forces Driving Global Change*, ed. T.M. Swanson, Cambridge: Cambridge University Press, 1995, pp. 99-110.

Gadgil, M. and R. Guha, *This Fissured Land*, New Delhi: Oxford University Press, 1992.

Gadgil, M. and V.D. Vartak, 'The Sacred Uses of Nature', in *Social Ecology*, ed. R. Guha, New Delhi: Oxford University Press, 1994, pp. 82-9.

Grove, R., *Green Imperialism: Colonial Expansion, Tropical Island Edens and the Origins of Environmentalism, 1600-1860*, Cambridge: Cambridge University Press, 1995.

Gupta, A., 'Altruism beyond Con-specifics: The Role of Nature Religions', *Eubios Journal of Asian and International Bioethics*, vol. 16, no. 5, 2006, pp. 134-40.

Gupta, A. and K. Guha, 'Tradition and Conservation in Northeastern India: An Ethical Analysis', *Eubios Journal of Asian and International Bioethics*, vol. 12, 2002, pp. 15-18.

Kellert, S.R., 'Perception of Animals in America', in *Perceptions of Animals in American Culture*, ed. R.J. Hoage, Washington DC: Smithsonian Institution Press, 1989, pp. 5-24.

———, *The Value of Life*, Washington DC: Island Press, 1996.

Kellert, S.R. and E.O. Wilson (eds.), *The Biophilia Hypothesis*, Washington DC: Island Press, 1993.

Leopold, L.B., 'Ethos, Equity and the Water Resource', *The Abel Wolman Distinguished Lecture, National Academy of Sciences*, USA, 1990, p. 14.

Little Bear, L., 'Jagged Worldviews Colliding', in *Reclaiming Indigenous Voice and Vision*, ed. Marie Battiste, Vancouver: UBC Press, 2000, pp. 77-85.

Martinez, M.A., Study on Treaties, Agreements and Other Constructive Arrangements (First Progress Report), (E/CN.4/Sub.2/1992/32; 25 August 1992).

Martell, L., *Ecology and Society: An Introduction*, Cambridge: Polity Press, 1994.

Odum, E.P., *Basic Ecology*, New York: Saunders College Publishing, 1983.

Parsons, R. and G. Prest, 'Aboriginal Forestry in Canada', *The Forestry Chronicle*, vol. 79, no. 4, 2003, pp. 779-84.

Rajan, R., 'Imperial Environmentalism or Environmental Imperialism? European Forestry, Colonial Foresters and the Agendas of Forest Management in British India 1800-1900', in *Nature and the Orient: The Environmental History of South and Southeast Asia*, R. Grove, V. Damodaran and S. Sangwan, New Delhi: Oxford University Press, pp. 324-71.

Rhi, B.Y., 'The Phenomenology and Psychology of Korean Shamanism', in *Contemporary Philosophy: A New Survey*, vol. 7: *Asian Philosophy*, Dordrecht: Kluwer Academic Publishers, 1993.

Saraswati, B., 'The Implicit Philosophy and Worldview of Indian Tribes', in *Contemporary Philosophy: A New Survey*, vol. 7: *Asian Philosophy*, Dordrecht: Kluwer Academic Publishers, 1993.

Sessions, G., 'Ecocentrism and the Anthropocentric Detour', in *Deep Ecology for the 21st Century*, ed. G. Sessions, Boston: Shambhala, pp. 156-83.

Singh, L.J., N.B. Singh and A. Gupta, 'Environmental Ethics in the Culture of Meeteis from North East India', in *Bioethics in Asia in the 21st Century*, ed. S.Y. Song, Y.M. Koo and D.R.J. Macer, 2003, Tsukuba: Eubios Ethics Institute, pp. 320-6.

van den Born, R.J.G., *Thinking Nature: Everyday Philosophy of Nature in the Netherlands*, Nijmegen: Radboud University Nijmegen, 2007.

Zweers, W., 'Radicalism or Historical Consciousness: On Breaks and Continuity in the Discussion of Basic Attitudes', in *Ecology, Technology and Culture*, ed. W. Zweers and J.J. Boersema, Cambridge: The White Horse Press, 1995, pp. 63-71.

CHAPTER 17

Opportunities for Indo-Canadian Cooperation in the Energy Sector

DALJIT SINGH

INTRODUCTION

As India is growing economically, it is caught in a difficult situation. On the one hand, it needs to dramatically increase energy services for a large section of its population to meet the Millennium Development Goals (MDG). On the other hand, such a rapid increase in energy consumption will lead to severe resource and environment constraints. In addition to these pressures, there is increasing evidence that we are stressing the global environment to dangerous levels. With more certainty being provided by science about the impacts of increased greenhouse gases (GHG) on the climate, there is urgency for a concerted international effort to curtail emissions of GHGs. Dramatic reductions in emissions are required if we are to avoid irreversible damage to the earth's climate. Together these conditions have created a difficult challenge for the energy policy of India: How to remove bottlenecks in economic development and attend to the energy needs of the poor on a priority basis while protecting the local and global environment?

Other countries, particularly the more technologically-advanced ones have also been looking at how to provide energy services to their populations more effectively. Can India draw from their experience in tackling some of these difficult issues, and are there opportunities for collaborative work in energy between India and these countries? In this paper, we explore whether there may be opportunities for cooperation between India and

Canada in the energy sector. We first provide an overview of the Indian energy sector and the challenges facing it, including issues related to global climate change. Then we discuss what needs to be done to face the challenge and look at some opportunities for Indo-Canadian cooperation in the energy sector.

THE ENERGY SCENARIO IN INDIA

Figure 17.1 shows the primary energy requirements for the country as projected under a high efficiency scenario. As can be seen, India's energy demand is expected to grow dramatically, by about four times between now and 2030. Industry and transport are the two major consumers of commercial energy. Over the period until 2032, industry's share of consumption is likely to remain at a little over half of the commercial energy. The share of transport is likely to increase from about 18 per cent now to 31 per cent in 2032.

Coal plays a dominant role in India's energy mix and is expected to continue to do so for the next few decades. It provides about 50 per cent of the country's energy needs. Coal production is carried out almost exclusively by government companies although recently some coal blocks have been allocated to private

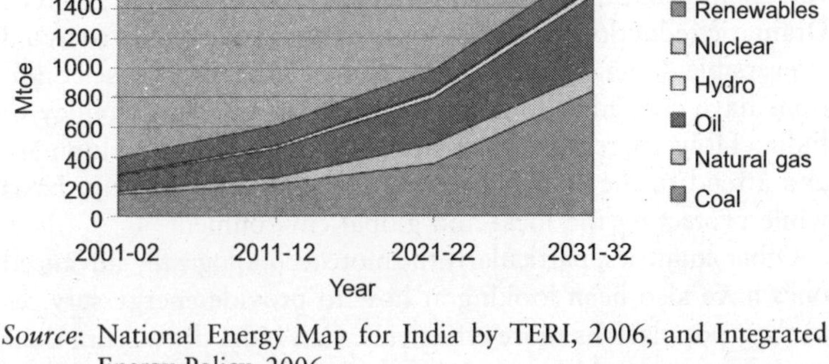

Source: National Energy Map for India by TERI, 2006, and Integrated Energy Policy, 2006.

FIGURE 17.1: TOTAL PRIMARY ENERGY REQUIREMENTS UNDER EFFICIENCY SCENARIO

players. Productivity of Indian coal mines is very low as compared to other countries. Further, known extractable resources are estimated to be about 42 bt, and if no further reserves are added it is expected to last for about 40 years assuming production increases at 5 per cent per year. Because only about 45 per cent of the potentially coal-bearing areas have been systematically explored, there is considerable uncertainty about the actual reserves of coal in the country.

Oil is the second largest fuel consumed in India after coal and accounts for about 35 per cent (145 mt) of the total commercial energy consumed in India, while gas accounts for about 10 per cent (43 mt) (TERI 2006). The established hydrocarbon reserves in India are about 7.5 bt. After being completely controlled and run by the government, the oil and gas sector has recently been opened up for private participation. In the upstream segment, the New Licensing and Exploration Policy (NELP) introduced in 1997-8 has attracted many national and international players to explore large unexplored parts of India.

Problems with Conventional Approach to Planning

The projected growth of energy requirements in India is unsustainable for several reasons. First, it would exceed by a large amount the domestic production capacity for all the fuels, greatly increasing India's dependence on imports. Even for the country's most abundant resource, coal, import dependence would increase. For oil, India already depends on imports for about 70 per cent of its requirements. By 2031, this would increase to 90 per cent of the requirement. Increased imports of fuels would be a drain on the country's foreign exchange reserves.

Second, this level of growth would exceed the capability to add energy infrastructure. At current levels of growth projections, by 2031 India would need to add over 40,000 MW of electric generating capacity every year—add a 1,000 MW power plant every 10 days or so. The country is already facing difficulties with siting of power plants due to local opposition, environmental concerns, and issues with displacement of people, and these difficulties are likely to multiply.

The third reason for unsustainability of the current approach is the effect on the environment of such growth in energy use. Global environmental concerns which we shall discuss in more detail in the next section, will constrain the path that India's energy policy follows. India's current GHG emissions at 1.6 tonnes per capita are a quarter of the world average, but they could grow to almost 4.5 tonnes per capita in 2030 as per the efficiency scenario if there are no significant changes in the fuel mix used. These emissions may be justified, particularly, if there is not much reduction of emissions by the developed countries. But in its role as a responsible member of the community of nations, India may not want to keep increasing its GHG emissions. In addition, local environmental effects will constrain the pattern of energy use in the country.

Global Climate Change

The Stern Report states that reductions of 75 per cent or more of 2,000 level of global emissions will be required by 2050 (Stern 2005). Much of the cumulative emissions have come from the developed countries as they grew since the industrial revolution. This responsibility is recognized in the United Nations Framework Convention on Climate Change (UNFCC) documents which talk about a 'common but differentiated responsibility', and in the Kyoto Protocol under which developed countries committed to reductions in emissions from their 1990 levels while developing countries did not have any commitments. However, most of the developed countries have not reduced their GHG emissions as required by their commitments.

The developed countries have now shifted the focus to emissions by fast developing countries, mainly India and China, saying that these countries' emissions must be constrained also. India and other developing countries are reluctant to commit to quantitative targets because they fear that their development will be jeopardized.

As this debate rages on, with a lot of hot air but little action, the poor countries and the poor people in these countries suffer and are likely to suffer further in the future. First, the poor are the most vulnerable to the impact of climate change, because of their geographic location and because they do not have the resources to adapt their lifestyles to dramatic changes in climate. Second, their prospects for development are curtailed as the required ecological space has shrunk due to the historical emissions of the wealthy. Third, many of the actions being taken by the wealthy, both within and outside the country, to mitigate emissions such as the push for bio-fuels, or building of large hydro-electric and nuclear plants create negative impacts that are borne mostly by the poor.

A Way Out of the Situation

Clearly, India cannot keep planning its energy infrastructure in this manner. The need for an alternative becomes more urgent when it is realized that 70 per cent of the infrastructure that will be there in 2030 is yet to be built. How cities and transportation networks are organized and whatever is built now—power plants, buildings, roads, industries, etc.—is going to be with us for a long time. Further, as experience in other countries has shown, as incomes increase, there is likely to be a dramatic increase in electricity usage as people start buying high-energy use appliances such as air-conditioners, washing machines, etc.

Most often options are selected based on considerations of cost (economic efficiency). However, we believe that environmental considerations and equity must also be factored into the selection of a particular option or energy path. Unfortunately, because environment-friendly solutions often cost more, and equity considerations imply additional costs (or subsidies), economic, environmental, and equity considerations are seen to be in opposition. But it does not have to be so. There are choices that satisfy all three considerations (3-E criteria). As Figure 17.2 illustrates, given the challenges faced by India, we must apply our creativity to find solutions that lie in the overlapping space of economic efficiency, environment-friendliness, and equity.

One good example of such an option is the promotion of public transportation. Increased public transport instead of personal transport, has tremendous positive impact on local air quality, reduces personal expenditures while reducing energy consumption, and benefits the poor the most. Another example

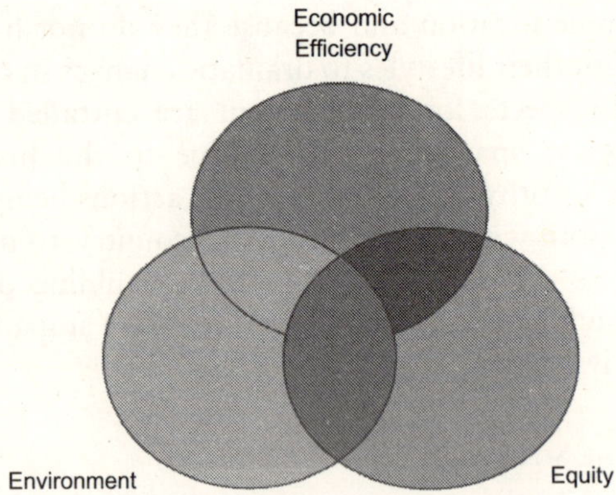

FIGURE 17.2. 3-E APPROACH TO ENERGY PLANNING

is promotion of solar PV based LED home lighting systems for the 40 per cent unconnected houses, rather than subsidization of grid connected MW size PV plants. The first route would promote PV technology and immediately offer lighting to 10 million houses while the second route would only put in place a couple of hundred MW of PV power plants—which would be too small for the grid to have any impact. Similar such examples can be seen in rural electrification, agricultural energy use, etc.

The equity considerations in the 3-E approach require the country's energy policy to be designed to provide lifeline energy to all citizens. In addition, the energy policy should fufill the following conditions to ensure energy security in a more conventional sense:

- Supply of energy at competitive prices.
- Supply at all times with a given level of confidence taking into consideration disruptions that can reasonably be expected.

These requirements including the 3-E criteria lead us to the following steps for developing energy plans: (1) reduce energy requirements; (2) reduce dependence on imports of fuels; (3) diversify fuel choices and supply sources.

OPPORTUNITIES TO COLLABORATE WITH CANADA

CANADA'S ENERGY SCENARIO (EIA 2007)

Canada is richly endowed with natural resources. In 2004 it produced 470 mt of energy. In contrast, India produced only about 180 mt of commercial energy supply sources. Its exports form a large share of the energy used in the US; with 11 per cent, 16 per cent, and 1 per cent of US oil, gas, and electricity respectively coming from Canada. At 180 billion barrels (24,480 mt), Canada's oil reserves are second only to Saudi Arabia and more than 30 times that of India. However, about 95 per cent of these reserves are in oil sands deposits which are difficult to extract and process. Canada is the largest producer of natural gas in the Western hemisphere after the US. Canada is also endowed with extensive hydro resources and is one of the world's largest producers of hydroelectricity. About 58 per cent of its electricity comes from hydro, about 25 per cent from thermal, 15 per cent from nuclear power, and about 2 per cent from renewables.

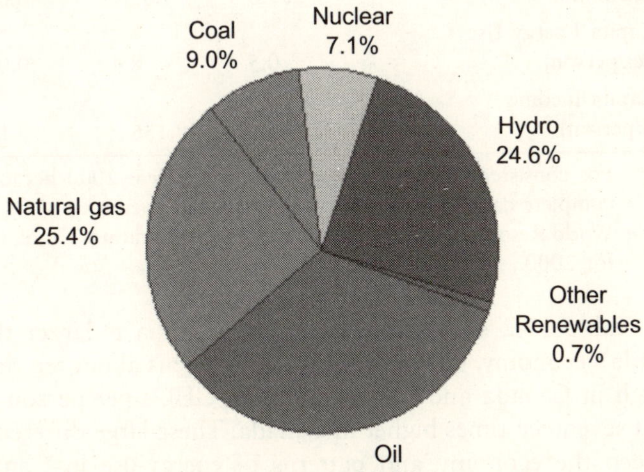

Source: *EIA International Energy Annual*, 2004.

FIGURE 17.3 TOTAL ENERGY CONSUMPTION IN CANADA, BY TYPE (2004)

Canada's commercial energy consumption is about 240 mt. Canada's per capita CO_2 emissions were 17 tonnes in 2004, which was more than three times the world average, and they are increasing by 0.7 per cent per year, or about 0.12 tonne per capita per year. Given the concerns with GHG emissions, Canada will face a tough challenge in reducing its emissions without significantly affecting the quality of life of its people.

There are large differences between the economies of India and Canada and how energy is used in the two countries. Table 17.2 highlights some of the differences.

TABLE 17.2 COMPARISON OF ENERGY-USE IN INDIA AND CANADA

Feature of Country	India	Canada	Ratio
Size of Economy (billion US $)	3,078	932	3.3
Energy Use—Annual (mt)	573	269	2.1
Population	1,079	32	33.7
Intensity of GHG Emissions (tonnes/million US $)	389.6	589.1	0.66
Per Capita Energy Use (tonnes/person)	0.5	8.4	0.06
Per Capita Income (US $/person)	2,851	29,136	0.10

Note: For consistency we have used data for the year 2000 because a complete data-set was not available for later years.

Source: World Resources Institute—Climate Analysis Indicators Tool; Data for 2000.

As Table 17.2 shows, the economy of India is larger than Canada's economy, but the per capita income is about ten times as high in Canada and the emissions of GHGs per person are about seventeen times higher in Canada. These large differences between the economy and patterns of energy-use in Canada and India must be kept in mind as we seek opportunities for cooperation in the energy sector. However, in spite of these differences, there are several areas where there may be opportunities for learning and cooperation. We look at those areas next.

Build an Equitable and Enforceable Global Emissions Reduction Regime

The most pressing issue in energy today is that of climate change and the need for drastic reductions in emissions of GHGs. So the most important area for cooperation would be for Canada and India to work together to break the political impasse by facilitating the development of an equitable and enforceable global reductions regime. Any global emissions reduction regime must meet the following requirements:

- It must recognize the responsibility of the wealthy nations for their historical cumulative emissions that have shrunk the ecological space left for development of the poorer countries.
- It must recognize the right to development of the poorer countries.
- Following from the above two requirements, it must require the wealthier nations to shoulder the additional cost burden of the poorer countries de-carbonizing their economies.
- It must ensure that the equity considerations between countries are also followed within a country. Thus the wealthy people in a country must shoulder the burden of providing for the development needs of their poorer country-men/women.
- It must ensure that the mitigation measures taken by wealthy countries/people such as production of bio-fuels or development of large hydro/nuclear power plants do not impose negative impacts on the poor.

One of the essential features of a global emissions reduction regime is an effective mechanism to provide adequate and predictable funds for technology transfer by the developed countries to the developing countries for emission reductions. The Stern Report estimates that the fund requirement would be around 1 per cent of World GDP[1] (Stern 2005), although some people estimate that the requirements would be significantly higher. In any case, assuming the estimate to be 1 per cent of GDP, the required funds would have been about US $550 billion in 2007.

In comparison with these estimates, the amount of fund transfer for climate change mitigation has been miniscule. The Global Environment Facility (GEF), helps developing countries fund projects and programmes that protect the global environment, and supports projects related to not just climate change, but also biodiversity, international waters, land degradation, the ozone layer, and persistent organic pollutants. In 2006, 32 donor countries pledged 3.13 billion US $ to fund operations for four years (GEF 2008); a mere 0.6 per cent of the amount estimated by the Stern Report. Another example of funds transfer is carbon trading through the CDM. Here too the volume of fund transfer has been miniscule compared to the requirements. Helme (2006) reports that the total volume of carbon traded under CDM in 2005 was about 2.5 billion US $.

Given the amounts involved, it is clear that a separate fund will be required to provide for technology transfer, acquisition and development by the developing countries to meet emission reduction targets. Furthermore, mechanisms must be implemented to ensure that the stream of funding from such a fund is predictable. In addition, the governance structure for such a fund must be equitable and not biased in favour of donor countries.

Development of End-use Energy Efficient Technology

In India while some attention has been paid to efficiency in the supply of energy, relatively less attention has been paid to improving efficiency at the end-use level. This situation is changing with the passage of the Energy Conservation Act in 2001 and the establishment of the Bureau of Energy Efficiency (BEE).

In Canada, the Office of Energy Efficiency (OEE) in Natural Resources Canada has been promoting overall energy efficiency through energy conservation, improvements in efficiency of end-uses, and promotion of alternate sources of energy (OEE 2006). OEE uses a strategy combining information programmes, support for voluntary programmes, financial incentives, and regulations setting minimum standards. In addition, OEE maintains strong links with Canada Centre for Mineral and Energy Technology (CANMET) which develops advanced energy efficient technology. Cooperation between BEE and OEE would allow Canada to share best practices with India in promoting energy efficiency.

In addition, Canada has an interdepartmental technology investment programme, Technology Early Action Measures (TEAM), to demonstrate promising technologies. Through TEAM, Canada has demonstration projects in several areas such as integrated and intelligent buildings, advanced industrial process technologies, and alternative-fuel vehicles (TEAM 2008). Collaborative research in these areas could also be explored.

Development of Low Energy Building Materials

Infrastructure creation consumes the largest share of energy in India when one considers both direct and indirect energy use. Given the fact that half of the population in India is yet to have robust homes and that over 60 per cent of the infrastructure that will be in use in 2030 is yet to be built, energy consumption due to buildings and other infrastructure is going to remain high in the coming decades. This feature of economic growth is common for many developing countries. Therefore, any effort to reduce energy use cannot ignore development of low energy building materials and building technology. Biomass based advanced building materials offers a ray of hope. Use of biomass as materials saves three to four times more energy than the energy generated from it by direct combustion or through the bio-fuels route, because the energy used in making steel, cement, etc., is saved.

Indo-Canadian collaboration can facilitate development of improved biomass materials and construction techniques, and adapt Canada's building standards for buildings using wooden materials. Efforts should be targeted at construction of houses, small bridges, and roads. Collaborative research would have to factor in that India can use only small timber based materials, unlike as in Canada.

Biomass-based Energy

Canada has been carrying out demonstration projects on conversion of waste to energy or biofuels (TEAM 2008). Opportunities should be explored to see if India can benefit from these programmes in several areas such as: using agricultural wastes more efficiently; energy from household waste; and production of biofuels.

Renewable Energy Technologies and Distributed Generation

As the concern of GHG emissions increases, alternatives to fossil fuels are going to become more important and renewable energy technologies will play a greater role in India's energy mix. Canada is carrying out research in many of these technologies such as wind turbines, wave energy, and solar energy (TEAM 2008). India should explore opportunities for cooperation in these areas.

Hydropower

The two countries could collaborate on forecasting potential impact of global warming on river runoffs. This is important for both countries for their own reasons. 58 per cent of Canada's electricity comes from hydropower and India is planning to build nearly 100,000 MW of new dams in northern India, which are largely fed by runoff from melting glaciers of the Himalayas. India can benefit from learning techniques of hydropower management especially scheduling.

Cleaner Coal Technologies

Coal is India's most abundant resource. However, there are concerns about the environmental impacts of using coal for electricity generation, and an interest in increasing efficiency in order to make the most of the coal resource. Therefore, it is natural that India looks for development of cleaner coal technologies (CCT) for electricity generation.

It is critical that India creates a strategic technology plan (road map) to evaluate the plethora of technology options in CCTs available, and to select and invest in appropriate options. Because of uncertainties in development of technologies, it should be emphasized that the roadmapping process needs to be dynamic and iterative.

Canada has already developed a road map and it would be very useful for India to learn from Canada's experience in bringing together diverse stakeholders. However, India will not be able to directly use the Canadian coal technologies road map because conditions in India are different. The Indian context for CCT development differs considerably from the Canadian context in terms of: (1) quality of coal; (2) economic considerations and availability of alternative fuels; and (3) CO_2 emission reduction requirements. Further, India may not be willing to pay substantially for the CCT technology while its emissions remain far below the world average emissions. India needs to develop its own technology development road map. Then it can explore how partnerships and collaborations with Canada and other countries can be used most appropriately.

CONCLUSION

India is facing a difficult challenge in the development of its energy policy as it tries to dramatically improve energy services for a large section of its population while coping with the severe resource and environmental constraints that such rapid growth is likely to bring. Clearly, conventional planning methods will not work and a shift in paradigm is required where energy is provided in ways that are economically efficient, equitable, and environment-friendly.

Much of this work will have to be done by India itself. However, cooperation with Canada can be of great value most importantly in the development of a global emissions reduction regime that is effective, enforceable, and equitable. Cooperation with Canada can also be explored in the areas of: end-use energy efficiency, low-energy building materials; biomass-based energy; renewable energy technologies; hydro-power; and cleaner-coal technologies.

NOTE

1. The Stern Report's estimate is based on bringing the level of CO_2 to 500-50 ppm which would still result in a temperature rise of about 3 °C with some consequent damages. If the CO_2 level in the atmosphere is stabilized at 450 ppm, damages will be lower, but costs of emissions reductions will of course be higher.

REFERENCES

EIA, Energy Information Administration, Department of Energy, Washington DC, USA: *Canada Country Brief*, April 2007, www.eia.doe.gov.

GEF, Global Environment Facility, GEF Secretariat, 1818 H Street, NW, MSN G6-602,Washington, DC: 20433, 2008 http://www.gefweb.org/

Helme, Ned, *The International Carbon Market: Myths and Realities*, Washington, DC: Tutorial for Inter-American Development Bank, 31 May 2006.

OEE, Office of Energy Efficiency, Natural Resources Canada, *State of Energy Efficiency in Canada, Report 2006*; Energy Publications, Office of Energy Efficiency, Natural Resources Canada, Ottawa, 2006.

Planning Commission, *Integrated Energy Policy—Report of the Expert Committee*, New Delhi: Government of India, Planning Commission, August 2006.

Stern, Nicholas, *Stern Review: The Economics of Climate Change*, Cambridge: Cambridge University Press, 2005.

TEAM, *Technology Early Action Measures*, Government of Canada, 2008, http://www.team.gc.ca/english/

TERI, The Energy and Resources Institute, *National Energy Map for India—Technology Vision 2030*, New Delhi: TERI Press, 2006.

CHAPTER 18

Theorizing Indo-Canadian Diaspora

Religion: The Missing Factor?*

OM P. JUNEJA

Rewarded for their loyalty to the Queen Empress during the Mutiny of 1857, the Sikh soldiers were invited to participate in the celebration of the Diamond Jubilee Celebrations of Queen Victoria in 1897 in England. On their return they passed through Canada and brought back the good news of God's plenty. Canada thus became the choice destination for the young farmers who wished to make it big. Sikhs were the first to emigrate from India to Canada. Bravely facing racial discrimination, social injustice and harsh climate, they numbered around three thousand five hundred in 1908. Though thousands of miles away, they maintained their relationship with their homes in the Punjab by visiting them regularly and also by buying land and other assets in their villages from the remittances they sent home. Eventually these immigrants also bought land and lumber mills in Canada and replicated the village of Paldi in British Columbia from the village with the same name in the Hoshiarpur district in the Punjab from where they had come.

The story of their migration to Canada is a fascinating narrative of courage, suffering, racism, resistance, hard work, camaraderie, and above all of believing. It is a story of the *Panthic* faithfuls who lived the three values of *seva*, *izzat* and *panth* highly cherished by Sikhism. Discussing the teleology of

* This research was initiated by UGC under Emeritus Fellowship awarded to the author.

return of these immigrants, I have argued in an earlier version of this paper that they were rooted in a spiritual homeland (Juneja 2004), though thousands of miles away from their homes in India.

Discussing the question of rootedness of the diasporic Indian, Parekh compares him with the banyan tree, 'like a banyan tree, the traditional symbol of the Indian way of life, he spreads out his roots in several soils, drawing nourishment from one when the rest dry up. *Far from being homeless, he has several homes, and that is the way he has come to feel at home in the world*' (Parekh 1993. Emphasis added).

Thus a Person of Indian Origin to use the terminology coined by the Government of India *Report of the High Level Committee on Indian Diaspora* can never be homeless (http://Indiaspora.nic.in/pressrelease.htm) like Bhikhu Parekh himself, a Lord in the House of Commons of the British Parliament and a very well established intellectual, who has homes both in the UK and in India and is at home both in the West and the East. Some others who would fall in this category are Amartya Sen, Zakir Husain, Ravi Shankar, Amitav Ghosh, Vikram Seth, and many others. For them nationality is a matter of passports and visas and not of (be)/longing.

However, homelessness of an émigré, an expatriate or an exile is proverbial. This has been celebrated by Joseph Conrad, Mikhail Bakhtin, Fyodor Dostoevsky, V.S. Naipaul, Salman Rushdie, Homi Bhabha among many as an epistemological privilege of being an outsider insider with all the significant creative possibilities that such a vision can offer. Bakhtin calls it 'oxotopy': a privileged position of the outsider insider:

> Being an expatriate, not directly involved in the mundane existence of the paternal land left behind, he is supposedly a non-aligned epistemological observer ambivalent in two or more cultures and has ontology of an outsider insider. The expatriate is therefore a privileged writer who appropriates the strategies of the outsider insider for abrogating the epistemologies of the outside culture to lighten up the ontological processes of the paternal culture. (Mikhail Bakhtin quoted in Juneja 2002)

Aritha van Herk, a second generation Dutch Canadian, argues that emigration/immigration is both a 'disguise' and 'damnation' in *In Visible Ink*. It acts as a disguise for creating a magic of the self:

> The act of emigration enables the new immigrant to fashion her or his own fiction and live it out. In short, the transformation does not require Rushdie's drastic explosion and miraculous survival (as in *The Satanic Verses*) but only a journey from one shore to another. *The immigrant becomes magician of the self.* (van Herk 1997: 174, emphasis added)

According to van Herk, there are three stories in emigration/immigration: overt, covert and absent. While the overt story is a simple story of migration from one country to another, the covert story is 'much more complex and multi-foliated'. They are 'same but differently tainted: oxymorons of themselves, a contradictory reflectance' and offer a difficult choice: 'No matter which goddess he favoured, Paris would have purchased disaster, but his choice has dictated the story we all know, of Helen and Menelaus and fallen Troy.' Emphasizing the need for making a choice between contradictory reflectants, which are not binary opposites, van Herk problematizes the crisis that an immigrant writer has to face to 'entext' the immigrant experience.

Once the overt and covert story of immigration has been somehow constructed for entexting the immigrant experience, the *I* of this story then faces a real challenge of entexting a tale that is ever changing and can perform a disappearing act, which results itself in a transformation, 'the staggered illusion of story built on story, one telling/resisting on the quicksand construction of the previous telling'.

Thus, after making a choice between contradicting reflectants of an overt and covert story and also facing the temptations of creating a fiction of fiction, the writer has now to indulge in the illusory/magical feat of imagining a possibility by its absence, which is the third story:

> The third *legerdemain* (an illusory feat considered magical by naïve observers) that has become evident is not the overlooked obvious or the secret/hidden story. This is the most illusive of all immigration's fiction. . . . It offers itself as possibility by its absence. . . . This is the story of this *I* would have been if her parents had not emigrated to Canada but to Australia (which is what her father wanted to do . . .) and so this too is a story that does not exist, but yet demands to be

told because it never happened, though it was invented. (van Herk 1997: 186)

Thus having written all the three overt, covert and the absent stories, the immigrant becomes a writer of the self and the other. 'The immigrant as the fiction writer of the self becomes then a creature of the imagination, and practical considerations aside, the inventor of a desired and desirable other' concludes van Herk.

Eli Mandel in his essay 'The Ethnic Voice in Canadian Writing' (1978) had noted a 'doubleness' or 'duplicity' that all immigrants live in and grapple with. Quoting him in her book *Splitting Images: Contemporary Canadian Ironies*, Linda Hutcheon says, 'The literature that comes out of this experience itself exists at the "interface of two cultures": a form concerned to define itself, its voice, in the dialogic self and other and the duplicities of self-creation, transformation, and identities.' She further explores this 'doubleness' and 'duplicity' and finds the location of the trope of irony in this. She therefore remarks:

> I have been suggesting that irony is one way of coming to terms with this kind of duplicity, for it is the trope that incarnates doubleness, and it does so in ways that are particularly useful to the 'other': irony allows other to address the dominant culture from within that culture's own set of values and modes of understanding, without being co-opted by it and without sacrificing the right to dissent, contradict, and resist. . . . The need to retain this right is specially clear in the work of those writers who belong to . . . 'visible minorities'. Perhaps this has a lot to do with the discrimination that they feel. (Hutcheon 1991: 49).

Elaborating further Hutcheon quotes Arun Mukherjee who argues that South Asian writers may be said to possess that double vision which comes only with alienation from the dominant group. Hutcheon concludes by arguing that this double vision is a fruitful ground for ironies that voice the contradictions that the outsider can see.

Tracing 'ironies' in real life situation of the minority communities thus privileges a mainstream critic, while a person from 'visible minority' may not be privileged to see this irony in a real life that she lives as is clear from the revised views of Arun

Mukherjee who discusses this kind of irony as 'racialized irony' in *Opposional Aesthetics* (1994) because the two readers from majority and minority communities read this irony differently.

For Aritha van Herk, an immigrant writer is a magician of the self. For Linda Hutcheon this writer has 'duplicity': a trope that incarnates 'doubleness' which has a trace of irony in it. For Mukherjee this 'irony' is 'racialized irony' which is read by the dominating and the dominated cultures differently. Her methods of readings from the hyphenated space of diaspora therefore are, 'oppositional to the dominant ideologies of literary and cultural analysis in Euro-America' (Mukherjee 1994).

Vijay Mishra, however, locates this irony in the real life situation of an Indo-Canadian. As in the poem 'Chameleons' by Sadhu Binning in which the poet, on his return visit to his homeland, forgets the pain and suffering caused by immigration. Recounting his journey back home flying from Vancouver to Delhi, the poet contemplates 'in a few hours/we change completely/like chameleons' and forgets all the pain while stooping and crawling in picking strawberries and other labour-intensive activities. He also forgets the racist stares that burn through his skin and also the pain of not speaking Punjabi with their children. The poem concludes ironically with 'what occupies our thoughts/is multiplication/faster than computers/we churn our figures/multiplying one with twenty-five/our pockets feel heavier' (Binning 1994: 43). This multiplication/conversion of one Canadian dollar to twenty-five Indian Rupees makes him jump the class.

This elevation of social status due to economic mobility of the Punjabi/Sikh emigrants from Paldi village in the Punjab in the first few decades of the twentieth century has been analysed by Archana B. Verma in a study of the immigrants in her book *The Making of the Little Punjab in Canada*, which is discussed later in this paper.

DIASPORAS OLD AND NEW

Vijay Mishra divides the Indian diaspora into two 'diasporas old and new, of classic and late capitalism respectively'. He notes:

2. The predominantly white host community did not accept them except as labourers;
3. A large number of these immigrants travelleved between Punjab and British Columbia as poly-seasonal migrants;
4. They came primarily to acquire capital to improve the economic and social status of their families at home;
5. They always viewed themselves through the eyes of their relatives and friends at 'home' who attached the highest value to *izzat* (honour) and *seva* (community service) defined in their rural community; and
6. They perceived themselves as 'sojourners' and not as settlers, though eventually some of them settled in Canada permanently.

Studying the sociological causes of the above characteristics, Verma suggests that the Punjabi immigrants remained bound to their homeland because of their kinship ties and also for considerations of status. She notes,

> Paldi emigrants, who continued to construct their identity in terms of village relationships, consistently worked towards higher status for their familial and caste kin back home. They achieved this by investing foreign earned capital in the traditional symbols of status, by maintaining close contact with their families and by continuing to respect the concept of *Izzat*, obligation, respect and honour, towards the kin group. Thus even though the two villages were half a world apart and existed in different socio-cultural environments, an intricate web of linkages connected them more closely than mere proximity would have done. . . . The predominant factor in this development was the home-village orientation of the immigrants and their focus on the Punjabi values of social standing and Seva or service to their kin in the homeland. (Verma 2002: 16)

Though a full examination of the concepts of *izzat* and *seva* can be done only when more data is collected and analysed, we can, however, surmise that it was this social and cultural capital that these early immigrants carried with them from their villages to Canada that sustained them to survive the cold climate of Canadian racism. Verma, however, seems to follow what Verne A. Dusenbury notes though in a different context a 'deep seated and recurrent Western ontological and sociological dualism (e.g.

spirit and matter, sacred and secular, religion and ethnicity)' that categorize Sikhs either as ethnic or a religious community (Dusenbury 2007). Agreeing with the dominant ethno-sociology, which is not premised on this dualism, Dusenbury argues that Sikhs do not neatly fall into familiar Western social categories and hence are both a social and religious group. Verma's readings of the internal social structure of the Mahton community are sociological and not socio-religious that Dusenbury cautions us about the Sikhs. Both the values highlighted by Verma, though significant, do not account for the success of this community of the faithfuls.

Thus, the aspect that has been completely neglected by Verma (2004) as by the others is the role that religion has played in the settlement of early immigrants who spent their first savings in building gurdwaras across British Columbia. N. Gerald Barrier (2007) in his essay tracing the transformation of information resources and values among the Sikh emigrants in the early twentieth century notes that this emigration happened during a dynamic phase of Sikh history when they became world travellers, as temporary unskilled workers, visitors or as emigrants. It is during this phase of revitalization and expansion, that the Sikhs built a network of communication between many institutions, communities and individuals. In some instances (like the creation of Paldi village in British Columbia) certain institutions and their values were transplanted in foreign lands: 'In some instances, Sikh and Punjab institutions were transferred or recreated and vital links established with the homeland. These contacts involved the transfer of resources, information, and values back and forth between Sikhs in the Punjab and abroad' asserts Barrier (2007). He further notes that many contemporary ideological issues and institutions of contemporary Sikhism have their roots in the cultural debates and revitalization that took place between 1875 and 1920.

Like the 'Hindu Tool Kit' (Mishra in Paranjpe 2001) the indentured labourers carried with them when they left their homeland to work on the sugar plantations in the Caribbean islands and Pacific Sea islands, the Sikhs carried with them the notion of the 'Sikh Panth' as a 'worship genus' composed of any and all persons who share the Guru's substances, acquired through their 'physiological engagement' with the scriptural Guru and corporate Guru, not with the land of Punjab, asserts Dusenbury (2007). The land of Punjab for many of those who established the village of Paldi in British Columbia thus conceptualised becomes a 'spiritual homeland', the birthplace of their Gurus and the site of historical shrines. Gurdwaras in British Columbia thus literally became the doors to the Guru for a physiological engagement with the scriptural Guru. Establishing a gurdwara, therefore, satisfied both the sociological and religious needs of the early Sikh immigrants, whose internal community structure was rooted in the three cardinal values of *izzat*, *seva* and *panth* (as discussed below).

Appreciating the faith and zeal of these immigrants, Walter W. Baer who attended the opening ceremony of the Sikh temple, Victoria, wrote the following in the *Canadian Courier* in May 1912:

> The temple cost nearly 10,000 and is a monument to religious zeal and faith of a people far from home, in a strange land which has not treated them justly and among a people to whom they are united by but two bonds. The first of these is their attachment to the throne empire of the British people whom delivered India and second is their unconquerable conviction that 'God hath made of one flesh all the nations of the earth.' It is the last rather than the first which makes the Sikh tolerant of the abuse and misrepresentation to which he has been subjected by the people who send missionaries to show him the way to salvation. (Baer cited in Singh 1989)

Commenting on the Zionists practice of crying before the Wailing Wall in Jerusalem for a return to their homeland, Baer further remarks,

> It is for the perpetuation of their reformed religion that the Sikhs have erected temple in British Columbia to share with their brethren in Victoria the glad event. The one dedicated on Sunday was the third in the province, for already there are Sikh temples at Vancouver and Abbotsford, B.C., the Sikhs evidently determined to keep their faith unspotted from the world. They do not intend to hang their harps upon the willows and remorsefully ask, 'How can we sing the songs of Zion in a strange land. (Baer cited in Singh 1989: 88)

For the early Sikh emigrants, who perceived themselves as

sojourners and not as settlers, home was constructed through the narratives of their kith and kin who visited their villages regularly. Unlike the indentured labourers, who could not come back to their villages in U.P., or Bihar, home was not fixed and fossilized on a point of departure, but was generally in a flux furbished and re-furbished by the long arduous journeys back home. They could replicate a village in a foreign land that was hostile to them due to their faith that taught them, as noted by Baer, 'God hath made of one flesh all the nations of the earth.'

The role of religion in shaping the culture of a nation, though ignored by some early scholars, is now being recognised in a post-industrial society like Canada:

Scholars have come to recognize that secularisation doesn't work for interpreting post-industrial societies. Yet the dominant ideologies of the governments, media and the arts appear to hold the view that only in a secular society can freedom and democracy flourish. . . . The pervasiveness of the secular ideology is measured by who and what it chooses to exclude and in this respect religions have become one of the most frequently excluded expressions of difference in Canadian society. That this negatively effects the Muslim, Jew, Christian, Hindu, and Sikh is simply a fact. (Bowlby 2003: 45-6)

Paul Bramadat, therefore, argues that the basic Canadian values are rooted in Christianity at the neglect of the values highlighted by other religions including Hinduism, Sikhism, and Islam. Making a case for the inclusion of other religions in the system of core Canadian values, he notes that they should also be allowed to contribute to this vast reservoir for building a multi ethnic, multi cultural and multi lingual Canadian society:

Consider this partial list of values and ideas: *notions of civility and moderation . . . the advanced or late capitalism . . . charity and commitment to solidarity* on which our social safety net is based; the justice and forgiveness on which aspects of our criminal justice are purportedly based; the patriarchy which is such a crucial . . . *heterosexual monogamous* model of marriage, *chastity* that guides some groups' sexual mores; *the objectification of natural world . . . the individualism.* These are just some of the dimensions of our society that spring directly or indirectly from certain forms of Christianity. Canada's non-Christian traditions also embrace and promote several of these values, but most emerged out of the dominant role of Christianity in Canadian society. (Bramadat 2003)

He pleads for a more inclusive system of values for Canada as it is increasingly becoming a real multi religious society every day.

Manjit Inder in his paper 'Between History and Cultural Politics: Reflections on the Punjabi Writings of the Diaspora' (Inder 2001) notes that for most of these writers the return to homeland is metaphorical existing in what Edward Said perceives as 'imaginative geography and history' and Anderson calls 'imagined community'. He asserts, 'Sikhs carried with them their own native cultural memories and problems of geographical assimilation—a significant offshoot of diasporic existential situation'. He however recognises the concept of *izzat* when he remarks, 'Punjabi pride in native history, tradition, folk, the great Gurus' teachings in the holy scripture, the richness of Punjabi language and literature basically stemmed from a strong sense of roots, principles and values in a collective authentication of their way of life and the overall philosophic world-view.'

He finds a contradiction (and therefore confusion?) in the diasporan Punjabi writing because of a pull between 'progression and retreat, euphoria and despair, swimming with and against the tide simultaneously, oscillating between a putative dream of permanent return and social transformations'. He goes on to argue that the Punjabi/Sikh diaspora has developed 'occupational cultures' within transnational cultures. Quoting Homi Bhabha, he asserts that the immigrant's final return to home and national culture 'is always mythic, a stuff of longing and prayers . . . as imagined it never happens, there is no final return'. He then notes that 'the diaspora, apart from its indigenous and shared features, centres on the religious idea of the *panth* (community) through which its cartography is constituted by heterogeneous movements of history that in turn link local formations'.

Manjit Inder, though under the influence of high theory finds contradictions in the diasporic Punjabi writings, however, recognizes the importance of the religious idea of *panth*. If further explored, the idea of *panth*, I would like to argue, is just not any community as Inder translates it, but as a religious community. As discussed earlier in this paper, the notion of the 'Sikh Panth' inclusive of the scriptural Guru and corporate Guru, would render a different reading to most poems that Inder analyses. These poems are rooted in the idea of the community of the faithful and not in the idea of a secularized community that one wishes to identify with in a post-industrial society defined by alienation. It is a community of the faithfuls who are bound to a faith through an internal structure of kith and kin as much as by the idea of the scriptural Guru and corporate Guru. For this community of faithfuls, India occupies a central place: the place of all the sacrifices of the ten Gurus for the sake of practising their faith against the tyranny of despots and emperors. These poets writing in Punjabi constantly look 'homeward' for replenishment through faith, which is located in India, their 'spiritual homeland' and not elsewhere geographically. Teleology of 'Return' of the Punjabi diaspora, thus, will have to take into account the key concepts of *izzat*, *seva* and *panth* and the significance of *Guru Granth* in the lives of the diasporan Sikhs for its definition.

Bhikhu Parekh in his paper mentioned in the beginning of this paper identifying the *Ramayana* as the central text of the Hindu diaspora, finds four reasons for its popularity. Explaining the first and the foremost reason, he says,

> First, its theme of exile, suffering, struggle and eventual return resonated with the experiences of the Hindu migrants, especially but not exclusively those of the indentured labourers. The *Ramayana* gave them conceptual tools to make sense of their predicament, articulated their fears, and showed them how to cope with these. Hindus were reluctant migrants, leaving India not in a mood of alienation or a spirit of adventure and curiosity but as an economic necessity. Not surprisingly they saw their migration as a semi-voluntary exile, very like that of Rama's, and constantly referred to as *vanvas*. The recent Hindu settlers do not see migration in this way. But they do remain deeply attached to India and her way of life, their parents, close relations and friends continue to live there and many of them would have preferred not to emigrate if the economic situation at home had been better. The idea of being in exile is not without some appeal to them either. (Parekh 1993)

Simple and uncomplicated nature of the text, the *Ramayana* as a social treatise and a relatively casteless text are the other reasons for its popularity among the migrants, argues Parekh. He, however, does not discuss the religious significance of this text, which was the central text in the imaginary of the diaspora of the indentured labourers. However, he recognizes that religion is one of the three modes of self-identification of the Indian diaspora, 'Overseas Hindus had three modes of self-identification, and thus three forms of social organization available to them, namely caste, religion and their region of origin.' Unlike the universalist religions of Islam and Christianity, Hinduism is an ethnic religion deeply embedded in the Hindu way of life and in the Indian soil. He claims that a Hindu has 'an acute sense of rootedness, of what is and is not its cultural home, and deep respect for cultural and territorial boundaries. For the Hindus, they belong to India, their religious and cultural home.' He agues, 'If the Hindus therefore went to live elsewhere, they were outsiders or guests. Given their mode of self-understanding, overseas *Hindus conceptualised themselves as guests in their countries of settlement*' (emphasis added).

When they could not come back to India, the indentured labourers of the colonial India replenished the memory of India in many ways: 'The old Indian diaspora replicated the space of India and sacralised the stones and rivers of the new lands,' asserts Vijay Mishra. To put it differently, the old diaspora carried with it a sort of 'Hindu toolbox' to Indianize its new surroundings:

> Their homeland is a series of objects, fragments of narratives that they keep in their heads or in their suitcases. Like hawkers, they can reconstitute their lives through the contents of their knapsacks: a Ganpati icon, a dog-eared copy of the Gita or the Quran, an old sari or other deshi outfit, a photograph of a pilgrimage or, in modern times, a videocassette of the latest hit from the home country. (Mishra in Paranjpe 2001)

Though the Sikh pioneers of the diaspora in British Columbia did not carry with them a 'Hindu tool box' described above by Mishra, they did carry, the *Guru Granth Sahib* with them and built temporary places of worship on the lands of the lumber mills in Vancouver and Victoria, where they worked around 1904. Soon after the foundation stone for building the Sikh Temple, Vancouver was laid in October 1907 and this temple was opened on 19 January 1908 under the management of Khalsa Diwan Society (Singh 1989). Building a gurdwara was an act of faith for this all male community of the faithfuls. Describing the effect of the temple on the lives of the immigrants, Jagpal writes,

> The temple played an important part in helping the newcomers. On landing it was usually their first stop. Here they could seek spiritual strength and salvation. They would thank God for their safe journey, offer a donation, eat a meal and check in with the temple officials. Here they could connect with relatives and friends who would find them housing and work. (Jagpal 1994: 56)

These temples thus were both places of worship, social, cultural and community centres. They became a safe haven for keeping the community with its traditions mostly intact. They also charged the internal structure of the community with *izzat*, *seva* and *panth*: the three cardinal values of social, communal and religious lives of the early Sikh emigrants.

Presenting a brief survey of the above theories in this paper, I have attempted to critique them with the help of the social reality of the Paldi village established by the Mahton Sikhs in British Columbia. The Punjabi/ Sikh diaspora of British Columbia, unlike that of the indentured labourers of the old diaspora, defines 'here' and 'there' not as two separate spaces divided by two countries and cultures, but as one 'community of faith' guided by the concepts of *izzat*, *seva* and *panth*. The questions of 'home' and 'homeland', therefore, will have to be framed differently for this community which has survived the racist regimes during the colonial period and is a thriving Indo-Canadian community in the post-colonial multi-cultural Canada. They cannot be raised either within the high metropolitan theory based on alienation of the urban elite mostly speaking from the ivory towers of the universities in the West or within the 'wailing wall' of the Fijian/Caribbean theories of the Old Diaspora. To theorise this experience, a new model of 'Spiral/circular' movement has been developed in this paper. This theory though seemingly close to that of the Pravasi Bharatiya Divas theorists, differs in its approach to India as a 'spiritual homeland'. In the case of these early emigrant Sikhs the notion of the 'spiritual homeland' was through their Sikh identity embedded in the three values of *izzat*, *seva* and *panth* with a clear locus in the Guru: that is, the history of the Gurus, and the philosophy of the *Adi Granth*, the *Guru Granth Sahib*. The notion of 'homeland' as *Bharat Mata* (Mother India) as the Pravasi Bhartiya Divas theorists seem to suggest, however, in the case of this community of the faithfuls, is not so much located in the physical geography of a sacred place as in the value system of the early Sikh identity.

This may be exemplified with the help of the some Gujarati emigrants from Kheda, Anand and Baroda districts of Gujarat who follow the Swaminarayan-BAPS, a sect of Hinduism. These Gujaratis like the Mahton Sikhs discussed in this paper follow the preaching and the value system embedded in the *Shikshapatri*, their holy book, written by Bhagwan Swaminarayan, the first proponent of the sect, originally in Sanskrit has 212 verses. It is the central rule book for all devotees of the Swaminarayan Sampraday and contains guidelines on how to lead a happy, peaceful, healthy and God-centred life as claimed in their website http://www.swaminarayan.org/publications/index.htm. Claiming their belief in the Hindu tradition and philosophy, the Swaminarayan Sampraday (BAPS sect) they have identified the basic concepts of service, obedience, tolerance, glory of the *sadhu*, faith, love for God, ever-presence of God, supremacy of God, etc., as their basic values, besides building temples around the globe. This thriving community of the faithfuls recently built Canada's most ornate Hindu temple—a 40-million dollar vision, hand-carved by Indian artisans out of 24,000 blocks of Italian marble and Turkish limestone. It was opened in Toronto in September 2007 for the public by BAPS. This Mandir is the largest initiative of its kind ever undertaken by the Indo-Canadian community.

Mandir, for this sect, like the gurdwara for the early Sikh Indo-Canadians, is a socio-cultural centre of the community of the faithfuls for the propagation and preservation of a value system and culture. Like the Sikhs of the Mahton community discussed earlier in this paper, they would like to locate themselves within the BAPS-Sampraday as much as associate themselves with their ancestral homes in the Charotar region of central Gujarat and not with the entire range of history and geography of India or even Gujarat that the Pravasi Bharatiya Divas theorists would wish to believe.

If we study the immigration practices of the Ismaili Khojas of Gujarat, who practice a specific sect of Islam and like Sikhs and Gujaratis are spread all over the world, the picture may not be much different. I would, therefore, like to argue that the role of religion and the consequent value system that it propagates in the lives of these immigrants cannot be ignored. In fact, any theory that ignores this is at risk of becoming irrelevant in the post-9/11 world.

Arguing for considering 'Diaspora' as an analytical category, Martin Baumann notes that a dispersed group of people forming diaspora has a certain type of consciousness that has religious implications with its emphasis on its 'geographic-sociological aspects' of 'relational facts of a *perpetual recollecting identification with a fictitious or a far away existent geographic territory and its cultural-religious traditions*' constituting such a consciousness (Barrier 2007 in Sahu and Maharaj: 73). A diaspora so defined places a lot of emphasis on enduring 'identification of people with a cultural-religious point of reference outside the current country of living' to form a collective identity. He further notes,

> More often than not it involves an identificational difference of the diaspora in contrast with the society's dominant cultural and religious norms and orientations. This difference of a cultural-religious identification bound to a region and culture outside the current culture of residence. . . . This emphasis if meant to (re)direct attention and awareness to the prototypical role of religious identity in situations of settlement after migration; of the perpetuation of a specific identificational difference; or . . . of the demarcation and strengthening of collective identity in a culturally foreign environment. (Barrier 2007 in Sahu and Maharaj: 73-4)

The identificational difference of the diaspora that may be contrasting to the dominant cultural and religious norms and orientations, in fact, is the crux of the matter that the modern state is engaged in most immigrant receiving societies. This crucial factor, however, has been ignored in the theorization of the diaspora, which cannot be complete without taking religion/ sect into consideration in the case of most diasporan communities like that of the Jews. The resilience and endurance in maintaining their religious/sectarian identity through a contact with their homeland, imagined or real, repudiate the construction the diaspora theories based on the famous Anderson pronouncement. For these faithfuls, home is real: neither imagined nor 'invented (Anderson 1983) as most of their fellow-members know each other, even if they do not meet each other or hear of them, they are in communion with each other because of their being a member of the community of the faithfuls. In this age of transnational migrations, such diasporan communities, in fact, have developed a close linkage or networking with motherland, real or imaginary, because of fast transportation, instant communication, international travel, global flow of capital and goods and networking technologies. Religious/sectarian identity is one of the main factors of these diasporan communities.

Do these value systems merge into the predominantly Christian value system of the Canadian society or are they a threat to the larger Canadian value system of—(a) notion of civility and moderation; (b) charity and commitment to stability and (c) justice and forgiveness, etc., is a matter for further research investigation?

REFERENCES

Anderson, Benedict, *Imagined Communities: Reflections on the Origin and Spread of Nationalism*, London: Verso, 1983.

Bramadat, Paul, 'From the Background to the Foreground: Understanding Religion in Canadian Society', *Canadian Diversity/Diversite Canadienne.* vol. 2, no. 1, Spring 2003, pp. 69-71.

Barrier, Gerald N., 'Sikh Emigrants and Their Homeland: The Transformation of Resources and Values in the Early Twentieth Century', in Ajaya Kumar Sahu and Brij Maharaj (eds.), *Sociology of Diaspora: A Reader*, vol. 2, Jaipur & New Delhi: Rawat Publications, 2007, pp. 663-91.

Binning, Sadhu, *No More Watno Dur*, Toronto: TSAR, 1994.

Bowlby, Paul W.R., 'Diasporic Religions in Canada: Opportunities and Challenges', *Canadian Issues: Themes Canadians*, 2003, pp. 45-6.

Dusenbery, Verne A., 'A Sikh Diaspora? Contested Identities and Constructed Realities', in *Sociology of Diaspora: A Reader*, vol. 2, Ajaya Kumar and Brij Maharaj Sahu, eds., Jaipur and New Delhi: Rawat Publications, 2007, pp. 692-717.

Hutcheon, Linda, *Splitting Images: Contemporary Canadian Ironies*, Toronto: Oxford University Press, 1991.

Inder, Manjit, 'Between History and Cultural Politics: Reflections on the Punjabi Writings of the Diaspora', in *Indiaspora: Theories, Histories, Texts*, ed. Makarand Paranjpe, New Delhi: Indialog Publications, 2001, pp. 93-116.

Jagpal, Sarjeet Singh, *Becoming Canadians: Pioneer Sikhs in Their Own Words*, Vancouver: Harbour Publishing, 1994.

Johnston, Hugh and Tara Singh Bains, *The Four Quarters of the Night: The Life Journey of an Immigrant Sikh*, Montreal: McGill Queen's University Press, 1995.

Juneja, Om P., 'Exotopy of the Non-aligned Epistemological Expatriate Writer: The Ontology of Naipaul and Mistry', *Critical Practice*, vol. IX, no. 1, 2002, pp. 26-40.

———, 'Where is Here? Teleology of Return: The Homeland of Punjabi Diaspora in British Columbia', in *Theorizing and Critiquing Indian Diaspora*, ed. Kavita Sharma, Adesh Pal and Tapas Chakrabarti, New Delhi: Creative Books, 2004.

Mishra, Vijay, 'Diasporas and the Art of Impossible Mourning', in *Indiaspora: Theories, Histories, Texts*, ed. Makarand Paranjpe, New Delhi: Indialog Publications, 2001, pp. 24-51.

Mukherjee, Arun, *Oppositional Aesthetics: Readings from a Hyphenated Space*, Toronto: TSAR, 1994.

Parekh, Bhikhu, 'Some Reflections on the Indian Diaspora', *Journal of Contemporary Thought*, no. 3, 1993, pp. 105-51.

Singh, Kesar, *Canadian Sikhs and Kamagata Maru (Part One)*, Surrey, B.C., Canada V3T 1C7: 30-1.

van Herk, Aritha, *In Visible Ink (Crypto-Fictions)*, Edmonton: Newest Press, 1991.

Verma, Archana B., *The Making of the Little Punjab in Canada: Patterns of Immigration*, New Delhi: Sage Publications, 2002.

CHAPTER 19

Journey of Indian Immigrants towards Canadian Nationhood: Gleanings from a Canadian-Punjabi Literary Periodical

RAJ KUMAR HANS

The movement of people from their place of birth to different and distant places in modern times has raised issues of geo-political, economic, cultural and psychological dimensions. If this process has opened up the democratic doors of multicultural existence and human rights it has also thrown up regressive religious and racial ideologies of fundamentalist nature to complicate the problems of migrants and diasporic communities. If there are xenophobic zealots to close the doors to 'strangers', there are ardent votaries of building bridges between different peoples and nations. The last quarter of the past century, the last decade more so, was a period of manifest 'liberalization' and 'globalization' when earlier notions of 'home' and 'nation-hood' came under serious strains. Indeed, globalization has led to the diffusion of the exclusivist attitudes and is facilitating a march forward without the past baggage. In this changing scenario, the people who had left their home countries and settled elsewhere have started redefining their notions of 'home', 'community' and 'country' with a degree of relaxed reflection. Poets, writers, journalists and intellectuals play a important role in easing up the tensions around the notions of the 'home country' and 'host country' when the latter gets suffused into the former. Despite some mute but also at times loud continuities of discrimination around notions of race, class, gender and ethnicity, a global change in attitudes about national identities has heralded a new era of more liberal and tolerant understanding of differences and diversities. This stands best exemplified in the case of people from India and Canada with their changing attitudes to each other. The paper shall address this change in attitude as far as it gets reflected in the creative and discursive writings of Punjabi settlers in Canada that appeared in a Punjabi literary and cultural magazine, namely *Watan*, published from Vancouver from 1989 to 1994. While the first part of the paper would try to contextualize the problematic in its historical settings of Indians in Canada and their attempts to reflect their diasporic experience in literary writings the second part would focus on the post-1970s literary expressions especially represented in *Watan*.

I

The history of Indians in Canada, who were mostly Punjabis, goes back to the beginning of the twentieth century. Over time, the community has grown in size and many among them have made their mark in economic, political, and social arenas of Canadian life. The literary production in Punjabi had started very early on the Canadian soil. Several papers made their appearance in Vancouver, the most important being *Free Hindustan, Swadesh Sewak, Khalsa Herald, The Aryan, Sansar, The Hindustanee*, and *Canada and India*, in the first two decades of the twentieth century (Buchignani 1977: 91-2; Tatla 1994; Hans 1998: 885). Early Punjabi literature in Canada was produced by people who were part of a revolutionary group, the Ghadar Party, founded in California to liberate India from the British. Munsha Singh Dukhi, Harnam Singh Tundilaat, Bhagwan Singh and Bhai Daljit Singh, are some of the better-known names. They felt rather uncomfortable with the prevalent racism and turned into revolutionaries. Thereafter there was a long lull as community continued to be small. By the end of the First World War, complete ban on South Asian immigration and the failure of the Ghadar had left the small community badly bruised and battered. And yet this listless collectivity found a counseling voice in Kartar Singh who encouraged his compatriots socializing with other Canadian people. Highly educated while in Punjab circumstances had taken him to Canada in 1912. He was well versed in Sikh religion and had received a warm welcome from the community in Vancouver. After initial years of Punjabi journalism spent in Vancouver, he left for Toronto where he continued his writings. His naturalization to Canada occurred very early and he very earnestly wished 'Canadianisation' of all the remaining east Indians. He came to acquire a command over English language as well as good knowledge of the dominant culture of Canada (Hans 1998: 885).

Besides editing magazines and other tracts, Kartar Singh edited a periodical called *India and Canada: A Journal of Interpretation and Information* from June 1929 to September 1936. It was a bilingual paper written in English and Punjabi and had two purposes:

> For its immediate usefulness, this publication will endeavour to place before the Canadian public the truth and nothing but the truth, about the people of North India, now resident in Canada. After giving examples and facts, its appeal will be to invite Canada to scientifically examine now—when sufficient practical results are available—the fitness or unfitness, the merits and demerits, of the Sikh settlers in Canada. The other aspect of the work of this journal will be to inform, through its Punjabee section, the people of North India here and at home, about the life, institutions, problems, requirements, standards and ideals of Canada.

It was very well written and informed the Punjabi community of significant events here and in India. Since many Sikhs of them did not socialize beyond their own family or neighbourhood, this journal added another dimension to their social lives. It helped in giving them some legitimacy. Seeing their affairs appear in print made the Punjabis feel more a part of Canadian society. It was well received by the Canadian press both in the West as well as in the East and Kartar Singh's efforts came to be lauded in their respective papers (Hans 1998: 885-6).

The 1940s were an economic boom time for Indians living in BC. Jobs were plentiful because of the wartime economy and the shortage of labour at the mills and elsewhere. Their businesses flourished as they took over lucrative contracts, their trucking businesses prospered, and their traditional investments in real estate grew. The community prospered economically through hard work, extensive social networking and better employment opportunities. However, this newfound prosperity did little to change their standing as Canadians. They still could not call Canada their home until they gained the franchise. This one issue dominated all others and became community's major goal. Eventually, east Indians were granted the municipal franchise as per enactment of 2 April 1947 and 15 September 1947. They had finally become Canadians, technically. 'Mr. Manga S. Jagpal says that on the day they got their rights the Sikhs got dressed up in their best suits and went downtown. There they proudly lined up to eat at the fancy restaurants that had previously refused them service. By law, they had to serve them now, and they did.' They could now call Canada their home (Jagpal 1994).

The ban on immigration also began to ease up and in the early 1950s and by 1960s, the number of Punjabis entering Canada slowly began to increase. The early 1970s, however, saw a dramatic increase that changed the composition and profile of the Punjabi community. The new wave of immigrants included a large number of educated youth. These young Punjabis had grown up in a free country and many of them had been exposed to the Naxalite movement in the Punjab. The degree of confidence and self-esteem these people carried was different than their earlier counterparts. Though Vancouver continued to remain the primary point of entry for the Punjabis, they also moved to metropolitan centres like Toronto and Montreal. The post-1970 immigrants constituted what is called the 'new community', which had to distinguish itself from the larger white community as well as from the older Punjabi community. (For details see Buchignani & Indra 1985; Chadney 1984; Judge 1998.)

Some of these newcomers were already writing in Punjabi while others got motivated after being in Canada. For instance, Gurcharan Rampuri was a well-established writer before coming to Canada in 1964. While some kept on writing about the need to change deplorable conditions in Punjab, others slowly began to focus on their experiences as immigrants in Canada. The increase in numbers of Punjabi writers led to the formation of cultural and literary organizations in and around Vancouver. The 'Punjabi Cultural Association of Vancouver' was formed in 1971. In the same year a literary magazine, *Jivan Sanjhan* (Life's Sharing) began its publication. The next year saw the formation of the 'Punjabi Literary Association of Vancouver' and the start of a monthly literary magazine *Watno Dur* (Far from Homeland). Punjabi writers began to meet twice a month and their writings started to appear in their own magazines. In a short time Vancouver appeared on the Punjabi literary map. There were similar developments in other Canadian cities wherever Punjabis had settled in large numbers. The 'Punjabi Literary Association' was formed at Edmonton in 1979 whereas at Winnipeg 'Punjabi Literature and Cultural Association' appeared in 1982. In 1983, theatre groups were launched: 'Vancouver Sath' at Vancouver and 'People's Cultural Theatre' at Calgary. 'Calgary School of Drama' was formed in 1988 whereas 'Punjabi Art Association' came up in 1991 (Binning & Hundal 2000).

Following the Great Britain, Canada is the second most active place for Punjabi writings outside the Punjab. The first anthology entitled, *Canadian Punjabi Poetry*, was produced by Vancouver's Punjabi Literary Association in 1979, which included 27 poets from across the country. Since then a large number of other collections have been published by various organizations and individuals across Canada. Though the main genre of expression for Punjabi writers in Canada continues to be poetry, a considerable number of short-story collections and novels have also been published. Writers such as Gurcharan Rampuri, Ajmer Rode, Surjit Kalsi, Navtej Bharti, Ravinder Ravi, Balbir Momi, Sadhu Binning and many others have all been living and writing in Canada for decades now and hold a place of considerable respect in Punjabi literature (Binning 2006).

II

Watan, that appeared on the literary horizon of the Canadian-Punjabi from 1989 to 1994, was a co-edited quarterly by Sadhu

Binning and Sukhwant Hundal. Both of them had earlier co-edited a monthly *Watno Dur* from 1976 to 1983. The very act of rechristening of *Watno Dur* to *Watan* is indicative of the transformation of minds of the educated immigrants how they steadily came to see, accept and identify Canada as their *watan* (country). So much so that towards the closure of *Watan*, Sadhu Binning published a book *No More Watno Dur* in 1995 to give an explicit expression to that process. Sadhu was born in India and immigrated to Canada in 1967. He has published several books of poetry, fiction, plays and research. A founding member of 'Vancouver Sath', a theatre collective, Sadhu is a central figure in the Punjabi literary and cultural community. He has been teaching Punjabi at UBC since 1988 and also working as a translator. Sukhwant Hundal is a writer, playwright, director, and journalist as he also co-hosts weekly radio programme in Punjabi and English CFRO-FM Vancouver and hosts the Punjabi edition of *Interactive* Channel M Vancouver. Like Sadhu and Sukhwant there are many well educated immigrants who through their thought process made Canada as their country. The contributors to the magazine, writers and readers, very well reflect this psychological change. Quite often, a complete collapse of the immigrants with the host national stream is seen in the third or fourth generation but what we find here with Punjabi writers and intellectuals is that the very first generation succeeds in achieving that goal. This became possible because of their education, literary sensibility, progressive ideology (most of them exposed to Marxism) and cultural activism.

The inaugural issue of the quarterly *Watan* (July-August-September 1989) was designed to be a special number devoted to *Kamagata Maru*, remembering the landmark episode in the history of Indo-Canadian community. The opening paragraph of the editorial was reflective of the changed situation since then:

> There are increasing literary and cultural activities in the last decade in Canada. The magazines and newspapers have contributed significantly towards development of Punjabi language, literature and culture. In this regard the role of *Watno Dur* from 1973 to 1986 is outstanding. We feel happy and take pride that we were an integral part of *Watno Dur*. Now at restarting the journal, while contemplating over several

issues along with its name we feel that it is not always healthy and wise to think of the country as a far away place. (All translations are mine unless otherwise stated.)

The editorial concludes on a conciliatory note:

> We demand from the Canadian Government to admit the mistake committed 75 years ago to take conciliatory measures. . . . We feel such admission by the government would create cordial feelings. Overcoming historic mistakes obviates occurrence of new ones. (*Watan*, 1.1.1989)

While the inaugural number of *Watan* brings out several old documents including photographs pertaining to *Kamagata Maru*, the poems, essays and research articles like Hugh Johnston's are published to give a balanced and objective view of the historic event. Ajmer Rode's poem 'Forgiveness' (*Muafi*) in the number (vol. 1, no. 1, 1989) is reflective of the changing attitude of the community in Canada. The opening stanza reads:

> I am a good citizen of this country
> At least that is what I think
> Not been to jail till now
> Never evaded taxes
> Nor I have taken LSD
> Not sold marijuana
> 'have not become a thug
> by selling Company shares underhand
> All have a right over UIC
> I have not procured even that.

Assertion of being Canadian is clear and loud in the Spring 1990 volume of *Watan*:

> We are not 'guests' in this country nor we have come here as 'visitors'. We must accept this reality that it is our own country and we should live here as it is our own home. Being citizens of this country we must perform all our duties and use all available rights.
>
> . . .
>
> It is the need of the time that while preserving our Punjabiness we should try to become part of the Canadian society. Its language must be learnt. Information and knowledge of its history and culture be gained. Punjabis in this country have their own history and it is our duty to research that for the sake of next generations.

Commenting on Canadian-Punjabis' obsessive anxieties during the peak of Sikh militancy in Punjab, the editors tried to diffuse that preoccupation:

> We cannot dispute the fact that being immigrants from Hindustan, what transpires there occupies special space in our lives and that we do get affected and do react to those happenings. *But now we have made Canada our own home and we and our children are to live our entire lives here. Therefore we should prioritize our attention to issues that are local and work for their resolutions. This is our biggest need.* (Emphasis added)

Sadhu Binning's deeply connecting, transformative poem 'WatnoN Dur NahiN' that was to become the title poem of his collection of poetry in 1995 first appeared in the Summer 1992 issue of *Watan*.

WatnoN Dur NahiN (Original Punjabi)	No More Watno Dur (Translation mine)
Sadee beet gayee hai is mitti te vichardiaN, khaNdiaN, peendiaN nuN jamdiaN, mardiaN nuN sadee beet gayee hai apne aap nuN wanton dur dasdiaN nuN	Hundred years have passed on this soil thinking, eating, drinking here being and dying here Hundred years have passed announcing myself 'far from the country'
hun tak main jo vee khat likhe khat jo main apni maN nuN likhe dost nuN likhe mahbub nuN likhe uh sab khat ik bigane deson apne desh nuN likhe	letters that I wrote so far to my mother to my friend to my beloved were all written from a foreign land to the motherland
par hune jo khat apne baap di maut bare likhia hai uh apne desoN paya hai main likhia hai bahut der pehlaN chhadia si ghar baap mere ki safar la ke murh khetaN baNne aa bahega	but the letter that I just wrote about my father's death is dispatched from my country I wrote: My father left his home a long time ago Dreaming to one day return to his fields

sukh 'ch bitaunn layee aakhri vare
par hun BC di barfeelee nadee 'ch
main khud taare uhde phul
te pal ku paani di teh 'te karke
alop huNde kinke
mere layee naviN asleeyat ujagar
kar gaye
mera baap is mitti 'ch milia hai
mera put is mitti chuN jamia hai
ih mitti hun watan hai mera
watnon dur nahiN hai

to spend the last of his days in
peace
Now I have immersed his remains
in the BC's icy river
The disappearing elements
in the small water
awakened me to the new truth
My father is immersed in this soil
my son is born of this soil
This soil is now my country
not far from country

The major poets appearing in the pages of *Watan* which included Ajmer Rode, Surinder Dhanjal, Iqbal Ramuwalia, Nadim Parmar, Sadhu, Surjit Kalsi, Shashi Samundra, Sukhinder Kamboj, Sukhpal, Darshan Gill, Navtej Bharati, etc., have expressed the anxieties of their community about notions of 'home', and 'nation' and had been at the forefront to confront even the latecomer Sikh militants in Canada. Discursive writings like essays, especially by Sukhwant Hundal, have covered the global issues: economic, political as well as ideological. Whether he talks about the American hegemony in the world, white racism, decline of Soviet socialism or about the health of the developing countries, he writes from a progressive/leftist perspective which itself is universal in character. Then titles of his essays are self-explanatory: 'Hunger in the World: Who is Responsible?'(*Watan*, 1, 2, Fall 1989); 'Why Rich Countries Give Aid to the Poor Countries? (*Watan*, 2, 2, Fall 1990); 'Merchants of Poison' (*Watan*, 3, 2, Fall 1991); 'International Terrorism and the United States' (*Watan*, 4, 1, Summer 1992); 'International Monetory Fund and Third World Countries' (*Watan*, Series 15, 4, 3, Spring 1993); 'Sex Selection' (*Watan*, Series 18, 5, 2, Fall 1993); 'International Media and Poor Countries' (*Watan*, Series 21-2, 6, 1-2, Fall 1993). Similarly, Joginder Singh Randhawa's essay 'Oil Crisis and Conflicts in Persian Gulf' (*Watan*, 2, 3, Winter 1991), Balinder Johal's 'Sexual Discrimination and New Technologies' (*Watan*, 2, 4, Spring 1991), Gurmit Tiwana's 'The Tragic End of the Russian Socialist Experiment: A View' (*Watan*, 4, 1, Summer 1992) and Sufi

Amarjit's 'Western Civilization and India' (*Watan*, 2, 4, Spring 1991) are few other essays in the same direction.

The regular columns were excellent educative material for the community to get attuned to their surroundings. 'Mental Health' by Dr. Rajpal Singh became a very popular column that highlighted complex problems of sex, drugs, addiction and those pertaining to cultural adjustments. 'Apne Lok' by Ajmer Rode was a humorous column bringing out conflicting bahaviour of the community in readjusting in different cultural setting. 'Activities', another column, informed the readers about various cultural programmes organized by the community. 'Book Introductions' kept the readers informed about the healthy appearances in Punjabi. 'And You Wrote' was a good interactive space for readers and writers for their comments and suggestions.

Publishing interviews with cultural ambassadors was an interesting features of the magazine. Interviews with Om Puri, Prof. Sayeed Firani Kammi, Dr Raghbir Singh, Sohan Kadri, Shashi Samundra and Film Director, Manjira Dutta explored possibilities of diffusing the prejudices about people belonging to different cultural backgrounds.

Overall, most of the contributors, whether poets, story writers, discursive writers or readers themselves, convey the sense of a need to come to terms with the changed cultural reality; while retaining linguistic and cultural traits they try to adapt to the objective material and social environment. Accepting Canada as a nation was felt no more a technical necessity but a cultural need to learn and share knowledge across boundaries. The Punjabis who have settled in Canada for a few decades have tried their best to adapt to the new milieu without throwing away their linguistic and cultural heritage. In the process they have understood the value of multiculturalism and tolerance of Canada so well to make full use of this liberal ethos to resituate their cultural aspirations. Literary periodicals like *Watan* have served as platforms for diverse expressions of Punjabi settlers as they have also helped building bridges between cultures. The importance of literary and cultural interventions can hardly be underrated if they cannot be overstated.

REFERENCES

Binning, Sadhu, 'Punjabi-Canadian Literature: A Brief Introduction', *Journal of Punjab Studies*, vol. 13, nos. 1 & 2, Spring Fall 2006, pp. 279-85.

Binning, Sadhu and Sukhwant Hundal, *Sangharsh de Sau Vre: Kanada vich Punjabi Pragatisheel Lahar* (One Hundred Years of Struggle: Punjabi Progressive Movement in Canada), Ludhiana: Chetna Prakashan, 2000.

Buchignani, Norman, 'Bibliography: A Review of the Historical and Sociological Literature on East Indians in Canada', in *Canadian Ethnic Studies*, vol. IX, no. 1, 1977, pp. 91-2

Buchignani, Norman, Doreen Indra and Ram Srivastava, *Continuous Journey: A Social History of South Asians in Canada*, Toronto, 1985.

Chadney, James G., *The Sikhs of Vancouver*, New York: AMS Press, 1984.

Hans, Raj Kumar, 'Punjabi Press and Immigrant Culture in British Columbia between Wars', *Economic and Political Weekly*, vol. XXXIII, no. 16, April 1998.

Hundal, Sukhwant and Sadhu Binning (eds.), *Katha Canada*, Ludhiana: Chetna Prakashan, 2000.

Jagpal, Sarjeet Singh, *Becoming Canadian: Pioneer Sikhs in Their Own Words*, Vancouver: Harbour Publishing, 1994.

Tatla, Darshan, 'Minor Voices: The Evolution of the Punjabi Press in North America', *International Journal of Punjab Studies*, vol. I, no. 1, 1994.

Wallia, C.J.S., 'Review of 'No More Watno Dur', *India Star Review of Books*, http://www.indiastar.com/wallia8.htm.

Watan—Literary and Cultural Quarterly of Punjabi (nos. 21-2), Vancouver, 1989-94.

CHAPTER 20

Political Autonomy and Economic Development of Indigenous Peoples: A Comparative Study of North-East India and British Columbia

H. SRIKANTH

When colonialism was making inroads into continents and countries little known to Europeans at large, both apologists as well as critics of colonialism in the West contended that the indigenous peoples inhabiting the colonies and semi-colonies would perish as communities unless they learnt to adapt themselves to the changing times.[1]

It was then assumed that penetration of the market economy, expansion of the institutions of private property, development of modern education, spread of Christianity, and growth of liberal values and practices in the colonized world would overshadow and replace the pre-capitalist structures and traditions and subsume the native communities in the capitalist mainstream. Such predictions, however, did not come true. Despite all the hardships and sufferings that they had to encounter, the indigenous peoples survived the onslaughts of colonialism and made their presence felt in the post-war world by leading many a struggle for recognition and restoration of the aboriginal identities and rights. Far from giving up their identities, the indigenous peoples are reorganizing themselves as communities and fighting for restoration of their dignity and rights as indigenous peoples. Compelled to address the indigenous peoples' demands, liberal democratic states like Canada and India are now amending their constitutions, restructuring their political and administrative structures and reviewing their development strategies.

To make sense of the ongoing indigenous peoples' struggles and their impact in liberal democratic countries, the present paper attempts to make a comparative study of the experiences and movements of Native Indians in British Columbia (BC) and hill tribes in north-east India and then analyse the responses of the governments in the two countries to the indigenous peoples' demands for autonomy and self-reliance. Since the histories of indigenous peoples in the two countries have different trajectories, the paper first presents the case of hill tribes of north-east India and then contrasts it with the experiences of Native Indians in British Columbia. Later it examines how far the governments in the two liberal democratic countries have been able to fulfil the indigenous peoples' aspirations for political autonomy and economic self-reliance.

HILL COMMUNITIES OF NORTH-EAST INDIA

The hill areas of north-east India are inhabited by several Mongoloid tribes belonging to different linguistic groups. The communities seem to have migrated to the region from the East and South-East Asian countries. While some of them like the Bodos and Karbis had migrated to the region several centuries ago, some like the Kukis came to settle only during the colonial rule. Prior to the British colonization, barring a few tribes like Jaintias, Dimasas and Bodos which were to some extent Hinduized, most hill tribes in the region did not have any cultural or economic contacts with the mainland India. The communities had village councils headed by tribal chiefs. Each tribal community had its own unique social and political organizations and they survived for centuries relying on shifting cultivation, food gathering and hunting. In times of scarcity, they were attacking the villages in the adjacent plains areas and plundering food and other essential items from the non-tribal communities. Inter-tribal conflicts and wars between hill tribes and adjacent kingdoms in the plains were common in the region. There were occasions when the kings in the adjoining plain areas defeated the tribal chiefs and punished the tribal communities who used to attack them.[2] But the hill communities at no point of time were subjected to the political rule of any kingdoms or empires that ruled the mainland India. It was only in nineteenth century that the hills were colonized and brought under the British colonial rule.

HILL TRIBES UNDER THE BRITISH RULE

By the middle of the eighteenth century almost all the territories in the mainland India came under the British colonial rule. But it took more than a century for the British to subjugate and tame the hill communities inhabiting the north-eastern region. In the mainland India the British did not make distinction between tribal and non-tribal areas. The colonial land and forest policies pursued during the British period deprived the tribes in the mainland India of control over their traditional land and other resources and subjected the tribal communities to worst forms of exploitation and oppression.[3] However, when it came to the hill areas of north-east India, the colonial authorities followed altogether a different kind of policy towards the native tribal communities. As these areas constituted the borders or frontier areas of British India, both for strategic and economic reasons the British felt it unnecessary to impose political and administrative institutions that were in force in mainland India. Instead they sought to realize their colonial objectives by taming the traditional tribal elite and using the traditional institutions. In the name of protecting the hill tribes from the plain people, different acts were enacted to keep the tribal areas aloof from the plains and even positive interactions between tribal and non-tribal communities were forbidden. Only the Christian missionaries were allowed to enter these hostile hill areas to preach the Gospel and to provide basic education and health facilities for the tribal communities. On their part, the colonial authorities did not make any sincere efforts to bring about drastic changes in the socio-economic base of the tribal communities. The hill districts that the British gave shape to were included as part of Assam, but the elected governments in Assam virtually had no control over the hill areas.[4] By confining the tribal communities to the hills and restraining their movements, the British made the tribal communities feel that they belong to the hills and only the hills belong to them. By developing scripts and by starting schools in tribal languages, the missionaries contributed to the formation of distinct ethnic identities as hill tribes.[5] As the Indian nationalist movement failed to touch most tribal communities, the natives in the hill areas could not fully identify themselves with the emerging Indian nation and Indian people.

HILL COMMUNITIES IN POST-COLONIAL INDIA

Despite the fact that the Indian nationalist struggle had little influence on the hill tribes, by mere accident of history the hill areas of north-eastern region became a part of independent India. On the eve of transfer of power, the hill tribes had their inhibitions and reservations against joining the Indian Union. They were afraid that they would lose their autonomy and their control over the resources once they become a part of Indian State. The native response to the post-colonial state's intention to integrate them into the Indian Union was not uniform. Most tribes in Northeastern Frontier Tracts bordering China and Bhutan (later NEFA) remained oblivious of the political processes taking place in the country. Whereas some like the Garos and the Khasis aspired for greater autonomy for themselves within the Indian Union, the Mizos found themselves divided. While the Mizo Union representing the emerging educated middle classes were in support of joining India, the Mizo chiefs were against it. But on the other extreme were the Nagas who were reluctant to be a part of the Indian Union right from the beginning.[6] The Indian nationalist leaders who had by then become the ruling political elite tried to accommodate the aspirations of the hill communities of composite Assam through the Sixth Schedule of the Indian Constitution which made special provision for autonomous district councils (ADC) and autonomous regional councils (ARC), granting the hill tribes of the state of Assam powers to protect their respective culture, social institutions and resources. Barring the Nagas who rose in revolt right in 1948, other major hill communities of composite Assam more or less accepted the Sixth Schedule and experimented with ADCs and ARCs. In order to contain the Naga insurgency, the Government of India created a separate state of Nagaland in 1963, guaranteeing greater powers to the Nagas within the Indian Union.[7] This political concession was, however, not palatable to the radicals among the Nagas, who continued to fight for independence from the Indian Union. Meanwhile, the communities that experimented with the Sixth Schedule also began to feel that they had too little powers and resources to control their destinies. The emerging educated middle-class elites among the hill tribes aspired for more powers and began to fight for separate hill states for the tribes. To accommodate their aspirations, the new states of Meghalaya, Mizoram and Arunachal Pradesh were created in course of time by reorganizing the north-eastern region.[8] Only North Cachar Hills and Mikir Hills inhabited by the hill tribes such as Dimasas and Karbis could be convinced to remain in the state of Assam by guaranteeing enhanced powers to their district councils. As on date, 90 per cent of seats in the district councils and the newly constituted tribal dominant states are in the control of the representatives of the indigenous tribal communities. The district councils and the tribal dominant states have enacted several laws to prevent land alienation and to protect the customs and traditions of native tribal communities. They exercise control over agriculture, horticulture, forests, education, health and police. The Government of India guarantees special concessions to these communities in matters relating to taxation and financial allocations. Practically these district councils and hill states of north-east India acquire special status in Indian federal set-up.[9]

As such the Indian State has gone far ahead of many other democratic nation states as far as accommodating the interests of the indigenous peoples is concerned. However, several critics hold the view that far from benefiting the natives, these initiatives have adversely affected these traditional communities. It is pointed out that introduction of modern constitutional political structures and practices have marginalized the traditional tribal institutions. After the district councils and tribal state governments came into existence traditional political institutions were either abolished, like the Mizo chieftainship, or were made weak and dependent. Assuming the role as protectors of tribal interests, the modern constitutional institutions now control and dominate all aspects of tribal life. As powers and roles of these formal institutions increased, community control over natural resources has gradually started diminishing. Class divisions started making their appearance in the tribal societies and the newly emerging middle class elite have started controlling the economy and politics of the hills, at times much to the detriment of the interests of majority of the tribal people. Hence it is often held that the formation of tribal dominant states has only benefited the ruling tribal elite. Further, the ethnic nature of the leadership in the ADCs and the state governments in the hill areas has widened the inter-tribal differences in the hill areas and compelled many other smaller tribal communities to come out with demands for separate states for themselves. Inability of the ADCs and state governments to mobilize internal sources makes them heavily dependent on the financial support from the central government. Naturally, they fail to innovate and implement programmes and policies appropriate and beneficial to the overall interests of the tribal communities.[10]

NATIVE CANADIANS IN BRITISH COLUMBIA

As was the case with north-east India, the province of British Columbia in Canada was also almost the last post of British colonialism in Canada. It was almost three hundred years after John Cobot claimed Terre Nova in the name of King Henry VII in 1497, that the British fur traders and adventurers began to move westward exploring the islands in and the territories around the Pacific Ocean.[11] British Columbia became the Crown colony only in the middle of the nineteenth century. Prior to their colonization the territory was inhabited by several indigenous communities. Each had its own social, cultural and political institutions. They spoke different languages and were at different stages of economic development. While the coastal communities such as the Haida and Nootka were surplus generating developed communities with highly structured and distinct social strata, the interior tribes like the Carrier, Beaver, Sekani, and Slave, etc., were mostly nomadic with rudimentary political organizations.[12]

Ignoring all these differences, the colonial powers labeled all of them as Native Indians. During the heydays of fur trade the colonizers entered into agreements with the native communities and took their help in hunting the fur-bearing game. In return for fur, the natives sought metal items, firearms and ammunition, blankets, tobacco and alcohol. The fur traders interfered little in the social and cultural lives of the Native Indian communities. Paying respect to the Royal Proclamation of 1763, which laid down certain guidelines for the British colonizers in their dealings with the native communities in North America, James Douglas, the first governor of British Columbia entered into formal treaties with some native communities to acquire the land for colonization. Although the agreements and treaties were unequal, still there existed some semblance of equality between the British colonizers and the native communities till mid-nineteenth century. Advantages that the native communities had during the period disappeared once the fur trade declined. But after the decline of fur trade, colonization took the form of permanent agricultural settlements and mineral exploration. During this period several thousands of white settlers entered these territories to make fortunes. They occupied and settled in the lands habited by the native communities. In the name of reducing tensions between the white settlers and the native communities, the colonial government compelled the native tribes to live in designated reserves with limited resources. Due to decline of incomes, loss of control over natural resources, intensification of inter-tribal conflicts and spread of diseases introduced by the white settlers, several indigenous communities were wiped off and the native population in British Columbia declined drastically in the second half of the nineteenth century. Taking the decline of Indian population as a pretext, the land base of the reserves was further reduced, leaving very little for the Indian communities to sustain themselves.[13]

Even after British Columbia joined the Canadian Federation in 1871, there was no positive change in the plight of Native Indians. The Canadian Indian Act of 1876 put an end to traditional political institutions and created uniform band governments for all Native Indian communities in Canada. Treating the indigenous communities as wards to be protected,

Canadian government denied political autonomy and granted very little financial and administrative powers to the band governments. With the avowed purpose of bringing the natives into Canadian mainstream, the governments imposed compulsory residential education for Native Indian children through missionary schools and insisted that they give up Indian status in lieu of Canadian citizenship. Traditional religious and cultural festivities such as Potlatch and Sun Dance were banned and the Indians found to be taking drinks outside the reserve areas were punished.[14] Unlike the hill communities in north-east India, who enjoyed considerable autonomy during the colonial regime, Native Indians in British Columbia had to put up with worst forms of colonial and racist discrimination. Initially for a few decades, the shattered Native Indian communities in British Columbia could not put up resistance to the colonial policies pursued by the provincial governments. However, since the beginning of the twentieth century, the Native Indian communities began to form associations to pressurize the governments to settle their land claims and to grant them more powers to govern themselves. In response, the Canadian government passed undemocratic Acts to prevent all political and legal initiatives taken up by the native organizations in pursuit of their aboriginal rights.[15] The governments and the white Canadians used to look at all activities of the native communities with suspicion. However, active participation of several Native Indians in Canada in the Second World War in support of the Allied Forces changed to an extent the perceptions of white Canadians about the indigenous communities and helped Canadian government to look at the native problem in a more positive light.

Following the changed perceptions of the white Canadians, the Canadian government began to take certain positive initiatives benefiting the Native Indians. The Indian Act was amended in 1951 lifting the ban on festivities and political activities of Indian communities. Taking advantage of these changes, the Native Indian communities in British Columbia began to organize themselves into tribal and regional level organizations and started mobilizing public opinion in support of their demands.[16] Responding to their demands several committees and commissions such as the Hawthorn Committee (1966), the Penner Committee (1983) and the Royal Commission on Aboriginal Peoples (1996) were constituted to study the problems of the Native Indians and to suggest appropriate remedies. Responding positively to some of the vital recommendations of these committees and commissions, Canadian governments began to delegate more and more administrative and financial powers to the band governments. The courts in Canada also played an important role in interpreting the meaning and status of aboriginal rights. The native organizations waged militant struggles forcing the Government of Canada to desist from policies that seek assimilation and recognize them as distinct communities, as First Nations. Their demands were partly fulfilled with the Constitution of 1982 recognizing them as aboriginal communities with distinct rights and later the governments accepting in principle to grant them self-government. The provincial government of BC was initially reluctant to concede to any demands for recognition of their right to autonomy and self-government.[17] But compelled by federal initiatives, court verdicts and militant movements of the aboriginal peoples, BC government had to formally acknowledge Indians' right to self-government and join the ongoing treaty negotiations that seek to arrive at honourable and mutually beneficial agreement between Canada and Native Indian communities.

Discourse on Strategy for Development of Native Indians

In the background of changes taking place in Canada in general and BC in particular, a lively debate has been taking place in Canada on issues concerning autonomy, self-reliance and future relations between Canadian governments and Native Indians. Although there has been a consensus among all parties involved in the discourse on the need to put an end to the racist and discriminatory Indian Act regime, there is no unanimity among them as to what could be the best possible arrangements necessary for promoting the interests of the native communities. A study of three dominant intellectual perceptions in the ongoing discourse on the future of Native Indians helps us to understand the future of indigenous peoples in Canada.

1. Liberal Cynicism

This point of view is effectively reflected in the writings of Tom Flanagan and Melvin Smith.[18] They contend that Native Indians should be treated like any other Canadian citizens and in their own interests the native communities should break down the thicket of laws, regulations, and procedures that separate them from their fellow Canadians and dissolve all stereotype attitudes and mindsets. In their view, self-government projects are disasters, producing wasteful, destructive, familistic factionalism. They advocate putting an end to federal treaty obligations and to pass out, over time, all native programmes, thus making existing federal and provincial programs applicable to all native peoples. In their view, possibilities of significant reserve-based economic development generating a reasonable standard of living are extremely limited. Concentration of all powers in band governments poses a threat to individual freedom and hence not conducive to economic efficiency. Aboriginal governments must be like municipal authorities subordinate to provincial and federal authorities. Native Indians can make progress only by acquiring the skills and attitudes that bring success in the market-oriented liberal democracies.

2. Radical Indigenous Perspective

In contrast, indigenous writers such as Menno Boldt and Noel Dyck[19] put forward a radical perspective, which views aboriginal peoples as distinct nations. In their view, recognition of the special status of Native Indians should become the starting point of treaty negotiations with indigenous communities. Coming out against all attempts aimed at political and cultural assimilation, the radicals argue that the indigenous peoples should be given the right to self-determination and internal sovereignty, so that they could protect and promote their aboriginal identities, interests and values. To restore aboriginal peoples to their place alongside Canada as First Nations, they advocate nation-to-nation relationship. They expect Indian self-governments to protect native culture and manage native lands and resources. In their view, Indian self-government should be radically different from the municipal governments. It should be administered by Indian leadership committed to Indian traditional philosophies and principles. Indian self-government should work to revive the communal patterns of the past and jettison the formal, bureaucratic institutions imposed by the Indian Act. It should make an effort to revitalize native cultures, languages and social systems.

3. *Citizens' Plus Approach*

This approach is advocated by scholars like Hawthorn, and Alain Cairns.[20] Opposing both liberal and radical perspectives, this approach advocates a middle path. It does acknowledge the deprivations that the Native Indians had experienced in the past and advocates that the native peoples should be treated as 'Citizens Plus', meaning citizens with additional rights. But at the same time this perspective views integration of natives with Canadian nation as something necessary and beneficial to the Native Indians. In their view, Native Indians are already a part of a common project, Canada. Future of both natives and non-Natives are interconnected. Aboriginal future is in Canada. The aboriginal peoples are not only Canadians, but are and should be thought of as such by others and by themselves. This perspective recognizes the structural constraints that impede the development of on-reserve Indians and believe that their future lies in the urban areas. Its advocates sympathize with the native struggles for autonomy and defend different self-government experiments taking place in Canada. They view native struggles not as reactionary movements aimed at taking them back to pre-Columbus days, but as progressive steps that seek to engage with the modern world without giving up aboriginal difference.

In the background of the intellectual discourse that has been taking place in Canada on issues concerning political autonomy and economic development, Native Indians are also debating over questions such as what kind of relations they should have with Canada in future; what should be the form of Indian self-government; what needs to be the primary focus of development—the reserves or the urban areas?; how should the Indian government mobilize resources for developmental activities?, and in what ways one could ensure auditing and accountability of Indian governments. Although there is no consensus on any of the issues as yet, the emerging dominant perception appears to be that the Native Indians are aspiring for justice and greater autonomy within the system and that they have no aspiration to break away from Canadian federation.[21] They desire to acquire adequate land base and make their reserves economically self-reliant, but at the same time wish to keep their development options open outside the reserve system. Although the native communities are not yet ready for own-taxation, they are exploring avenues to generate adequate resources so that they could plan and implement their own activities for development of their respective communities. The native communities detest the Canadian governments' intervention in the name of auditing and accountability, but they do accept the need for the Indian self-government to be responsible to their respective communities.[22]

Self-Government Experiments in Action

While most native communities accept the need for an elected leadership there are still many like Gitksan and Wet'suwet'en citizens who think that reverting to traditional systems of governance is necessary to realize self-government.[23] Some like Hupasceth First Nation look for a middle ground, seeking to take advantage of the best of both worlds. Even in communities where there has been demand for handing over power to the traditional leadership it is accepted in principle that all decisions of the leadership have to be taken in public in consultation with all members of the First Nation. Native women's organizations have made considerable inroads to make their viewpoints clear and have been pressurizing the Indian leaders to accommodate their interests in the emerging political set-up. Several educated women are coming forward to take up executive and administrative positions in the Indian governments. About 20 per cent of the First Nations' leaders in Canada today are women.[24]

It is true that incidences of corruption, wastage, and mismanagement of funds are visible here and there, as Flanagan and others have pointed out. It would, however, be premature at this moment to conclude that the First Nation governments have failed in all respects. If one evaluates the performance of Native Indian governments from modern administrative yardsticks one would probably jump only to negative conclusions. For, most Indian governments are inexperienced and lack professionalism. But if one evaluates their performance from the perspective of the needs of the Native Indians their achievements do not appear to be all that bad. Many have been trying to do justice to their communities by shouldering different responsibilities. Realizing the need for an adequate land base, all First Nations are pursuing the land claims. Many First Nations are negotiating agreements with different state agencies and private business enterprises to start joint business/development ventures. They have forced enterprises like BC Hydro and Royal Bank to take up initiatives for education, training, and employment of Native Indians in their projects.[25]

Today, not all Indian reserves are poor and underdeveloped. Taking advantage of their location, physical resources, and social capital, some First Nations have initiated economic development programmes that suit their interests and needs. By imposing taxes on non-aboriginal citizens, leasing reserve lands for commercial purposes, claiming royalties from non-aboriginal business enterprises operating on reserves, and entering into mutually-beneficial agreements with the corporate sector and state enterprises, the First Nations have been able to mobilize considerable resources for their governments. Gradually, many aboriginal Indians are entering business activities: approximately 20,000 aboriginal businesses are registered across Canada, about 4,700 of them in British Columbia. Native Indian enterprises are visible in the primary sector, manufacturing, and service sectors. Although most of them are small-scale enterprises catering to local markets, some even target international markets. About 72 per cent of aboriginal entrepreneurs reported profits in 2002; and 70 per cent of aboriginal entrepreneurs residing in BC anticipated growth in the next two years as well. Making use of different tax concessions granted to them Native Indian entrepreneurs are trying to create their own niche in the market in certain domains where they have advantages.[26] Since they earn their livelihood basically from land, seas, and forests, Native

Indians value the need for protecting biodiversity and advocate sustainable developmental strategies for development. Canadian government agencies and business enterprises operating in the reserve areas are, therefore, compelled to fall in line with First Nations' aspirations and reorient their development and business strategies in areas inhabited by aboriginal Indians. In collaboration with non-aboriginal business enterprises some First Nations have initiated culturally sensitive and environmentally sustainable development projects in forestry, horticulture and tourism. As such, hundreds of experiments in Indian self-government have been taking place on the reserves and in urban areas.

CONCLUSION

The comparative study of the experiences of hill communities in north-east India and Native Indians in BC show certain similarities as well as differences. These native communities are racially, culturally and historically different from other citizens who share the dominant political ethos of the respective nations. They remain peripheral to national polities and economies, and are apprehensive of integrating themselves into the national mainstream. Conscious of their identity as indigenous peoples, they aspire to preserve their aboriginal identities and look for development that is in conformity with their traditional values and culture. Despite their demographic disadvantages, the native communities in Canada as well as in India waged many a struggle to preserve their autonomy and identities. Their uncompromising struggles and movements had brought pressure on the governments in both countries to initiate constitutional and political changes to accommodate the interests and aspirations of the aboriginal people within the broad framework of liberal democracies.

These commonalities apart, if one looks at the trajectories of the struggles and movements of hill communities of north-east India and Native Indians in BC, one can notice considerable differences in the experiences of these communities and also in the governments' responses to the demands and aspirations of the indigenous peoples. During the colonial period the hill tribes in north-east India enjoyed greater autonomy, compared to

Native Indians in Canada. Although both Canada and India were the colonies of the British, the colonial interests compelled them to act differently in different regions. While the geographic and military compulsions compelled the British to leave the hill communities in north-east India almost unadministered, the economic considerations and also the need to facilitate the white settlements forced the colonial government in BC to ignore the promises that the Crown had earlier made to the Native Indians in North America and impose highly discriminatory and authoritarian regime over the Native Indians. Transition from colonial to post-colonial regime in Canada mattered little to Native Indians since the political power continued to remain in the hands of the white people even after the formation of Canada in 1867. In contrast there was a distinct change in the nature of political power in India after 1947, as the nationalist elite took over the political power after India became politically independent. This change did affect the hill tribes in north-eastern region, who are racially, culturally and historically different from the people in the mainland India. While the Native Indians had to fight against the continuing colonial and assimilatory policies of Canadian governments, the hill communities had to organize themselves to defend their autonomy and identity against the possible encroachment by the post-colonial regime in India. Unlike Canadian State which remained indifferent to the aspirations of the aboriginal peoples for decades, the post-colonial state in India did take several constitutional and political initiatives, almost immediately after Independence, to accommodate the political aspirations of the indigenous tribes within the constitutional framework. Indian State has given state (provincial) status to some of the erstwhile hill districts inhabited by the native communities. But in Canada even to this day, none of the territorial units peopled by the indigenous peoples enjoy the status of a province.

These differences, however, should not lead one to conclude that the conditions of tribal communities in India are better than that of Native Indians in Canada. Many critics in India have pointed out that far from protecting the aspirations and interests of tribal communities, the creation of district councils and state governments have led to the decline of traditional communitarian institutions and practices among the tribes. Financial dependence of these politico-administrative units on central government allow them limited opportunities for innovating and implementing developmental projects that suit the tribal milieu. In this respect, Native Indians in Canada seem to be making a slow but steady progress. They have been asking the right questions and exploring indigenous alternatives both within and outside the constitutional framework. They are pragmatic enough to understand that in the prevailing international situation they can aspire only for internal autonomy and not for independence from Canada. From experience, they realize that political autonomy makes sense only when they are economically self-reliant. Hence they are making efforts to seek maximum concessions from federal and provincial governments in the form of land and other resources. In this respect most hill tribes in north-east India appear to be bit impractical and adventurous. They have been indulging in violent and self-defeating struggles for autonomy or independence without realizing their own limitations. On its part, the Indian State did all that it could do within the limits of its underdeveloped capitalist economy and has reached its limits. It realizes that it cannot go on creating more and more states to accommodate the political aspirations of different tribal communities. India's economy and its over population will also not allow the Indian State to grant economic concessions beyond a point. Unable to handle the ever increasing and at times conflicting tribal aspirations in a democratic way, the Indian State is relying more and more on its armed powers to deal with the indigenous challenge. But in Canada, since 1990s the governments are coming forward to negotiate honourable and mutually beneficial treaties, guaranteeing considerable freedom for the native communities to determine their own forms of rule within the Canadian polity. Realizing the need for peace and development, the Canadian State is making economic and political concessions to the indigenous peoples, ignoring the white lobbies opposing such indulgences. Developing countries like India which have limited resources and more claimants aspiring for a share cannot afford to imitate developed countries like Canada which have resources to share with its indigenous peoples. Because of all these factors, despite the similarities in political systems and ideologies, Canadian State appears to be better placed than its Indian counterpart in handling the challenges posed by the indigenous peoples.

NOTES

1. Karl Marx and Frederick Engels, *Selected Works*, vol. I, Moscow: Progress Publishers, 1977, pp. 488–99; David Bedford, 'Marxism and the Aboriginal Question: The Tragedy of Progress', *Canadian Journal of Native Studies*, vol. 14: 1, 1994, pp. 101–16; Louis Proyect, 'Colonialism, Indigenous Peoples and Split in European Socialism', *Marxism Mailing List Archive*, 26 November 1999, http://archives.econ.utah.edu/archives/marxism/1999w47/msg00201.htm accessed on 4 July 2008; For arguments of colonial apologists refer, Niall Ferguson, *Empire: How Britain Made the Modern World* (London: Penguin, 2002); Lawrence James, *Raj: The Making and Unmaking of British India*, New York: St Martin's Press, 1999; A.P. Thornton, *Doctrines of Imperialism*, New York: John Wiley, 1965.
2. H.K Barpujari, *Problem of the Hill Tribes North-East Frontier*, vol. I, Shillong: North-Eastern University Publications, 1998, pp. 20-3.
3. Christopher von Furer Haimendorf, 'Aboriginal Rebellions in Deccan', *Man in India*, vol. 25, no. 4, December 1945, pp. 208-16; Prakash Chandra Jain, *Social Movements Among Tribals*, Jaipur: Rawat Publishers, 1994, pp. 26–55.
4. R.S. Lyngdoh, *Government and Politics in Meghalaya*, New Delhi: Sanchar Publishing, 1996, pp. 136–50; Piketo Sema, *British Policy and Administration in Nagaland, 1881–1947*, New Delhi: Scholar Publications, 1992, pp. 29–36; Amiresh Ray, *Mizoram*, New Delhi: Regency Publications, 1998, pp. 147-50; Robert Reid, *History of the Frontier Areas Bordering Assam, 1883–1941*, Delhi: Eastern Publishing House, 1983.
5. O.L. Snaitang, *Christianity and Social Change in Northeast India*, Shillong: Vendrame Institute, 1983, pp. 65–95; Lal Dena, *Christian Missions and Colonialism: A Study of Missionary Movement in North East India with Particular Reference to Manipur and Lushai Hills, 1894–1947*, Shillong: Vendrame Institute, 1988, p. 21.
6. Sajal Nag, *Contesting Marginalities: Ethnicity, Insurgency and Subnationalism in North-East India*, New Delhi: Manohar, 2002, pp. 129-32.

7. V. K. Nuh (ed.), *The Naga Chronicle*, New Delhi: Regency Publications, 2000, pp. 195-8; Udayon Misra, *The Periphery Strikes Back*, Shimla: Indian Institute of Advanced Studies, 2000, 158.
8. S.K. Chaubey, *Hill Politics in Northeast India*, New Delhi: Orient Longman, 1999, pp. 136-84.
9. S.K. Chaubey, *Hill Politics in Northeast India*, pp. 253-9.
10. *Some of the weaknesses of modern constitutional institutions working in the hill areas are pointed out in different writings. Refer, A Consultation Paper on Empowering and Strengthening of Panchayati Raj Institutions/Autonomous District Councils/Traditional Tribal Governing Institutions in North-East India*, New Delhi: National Commission to Review the Working of the Constitution, 2001; R.N. Prasad, 'Sixth Schedule and Working of the District Councils in North-Eastern States', *Dialogue*, vol. 6, no. 2, October-December 2004, www.asthabharati.org/Dia_Oct04/prasad.htm accessed on 12 December 2007; B.K. Roy Burman, 'Sixth Schedule of the Constitution', in *Autonomous District Councils*, ed. L.S. Gassah, New Delhi: Omsons Publications, 1997, p. 33; Tiplut Nongbri, *Development, Ethnicity and Gender*, New Delhi: Rawat Publications, 2003, pp. 121-59.
11. George Woodcock, *British Columbia: A History of the Province*, Vancouver and Toronto: Douglas & McIntyre, 1994, pp. 15-32.
12. Allan D. McMillan Elder Yellowhorn, *First Peoples in Canada*, Vancouver: Douglas McIntyre, 2004, pp. 189-232; Robert J. Muckle, *The First Nations of British Columbia: An Anthropological Survey*, Vancouver: UBC Press, pp. 117-22.
13. Cole Harris, *Making Native Space: Colonialism, Resistance, and Reserves in British Columbia*, Vancouver: UBC Press, 2002, pp. 56-69.
14. John L. Tobias, 'Protection, Civilization, Assimilation: An Outline History of Canada's Indian Policy', in Ian Getty and Antoina Lussier, *As Long as the Sun Shines and the Water Flows*, Vancouver: UBC Press, 1983, pp. 39-53.
15. Chief Joe Mathias and Gary R. Yabsley, 'Conspiracy of Legislation: The Suppression of Indian Rights in Canada', *BC Studies*, vol. 89, Spring 1991, p. 35.
16. Paul Tennant, 'Native Indian Political Organization in British Columbia, 1900-69: A Response to Internal Colonialism', *BC Studies*, no. 55, 1981, pp. 26-49.
17. Paul Tennant, 'Aboriginal Peoples and Aboriginal Title in British Columbia Politics', *in Politics, Policy and Government in British Columbia*, ed. R.K. Carty, Vancouver: UBC Press, 1996, pp. 26-43.
18. Melvin Smith, *Our Home or Native Land?: What Government's Aboriginal Policy Is Doing to Canada*, Toronto: Stoddart Publishing

Co. Limited, 1995, Tom Flanagan, *First Nations? Second Thoughts*, Toronto: McGill-Queen's University Press, 2000, pp. 195-8.

19. Menno Boldt, *Surviving As Indians: The Challenge of Self-Government*, Toronto: University of Toronto Press, 1993, 265; Noel Dyck, *What is the Indian Problem?: Tutelage and Resistance in Canadian Indian Administration*, St. Johns, Newfoundland: Institute of Social and Economic Research, 1991, pp. 139-62; Michael Asch, 'Aboriginal Self-Government and Canadian Constitutional Identity: Building Reconciliation', *in Ethnicity and Aboriginality: Case Studies in Ethno-Nationalism*, ed. Michael D. Levin, Toronto: University of Toronto Press, 1983.
20. Allan C. Cairns, *Citizens Plus: Aboriginal Peoples and the Canadian State*, Vancouver: UBC, 2000; H.B. Hawthorn, *A Survey of Contemporary Indians in Canada: A Report of the Economic, Political, Educational Needs and Policies*, vol. 1, Ottawa: Canadian Department of Indian Affairs and Northern Development, 1966.
21. Anthony J. Long, Leroy Little Bear and Menno Boldt, eds., *Pathways to Self-Determination: Canadian Indians and the Canadian State*, Toronto: University of Toronto Press, 1984, p. 79.
22. Robert Sheperd and Russel Diabo, 'A Government-First Nations Dialogue on Accountability: Reestablishing Understanding on the Basics of a Complex Relationship', *Native Studies Review* 15, no. 2, 2004, pp. 61-81.
23. Dan Smith, *The Seventh Fire: The Struggle For Aboriginal Government*, Toronto: Key Porter Books, 1993, pp. 209.
24. See Phil Fontaine's address to the First Nations Women Leaders Forum, Vancouver, British Columbia, February 2007, http://www.turtleisland.org/discussion/viewtopic.php?p=7997&sid=c94cc136f052e280bc19ab5fa4107c74 accessed on 14 December 2007.
25. See 'Initiatives', BC Hydro, http://www.bchydro.com/ard/initiatives/initiatives905.html accessed on 14 December 2007; 'RBC Aboriginal Student Awards Program', Royal Bank of Canada (12 May 2005), http://www.rbc.com/uniquecareers/campus/aboriginal-student-awards.html accessed 14 December 2007.
26. 'Aboriginal Entrepreneurs Survey 2002', Daily, 27 September 2004, http://www.statcan.ca/Daily/English/040927/d040927d.htm accessed 14 December 2007; Aboriginal Business Service Network, 'BC Aboriginal Entrepreneurs: A Growing Force: BC Aboriginal Small Business Profile', http://www.firstbusiness.ca/guides/bc_aes_profile.pdf accessed on 14 December 2007.

CHAPTER 21

Acculturation and Social Cognition: A Study of Prosociality among the Indo-Canadians

NEERJA CHADHA

'Prosocial behavior' is the general term for behaviour assumed to be intentionally beneficial to others; not necessarily without self-interest. Every society depends heavily on the willingness of its members to help others in need, to contribute to a common good, and to be fair and considerate. While this is widely accepted and fairly obvious, what makes people behave prosocially in one situation and refrain from doing so in another is something which is much less obvious and discernible. The fact remains that prosocial behaviour varies not only between individuals, but also situationally within the same individual. What is more, it is not merely behaviour that varies situationally for the same person; the core motivation to act prosocially varies from one context to another within the same person. It is important to take cognizance of the fact that our behavior changes between situations and relationships (Ross & Nisbett 1991; Smeeters et al. 2003). The processes of cognition, motivation, and behaviour are closely linked (Gollwitzer & Bargh 1996), and reflective and emotional processes strongly interact in bringing about social behaviour of any kind (Strack & Deutsch 2004). This

*This research study was carried out under the aegis of the Canadian Studies Faculty Research Fellowship of the Shastri Indo-Canadian Institute, through institutional affiliation with the University of British Columbia, Vancouver, B.C., Canada, and with the approval of the Behavioral Research Ethics Board of UBC.

being the case, it is important to examine the cognitive processes that influence an individual's prosociality by mediating the influence of both the personality of the individual and the situation in which the behavior takes place.

In the domain of social psychology, research initiatives with respect to prosociality were dominated for a long time by an attempt to identify situational determinants of helping behaviour. The 'empathy-altruism hypothesis' was confirmed in many empirical studies (Bierhoff 2002). Another important line of research is related to the development of prosocial reasoning in children and adolescents. Pioneering work in this field has been done by Eisenberg and colleagues (e.g. Eisenberg 1982, 1986, 1990; Eisenberg et al. 2005; Eisenberg & Fabes 1998; Eisenberg, et al. 1991; Eisenberg & Shell 1986; Eisenberg et al. 1987; Eisenberg-Berg 1979), who found that the prosocial reasoning of American children (preschoolers through adolescents) was primarily hedonistic, stereotyped, approval and interpersonally and needs and direct reciprocity-oriented. Studies on prosocial reasoning of children and adolescents in countries other than the US, for example, Brazil (Carlo et al. 1996), Germany (Eisenberg et al. 1985), Japan (Munekata & Ninomiya 1985), and Israel (Eisenberg, Hertz-Lazarowitz & Fuchs 1990; Fuchs, et al. 1986) yielded similar findings. Some cultural differences, however, have also been reported. For instance, Eisenberg, Hertz-Lazarowitz, and Fuchs as well as Fuchs et al., found that city children in Israel verbalized more hedonistic and pragmatic reasoning. Kibbutz children, on the other hand, made more references to the humanness of the needy others and to direct reciprocity. These differences in reasoning were attributed basically to the Kibbutz ideology. In the Indian context (Chadha & Misra 2004, 2006), children's prosocial reasoning has been found to be characterized mainly by concern for needs of others, hedonism, authority/punishment orientation, pragmatism, orientation to affectional relationship, stereotypes of a good/bad person or behavior, internalized norms and value orientation, mutual gain and direct reciprocity considerations, orientation to honouring requests made, and shame orientation. Findings indicated that the mode of reasoning adopted varied as a function of the nature and parameters of the context in which the reasoning was elicited. Further, it was observed that though Indian children made use of many of the modes of reasoning used by children from the US and other Western countries, they also reflected some unique lines of reasoning, indicating the influence of some significant aspects of the cultural ethos on children's prosocial reasoning. Chadha (2007) emphasizes that prosocial reasoning and behaviour of children is influenced by a variety of factors; that include cognitive developmental factors, other individual factors including personality and other variables, socialization experiences and other life experiences. The socio-cultural milieu plays an important role. In fact, the importance of culture in understanding and explaining social cognition processes, including those in the prosocial domain, is now being increasingly recognized (e.g. Chadha 2007; Miller 1997; Misra 2001; Shweder 2003; Sinha & Kao 1997).

Against this background, the study reported here examines prosocial development of Indo-Canadian children. The purpose is to draw insights about the socio-cultural influences on prosocial reasoning; and to derive implications in the broader context of acculturation and social cognition.

METHOD

Participants

Thirty Indo-Canadian children, between 8 and 14 years of age, participated in the study. While the original criterion had been that the participant should have primarily lived in Canada for at least the last five years, as it turned out, all the participants were born and brought up in Canada. Twenty of the participants were in the age group of 8-11 years (10 boys and 10 girls) while 10 participants (8 boys and 2 girls) were in the age group of 11-14 years. The participants were identified through the snowballing method, and interviewed after taking parental consent and subject's assent as per the procedures laid down by the Behavioural Research Ethics Board of the University of British Columbia, Vancouver, Canada.

Measure

The prosocial reasoning of children was examined through individual interviews, in the course of which the researcher (author) presented five hypothetical situations, involving prosocial dilemmas, to each participant. Each hypothetical situation was presented in a story form, with the help of a colourful vignette illustrating the dilemma situation. In each story, a situation was depicted in which a child had an opportunity to behave prosocially toward another child. Narration of each story was followed by asking the participant how the protagonist would respond in the situation; and seeking the reason for that behaviour (by asking 'why').

This measure is essentially the same as had been used in a prior study (Chadha & Misra 2004), with children of a similar age-group in India. The prosocial dilemma situations comprising this measure are primarily from the children's world, and are adaptations of stories used in earlier research studies in this area (Bar-Tal, Raviv, & Shavit 1981; Eisenberg-Berg & Hand 1979). The themes of the five stories are: (1) helping a peer in a task (picking up crayons from the floor); (2) helping a child being beaten by a bully; (3) comforting a hurt peer; (4) sharing one's toy with another child; and (5) sharing tiffin with a hungry classmate.

Procedure

The stories were narrated individually to each child, with the help of vignettes. The sex of the protagonist and the other characters in each story was matched to the sex of the child to whom the stories were being presented. The content of the stories was essentially the same for boys and girls. After narrating each story, children were asked what the protagonist would do, followed by probes pertaining to why they thought the protagonist would, or would not, behave prosocially in the given situation. After presenting the bully, situation, as also after the toy-sharing story, in addition to the general question about what the protagonist would do, the child was also asked about how the protagonist would behave if the potential recipient were his brother, friend, or a stranger. Again, the reason for that behaviour was sought by asking the question 'why'. Supplementary questions were also asked, if needed, to seek further clarification of the answer or obtain more information in that regard. Children's responses to probes were audio-recorded or written down on paper by the researcher; as per the consent and assent of the parent and child respectively. The audio recordings were transcribed and all the responses analysed. To maintain confidentiality, the name and contact details were deleted from the response sheets (on which the interview responses were written, or transcribed from the audio tapes), prior to analysis.

Coding and Scoring

Prosocial Reasoning

The responses of children to probes were analysed in terms of their content. For the purpose of analysis, the comprehensive range of prosocial reasoning categories formulated by Eisenberg-Berg (1979); that have used in the majority of studies carried out in the field of prosocial reasoning (e.g. Eisenberg et al. 1985, 1987, 1991, 2002, 2005), was utilized in its marginally adapted form, made use of in the studies on prosocial reasoning (Chadha & Misra 2004, 2006) in India. For analysing children's prosocial reasoning in the context of the varied role-relationships portrayed in two of the hypothetical situations, instead of comparing across the vast multitude of categories, the concept of reasoning levels was used. The framework of reasoning levels was basically the one proposed and used by Eisenberg and her colleagues (e.g. Eisenberg 1982, 1986; Eisenberg, Lennon, & Roth 1983). The reasoning levels used are as follows: self-focused orientation; needs orientation; approval and interpersonal orientation and/or stereotyped orientation; empathic orientation and internalization.

For analysing children's reasoning responses, scores were assigned to indicate the usage of the various prosocial reasoning categories (3 = clear use of the category; 2 = ambiguous use of the category; 1 = no use of the category). For each child, the scores for each reasoning category were summed across the five hypothetical situations presented, and divided by 5 (the number of stories), thus obtaining summary scores in the possible range of 1 to 3. These summary scores were used for further analyses. Likewise, the use of reasoning levels with respect to each child and context presented was also expressed in terms of scores ranging from 1 to 3.

Prosocial Behaviour

For each child, the percentage of prosocial dilemma situations for which the child gave a prosocial response was calculated, and used as a measure of prosociality in analyses.

RESULTS

Table 21.1 reflects the means and standard deviations indicative of the use of the various prosocial reasoning categories by the children, as well as the percentage of prosocial responses.

Patterns of Prosocial Reasoning

On examining the mean scores indicative of the use of the various prosocial reasoning categories, one finds that the prosocial reasoning of Indo-Canadian children was characterized primarily by stereotypes of a good/bad person or behaviour; concern for physical and material needs of the other person; orientation to affectional relationship; hedonism; interpersonal orientation; pragmatism; concern for psychological needs of the other person; mutual gain orientation; and direct reciprocity considerations. M for these categories was at least 1.1.

Stereotypical reasoning was evident most often. In other words, there was a predominance of the orientation to stereotypical images of a good/bad person or behaviour, as indicated in responses such as 'He would comfort him first because it is a good thing to do', 'I think she would share her tiffin because that shows that you are not greedy; you are kind', and 'He'd help him in picking up the crayons because it wouldn't be nice if he didn't help him and carried on colouring.'

TABLE 21.1: MEANS AND STANDARD DEVIATIONS FOR USE OF PROSOCIAL REASONING CATEGORIES AND PERCENTAGE OF PROSOCIAL RESPONSES

Measure	M	SD
Reasoning category		
Stereotypes of a good/bad person or behaviour	1.59	0.48
Concern for physical needs of others	1.58	0.39
Affectional relationship	1.36	0.4
Hedonistic gain to the self	1.33	0.37
Interpersonal orientation	1.16	0.27
Pragmatism	1.15	0.23
Concern for psychological needs of others	1.13	0.19
Mutual gain orientation	1.11	0.23
Direct reciprocity	1.1	0.17
Role taking	1.07	0.21
Internalized norms and values orientation	1.06	0.14
Positive affect related to consequences	1.05	0.13
Generalized reciprocity	1.03	0.1
Authority/punishment orientation	1.01	0.07
Reference to and concern with humanness	1.01	0.07
Internalized positive affect from living up to one's values	1.01	0.04
Stereotypical images of majority behaviour	1	0
Stereotypical images of others and their roles	1	0
Approval orientation	1	0
Sympathetic orientation	1	0
Internalized negative affect over consequences of behaviour	1	0
Internalized negative affect due to not living up to one's values	1	0
Concern with individual rights and justice	1	0
Concern with the condition of society	1	0
% of prosocial responses	84	18.5

Note: Scores could range from 1 to 3.

Orientation to the physical and material needs of others was also prominent. A number of children gave responses such as 'She can have one and give one to her because this other girl is also very hungry', 'Give him half, because you wouldn't want this other guy to starve', 'He'd go stop the bully. May be that guy may get hurt, may be he might break his arm—so he'd help him', 'Stop the bully because otherwise the kid would get hurt really badly.'

Orientation to affection relationship was also evident in a number of responses; for instance, 'He will help him because they are friends' and 'If this girl is her friend, she'll help.'

Hedonistic gain to the self, or putting one's own needs before those of another, was evident not only in the case of non-prosocial responses, but also in case of some prosocial ones. Consider the following examples of this line of reasoning articulated: 'No, he would not share his tiffin because he is hungry', 'It depends on how much he has. Because if he has only a little bit, I'd say he would eat it and it is that person's responsibility to get his own lunch', 'He wouldn't share because the other kid may steal the car', and 'He'll help put the crayons back. Because if you are drawing and you have only one crayon, then you would need other colors too'.

Interpersonal orientation, or orientation to making new friends or strengthening existing friendship, was also evidenced; for instance 'Yes. Both could play turn by turn. Because he could then make a new friend' and 'He is his classmate. Well, I think he would share. He would then become his friend'. Pragmatism, or orientation to practical concerns that are unrelated to selfish considerations, found expression as in 'I think he will help him pick up the crayons. It would be faster if he helped'. Concern for psychological needs of others was expressed by the children through responses like 'She would comfort to make her happy and not cry' and 'He would first come and start helping him up so that that boy can cheer up and they can both play together'. The latter statement exemplifies mutual gain orientation as well. Orientation to direct reciprocity also found expression in the reasoning articulated by children, for example 'I think he would share. Then in future, if he needs help, then he would also help'. Role taking was evident in statements like 'I think he would go to his help, because if it was he who was being bullied, and nobody came to help him, then he wouldn't have liked it' and 'He would share his lunch with Rehman. Because the way he missed a meal, he doesn't want Rehman to miss a meal as well'. Responses like 'I think he should help the little kid because I have learnt from my dad that a strong man stands up for himself and a strong man stands up for others' provided a glimpse of internalized norms and values orientation. Likewise, internalized positive affect was indicated in responses such as 'He'll help because you feel a sense of joy when you help someone'.

There were infrequent, but interesting references to authority/ punishment orientation as well; for example 'He'll comfort him. Because the person is hurting and you don't know how bad it is. If its serious, people would blame you!'

Prosocial Responses

As is evident from Table 21.1, the majority of responses (84 per cent) to the hypothetical situations presented were prosocial. In other words, when answering the probe about what the protagonist would do in a given situation, most of the children stated a prosocial course of action.

Relationship between Prosocial Reasoning and Behaviour

The relationship between prosocial reasoning and behaviour was investigated by assessing the extent to which the use of the various prosocial reasoning categories is correlated with the percentage of prosocial responses articulated with respect to the dilemma situations presented. In other words, the purpose was to ascertain if a higher percentage of prosocial responses, and greater or lesser use of certain reasoning categories, go together. It was found that the percentage of prosocial endings suggested by children ($N = 30$) was significantly positively related to orientation to the psychological needs of others ($r = 0.37$, $p < 0.05$), and strongly negatively related to hedonistic reasoning ($r = -0.81$, $p < 0.01$).

Prosocial Reasoning and Behaviour in Relation to Role-Relationships

In the context of the bully and toy-sharing situations, the children had also answered questions about what the protagonist would do, given the situation depicted in the story, if the potential recipient were (a) a sibling, (b) a friend, or (c) a stranger; and why. The idea was to assess whether the protagonist would be said to behave prosocially, more in the context of one role-relationship rather than the other, and if there are any changes in the underlying reasoning.

Table 21.2 presents the means and SDs for the nature (prosocial/non-prosocial) of responses suggested and the reasoning

TABLE 21.2: NATURE OF RESPONSES (PROSOCIAL/NON-PROSOCIAL) AND USE OF REASONING LEVELS UNDER CONDITIONS OF PORTRAYAL OF DIFFERENT ROLE-RELATIONSHIPS IN THE BULLY AND TOY-SHARING SITUATIONS: MEANS AND STANDARD DEVIATIONS

Measure	M	SD
Bully situation: Relationship portrayed—Sibling		
Response^	1	0
Reasoning level*		
Self-focused orientation	1.13	0.51
Needs orientation	1.67	0.96
Stereotyped orientation	2.57	0.82
Empathic orientation 1	0	
Internalization	1.47	0.86
Bully situation: Relationship portrayed—Friend		
Response^	1.03	0.18
Reasoning level*		
Self-focused orientation	1.07	0.37
Needs orientation	1.27	0.69
Stereotyped orientation	2.7	0.69
Empathic orientation	1	0
Internalization	1.4	0.82
Bully situation: Relationship portrayed—Stranger		
Response^	1.43	0.5
Reasoning level*		
Self-focused orientation	1.93	1.01
Needs orientation	1.5	0.86
Stereotyped orientation	1.33	0.76
Empathic orientation	1.2	0.61
Internalization	1.07	0.37
Toy-sharing situation: Relationship portrayed—Sibling		
Response^	1	0
Reasoning level*		

Self-focused orientation	1.6	0.93
Needs orientation	1	0
Stereotyped orientation	2.4	0.93
Empathic orientation	1	0
Internalization	1.33	0.76
Toy-sharing situation: Relationship portrayed—Friend		
Response^	1	0
Reasoning level*		
Self-focused orientation	1.5	0.86
Needs orientation	1.1	0.4
Stereotyped orientation	2.4	0.93
Empathic orientation	1	0
Internalization	1.07	0.37
Toy-sharing situation: Relationship portrayed—Stranger		
Response^	1.77	0.43
Reasoning level*		
Self-focused orientation	2.47	0.9
Needs orientation	1	0
Stereotyped orientation	1.53	0.9
Empathic orientation	1	0
Internalization	1	0

Notes: ^ Means range from 1 to 2, with 1 indicating a prosocial response and 2 reflecting a non-prosocial response.
* Means range from 1 to 3, with 1 indicating no use and 3 reflecting clear, unambiguous use.

levels used by the children in the context of varied role-relationships portrayed in the bully and toy-sharing situations. Looking at the means, we find that in both the situations, the number of children who said that the protagonist would act prosocially was much more when the potential recipient was a sibling or friend, than when it was a stranger. Further, while prosocial responses were articulated to a similar extent across the two situations, as long as the relationship portrayed between the protagonist and the potential recipient was that of a sibling or a friend, they were considerably less forthcoming in the context of sharing with a stranger, as compared to the helping situation.

Coming to the use of reasoning levels (Table 21.2), we find that in both the situations, in the case of a sibling or a friend being the potential recipient, the reasoning articulated was mostly at the stereotyped level, with the children's reasons touching on the affectional relationship and the norm of helping (or sharing with) siblings and friends (e.g. 'He'll obviously go and help – that bully is beating up his brother!', 'Yes, he'll let him play, because he is a friend', and 'We should share our toys with our friends').

In the context of the relationship being that of a sibling/friend, the next most commonly used reasoning level was needs orientation with respect to the bully situation (concern about sibling/friend getting hurt) and self-focused orientation with respect to the toy-sharing situation (with emphasis on mutual gain such as 'playing together and having more fun' and direct reciprocity). The reasoning pattern was a bit different when a stranger was portrayed as thc potential recipient. In this case, with respect to both the situations, it was hedonism and self-focussed orientation that predominated.

DISCUSSION

The prosocial reasoning of participants was found to be characterized primarily by orientation to stereotypes of a good/bad person or behaviour, physical and psychological needs of others, affectional relationship, hedonistic considerations, enhancing interpersonal relationship, pragmatism, mutual gain, and direct reciprocity considerations. These findings, by and large, approximate those obtained with respect to children in India (Chadha & Misra 2004)!

While the broad lines of reasoning obtained with respect to children in India and the Indo-Canadian children are similar, some qualitative differences do emerge as one looks at the content of responses given by the children. For instance, in the toy-sharing situation, justifying non-sharing by referring to the risk of losing the toy was something that was encountered primarily in the case of children from the low socio-economic background in the Indian context. And yet, this fear was frequently articulated by Indo-Canadian children. Further, reasoning focussing on themes like 'One should not talk to strangers', 'You are not supposed to talk to a stranger', 'You can't trust strangers', and 'No, because we are not allowed to give things or take things from strangers', which predominated the responses given by Indo-Canadian children particularly with reference to sharing one's toy with another child who has expressed a desire to play with it, was mentioned only infrequently in the Indian context. The socio-cultural milieu in India comes across as much more open, trusting and welcoming with respect to strangers as compared to the Canadian.

Yet another prominent discernible difference is the much greater reliance on formal systems rather than taking matters in one's own hands—this aspect predominated the responses of Indo-Canadian children, particularly in the bully situation. The situation that had been presented to the children was as follows:

> Kamal was playing with his ball. And then he saw that some distance away, a big boy, who was generally a bully of that area, picked on a small boy, and without any reason, started beating him up. Kamal knows that if he would go and try to stop the bully from hitting the small boy, the bully might hit him also.
>
> What will Kamal do? Will he go and try to help the small boy or try and stop the bully from hitting him, or no? Why?

In the Indian context, the children by and large focused on intervention with respect to the protagonist directly. The majority of Indo-Canadian children, however, refrained from suggesting any direct intervention on behalf of the protagonist, and opined, for instance: 'She will go to the nearest adult and tell the adult', 'He'll go call an adult. Get help', 'She should tell a grown up around her' and 'She should call her mom to tell her to stop to hit'.

The much greater emphasis to politeness and 'correct' way of requesting also surfaced prominently in the context of Indo-Canadian children. For example, consider the following reasons articulated for non-sharing: 'If she said please she would share. But she didn't, so she wouldn't' and 'No. Because the kid didn't use his manners' (in the story presented, the request made did not include the word 'please'!). With respect to the Indian sample, this line of reasoning was not encountered even once!

On the other hand, the distinctive lines of reasoning that

could be observed in the reasoning responses of children in India (Chadha 2007; Chadha & Misra 2004), viz., orientation to community brotherhood (orientation to viewing others, even strangers, as one's own brothers and sisters); orientation to honouring request made (orientation to doing something simply because someone has requested one to do so); shame orientation (orientation to doing something because of a concern about how one appears to others; what kind of impression one is making); and immanent justice (expression of anxiety about divine justice being meted out, in the form of some suffering, resulting from not having behaved prosocially), were conspicuous by their absence in the case of the Indo-Canadian children.

A common research fallacy is that culture is often portrayed as distal to the behavior and social interactions that take place during development. To be closer to reality, what the contemporary human developmental models need to do is to incorporate two or more cultures in contact, and identify how these influence the developmental outcome. For doing so, it has been suggested that acculturation should be seen as an integral part of, or as embedded within, development (Sam & Berry 2006). The emergence of the autonomous-related self, in fact, is a likely outcome in the context of acculturation (Kagitcibasi 2005 for a review). The prosocial reasoning responses of the Indo-Canadian participants in the present study exemplify this aspect.

The most important function of family as a primary socialization agency has often been stressed in the social and behavioural sciences. The immigrant family as a socialization agency has a major influence on the acculturation orientations of its members (Nauck 2001). Perceived family support can reduce stress levels for the acculturating individual (Castillo, Conoley & Brossart 2004). The socialization strategies that parents adopt emphasize the development of whatever instrumental competencies are needed for being successful in the environment in which the family lives as well as those valued in their culture of origin; and these two views are not mutually exclusive. A model of parenting and child development that integrates cultural traditions and legacies with current conditions is necessary to acculturation. The Indian community in Canada does come across as trying to implement this model in realistic terms.

When immigrants from collectivist cultures, like India, move to a more individualistic culture (like most of the Western cultures, including Canada), they are confronted with a culture in which family relationships differ from their culture of origin. Three models regarding acculturation and family relationships have been proposed. The first one, based on the modernization theory, holds that acculturation leads to a unidirectional shift in family characteristics and relationships toward the Western pattern. According to the second model, some aspects of the family undergo changes, while others remain unaffected. Emotional dependencies may continue (or even increase), even if material dependencies show a decline over generations with increased affluence (Kagitcibasi 1996). The third model propounds that family relationships are strengthened as a result of acculturative stress. Families provide the buffer for immigrants to cope with acculturative stress. There is some evidence that children use cultural information from their mesosystems to help socialize their parents around new modes of communication and emotional expression (Chun 2006).

Further, assimilation and contrast are pervasive phenomena in social perception, social judgement, and social behaviour (Stapel & Sals 2007). Acculturation is a major transforming force on family life and human development. Immigrants face multiple challenges in acculturating; including deciding which cultural behaviours or beliefs to adopt from the culture within which they reside, and which to retain from their culture of origin (Bornstein & Cote 2006). According to the assimilationist model, once immigrants have lived in their new culture for a time, their beliefs and behaviours come to resemble those of the extant majority and they forever relinquish those of their country of origin. Contemporary researchers, however, have tended to define acculturation as a multidimensional and bidirectional process, in which an individual or group retains cognitions and practices of its heritage and simultaneously adopts those of another group with which there is repeated or prolonged contact. Acculturation thus is the dual process of cultural and psychological change that takes place as a result of contact between two or more cultural groups and their individual members. At the group level, it involves changes in social structures and institutions and in cultural practices. At the individual level, it involves changes in a person's behaviour repertoire (Berry 2006). Culture is composed of the ways in which people process and make sense of their experiences. Much of the contemporary research on acculturation has been concerned with how ethnocultural groups relate to one another and change as a result of their attempts to live together in culturally plural societies (Sam & Berry 2006, for an international perspective). At the individual level, we need to consider the psychological changes that individuals undergo, and their eventual adaptations to their new situations. This process is often termed as 'adjustment', because virtually all the adaptive changes take place in the acculturating individual, with few changes occurring among members of the larger society (Ward, Bochner & Furnham 2001). Ideal would be a multicultural orientation in the dominant society that matches the preference for integration among the non-dominant groups. Integrative strategies and multiculturalism have been found to be associated with better adaptations (Berry 2000; Berry et al. 2006; Curran 2003). The internationalization of the norms, values and desired behavioural responses of the Canadian society by the Indo-Canadian children provides support in this regard.

In an international study of immigrant adolescents (Phinney et al. 2006), significant support was found for the conceptually derived model of four acculturation strategies (Berry et al. 1989); namely integration, separation, assimilation and marginalization. Phinney and colleagues reported that the most frequently occurring profile that appeared to be comfortable in both ethnic and national contexts, consisted of adolescents whose attitudes and behaviours reflected integration.

Research and theories on immigrant children's adaptation are surprisingly lacking considering that immigrant children constitute the fastest growing sector of the population in many Western industrialized countries (Aronowitz 1984; Sam 2006). This trend is indicated for Canada as well (www12.statcan.ca/english/census01). It is only in recent years that some research attention has been aimed at understanding how the immigrant children adapt to the two often opposing cultures they face at home and within the larger society they live in. Early research efforts with respect to immigrant children were more concerned with how well they were adapting, particularly in the light of postulations that children may be particularly vulnerable to the stresses of migration (Bashir 1993; Evans 1987; McKay, Macintyre & Ellaway 2003). As Fuligni (2003) pointed out, results from these studies indicate that at least in the US, immigrant children and adolescents show remarkably good adjustment, ranging from good school adjustment and academic records (Fuligni 1997, 1998) to comparably good psychological adjustment (Harris 1999). In recent years, similar findings have been reported in other countries (Berry et al. 2006). It would be natural to expect that the paradox presented; that is, good adaptation in spite of poor socio-economic background and the hardships associated with migration, calls for an explanation. Unfortunately, there is a dearth of theories that can account for immigrant children's successful adaptation (Garcia & Magruson 1997). There have been only a few attempts in the field of acculturation of children (Sam 1995). The developmental perspective is conspicuous by its absence in acculturation theories about children (Sam, Kosic & Oppedal 2003).

From a developmental perspective, change arises from an interaction between biological and maturational processes on the one hand, and environmental learning experiences on the other (Lerner 2001). Acculturation is often explained in terms of being a coping mechanism in response to a stressful situation that is induced by an encounter with an unfamiliar cultural context, or as a need on the part of an individual to learn specific cultural skills that are adaptive and functional (Ward 2001). Nevertheless, a significant aspect that needs to be taken into consideration is that some changes in individuals that are attributed to acculturation, may in reality be developmental changes. For instance, it is often assumed that with the passage of time, immigrant children and their parents may differ in cultural values, and these value discrepancies may be the basis for psychological maladjustment. And yet, a number of studies have not found support for the hypothesis that intergenerational value discrepancies are particularly larger in immigrant families than in host national families (Sam & Virta 2003; Phinney, Ong & Madden 2000), and indicate that any problems observed could well be normal developmental processes (Kwak 2003 for a review). With respect to children, an aspect which is usually not taken into cognizance is that other than those with refugee background, many children migrated as part of family re-unification process, or were actually born in the host country to an immigrant family. This latter group has not had direct experience with the uprooting part of immigration. Thus, studying them using models developed for first generation adults may not be appropriate. It should therefore not be surprising that, in contrast to the earlier studies that contended that immigrant children were poorly adapted (Bagley 1972; Minde & Minde 1976), recent studies on immigrant children suggest that they adapt very well (Berry et al. 2006; Fuligni 1998). One possible explanation for this is that the children are now being studied in their own right, through perspectives and models developed specifically for their situation; namely that they are undergoing both acculturation and development. The present study supports this premise.

ACKNOWLEDGEMENTS

The author would like to extend heartfelt appreciation to the participants for their unhesitant and warm involvement in the study. Thanks are also due to the Indian community in Vancouver, for facilitating the identification of participants.

REFERENCES

Aronowitz, M., 'The Social and Emotional Adjustment of Immigrant Children: A Review of Literature', *International Migration Review*, no. 18, 1984, pp. 237-57.

Bagley, C., 'Deviant Behavior in English and West Indian School Children', *Research in Education*, no. 8, 1972, pp. 47-55.

Bar-Tal, D., A. Raviv and N. Shavit, 'Motives for Helping Behavior: Kibbutz and City Children in Kindergarten and School', *Developmental Psychology*, no. 17, 1981, pp. 766-72.

Bashir, M.R., 'Issues of Immigration for the Health and Adjustment of

Young People', *Journal of Pediatrics and Child Health*, vol. 9, 1993, pp. 42-5.

Berry, J.W., 'Socio-psychological Costs and Benefits of Multiculturalism: A View from Canada', in *Governance and Cultural Diversity,* ed. J.W. Dacyl and C. Westin, Stockholm: UNESCO & CIEFO, Stockholm University, pp. 297-354.

Berry, J.W., 'Acculturation: A Conceptual Overview', in *Acculturation and Parent-Child Relationships: Measurement and Development*, M.C. Bornstein and L.R. Cote, eds., New Jersey: Lawrence Erlbaum, Mahwah, 2006, pp. 13-32.

Berry, J.W. et al., 'Acculturation Attitudes in Plural Societies', *Applied Psychology: An International Review*, vol. 38, 1989, pp. 185-206.

Berry, J.W. et al., eds., *Immigrant Youth in Cultural Transition: Acculturation, Identity, and Adaptation across National Contexts*, New Jersey: Lawrence Erlbaum, Mahwah, 2006.

Bierhoff, H.W., *Prosocial Behavior*, New York: Psychology Press.

Bornstein, M.C. and L.R. Cote, eds., 'Introduction', in *Acculturation and Parent-Child Relationships: Measurement and Development*, New Jersey: Lawrence Erlbaum, Mahwah, 2006, pp. 1-12.

Carlo, G. et al., 'A Cross-national Study on the Relations Among Prosocial Moral Reasoning, Gender Role Orientations, and Prosocial Behaviours', *Developmental Psychology*, vol. 32, pp. 231-40.

Castillo, L.G., C.W. Conoley and D.F. Brossart, 'Acculturation, White Marginalization, and Family Support as Predictors of Perceived Distress in Mexican American Female College Students', *Journal of Counselling Psychology*, vol. 51, 2004, pp. 151-57.

Chadha, N., *Prosocial Development in Children*, New Delhi: Mittal Publications, 2007.

Chadha, N. and G. Misra, 'Patterns of Prosocial Reasoning in Indian Children', *Psychology and Developing Societies*, vol. 16, no. 2, 2004, pp. 159-86.

———, 'Prosocial Reasoning and Behavior Among Indian Children: A Naturalistic Study', *Psychology and Developing Societies*, vol. 18, no. 2, 2006, pp. 167-99.

Chun, K.M., 'Conceptual and Measurement Issues in Family Acculturation Research', in *Immigrant Youth in Cultural Transition*, J.W. Berry et al., eds., New Jersey: Lawrence Erlbaum, Mahwah, pp. 63-78.

Curran, M.J., 2003, *Across the Water—The Acculturation and Health of Irish people in London*, Dublin: Trinity College and Allen Library.

Eisenberg, N., 'The Development of Reasoning about Prosocial Behavior', in *The Development of Prosocial Behavior*, ed. N. Eisenberg, New York: Academic Press, 1982, pp. 219-49.

———., *Altruistic Emotion, Cognition and Behavior*, New Jersey: Lawrence Erlbaum, Hillsdale, 1986.

———, 'Prosocial Development in Early and Mid-adolescence', in *Advances in Adolescence*, vol. 2: *From Childhood to Adolescence: A Transitional Period?*, ed. R. Montemayor, G.R. Adams and T.P. Gullotta, 1990, Newbury Park, CA: Sage, pp. 240-69.

Eisenberg, N. et al., 1985, 'The Development of Prosocial Behavior and Cognition in German Children', *Journal of Cross-Cultural Psychology*, no. 16, 1985, pp. 69-82.

Eisenberg, N. et al., 'Age Changes in Prosocial Responding and Moral Reasoning in Adolescence and Early Adulthood', *Journal of Research on Adolescence*, vol. 15, no. 3, pp. 235-60.

Eisenberg, N. and R.A. Fabes, 'Prosocial Development', in *Handbook of Child Psychology*, ed. W. Damon, vol. 3: *Social, Emotional, and Personality Development*, ed. N. Eisenberg, New York: Wiley, 1998, pp. 701-78.

Eisenberg, N., R. Hertz-Lazarowitz and I. Fuchs, 'Prosocial Moral Judgment in Israeli Kibbutz and City Children: A Longitudinal Study', *Merrill Palmer Quarterly*, vol. 36, pp. 273-85.

Eisenberg, N., R. Lennon and K. Roth, 'Prosocial Development in Childhood: A Longitudinal Study', *Developmental Psychology*, vol. 19, 1983, pp. 846-55.

Eisenberg, N. et al., 'Prosocial Development in Adolescence: A Longitudinal Study', *Developmental Psychology*, vol. 27, pp. 849-57.

Eisenberg, N. and R. Shell, 'Prosocial Moral Judgment and Behavior in Children: The Mediating Role of Cost', *Personality and Social Psychology Bulletin*, vol. 12, 1986, pp. 426-33.

Eisenberg, N. et al., 'Prosocial Development in Middle Childhood: A Longitudinal Study', *Developmental Psychology*, vol. 23, 1987, pp. 712-18.

Eisenberg-Berg, N., 'Development of Children's Prosocial Moral Judgment', *Developmental Psychology*, vol. 15, pp. 128-37.

Eisenberg-Berg, N. and M. Hand, 'The Relationship of Preschoolers' Reasoning about Prosocial Moral Conflicts to Prosocial Behavior', *Child Development*, vol. 50, 1979, pp. 356-63.

Evans, J., 'Introduction: Migration and Health', *International Migration Review*, vol. 21, 1987, pp. v-xiv.

Fetchenhauer, D. et al., 'Solidarity and Prosocial Behavior: A Framing Approach', in *Solidarity and Prosocial Behavior: An Integration of Sociological and Psychological Perspective*, ed. D. Fetchenhauer, et al., New York: Springer, 2006, pp. 3-22.

Fuchs, I. et al., 'Kibbutz, Israeli City, and American Children's Moral Reasoning about Prosocial Moral Conflicts', *Merrill-Palmer Quarterly*, vol. 32, 1986, pp. 37-50.

Fuligni, A.J., 'The Academic Achievement of Adolescents from Immigrant Families: The Role of Family Background, Attitudes and Behavior', *Child Development*, vol. 68, 1997, pp. 261-73.

———, 'The Adjustment of Children from Immigrant Families', *Current Directions in Psychological Sciences*, vol. 7, no. 4, 1998, pp. 99-103.

———, 'The Adjustment of Children from Immigrant Families', *Newsletter of International Society for the Study of Behavioral Development*, vol. 44, 2003, pp. 2-11.

Garcia Coll, C. and K. Magruson, 'The Psychological Experience of Immigration: A Developmental Perspective', in *Immigration and the Family: Research and Policy on US Immigrants,* ed. A. Booth et al., New Jersey: Lawrence Erlbaum, Mahwah, 1997, pp. 91-132.

Gollwitzer, P.M. and J. Bargh, eds., *The Psychology of Action: Linking Cognition and Motivation to Behavior*, New York: Guilford, 1996.

Harris, K.M., 'The Health Status and Risk Behaviors of Adolescents in Immigrant Families', in *Children of Immigrants: Health, Adjustment and Public Assistance*, ed. D. J. Hernandez, Washington, DC: National Academic Press, 1999, pp. 286-315.

Kagitcibasi, C., *Family and Human Development Across Cultures: A View from the Other Side*, New Jersey: Lawrence Erlbaum, Mahwah, 1996.

———, 'Autonomy and Relatedness in Cultural Context: Implications for Self and Family', *Journal of Personality and Social Psychology*, vol. 36, no. 4, 2005, pp. 403-22.

Kim-Jo, T., 'Cultural Values among Korean and Korean-American Adolescents', unpublished Master's thesis, California State University, LA, 2003.

Kwak, K., 'Adolescents and Their Parents: A Review of Intergenerational Family Relations for Immigrant and Non-immigrant Families', *Human Development*, vol. 46, 2003, pp. 115-236.

Lerner, R.M., *Concepts and Theories of Human Development* (3rd edn.), New Jersey: Lawrence Erlbaum, Mahwah, 2001.

Lindenberg, S., 'Prosocial Behavior, Solidarity, and Framing Processes', in *Solidarity and Prosocial Behavior: An Integration of Sociological and Psychological Perspective*, ed. D. Fetchenhauer, New York: Springer, 2006, pp. 23-44.

McKay, L., S. Macintyre and A. Ellaway, *Migration and Health: A Review of the International Literature, Occasional Paper 12*, Glasgow: Scotland Medical Research Council, 2003.

Miller, J.G., 'Taking Culture into Account in Social Cognitive Development', *Psychology and Developing Societies*, vol. 9, 1997, pp. 9-34.

Minde, K. and R. Minde, 'Children of Immigrants: The Adjustment of Ugandan Asian Primary School Children', *Canadian Psychiatric Association Journal*, vol. 21, 1976, pp. 31-381.

Misra, G., 'Culture and Self: Implications for Psychological Inquiry', *Journal of Indian Psychology*, vol. 19, 2001, pp. 1-20.

Munekata, H. and K. Ninomiya, 'The Development of Prosocial Moral

Judgments', *Japanese Journal of Educational Psychology*, vol. 33, 1985, pp. 157-64.

Nauck, B., 'Intercultural Contact and Inter-generational Transmission in Immigrant Families', *Journal of Personality and Social Psychology*, vol. 32, 2001, pp. 159-73.

Phinney, J., 'Ethnic Identity and Acculturation', in *Acculturation: Advances in Theory, Measurement and Applied Research*, ed. K. Chen, Organista, and G. Marin, Washington, DC: American Psychological Association, pp. 39-60.

———, 'Acculturation is not an Independent Variable: Approaches to Studying Acculturation as a Complex Process', in *Immigrant Youth in Cultural Transition: Acculturation, Identity, and Adaptation Across National Contexts*, ed. J.W. Berry et al., New Jersey: Lawrence Erlbaum, Mahwah, 2006, pp. 79-96.

Phinney, J. et al., 'The Acculturation Experience: Attitudes, Identities and Behaviors of Immigrant Youth', in *Immigrant Youth in Cultural Transition: Acculturation, Identity, and Adaptation Across National Contexts*, ed. J.W. Berry, et al., New Jersey: Lawrence Erlbaum, Mahwah, 2006, pp. 167-84.

Phinney, J. et al., 'Autonomy and Relatedness in Adolescent-Parent Disagreements: Ethnic and Developmental Factors', *Journal of Adolescent Research*, vol. 20, 2005, pp. 8-39.

Phinney, J., A. Ong and T. Madden, 'Cultural Values and Intergenerational Value Discrepancies in Immigrant and Non-immigrant Families', *Child Development*, vol. 71, 2001, pp. 528-9.

Ross, L. and R.E. Nisbett, '*The Person and the Situation: Perspectives of Social Psychology*, New York: McGraw Hill, 1991.

Sam, D., 'Acculturation Attitudes among Young Immigrants as a Function of Perceived Parental Attitudes Towards Cultural Change', *Journal of Early Adolescence*, vol. 15, 1995, pp. 238-58.

———, 'Adaptation of Children and Adolescents with Immigrant Background: Acculturation or Development?', in *Immigrant Youth in Cultural Transition: Acculturation, Identity, and Adaptation across National Contexts*, ed. J.W. Berry et al., New Jersey: Lawrence Erlbaum, Mahwah, 2006, pp. 97-112.

Sam, D. and J.W. Berry, eds., *Cambridge Handbook of Acculturation Psychology*, Cambridge: Cambridge University Press, 2006.

Sam, D., A. Kosic and B. Oppedal, 'Where is "Development" in Acculturation Theories?', *ISSBD Newsletter*, vol. 44, 2003, pp. 4-27.

Sam, D. and E. Virta, 'Intergenerational Value Discrepancies in Immigrant and Host-National Families and Their Impact on Psychological Adaptation', *Journal of Adolescence*, vol. 26, 2003, pp. 213-31.

Shweder, R.A., *Why do Men Barbecue? Recipes for Cultural Psychology*, Cambridge MA: Harvard University Press, 2003.

Sinha, D. and H.S.R. Kao, 'The Journey to the East: An Introduction', in *Asian Perspectives on Psychology*, ed. H.S.R. Kao and D. Sinha, New Delhi: Sage, 1997, pp. 9-22.

Smeesters, D. et al., 'Do Not Prime Hawks with Doves: The Interplay of Construct Activation and Consistency of Social Values on Cooperative Behavior', *Journal of Personality and Social Psychology*, vol. 84, 2003, pp. 972-87.

Stapel, D.A. and J. Sals, eds., *Assimilation and Contrast in Social Psychology*, New York: Psychology Press, 2007.

Strack, F. and R. Deutsch, 'Reflective and Impulsive Determinants of Social Behaviour', *Journal of Personality and Social Psychology Review*, vol. 8, 2004, pp. 220-47.

Ward, C., 'The ABCs of Acculturation', in *Handbook of Psychology and Culture*, ed. D. Matsumoto, Oxford, UK: Oxford University Press, 2001, pp. 411-45.

Ward, C., S. Bochner and A. Furnham, *The Psychology of Culture Shock*. London: Routledge, 2001.

CHAPTER 22

The Future of South Asian Canadian Literature

DEVIKA KHANNA NARULA

Migration is the most defining trope of the twentieth century and has brought people of different cultures into close socio-cultural contact with each other. The multicultural mosaic in Canada, too, incorporates in itself 'different' ethnic groups along with their 'different' cultures. The concept of multiculturalism is positive in its scope since it does not believe in submerging 'different' identities into homogeneity, but rather endeavours to preserve the 'difference' in cultures while attempting to assimilate them into a harmonious amalgam. Janice Kulyk Keefer in her essay, 'The Sacredness of Bridges: Writing Immigrant Experience' speaks about the racialism and marginalization that immigrants had to face initially in Canada, but then she goes on to talk about the changing climate in the country where there is now an effort being made to understand each other's 'differences'. The attempt to understand each other and accommodate to the changing demography of the country, is expressed by her as 'building a bridge' across the 'chasm' of the unknown, which is done by creating a familiarity, an understanding and an acceptance of the variety of cultural ethos that co-exists in a multicultural society.

Literature becomes the best medium of creating such familiarity with immigrant experiences which are as varied as the individuals making up a society. Janice Kulyk Keefer emphasizes in her essay on the variety of personal experiences and warns against lumping all immigrants into a homogenized whole:

In referring to 'immigrant experience' I deliberately refuse to preface this phrase by the definite article. I'm uncomfortable with the universalizing ring 'the immigrant experience' conveys, as if there were only one kind of immigrant, one narrative of experience to be told.
(Keefer 1998: 97)

Janice Kulyk Keefer is very obviously referring to the multicultural society that exists in any given place because of the vast world of new opportunities that was opened to people of all races and cultures with the advent of new modes of travelling. Whether the situation proved to be one of harmony and cooperation or of antagonism and hostility, depending from place to place and from nationality to nationality, but the fact remains that people of different races have been brought together in proximity to each other and have in some way become interdependent on each other, the causes for which may vary from technological reasons to trade interdependence or to any other factor. The significant fact is that now people are trying to extend the hand of friendship to each other. Hence Keefer's plea is that, given such a situation, it is better to live in harmony though not in homogeneity. It is a plea for the co-existence of different diasporas in the multicultural society of Canada:

It's a bridge . . . in which mobility vies with stability, a bridge over which people are constantly passing, jostling one another and stopping to exchange opinions or interpretations of the view. This kind of bridge points as much to the intractable chasm it was built to span as to the fact that a means of crossing that chasm now exists. (Keefer 1998: 101)

The South Asian Diaspora in Canada is an important factor since its strength is second only to the Chinese, which is the largest ethnic group. It is a very vibrant multicultural diaspora, containing in itself many vivid cultures and languages, and has an abundance of publications in English as well as in ethnic languages. It has works of excellent literary value which have been recognized worldwide as is obvious by the number of awards won by the South Asian Canadian writers' writing in English. The contribution of this corpus of writing lies in the variety of new ideas and philosophies it has contributed to Canadian literature, and through its many languages, it has also made available new words to enrich the Canadian vocabulary. New techniques and new forms of literature, culled from their own culture, have added a new depth and poignancy to Canadian literature. In her introduction to the collection of South Asian writings, *The Geography of Voice*, Diane McGifford praises South Asian literature for its thematic range and structural experimentation and comments on the variety of authorial perspectives in the South Asian Canadian writers. She declares, 'The dark days for South Asian Canadian writing are over. It has caught on and its campaign for recognition as real Canadian literature, to be taught as Canadian literature in schools and universities, is well underway' (McGifford 1992: xii). No doubt that South Asian literature is definitely an academic area to be interpreted and debated. It is a body of writing that deals with the ongoing dialectics of the post-modern contemporary society since it delves into the constant changes in intra-community and intra-racial tensions of the fabric of social intercourse. Arun Prabha Mukherjee in her essay 'How Shall We Read South Asian Canadian Texts?' refers to the acknowledgement and recognition of the South Asian writings, even though not directly as mainstream Canadian Literature, but definitely as post-colonial literature:

> Thus there is now definitely an object of knowledge called South Asian Canadian Literature that is being interpreted and debated. To the extent that South Asian Canadian writers share certain commonalities such as culture, memory and a repertoir of linguistic signs, they can be seen as producers of an entity called South Asian Canadian Literature that lends itself to analysis. (Mukherjee 1998: 30)

The South Asian Canadian diaspora has evolved into a force to be reckoned with, not only as a workforce but also in the literature that it produces in English which is of an excellence comparable to that of the mainstream writers.

The last decade has shown a keen awareness in diasporic literature all over the world. There has been a spurt of interest in the works of writers from different diasporas who privilege the recent history of their race and the life that they lived in their homeland or in the land from where they migrated; they present a chronicled account of the history of their race through a narration of their personal histories, which were neglected in the mainstream historical accounts. The concepts of ethnicity and race, being significant to such personal narratives, have become important theoretical tools for the analysis and critical evaluation of the literature produced by different diasporas. The South Asian diaspora has been prolific in their literary output since most of the immigrants of this particular diaspora, migrating after the 1960s, were fluent in English and used it as the medium of their writings. Meenakshi Mukherjee, at a conference on 'Interrogating Post-Colonialism' held in Shimla in October 1994, comments on this practice of using English as the language of expression. She highlights the 'professional compulsion to speak the same language and adopt the same frame of discourse that people from our discipline are doing all over the world, in order to belong to an international community' (Mukherjee 1998: 28) and points out the pressures of globalization on writers desiring a wider reach of audience. She also warns against its obverse effect of 'making the specific configuration of circumstances in particular regions subservient to a global paradigm' (ibid).

In the works of the immigrant writers, however, the Queen's English, though being the language of the coloniser, is now being appropriated with a twist to its syntax and format. Writers are freely using the colloquial/regional English that the colonized people had been speaking, with the syntax of their own regional vernacular thrown in. Such adaptation of the language shows an ironic usurpation of the coloniser's language and such appropriation makes it an effective, subjective, post-colonial tool of expression. This new format of the English language is also in effect the birth of a new language that has been churned out of the crucible of colonialism. The post-colonial reworking of the heritage of colonialism is the most vivid and realistic representation of colonialism itself.

The use of English as the medium of writing invariably invites evaluation of literary works on the basis of Eurocentric critical theories, but the literatures of different diasporas, evolving out of erstwhile colonies, should not be subjected to the hegemonic norms of Eurocentric literary critical theories of Europe and

America since they are writing out of a different context and with a different ideology. The need to have a new perspective of evaluation for alternative literatures is very evident from the fact that they do not have themes and objectives which are similar to the European white 'dead' writers, to use Arun Prabha Mukherjee's phrase. Critics of ethnic literature have to forge their own critical vocabulary. They have to work at many levels simultaneously because the holistic perception of diasporic literature and the critical norms which should be applied to it are totally different from the Eurocentric tradition. The diasporic writer is writing to make his 'voice' heard , to make his presence felt, to forge an identity in a new world where he is not known, recognized or understood. Hence, the critic must realize the complicity of the situation as he has to review a work where a new identity and a new awareness are being forged.

The immigrant writers do not write novels centering around ideologies, philosophies, or romantic involvements; they do not even position themselves as the voice of the 'colonized', what they do write about is the mundane day-to-day living of their communities along with their small joys and the everyday struggles of life. In addition to this, all immigrant writers cannot be seen with a homogenized critical perspective since each writer has his own peculiar lived experience, the history of his own community, his own individualized technique and style. Narrating personal histories, each writer must be judged on the basis of sincerity, consistency and technical/stylistic quality since the ideology that gives impetus to diasporic writing is the impulse to create a consciousness of the multiplicity of voices clamouring to be heard, which had retreated into oblivion since they had no place in the master narratives of history. Their objective is to record and preserve the socio-cultural nuances of the history of their race retrieved from the past and to create an awareness of themselves. Thus, alternative literatures, that is literatures other than that of the mainstream, provide an insight into the 'otherness' of different diasporas and familiarize the Western world with contemporary realities of the 'other', but in order to achieve this they need to preserve their identity and their 'otherness', which simultaneously and ironically positions their marginality as well. While evaluating or studying diasporic literature, the new ideology and socio-cultural ethos that informs it and privileges it has to be kept in mind.

Arun Prabha Mukherjee, in her essay 'Writing From A Hard Place: The African Fiction of M.G. Vassanji' states that reading *The Gunny Sack* was her first introduction to the historical fact of an Indian presence in East Africa. The immigrant community of Indians were traders in East Africa in the wake of, and even before, the British empire's presence there, but they are overlooked in the master narratives since they have no relevance to the chroniclers of Indian or British history. It is Vassanji who has retrieved their history and brought it to the knowledge of the outside world because:

> Vassanji . . . refuses to participate in the heroic narratives of freedom struggles. Unlike many other African and Indian novelists, he refuses to write about 'the people'. Instead, he writes about the distinct ethnic groups, of the Arabs, the Mangati, the Swahili, the Masai, the Khoja, the Goan, the Bohra, the Bhatias and on and on the list goes. (Begum 1996: 68)

The value of South Asian Canadian literature lies in its representation of the lived experience in different locations and different situations through the course of their various historic migrations. It becomes a documentation of their history of migration and their living experience which may otherwise be lost for ever. The literary work of the South Asian Canadians is not about resistance or about heroic deeds; it is rather a retrieval of the history of a people.

South Asian Canadian writers do not speak of a common national identity since they come from different countries in South Asia, with a vast diversity in culture, language, socio-religious background and historical experiences which are reflected in a vital and dynamic way in their works. However, underlying this very individualized and personalized writing, there are recurring themes and patterns that are common to their works as presentations of immigrant experiences. Professor Mavor Moore narrates in an interesting anecdote in the article 'Cultural Exchange' in the Bicentennial Conference Proceedings, 1985, York University Archives, Two Hundred Years—Learning to Live Together, how, while conducting economic negotiations in China, he was told that while economic matters were important, they were not important enough to postpone discussions about culture. The message that he immediately sent to Canada was, 'Please try to convince them in Ottawa that cultural exchange has to come before trade and commerce, not after. People have to get to know us before they'll do business with us'. This anecdote clearly projects the significance of 'knowing' each other before any kind of economic or political links can be established. The South Asian diaspora, through its writings, is contributing to this kind of an awareness of each other, of the lifestyle and customs, the religious beliefs and culinary habits, of socio-cultural systems. Professor Moore's logic establishes the significance of the exchange of culture in the basic role of 'opening doors', 'building bridges', 'getting the people to know one another' and 'enhancing and projecting a favourable self-image'. Hence the arts and literature of a race or ethnic group are strong containers of culture in a larger sense which includes lifestyles, attitudes, social and individual values, relationships, worldview, philosophy, myth and religion, history and above all, a certain mythic sense about the non-manifest reality behind the manifested universe that we populate. In this sense South Asian Canadian writers are cultural ambassadors who motivate and encourage a Canadian readership to South Asian Canadian literature, and through their fiction make the world aware of the historical realities of their people diaspora.

The increasingly complex development of the South Asian Canadian literature implies the need for a corresponding evolution and expansion of the critical approaches used in the analysis of the texts. Coherent investigation must delve into not only what the texts mean, but how they have to be understood and in what perspective, literary techniques and styles inviting as much introspection and revealing as many insights as the contents themselves. The appropriation of an established form by the writers with renewed creative and imaginative sensibilities heightens the literary experience as they gesture towards a new perception of cultural contexts and choices by renovating the content of an established form. The use made by them of the short story cycle, the diary or even the novel, has demonstrated how a traditional literary form is converted into a transnational literary phenomenon that can negotiate geographic, cultural, ethnic, and even linguistic boundaries so that the writers are able to achieve the integration of heritage with the socio-cultural traditions of the adopted land. Michael Fischer calls it a 'mirror of bifocality . . . seeing others against a background of ourselves, and ourselves against a background of others' (Davis 2001: 19). This 'reciprocity of perspectives' (Davis 2001: 19) to use Fischer's terminology, invites interdependence and formulates multiple meanings while creating something totally new: a metaphor for the task of negotiating identity. The dynamic process of ethnic awareness of ethnicity, thus, involves a (re)invention and (re) formulation of their own culture and history, thereby progressing to a forging and communicating of identity. The works of Bapsi Sidhwa, Rohinton Mistry, M.G. Vassanji, Lakshmi Gill, Farida Karodia, Uma Parameswaran, Surjeet Kalsi, Ajmer Rode and others, clearly projects the discerning negotiation of events and causes with an aim of establishing one's credentials and positioning oneself in the new context. This process is not an end in itself but a continuous process, as is also evident from the words of M.G. Vassanji in the foreword to *Floating the Borders*. He commends the title because he feels that recent multicultural fiction in Canada has become a process of

> not uprooting and moving boundaries, but simply setting them afloat and free, for an identity, a literature, in the broad sense, to grow, explore, find and define itself; and perhaps keep on defining itself.
>
> (Aziz 1999: viii)

Diasporic literature, as a distinct minority literature, has become a space for cultural contestation between hegemonic forces parleying for its containment and exclusion, and the more progressive and realistic forces negotiating for its enlargement and inclusion. The ethnic is no longer disparaged, in fact their exclusion from the centre of political power has placed them at the advantageous position of an observer and commentator. The South Asian Canadian writer, conscious of a multiple literary inheritance, within what has been a largely hegemonic framework of literary and cultural studies, exemplifies in his work the nature and boundaries of this body of literature, its categorization and composition, the interpretations and evaluations brought to bear on it, and, hence, foregrounds the plural categories of cultural classification that have worked in the production of knowledge and counter-knowledge inherent in it. The resulting hybrid text focuses on the continual and mutual development of the traditions from which it has evolved and of the post-colonial/postmodern forms it contends with Hence, instead of a multicultural literary scene, it is better to use Janice Kulyk Keefer's term and call the Canadian literary scene 'transcultural' because it is a more appropriate way of referring to the manner in which the dominant culture

> becomes part of a larger, looser structure within which literary texts which foreground the experience of 'minority' as opposed to 'dominant' groups both present themselves and are received as representative, even paradigmatic forms for an entire social formation, and not just for the ethnic or racial group with which the text's author is associated. (Davis 2001: 8)

Keefer prefers to use the term 'transcultural' to 'multicultural' since the latter can refer to a social formation, but not to that of a literary work because, as she says:

> what is important in transcultural writing is the circulation and exchange of ideas, energies, vision between different ethno-cultural groups as well as between 'center' and 'margin', 'dominant' and 'minority' groups'. (Davis 2001: 8)

Since social circumstances and social structures/constructs determine the personality of an individual, and since migration involves physical dislocation from one geo-cultural location to another, the trajectory of an individual's life in its social and political terms as well as spatial and temporal terms, defines the transcultural influences that have moulded his personality.

Jameson defines postmodernism as a periodizing concept 'whose function is to correlate the emergence of new formal features in culture with the emergence of a new type of social life and a new economic order' (Hutcheon 1988: 37). This postmodern positioning of literature/culture is reflected in all diasporic literature, that projects the new global social order where migration and mobility have become the natural order of the day. It acknowledges the human urge to make order, while pointing out that the ordered situations and contexts that we create are just human, transcultural constructs, not natural or given entities. This is precisely why the essential features of the literary life in Canada call for an interdisciplinary approach to literary history because the demographic topography of the country is constantly changing with the constant pouring in of different migrant races. Besides literature in French and English, there is in Canada a mosaic of other users of words, ranging from the oral traditions of the Inuit and the North American Indians to the literary works in the language of the immigrants. This important aspect of the Canadian experience, the creativity of the minorities had largely remained as 'the unheard voices' of the minorities, but now the scene is changing with new journals and collections of ethnic writers flooding the Canadian market. As the diasporic writing has become more and more prolific even in other ex-colonies like Australia, Africa, the Caribbean islands and other places, one can say that diasporic writing, in general, has become a significant part of International English Literature.

It is pertinent to say that in the postcolonial and post-modern era, with the significance attached to personal histories, diasporic writing has already foregrounded itself as a means of giving 'voice' to the unheard and the marginalized. In the contemporary context of Canada, South Asian diasporic writing is emerging as a major socio-cultural force, a compendium of writing that has a biographical dimension which introduces the reader to the sociocultural, political, historical, psychological and economic realities of the various 'different' minorities that comprise the population of Canada, both in their past and present circumstances. It is also a major literary force by magnitude of its contribution, in the vast number of publications and writers of note belonging to the diaspora. They have established themselves as a body of literature to be read and evaluated by the perspective which emerges from the fact that their writings have evolved out of their physical dislocation and cultural displacement, and is shaped by their immigrant experiences. They cannot be studied as an off-shoot of Eurocentric literature since their themes, concerns and objectives are very different from those of the Eurocentric writers. The works of the South Asian Canadian writers are the celebration of the life that their community has lived and which they have helped to retrieve from anonymity and oblivion. There appears to be, within them, a compulsion to write and express their personal 'histories' and they have a passionate faith in themselves and in their writings, because 'honesty' and 'plain speaking' are the two most important features of their work. Though they write about their homeland from where they have come, yet they consider themselves as Canadians writing Canadian literature and object to being called ethnic/immigrant writers, the term having been coined to distinguish them from British/American/French-Canadian writers. In her article 'Literature of the Indian Diaspora in Canada: An Overview', Uma Parmeswaran writes:

> Art and literature do not rise full blown like Venus from the sea. Their creation is a slow and cumulative process. This is especially true of immigrant literature; it starts off as a transplant, with its major referential points centred in the original homeland, and whatever it says is implicitly or explicitly comparative at this stage. (Begum 1999: 15)

But as it gains momentum and comes into its own, it takes its place in Canadian literature and as Ronald Sutherland says it has become one of the richest and most rapidly growing new components of Canadian literature because:

> they distill their experiences of Canada through a variety of rich cultural heritages. Perhaps it is this very process of diverse cultural distillation that will become the distinctive characteristic of Canadian literature. (Vassanji 1985: 76)

The road lies open to South Asian Canadian writers to forge ahead and this is definitely not the last word on them because, to use Diane McGifford's words, 'Unquestionably South Asian Canadian literature is here to stay'.

REFERENCES

Aziz, Nurjehan (ed.), *Floating the Borders: New Contexts in Canadian Criticism*, Toronto: TSAR Publications, 1999.

Begum, Jameela and Maya Dutt (ed.), *South Asian Canadiana*, Madras: Anu Chitra Publications, 1996.

Davis, Rocio G., *Transcultural Reinventions: Asian American and Asian Canadian Short-Story Cycles*, Toronto: TSAR Publications, 2001.

Hutcheon, Linda, *A Poetics of Postmodernism: History, Theory, Fiction*, London: Routledge, 1988.

Keefer, Janice Kulyk, ' "The Sacredness of Bridges": Writing Immigrant Experience', in Christl Verduyn (ed.), *Literary Pluralities*, Toronto: Broadview Press/Journal of Canadian Studies, 1998.

McGifford, Diane, *The Geography of Voice: Canadian Literature of the South Asian Diaspora*, Toronto: TSAR Publications, 1992.

Mukherjee, Arun, *Postcolonialism: My Living*, Toronto: TSAR Publications, 1998.

Sutherland, Ronald, 'The Mainstream of Canadian Literature', in M.G. Vassanji (ed.), *A Meeting of Streams: South Asian Canadian Literature*, Toronto: TSAR Publications, 1985.

Contributors

LOPAMUDRA BANDYOPADHYAY is a fellow of Global India Foundation, Kolkata.

NEERJA CHADHA is Associate Professor in the School of Continuing Education, Indira Gandhi National Open University, New Delhi.

YVON DANDURAND is Associate Vice-President Research and Graduate Studies, University of Fraser Valley, British Columbia, Canada.

PATRICIA DOLD is Assistant Professor, Department of Religious Studies, Memorial University of Newfoundland, St. John's, Newfoundland and Labrador, Canada.

ABHIK GUPTA is Professor of Environmental Studies at Assam University, Silchar.

RAJ KUMAR HANS is Reader at Department of History, Maharaja Sayajirao University of Baroda, Vadodara.

STEPHEN INGLIS is Senior Curator at Canadian Museum of Civilization, Gatineau, Quebec.

OM P. JUNEJA is Founding Director, Centre for Canadian Studies and former Professor and Head, Department of English Maharaja Sayajirao University of Baroda, Vadodara.

JYOTIRMAYEE KAR is a Professor of Economics at ICFAI Business School, Bhubaneswar.

G. KARUNANITHI is Professor and Head, Deptt. of Sociology, Manonmaniam Sundarnar University, Tirunelveli, Tamil Nadu.

KRISHNA K. KAUSHIK is Professor of Economics at Himachal Pradesh University, Shimla.

G. GOPA KUMAR is Professor of Political Science at University of Kerala, Thiruvananthapuram.

K.R.G. NAIR is Honorary Research Professor, Centre for Policy Research, New Delhi.

ARTI NANAVATI is a Professor of Economics, Deptt. of Economics and Director of Centre for Canadian Studies, Maharaja Sayajirao University of Baroda, Vadodara.

A.S. NARANG is Professor of Political Science at Indira Gandhi National Open University, New Delhi.

DEVIKA KHANNA NARULA is Reader in English, Delhi College of Commerce & Arts (University of Delhi), New Delhi.

SAYANTANI SEN is a Fellow at Global India Foundation, Kolkata.

DALJIT SINGH is Research Fellow, Pryas Energy Group, Pune.

TEJ PRATAP SINGH is Associate Professor of Political Science at Banaras Hindu University, Varanasi.

H. SRIKANTH is Reader at Department of Political Science, North-Eastern Hill University, Shillong.

GARY VAN LOON is Professor of Chemistry, Queens University, Kingston and former President of Shastri Indo-Canadian Institute, Canada.

V.K. VASAL is Director, Centre for Canadian Studies and Professor, University of Delhi (South Campus), New Delhi.

Index